JUST *the* WORDS *and* TEACHINGS *of* JESUS CHRIST

Inclusion—הללכה—*in His Resurrected Life*

MICHAEL D. MICHELUCCI

Just the Words and Teachings of Jesus Christ: Inclusion—הלּלכה—in His Resurrected Life

Trilogy Christian Publishers

A Wholly Owned Subsidiary of Trinity Broadcasting Network

2442 Michelle Drive

Tustin, CA 92780

Copyright © 2024 by Michael D. Michelucci

All Scripture quotations are taken from the Complete Jewish Bible, Copyright ©1998 and 2016 by David H. Stern. Used by permission. All rights reserved worldwide. Scripture quotations marked NKJV are taken from the New King James Version®. Copyright © 1982 by Thomas Nelson. Used by permission. All rights reserved.

All other pictures are sourced from httPs //pixabay.com/. Pixabay is a vibrant community of creatives, sharing over 4.1 million+ high quality stock images, videos, audio, and other media. All content is released under the Content License, which makes it safe to use without asking for permission or giving credit to the artist—even for certain commercial purposes.

All rights reserved, including the right to reproduce this book or portions thereof in any form whatsoever.

For information, address Trilogy Christian Publishing

Rights Department, 2442 Michelle Drive, Tustin, Ca 92780.

Trilogy Christian Publishing/ TBN and colophon are trademarks of Trinity Broadcasting Network.

For information about special discounts for bulk purchases, please contact Trilogy Christian Publishing.

Trilogy Disclaimer: The views and content expressed in this book are those of the author and may not necessarily reflect the views and doctrine of Trilogy Christian Publishing or the Trinity Broadcasting Network.

10 9 8 7 6 5 4 3 2 1

Library of Congress Cataloging-in-Publication Data is available.

ISBN 979-8-89041-762-6

ISBN 979-8-89041-763-3 (ebook)

"Look! He is coming with the clouds! Every eye will see Him, including those who pierced Him; and all the tribes of the Land will mourn Him. Yes! Amen! 'I am the "A," and the "Z" says Adonai, God of heaven's armies, the One who is, who was and who is coming'" (Revelation 1:7–8).

Cover picture taken by my son Brandon in April 2012 at Passover in Stockton, California.

Front cover picture copyright registration #1–12598484991.

DEDICATION

To the wounded and broken in spirit, soul, and body, yearning for truth regarding Jesus Christ, Son of God, yet by various means kept from knowing or experiencing Him. Individuals and groups of people who believe and feel they are or have been excluded in many ways of their lives. Especially for the reader regarding their life here on earth and here after.

To those sincerely proclaiming to be born again, possibly still suffering from strongholds of real afflictions or imaginations inside and outside themselves. Deeply desiring to be made free and wanting the clearer path of life.

Peace and blessings be unto you all as you sit down and read Just the Words and Teachings of Jesus: Inclusion—הללכה—in His Resurrected Life. May Jesus's words be louder than those of the world's, Satan's, or your own imaginations and His teachings become your new reality within His resurrected life.

ACKNOWLEDGMENTS

To my Lord and Savior Jesus the Messiah, who saved me from my adversaries: Satan, the world, my own sinful nature, and greatest enemy, which is eternal death and separation from God.

To the mothers of my children, who by God's grace survived and came out from under the tyranny of my addictions.

To our four children and their families. May Jesus reveal Himself to you all in such a personal and undeniable way. There is nothing more important that I can ever give or leave to you on this side of heaven except the gospel of Jesus, the living Christ. Despite my sincere efforts in our relationships, I realize at times I gave you cause to believe and say otherwise. This I know and believe with my whole heart. Jesus is the One who forgives, saves, and will guarantee your salvation and eternal life into heaven. Father God is a much better father than I have been, and Jesus, His Son, a much better man than I could ever possibly be by myself. I pray you all will hear and answer His call if you haven't done so already.

To the body of Christ, for we were all the same in desperate need of the cross and, most importantly, Jesus's resurrection daily. I pray you embrace Jesus's love and teachings even more in the understanding of your living in His kingdom here on earth and as it is in heaven. To be first is to become a servant. To be a son or daughter is divine in His nature.

To all those who have deeply impacted my life leaving lasting imprints within, both as friends and some as foes. For those who have loved and befriended me, thank you for the privilege. For the foes, you have caused me to find better ways in Jesus's teachings to deal with conflict.

For those I have offended and hurt somehow, please forgive me. Because of all of you, I have come to realize this is the way of the human experience that is necessary for me, and I thank you!

Finally, I wish to thank all the wonderful people at Trilogy Publishing for their masterful work and encouragement throughout this process. Making this book a reality for the glory unto God and promised salvation for any reader who becomes born again in Jesus's resurrected life.

TABLE OF CONTENTS

Part 1: What Is This Book All About?..13

Part 2: Author's Directives 15

Part 3: "180" Subtopic Teachings—Matthew, Mark, and Luke 17

Part 4: Subtopic Scriptural Alignment View—Matthew, Mark, and Luke 27

Part 5: "75" Subtopic Teachings—Gospel of John.....................................279

Part 6: Subtopic Scriptures—Gospel of John 283

Part 7: Glossary of Words and Meanings..327

Part 8: Commentaries...347

Part 9: Inclusion—הלּלכה—in the Resurrected Life of Jesus the Messiah 359

Part 10: Michael's Testimony 385

Part 11: Conclusion 395

Part 12: Space for Personal Notes 397

PART 1:

WHAT IS THIS BOOK ALL ABOUT?

*T*his book consists of a combination of Jesus's "255" subtopic teachings within chapters of the Bible's four Gospels and an understanding of what "Inclusion—הללכה—in the Resurrected Life of Jesus the Messiah" can mean for you. Giving the reader a resource and allowing you and Jesus to have a very personal and intimate one-on-one sit-down together.

Is the ultimate goal of this book for the reader to get to know Jesus in such a personal way that is so undeniable that you willfully choose to believe in Him and become a follower of His way, truth, and life? If my prayers are answered, then absolutely, but only you and Jesus will decide that. Without the pretense of any labels or opinions from others of what your conclusion and walk going forward may or may not be, especially based on your individual back story that some may or may not know.

Jesus already knows who you are and your entire life's story. He's simply waiting for you to sit down and get to know Him personally. I will not be taking away from or adding anything to His specific scriptures within their context found in the contents of the Holy Scriptures. Nor the call on a pastor, teacher, rabbi, or lay person's life to educate and disciple others into a relationship with God and His Son, Jesus.

Have you ever asked yourself what Jesus Himself really had to say about certain questions you might have regarding Him, yourself, or different subject matters, such as:

- How come I haven't ever heard of Jesus before?
- Do I know about Jesus, or do I really know Jesus?
- Is Jesus really the Savior of the world?
- Do I need to be saved? If so, from what and why?
- Does He really want someone like me, just the way I am?
- Did He or can He really forgive and save me? If so, how?
- What are His specific words and His teachings on various subjects?
- What are His promises specifically for me?
- Will He answer my questions?

- Where is He now?
- What is His resurrected life really all about as it relates to me?
- Do I judge people who proclaim to be a "Christian"?
- Etc.

To be in an intimate relationship with anyone, we need to have regular conversations with them. Jesus wants us to believe in Him and have an intimate relationship, so we need to be having regular conversations. The most important one is the first one. If, by reading on further, this will be your first conversation or your first real and honest conversation, I applaud you in advance. In Jesus's words and teachings, He explains how it's possible, if we choose, to have conversation; His understanding of life teachings, love for Father God and others, forgiveness, salvation, sanctification unto transformation into His image, and ultimately inclusion in an intimate relationship within His resurrected life.

The reader will be able to make a very informed decision on whether or not they want to be in a relationship with Jesus. He is more than just a man; He is the Son of God and is God. No matter what we may or may not choose regarding Him. Whatever our decision, please understand that it is directly relational on our part because either will take a "self-willed" decision on our part.

Jesus does an excellent job explaining both sides of the relationship in the Scriptures, as well as the benefits and consequences, but you get to decide.

I encourage you to continue reading Just the Words and Teachings of Jesus in parts 3 through 6, then "Inclusion—הללכה—in the Resurrected Life of Jesus the Messiah" in part 9. May my testimony in part 10 be a witness and inspire you to really count the cost before you make your choice or even rededicate your life. You will have to decide one way or the other, as making no decision is a decision that would ultimately not benefit you anything as a person in this life or life hereafter. So choose wisely.

I sincerely pray you and Jesus will find each other in His words and teachings. Now, how about, together, you and Jesus get started in a conversation? I guarantee your life will never be the same!

Shalom,
Michael Michelucci

PART 2:

AUTHOR'S DIRECTIVES

- It is especially important, when reading biblical scriptures of Just the Words and Teachings of Jesus, that the reader also go into the Bible and read all other scriptures within the specific subtopic chapter for relevant context of the content. Context within content is the only pathway of discernment and understanding to gain biblical wisdom given by Jesus with help from the Holy Spirit.

- For some subtopic teachings, there is only one apostolic Gospel writer. For other subtopics, there are two, three, or four Gospel writers. All written words of each writer are inspired and were intentionally given to them by the Holy Spirit, as the writers are witnesses to the life and times of Jesus's ministry, teachings, sacrifice, death, burial, and resurrection. When more than one subtopic is written about by more than one of the writers, it is self-evident there is an emphasis regarding Jesus's teaching that the Holy Spirit wants the reader to understand. The greater the emphasis, the greater the need for prayer and discernment. Please ask the Holy Spirit for increased understanding, wisdom, and, of course, help being obedient to act on Jesus's teachings.

- Two separate indexes of the four Gospel subtopic titles are listed for the reader as reference points of Jesus's teachings.
    - Part 3: "180" within the Gospels of Matthew, Mark, and Luke.
    - Part 5: "75" within the Gospel of John.

- Two sets of scriptures found within the subtopic listings are written out completely for the reader. Along with OT and NT scriptures as concordance references.
    - Part 4: the Gospels of Matthew, Mark, and Luke.
    - Part 6: the Gospel of John.

- All (OT/Tanakh) and (NT/B'rit Hadashah) concordance reference scriptures are noted within a subtopic scripture.
    - (OT/Tanakh) reference scriptures are capitalized as (A, B, C, D, E, etc.).
    - (NT/B'rit Hadashah) reference scriptures are noted as (a, b, c, d, etc.).
    - I highly recommend the reader take time to look up these reference scriptures as noted within a scripture to help gain contextual relevance regarding the subtopic content Jesus is speaking and teaching about.

- "Part 7: Glossary Words and Meanings" of Hebrew and various other words within a specific scripture are noted with an asterisk (*) and italicized. With the definition of a word found in the glossary section in mind, go back and reread the scripture from which it came to possibly gain greater revelations of Yeshua's words and teachings.

- Jesus is written as Yeshua, which is His Hebrew name. I will address Him as Yeshua going forward in this book.

- All pronoun references for Father God, Yeshua, and the Holy Spirit are capitalized within the scriptures out of respect for the One. See Deuteronomy 6:4, the "Sh'ma."

- Please pray for yourself and others seeking the narrow path to the resurrected life. Have pen and paper at hand or enter your personal notes within the pages allocated at the end of this book, part 12. As wisdom gained is life in the Spirit. "Now He is not the God of the dead, but of the living—to Him all are alive." See Luke 20:38.

PART 3:

"180" SUBTOPIC TEACHINGS—MATTHEW, MARK, AND LUKE

Starting on Page 28:

The Boy Amazes the Torah Teachers: Luke 2:49

Yochanan (John) Baptizes Yeshua: Matthew 3:15; Luke 3:21–22

Starting on Page 29:

Satan Tempts Yeshua: Matthew 4:4, 7, 10; Luke 4:4, 12, 8

Yeshua Begins His Galilean Ministry, Yeshua Rejected at Nazareth: Matthew 4:17; Mark 1:15; Luke 4:21–27

Starting on Page 31:

Four Fishermen Called as Disciples: Matthew 4:19; Mark 1:17, 20; Luke 5:4, 10

Starting on Page 32:

Yeshua Casts Out an Unclean Spirit: Mark 1:25; Luke 4:35

Yeshua Preaches in Galilee: Mark 1:38; Luke 4:43

The Beatitudes: Matthew 5:3–12; Luke 6:20–23

Starting on Page 35:

Believers Are Salt and Light, Tasteless Salt Is Worthless: Matthew 5:13–16; Luke 14:34–35

Starting on Page 36:

Christ Fulfills the Law: Matthew 5:17–20

Starting on Page 37:

Murder Begins in the Heart: Matthew 5:21–26

Starting on Page 38:

Adultery in the Heart: Matthew 5:27–30

Starting on Page 39:

Marriage Is Sacred and Binding; The Law, the Prophets, and the Kingdom: Matthew 5:31–32; Luke 16:18

Starting on Page 40:

Yeshua Forbids Oaths: Matthew 5:33–37

Starting on Page 41:

Go the Second Mile: Matthew 5:38-42

Love Your Enemies: Matthew 5:39–48; Luke 6:27–28, 6:29–30, 35, 31–34, 36

Starting on Page 44:

Make Peace with Your Adversary: Luke 12:57–59

Do Good to Please God, Yeshua Pronounces Woes: Matthew 6:1–4; Luke 6:25, 24, 26

Starting on Page 45:

The Parable of the Good Samaritan: Luke 10:26–28, 30–37

Starting on Page 48:

Mary and Martha Worship and Serve: Luke 17:41–42

Part 3: "180" Subtopic Teachings—Matthew, Mark, and Luke   17

Faith and Duty: Luke 17:6–10

Starting on Page 50:

A Friend Comes at Midnight: Luke 11:5–8

Starting on Page 51:

The Model Prayer: Matthew 6:5–15; Luke 11:2–4

Starting on Page 54:

Fasting to Be Seen Only by God: Matthew 6:16–18

Layup Treasures in Heaven, Do Not Worry: Matthew 6:19–21; Luke 12:33–34

Starting on Page 55:

The Rich Man and El'azar (Lazarus): Luke 16:19–34;

Starting on Page 58:

The Lamp of the Body: Matthew 6:23; Luke 11:33–36

Starting on Page 59:

The Parable of the Unjust Servant: Luke 16:1–8

Starting on Page 62:

You Cannot Serve God and Riches, The Parable of the Unjust Servant Continued: Matthew 6:24; Luke 16:9–13

Starting on Page 62:

Do Not Worry: Matthew 6:25–34; Luke 12:22–32

Starting on Page 65:

Do Not Judge: Matthew 7:1–6; Luke 6:37, 36, 38–41, 42

Starting on Page 67:

Keep Asking, Seeking, Knocking: Matthew 7:7–12; Luke 11:9–10

Starting on Page 68:

The Narrow Way, Key to the Narrow Way: Matthew 7:13-14, Luke 13:24

Starting on Page 69:

You Will Know Them by Their Fruits, A Tree Is Known by Its Fruit: Matthew 7:15–20; Luke 6:44, 43, 45, 44

Starting on Page 71:

Repent or Perish: Luke 13:2–5

Starting on Page 72:

I Never Knew You, The Narrow Way: Matthew 7:21–23; Luke 13:25–30, 32–33

Starting on Page 74:

Build on the Rock: Matthew 7:24–27; Luke 6:46–49

Starting on Page 75:

Yeshua Cleanses a Leper: Matthew 8:3–4; Mark 1:41–44; Luke 5:13–14

Starting on Page 76:

Ten Lepers Cleansed: Luke 17:14, 17–19

Yeshua Heals a Centurion's Servant: Matthew 8:7, 10–13; Luke 7:9

Starting on Page 78:

Yeshua Raises Son of the Widow of Nain: Luke 7:13–14

The Cost of Discipleship: Matthew 8:20, 22; Luke 9:58–60, 62

Starting on Page 79:

Wind and Wave Obey Yeshua: Matthew 8:26; Mark 4:35, 39–40; Luke 8:22, 24–25

Starting on Page 80:

Two Demon-Possessed Men Healed, A Demon-Possessed Man Healed: Matthew 8:32; Mark 5:8–9, 19; Luke 8:29–30, 32, 39

Starting on Page 82:

Yeshua Forgives and Heals a Paralytic: Matthew 9:2, 4–6; Mark 2:2, 5, 8–11; Luke 5:20, 22–24

Starting on Page 83:

A Sinful Woman Is Forgiven: Luke 7:40–50

Starting on Page 85:

Matthew, the Tax Collector: Matthew 9:9; Mark 2:14; Luke 5:27

Who Really Needs a Doctor?: Matthew 9:12–13; Mark 2:17; Luke 5:31–32

Starting on Page 86:

Yeshua Is Questioned about Fasting: Matthew 9:15–17; Mark 2:19–22; Luke 5:34–39

Starting on Page 88:

A Girl Restored to Life and a Woman Healed: Matthew 9:22, 23–24; Mark 5:30, 34, 36, 39, 41; Luke 8:45–46, 48, 50, 52, 54–55

Starting on Page 89:

Two Blind Men Healed, Blind Man Healed at Bethsaida: Matthew 9:28–30; Mark 8:23, 26

Starting on Page 90:

The Compassion of Yeshua: Matthew 9:37–38

Starting on Page 92:

Sending Out the Twelve: Matthew 10:5–7, 8–15; Mark 6:8–11; Luke 9:3–5

Starting on Page 93:

The Seventy Sent Out: Luke 10:2–12

Starting on Page 95:

The Seventy Return with Joy: Luke 10:18–20

Starting on Page 97:

Yeshua Rejoices in the Spirit: Luke 10:21–24

Starting on Page 98:

Persecutions Are Coming: Matthew 10:16–26; Luke 6:40

Starting on Page 101:

Yeshua Teaches the Fear of God: Matthew 10:27–31; Luke 12:4–7

Starting on Page 102:

Confess Christ before Men: Matthew 10:32–33; Luke 12:8–12

Starting on Page 103:

Christ Brings Division: Matthew 10:34–39; Luke 12:49–53

Starting on Page 105:

Leaving All to Follow Yeshua: Luke 14:26–33

Starting on Page 107:

A Cup of Cold Water: Matthew 10:40–42

Starting on Page 108:

Yochanan the Immerser (John the Baptist) Sends Messengers to Yeshua: Matthew 11:4–19; Luke 7:22–28, 31–35

Starting on Page 112:

Woe to the Impenitent Cities: Matthew 11:20–24; Luke 10:13–16

Part 3: "180" Subtopic Teachings—Matthew, Mark, and Luke   19

Starting on Page 113:

Yeshua Gives True Rest: Matthew 11:25–30

Starting on Page 115:

Yeshua Is Lord of the Sabbath: Matthew 12:3–8; Mark 2:25–28; Luke 6:3–5

Starting on Page 116:

Healing on the Sabbath: Matthew 12:11–13; Mark 3:3–5; Luke 6:8–10

Starting on Page 117:

A Spirit of Infirmity: Luke 13:12, 15–17

Starting on Page 118:

Healing on the Sabbath, A Man with Dropsy Healed on the Sabbath: Matthew 12:11–12; Luke 14:3, 5

Starting on Page 119:

A House Divided Cannot Stand: Matthew 12:25–30; Mark 3:23–27; Luke 11:18–23

Starting on Page 121:

The Unpardonable Sin: Matthew 12:31–32; Mark 3:28–29

A Tree Known by Its Fruit: Matthew 12:33–37; Luke 6:44–45

Starting on Page 123:

Keeping the Word: Luke 11:28

The Scribes and Pharisees Ask for a Sign, Seeking a Sign: Matthew 11:39–42; Luke 11:29–30, 32, 31

Starting on Page 124:

An Unclean Spirit Returns: Matthew 12:43–45; Luke 11:24–26

Starting on Page 125:

Yeshua's Mother and Brothers Send for Him: Matthew 12:48–50; Mark 3:33–35; Luke 11:21

Starting on Page 126:

Parable of the Sower: Matthew 13:3–9; Mark 4:3–9; Luke 8:5 12, 6, 13, 7, 14–15, 8

Starting on Page 129:

The Purpose of Parables: Matthew 13:11–17; Mark 4:11–13; Luke 8:10

Starting on Page 131:

The Parable of the Sower Explained: Matthew 13:18–23; Mark 4:14–20; Luke 8:11–15

Starting on Page 133:

Light under a Basket, The Parable of the Revealed Light: Mark 4:21–25; Luke 8:16–18

Starting on Page 134:

The Parable of the Wheat and the Tares, The Parable of the Growing Seed: Matthew 13:24–30; Mark 4:26–29

Starting on Page 136:

The Parable of the Mustard Seed: Matthew 13:31–32; Mark 4:30–32; Luke 13:18–19

Starting on Page 137:

The Parable of Leaven: Matthew 13:33; Luke 13:20–21

Prophecy and the Parables: Matthew 13:34–35

Starting on Page 138:

The Parables of the Tares Explained: Matthew 13:37–43

Starting on Page 139:

The Parable of the Hidden Treasure: Matthew 13:44

The Parable of the Pearl of Great Price: Matthew 13:45–46

Starting on Page 140:

The Parable of the Dragnet: Matthew 13:47–52

Starting on Page 141:

Yeshua Rejected at Nazareth, A Samaritan Village Rejects the Savior: Matthew 13:57; Mark 6:4; Luke 9:54–56

Starting on Page 142:

Feeding the Five Thousand: Matthew 14:16, 18; Mark 6:31, 37, 38; Luke 9:13, 14

Yeshua Walks on the Sea: Matthew 14:27, 29, 31; Mark 6:50

Starting on Page 143:

Defilement Comes from Within: Matthew 15:3–11, 13–14, 16–19, 20; Mark 7:10–13, 8–9, 6–7, 14–16, 18–21, 22–23

Starting on Page 148:

A Gentile Shows Her Faith: Matthew 15:24, 26, 28; Mark 7:27, 29

Yeshua Heals a Deaf Mute: Mark 7:34

Feeding the Four Thousand: Matthew 15:32, 34; Mark 8:2–3, 5

Starting on Page 149:

The Pharisees and Sadducees Seek a Sign: Matthew 16:2, 3–4; Mark 8:12; Luke 12:54–56

Starting on Page 150:

The Leaven of the Pharisees and Sadducees, Beware the Levan of the Pharisees and Herod, Beware of Hypocrisy: Matthew 16:6, 8–11; Mark 8:15, 17–21; Luke 12:1–3

Starting on Page 152:

Peter Confesses Yeshua as the Christ (the Son of the Living God): Matthew 16:13, 15, 17–20; Mark 8:27, 29; Luke 9:18, 20–22

Starting on Page 154:

Yeshua Predicts His Death and Resurrection: Matthew 16:23; Mark 8:33

Take up the Execution Stake (Cross) and Follow Him: Matthew 16:24–28; Mark 8:34–38 (plus 9:1); Luke 9:23–27

Starting on Page 156:

Leaving All to Follow Yeshua: Luke 14:27

Yeshua Transfigured on the Mount: Matthew 17:7, 9, 11–12; Mark 9:7, 12–13; Luke 9:35

Starting on Page 157:

A Boy Is Healed: Matthew 17:17–18, 20; Mark 9:16, 19, 21, 23, 25, 29; Luke 9:41 (plus 4:41)

Starting on Page 158:

A Boy Is Healed Continued: Matthew 17:20; Mark 9:21, 23, 25, 29; Luke 9:42

Starting on Page 159:

Yeshua Again Predicts His Death and Resurrection: Matthew 17:22–23; Mark 9:31; Luke 9:44

Starting on Page 160:

Who Is the Greatest? Greatness Is Serving: Matthew 18:3–5; Mark 9:33, 35, 37; Luke 9:48

Starting on Page 161:

Yeshua Warns of Offenses: Matthew 18:6–9; Mark 9:42–50; Luke 17:2, 1

Starting on Page 163

The Disciples Argue about Greatness: Luke 22:25–30

Starting on Page 165:

Yeshua Forbids Sectarianism: Mark 9:39–41; Luke 9:50

The Parable of the Lost Sheep: Matthew 18:10–14; Luke 15:4–7

Starting on Page 165:

The Parable of the Lost Sheep Continued: Matthew 18:14; Luke 15:7

The Parable of the Lost Coin: Luke 15:8–10

Starting on Page 167:

The Parable of the Lost Son: Luke 15:11–32

Starting on Page 171:

Dealing with a Sinning Brother: Matthew 18:15–20; Luke 17:3

Starting on Page 173:

The Parable of the Unforgiving Servant: Matthew 18:22–35; Luke 17:4

Starting on Page 175:

Marriage and Divorce: Matthew 19:4–6, 8–9; Mark 10:3, 5–9, 11–12

Starting on Page 177:

Yeshua Teaches on Celibacy: Matthew 19:11–12

Yeshua Blesses Little Children: Matthew 19:14; Mark 10:14–15; Luke 18:16–17

Starting on Page 178:

Yeshua Counsels the Rich Young Ruler: Matthew 19:16–19, 21; Mark 10:18–19, 21; Luke 18:19–20, 22

Starting on Page 180:

The Parable of the Rich Fool: Luke 12:14–21

Starting on Page 181:

With God All Things Are Possible: Matthew 19:23, 24, 26, 28–30; Mark 10:23–25, 27, 29–31; Luke 18:24–25, 27, 29–30

Starting on Page 183:

The Parable of the Workers in the Vineyard: Matthew 20:1–16

Starting on Page 187:

Yeshua a Third Time Predicts His Death and Resurrection: Matthew 20:18–19; Mark 10:33–34; Luke 18:31–33

Starting on Page 188:

Greatness Is Serving: Matthew 20:21–23, 25–28; Mark 10:36, 38–39, 40, 42–45

Starting on Page 191:

Two Blind Men Receive Their Sight, Yeshua Heals Blind Bartimaeus, A Blind Man Receives His Sight: Matthew 20:32–33; Mark 10:49, 51–52; Luke 18:40–42

Starting on Page 191:

Yeshua Comes to Zakkai (Zacharia) House: Luke 19:5, 9–10

Starting on Page 192:

The Triumphal Entry of Yeshua: Matthew 21:1–5; Mark 11:2–3; Luke 19:30–31, 40

Starting on Page 193:

Yeshua Cleanses the Temple: Matthew 21:13, 16; Mark 11:17; Luke 19:46

Starting on Page 194:

The Fig Tree Withered, Yeshua Cursed the Fig Tree: Matthew 21:19; Mark 11:14

The Parable of the Barren Fig Tree: Luke 13:6–9

Starting on Page 195:

The Lesson of the Withered Fig Tree: Matthew 21:21–22; Mark 11:22–25

Starting on Page 196:

Yeshua's Authority Questioned: Matthew 21:24–25, 27; Mark 11:29–30, 33; Luke 20:3, 8

Starting on Page 197:

The Parable of the Two Sons: Matthew 21:28–32

Starting on Page 198:

The Parable of the Wicked Vinedressers: Matthew 21:33–44; Mark 12:1–11; Luke 20:9–18

Starting on Page 201:

The Parable of the Wedding Feast, The Parable of the Great Supper: Matthew 22:1–14; Luke 14:16, 18, 17, 19–24

Starting on Page 204:

Take the Lowly Place: Luke 14:7–14

Starting on Page 206:

The Parable of the Persistent Widow: Luke 18:1–8

Starting on Page 207:

The Parable of the Pharisee and the Tax Collector: Luke 18:9–14

Starting on Page 209:

Peter and His Master Pay Their Taxes: Matthew 17:25–27

Starting on Page 210:

The Pharisees: Is It Lawful to Pay Taxes to Caesar? Matthew 22:18–21; Mark 12:15–17; Luke 20:23–25

Starting on Page 211:

The Sadducees: What about the Resurrection? Matthew 22:29–32; Mark 12:24–27; Luke 20:34–38

Starting on Page 213:

The Scribes: Which Is the First Commandment of All? Matthew 22:37–40; Mark 12:29–31, 34

Starting on Page 214:

Yeshua: How Can David Call His Descendant Lord? Matthew 22:41–45; Mark 12:35–37; Luke 20:41–44

Starting on Page 215:

Beware of the Scribes, Woe to Pharisees and Lawyers: Matthew 23:14 (NKJV); Mark 12:38–40; Luke 20:46–47, 11:42, 39–41, 44, 47–48

Woe to the Scribes and Pharisees: Matthew 23:2–20, 21–31; Luke 11:46, 43, 52

Starting on Page 223:

Woe to the Scribes and Pharisees Continued, Woe to the Pharisees and Lawyers Continued: Matthew 23:32–36; Luke 11:49, 51, 50

Starting on Page 224:

The Widow's Two Mites: Mark 12:43–44; Luke 21:3–4

Starting on Page 225:

Yeshua Laments over Jerusalem: Matthew 23:37–39; Luke 13:34–35

Yeshua Predicts the Destruction of the Temple: Matthew 24:2; Mark 13:2; Luke 21:6

Starting on Page 226:

The Signs of the Times and the End of the Age: Matthew 24:4–8, 14; Mark 13:5–13; Luke 21:8–17, 19, 18

Starting on Page 230:

The Great Tribulation, The Destruction of Yerushalayim: Matthew 24:15–25, 26–28; Mark 13:14–23; Luke 21:20–24

Starting on Page 233:

The Coming of the Kingdom: Luke 17:37

The Coming of the Son of Man: Matthew 24:29–31; Mark 13:24–27; Luke 21:25–28

Starting on Page 235:

The Parable of the Fig Tree: Matthew 24:32–35; Mark 13:28–31; Luke 21:29–33

Starting on Page 236:

The Importance of Watching: Luke 21:34–36

Starting on Page 237:

No One Knows the Day and Hour, The Coming of the Kingdom: Matthew 24:36, 37–44; Mark 13:32–37; Luke 17:20–35; 12:39–4

Starting on Page 242:

The Faithful Servant and the Evil Servant: Matthew 24:45–51; Luke 12:35–37, 42–43, 38, 44–48

Starting on Page 244:

The Parable of the Wise and Foolish Virgins: Matthew 25:1–13

Starting on Page 246:

The Parable of the Talents, The Parable of the Minas: Matthew 25:14–30; Luke 19:12–13, 16, 17, 14–15, 18–19, 21, 20, 22–24, 26–27

Starting on Page 250:

Yeshua Weeps over Jerusalem: Luke 19:41–44

Starting on Page 251:

The Son of Man Will Judge the Nations: Matthew 25:31–46

Starting on Page 255:

The Plot to Kill Yeshua: Matthew 26:2

Anointing at Bethany: Matthew 26:10–13; Mark 14:6–9

Starting on Page 256:

Yeshua Celebrates Pesach (Passover) with His Disciples and Foretells of His Betrayer: Matthew 26:18, 21, 23, 24–25; Mark 14:13–15, 18, 20–21; Luke 22:8, 10–12, 21–22

Starting on Page 259:

Yeshua Institutes the Lord's Supper (Seder): Matthew 26:26–29; Mark 14:21–22, 24–25; Luke 22:22, 15–16, 19, 17, 20, 18

Starting on Page 261:

Yeshua Predicts Peter's Denial: Matthew 26:31, 34; Mark 14:27, 30; Luke 22:31–32, 34

Starting on Page 262:

Supplies for the Road Luke: 22:35–38

24   *Just the Words and Teachings of Jesus Christ*

Starting on Page 263:

The Prayer in the Garden: Matthew 26:36–37, 38–42, 45–46; Mark 14:32, 34, 36–38, 41–42; Luke 22:40, 42, 46

Starting on Page 265:

Betrayal and Arrest in the Garden of Gethsemane: Matthew 26:50, 52–56; Mark 14:48–49; Luke 22:48, 51–53

Starting on Page 267:

Peter Denies Yeshua and Weeps Bitterly: Luke 22:61–62

Yeshua Faces the Sanhedrin: Matthew 26:64; Mark 14:62; Luke 22:67–70

Starting on Page 268:

Yeshua Faces Pontius Pilate, Yeshua Handed Over to Pontius Pilate: Matthew 27:11; Mark 15:2; Luke 23:3

Starting on Page 269:

The King on the Cross: Luke 23:28–31, 34, 43

Starting on Page 270:

Yeshua Dies on the Cross (Execution Stake): Matthew 27:46, 50; Mark 15:34, 37; Luke 23:46

Starting on Page 271:

The Women Worship the Risen Lord: Matthew 28:9–10

The Road to Emmaus: Luke 24:17, 19, 25–27

The Disciples' Eyes Opened: Luke 24:30–32

Starting on Page 273:

Yeshua Appears to His Disciples: Luke 24:38–39, 41

Scriptures Opened to Their Minds: Luke 24:44–51

Starting on Page 276:

The Great Commission: Matthew 28:18–20; Mark 16:15–18

PART 4:

SUBTOPIC SCRIPTURAL ALIGNMENT VIEW—MATTHEW, MARK, AND LUKE

(OT/Tanakh and NT/B'rit Hadashah References Included)

Luke 24:44-48

Yeshua, said to them, "This is what I meant when I was still with you and told you that everything written about Me in the Torah of Moshe, the Prophets and the Psalms had to be fulfilled." Then He opened their minds, to that they could understand the Tanakh, telling, "Here is what it says: The Messiah is to suffer and to rise from the dead on the third day; and in His name repentance leading to forgiveness of sins is to be proclaimed to people from all nations, starting with Yerushalyim. You are witnesses of these things.

~ May Yeshua open your minds and hearts as well. ~
As He talks to you with just His words and teaching

Gospel of Mattityahu "Matthew"	OT/NT References	Gospel of Mrk "Mark"	OT/NT References	Gospel of Luk "Luke"	OT/NT References
				Chapter 2 **The Boy Yeshua Amazes the Torah Teachers**	
				v. 49: "He said to them, 'Why did you have to look for Me? Didn't you know that I had to be (a) concerning Myself with (b) My Father's affairs?'"	a). John 9:4 b). Mark 1:22; Luke 4:22, 32; John 4:34 John 5:17, 36
Chapter 3 **Yochanan (John) Baptizes Yeshua**				**Chapter 3** **Yochanan (John) Baptizes Yeshua**	
v. 15: However, *Yeshua* answered him, "Let it be this way now, because we should do everything righteousness requires."				v. 21: "While all the people were being immersed, (a) *Yeshua* too, was immersed. As He was praying, heaven was opened."	a). Matthew 3:13–17; John 1:32
				v. 22: "The *Rauch HaKodesh* came down on Him in physical form like a dove, and a * voice came from heaven, 'You are My Son, whom I love; I am (A) well pleased with You.'" (See "Commentaries.")	A). Psalm 2:7; Isaiah 42:1; Matthew 3:17; 17:5; Mark 1:11; Luke 1:35; 9:35; 2 Peter 1:17

28 *Just the Words and Teachings of Jesus Christ*

Gospel of Mattityahu "Matthew"	OT/NT References	Gospel of Mrk "Mark"	OT/NT References	Gospel of Luk "Luke"	OT/NT References
Chapter 4 **Satan Tempts Yeshua**				**Chapter 4** **Satan Tempts Yeshua**	
v. 4: "But He answered, 'The *Tanakh says, (A) "Man does not live on bread alone, but on every word that comes from the mouth of [the Lord]."'"	A). Deuteronomy 8:3			v. 4: "*Yeshua answered him, 'The *Tanakh says, (A) "Man does not live on bread alone."'"	A). Deuteronomy 8:3
v. 7: "*Yeshua replied to him, 'But it also says, (A) "Do not put *Adonai your God to the test."'"	A). Deuteronomy 6:16			v. 12: "*Yeshua answered him, 'It also says, (A) "Do not put *Adonai your God to the test."'"	A). Deuteronomy 6:16
v. 10: "'Away with you, *Satan!' *Yeshua told him, 'For the *Tanakh says, (A) "Worship *Adonai your God and serve only Him."'"	A). Deuteronomy 6:13; Deuteronomy 10:20; Josh 24:10			v. 8: "*Yeshua answered him, 'The *Tanakh says, (A) "Worship *Adonai your God and serve Him only."'"	A). Deuteronomy 8:3
Chapter 4 **Yeshua Begins His Galilean Ministry**		**Chapter 1** **Yeshua Begins His Galilean Ministry**		**Chapter 4** **Yeshua Rejected at Nazareth**	
v. 17: "From that time on, *Yeshua began proclaiming, (a) 'Turn from your sins to God, for the Kingdom of Heaven is near!'"	a). Mark 1:14–15; Matthew 3:2; 10:7	v. 15: (A) "The time has come; (b) God's Kingdom is near! Turn to God from your sins and believe the Good News!"	A). Daniel 9:25; Galatians 4:4; Ephesians 1:10; 1 Timothy 2:6; Titus 1:3; b). Matthew 3:2; 4:17; Acts 20:21	v. 21: "He started to speak to them: (a) 'Today, as you heard it read, this passage of the *Tanakh was fulfilled!'"	a). Matthew 1:22–23; Acts 13:29

Gospel of Mattityahu "Matthew"	OT/NT References	Gospel of Mrk "Mark"	OT/NT References	Gospel of Luk "Luke"	OT/NT References
				Chapter 4 Yeshua Rejected at Nazareth Continued	
				v. 23: "Then *Yeshua* said to them, 'No doubt you will quote to Me this proverb—"Doctor, cure yourself!" We've heard about all the things that have been going on over in (a) *K' far-Nachum*; now do them here in (b) your home town!'"	a). Matthew 4:13; 11:23 b). Matthew 13:54; Mark 6:1
				v. 24: "'Yes!' He said, 'I tell you that no (a) prophet is accepted in his home town.'"	a). Matthew 13:57; Mark 6:4; John 4:44
				v. 25: "It's true, I'm telling you—(A) when *Eliyahu* was in *Isra'el*, and the sky was sealed off for three-and-a-half-years, so that all the Land suffered a severe famine, there were many widows."	A). 1 Kings 17:9; James 5:17
				v. 26: "But *Eliyahu* was sent to none of them, only to a widow in *Tzarfat* in the land of *Tzidon*."	

30 *Just the Words and Teachings of Jesus Christ*

Gospel of Mattityahu "Matthew"	OT/NT References	Gospel of Mrk "Mark"	OT/NT References	Gospel of Luk "Luke"	OT/NT References
				Chapter 4 **Yeshua Rejected at Nazareth Continued**	
				v. 27: (A) "Also there were many people with *tzara'at* in *Isra'el* during the time of the prophet	A). 2 Kings 5:1–14
Chapter 4 **Four Fishermen Called as Disciples**		**Chapter 1** **Four Fishermen Called as Disciples**		**Chapter 5** **Four Fishermen Called as Disciples**	
				v. 4: "When He had finished speaking, He said to *Shim'on*, (a) 'Put out into deep water, and let down your nets for a catch.'"	a). John 21:6
v.19: "Come after Me, and (a) I will make you fishers for men!"	a). Luke 5:10	v. 17: "*Yeshua* said to them, 'Come, follow Me, and I will make you (a) fishers for men!'"	a). Matthew 13:47–48	v. 10: "And likewise both *Ya'akov* and *Yochanan*, *Shim'on*'s partners. 'Don't be frightened,' *Yeshua* said to *Shim'on*, (a) 'from now on you will be catching men—alive!'"	a). Matthew 4:19; Mark 1:17
		v. 20: "Immediately He called them, and they left their father *Zavdai* in the boat with the hired men and went after *Yeshua*."			

Gospel of Mattityahu "Matthew"	OT/NT References	Gospel of Mrk "Mark"	OT/NT References	Gospel of Luk "Luke"	OT/NT References
		Chapter 1 **Yeshua Casts Out an Unclean Spirit**		**Chapter 4** **Yeshua Casts Out Unclean Spirit**	
		v. 25: (a) "Be quiet, and come out of him!"	a). Luke 4:39	v. 35: But *Yeshua rebuked it: (a) "Be quiet, and come out of him!"	a). Lit: Be Muzzled
		Chapter 1 **Yeshua Preaches in Galilee**		**Chapter 4** **Yeshua Preaches in Galilee**	
		v. 38: "He answered, (a) 'Let's go somewhere else—to the other villages around here. I have to proclaim the message there too—(B) in fact, this is why I came out.'"	a). Luke 4:43 B). Isaiah 61:1–; Mark 10:45; John 18:28; 17:4, 8	v. 43: "But He said to them, (a) 'I must announce the Good News of the Kingdom of God to the other towns too—this is why I was sent.'"	a). Mark 1:14; John 9:4
Chapter 5 **The Beatitudes**				**Chapter 6** **The Beatitudes**	
v. 3: "How (A) blessed are the poor in spirit! For the Kingdom of Heaven is theirs."	A). Proverbs 16:19; Isaiah 66:2; Luke 6:20–23			v. 20: "He looked at His *Talmidim and said: (a) 'How blessed are you poor! For the Kingdom of God is yours.'"	a). Matthew 5:3–12; 11:5; Luke 6:20–23; James 2:5
v. 4: "How (A) blessed are those who mourn! For they will be comforted."	A). Isaiah 61:2–3; Luke 6:21; John 16:20; Acts 16:34; 2 Corinthians 1:7; Revelation 21:4				

Gospel of Mattityahu "Matthew"	OT/NT References	Gospel of Mrk "Mark"	OT/NT References	Gospel of Luk "Luke"	OT/NT References
Chapter 5 **The Beatitudes Continued**				**Chapter 6** **The Beatitudes Continued**	
v. 5: (A) "How blessed are the meek! (b) For they will inherit the Land!"	A). Psalm 37:11; Isaiah 29:19 b). Romans 4:13				
v. 6: (a) "How blessed are those who hunger and thirst for righteousness! (B) For they will be filled."	a). Luke 1:53; Acts 2:4 B). Isaiah 55:1; 65:13; John 4:14; 6:48; 7:37			v. 21: (A) "How blessed are you who are hungry! (b) For you will be filled. (C) How blessed are you who are crying now! (D) For you will laugh."	A). Isaiah 55:1; 65:13; Matthew 5:6 b). Revelation 7:16 C). Isaiah 61:3; Revelation 7:17 D). Psalm 126:5
v. 7: "How blessed are those who show mercy! (A) For they will be shown mercy."	A). Psalm 41:1; Mark 11:25				
v. 8: (A) "How blessed are the pure in heart! (b) For they will see God."	A). Psalm 16:2; 24:4; Hebrews 12:14 b). Acts 7:55–56; 1 Corinthians 13:12				

Part 4: Subtopic Scriptural Alignment View—Matthew, Mark, and Luke

Gospel of Mattityahu "Matthew"	OT/NT References	Gospel of Mrk "Mark"	OT/NT References	Gospel of Luk "Luke"	OT/NT References
Chapter 5 **The Beatitudes Continued**				**Chapter 6** **The Beatitudes Continued**	
v. 9: "How blessed are those who make peace! For they will be called sons of God."					
v. 10: (a)"How blessed are those who are persecuted because they pursue righteousness! For the Kingdom of Heaven is theirs."	a). 2 Corinthians 4:17; 1 Peter 3:14				
v. 11: (a) "How blessed you are when people insult you and persecute you and (b) tell all kinds of vicious lies about you because you follow Me!"	a). Luke 6:22 b). Peter 4:14			v. 22: (a) "How blessed you are whenever people hate you and ostracize you and insult you and (b) denounce you as a criminal on account of the Son of Man!"	a). Matthew 5:11; 1 Peter 2:19; 3:14; 4:14 b). John 16:2
v. 12: (a) "Rejoice, be glad, because your reward in heaven is great—(B) they persecuted the prophets before you in the same way."	a). Luke 6:23; Acts 5:41; 1 Peter 4:13–14 B). 2 Chronicles 36:16; Nehemiah 9:26; Matthew 23:37; Acts 7:52; 1 Thessalonians 2:15; Hebrews 11:35–37; James 5:10			v. 23: (a) "Be glad when that happens; yes, dance for joy! Because in heaven your reward is great. (b) For that is just how their fathers treated the prophets."	a). Matthew 5:12; Acts 5:41; Colossians 1:24; James 1:2 b). Acts 7:51

Gospel of Mattityahu "Matthew"	OT/NT References	Gospel of Mrk "Mark"	OT/NT References	Gospel of Luk "Luke"	OT/NT References
Chapter 5 **Believers Are Salt and Light**				**Chapter 14** **Tasteless Salt Is Worthless**	
v. 13: "You are salt for the Land. (a) But if salt becomes tasteless, how can it be made salty again? It is no longer good for anything except being thrown out for people to trample on."	a). Mark 9:50; Luke 14:34			v. 34: (a) "Salt is excellent. But if even the salt becomes tasteless, what can be used to season it?"	a). Matthew 5:13; Mark 9:50
				v. 35: "It is fit for neither soil nor manure—people throw it out. Those who have ears that can hear, let them hear!"	
v. 14: (A) "You are light for the world. A town built on a hill cannot be hidden."	A). Proverbs 4:18; John 8:12; Philippians 2:15				
v. 15: "Likewise when people (a) light a lamp, they don't cover it with a bowl but put in on a lampstand, so that it shines for everyone in the house."	a). Mark 4:21; Luke 8:16; Philippians 2:15				
v. 16: "In the same way, let your light shine before people, (a) so that they may see the good things you do and (b) praise your Father in heaven."	a). 1 Peter 2:12 b). John 15:8; 1 Corinthians 14:25				

Part 4: Subtopic Scriptural Alignment View—Matthew, Mark, and Luke

Gospel of Mattityahu "Matthew"	OT/NT References	Gospel of Mrk "Mark"	OT/NT References	Gospel of Luk "Luke"	OT/NT References
Chapter 5 Christ Fulfills the Law					
v. 17: (a) "Don't think that I have come to abolish the *Torah* or the Prophets. I have come not to abolish but to complete."	a). Romans 10:4				
v. 18: "Yes indeed! I tell you that (a) until heaven and earth pass away, not so much as a *yud* or a stroke will pass from the *Torah*—not until everything that must happen has happened."	a). Matthew 24:35; Luke 16:17				
v. 19: (a) "So whoever disobeys the least of these *mitzvoth* and teaches others to do so will be called the least in the Kingdom of Heaven. But whoever obeys them and so teaches will be called great in the Kingdom of Heaven."	a). James 2:10				
v. 20: "For I tell you that unless your (a) righteousness is far greater than that of the *Torah-teachers* and *P'rushim*, you will certainly not enter the Kingdom of Heaven!"	a). Romans 10:3				

36   *Just the Words and Teachings of Jesus Christ*

Gospel of Mattityahu "Matthew"	OT/NT References	Gospel of Mrk "Mark"	OT/NT References	Gospel of Luk "Luke"	OT/NT References
Chapter 5 Murder Begins in the Heart					
v. 21: "You have heard that our fathers were told, (A) 'Do not murder', and that anyone who commits murder will be subject to judgement."	A). Exodus 20:13; Deuteronomy 5:17				
v. 22: "But I tell you that (a) anyone who nurses anger against his brother will be subject to judgment; that whoever calls his brother, (b) 'You good-for-nothing!' will be brought before the *Sanhedrin*: that whoever says, 'Fool!' incurs the penalty of burning in the fire of *Gei-Hinnom!*"	a). 1 John 3:15 b). James 2:20; 3:6				
v. 23: "So (a) If you are offering your gift at the Temple altar and you remember there that your brother has something against you."	a). Matthew 8:4				
v. 24: (A) "Leave your gift where it is by the altar, and go, make peace with you brother. Then come back and offer your gift."	A). Job 42:8; 1 Timothy 2:8; 1 Peter 3:7				

Part 4: Subtopic Scriptural Alignment View—Matthew, Mark, and Luke

Gospel of Mattityahu "Matthew"	OT/NT References	Gospel of Mrk "Mark"	OT/NT References	Gospel of Luk "Luke"	OT/NT References
Chapter 5 Murder Begins in the Heart Continued					
v. 25: "If someone sues you (A) come to terms with him quickly, (B) while you and he are on the way to court; or he may hand you over to the judge, and the judge to the officer of the court, and you may be thrown in jail!"	A). Proverbs 25:8; Luke 12:58–59 B). Psalm 32:6; Isaiah 55:6				
v. 26: "Yes indeed! I tell you, you will certainly not get out until you have paid the last penny."					
Chapter 5 Adultery in the Heart					
v. 27: "You have heard that our fathers were told, 'Do not commit adultery.'"					
v. 28: "But I tell you that a man who even (A) looks at a woman with the purpose of lusting after her has already committed adultery with her in his heart."	A). 2 Samuel 11:2–5; Job 31:1; Proverbs 6:25; Matthew 15:19; James 1:14–15				

Gospel of Mattityahu "Matthew"	OT/NT References	Gospel of Mrk "Mark"	OT/NT References	Gospel of Luk "Luke"	OT/NT References
Chapter 5 **Adultery in the Heart Continued**					
v. 29: (a) "If your right eye makes you sin, (b) gouge it out and throw it away! Better that you should lose one part of you than have your whole body thrown into *Gei-Hinnom*."	a). Mark 9:43 b). Colossians 3:5				
v. 30: "And if your right hand makes you sin, cut it off and throw it away! Better that you should lose one part of you than have your whole body thrown into *Gei-Hinnom*."					
Chapter 5 **Marriage Is Sacred and Binding**				**Chapter 16** **The Law, the Prophets, and the Kingdom**	
v. 31: "It was said, (A) 'whoever divorces his wife must give her a *get*.'"	A). Deuteronomy 24:1; Jeremiah 3:1; Matthew 10:2				
v. 32: "But I tell you that (a) anyone who divorces his wife, except on the ground of fornication makes her an adulteress; and that anyone who marries a divorcee' commits adultery."	a). Matthew 19:9; Mark 10:11; Luke 16:18; Romans 7:3; 1 Corinthians 7:11			v. 18: (a) "Every man who divorces his wife and marries another woman commits adultery, and a man who marries a woman divorced by her husband commits adultery."	a). Matthew 5:32; 19:9; Mark 10:11; 1 Corinthians 7:10–11

Gospel of Mattityahu "Matthew"	OT/NT References	Gospel of Mrk "Mark"	OT/NT References	Gospel of Luk "Luke"	OT/NT References
Chapter 5 **Yeshua Forbids Oaths**					
v. 33: "Again, you have (a) heard that our fathers were told, (B) 'do not break your oath,' and (C) 'Keep your vows to the LORD.'"	a). Matthew 23:16 B). Exodus 20:7; Leviticus 19:12; Numbers 30:2 C). Deuteronomy 23:23				
v. 34: "But I tell you (a) not to swear at all—not 'by heaven,' because it is (B) God's throne."	a). Matthew 23:16; James 5:12 B). Isaiah 66:1				
v. 35: "Not by the earth, 'because it is His footstool;' and not 'by *Yerushalayim*.' Because it is the city of (A) the Great King."	A). Psalm 48:2; Matthew 5:2; 19:6–10				
v. 36: "And don't swear by your head, because you can't make a single hair white or black."					
v. 37: (a) "Just let your 'Yes' be a simple 'Yes.' And your 'No' a simple 'No'; anything more than this has its origin in evil."	a). Colossians 4:6; James 5:12				

Gospel of Mattityahu "Matthew"	OT/NT References	Gospel of Mrk "Mark"	OT/NT References	Gospel of Luk "Luke"	OT/NT References
Chapter 5 Go the Second Mile				**Chapter 6 Love Your Enemies**	
v. 38: (A) "You have heard that our fathers were told, 'Eye for eye and tooth for tooth.'"	A). Exodus 21:24; Leviticus 24:20; Deuteronomy 19:21				
v. 39: (A) "But I tell you not to stand up against someone who does you wrong. (B) On the contrary, if someone hits you on the right cheek, let him hit you on the left cheek too!"	A). Proverbs 20:22; Luke 6:29; Romans 12:17; 1 Corinthians 6:7; 1 Peter 3:9 B). Isaiah 50:6; Lamentations 3:30			v. 29: (a) "If someone hits you on one cheek, offer the other too."	a). Matthew 5:39–42
v. 40: "If someone wants to sue you for your shirt, let him have your coat as well!"				v. 29: (b) "If someone takes your coat, let him have your shirt as well."	b). 1 Corinthians 6:7
v. 41: "And if a soldier (a) forces you to carry his pack for one mile, carry it for two!"	a). Matthew 27:32				
v. 42: "When someone asks you for something, give it to him; (A) when someone wants to borrow something from you, lend it to him."	A). Deuteronomy 15:7–11; Luke 6:30–34; 1 Timothy 6:18			v. 30: (A) "If someone asks you for something, give it to him; if someone takes what belongs to you don't demand it back."	A). Deuteronomy 15:7–8; Proverbs 3:27; 21:26; Matthew 5:42

Part 4: Subtopic Scriptural Alignment View—Matthew, Mark, and Luke

Gospel of Mattityahu "Matthew"	OT/NT References	Gospel of Mrk "Mark"	OT/NT References	Gospel of Luk "Luke"	OT/NT References
Chapter 5 Love Your Enemies Continued				**Chapter 6 Love Your Enemies Continued**	
v. 43: (A) "You have heard that our fathers were told, 'Love your neighbor'—(B) and hate your enemy.'"	A). Leviticus 19:18 B). Deuteronomy 23:3–6; Psalm 1:10			v. 27: (A) "Nevertheless, to you who are listening, what I say is this: "Love your enemies! Do good to those who hate you."	A). Exodus 23:4; Proverbs 25:21; Matthew 5:44; Romans 12:20
v. 44: "But I tell you, (a) love your enemies! (b) Pray for those who persecute you!"	a). Luke 6:27; Romans 12:14; Romans 12:20 b). Luke 23:34; Acts 7:60; 1 Corinthians 4:12; 1 Peter 2:23			v. 28: (a) "Bless those who curse you, (b) pray for those who mistreat you."	a). Romans 12:14 b). Luke 23:24; Acts 7:60
v. 45: "Then you will become children of your Father in heaven. (A) For He makes His sun shine on good and bad people alike, and He sends rain to the righteous and the unrighteous alike."	A). Job 25:3; Psalm 65:9–13; Luke 2:16–17; Acts 14:17			v. 35: "But (a) love your enemies, (b) do good, and (C) lend expecting nothing back! Your reward will be great, (d) and you will be children of *Ha'Elyon*; for He is kind to the ungrateful and the wicked."	a). Romans 13:10 b). Hebrews 13:16 C). Leviticus 25:35–37; Psalm 37:26 d). Matthew 5:46
				v. 31: (a) "Treat other people as you would like them to treat you."	a). Matthew 7:12

42 *Just the Words and Teachings of Jesus Christ*

Gospel of Mattityahu "Matthew"	OT/NT References	Gospel of Mrk "Mark"	OT/NT References	Gospel of Luk "Luke"	OT/NT References
Chapter 5 Love Your Enemies Continued				**Chapter 6 Love Your Enemies Continued**	
v. 46: (a) "What reward do you get if you love only those who love you? Why, even tax-collectors do that!"	a). Luke 6:32			v. 32: (a) "What credit is it to you if you love only those who love you? Why, even sinners love those who love them."	a). Matthew 5:46
v. 47: "And if you are friendly only to your friends, are you doing anything out of the ordinary? Even the *Goyim* do that!"				v. 33: "What credit is it to you if you only do good to those who do good to you? Even sinners do that."	
				v. 34: (a) "What credit is it to you if you lend only to those who you expect will pay you back? Even sinners lend to each other, expecting to be repaid in full."	a). Matthew 5:42
v. 48: (A) "Therefore be perfect just (b) as your Father in heaven is perfect."	A). Genesis 17:1; Leviticus 11:44; 19:2; Luke 6:36; Colossians 1:28; 4:12; James 1:4; 1 Peter 1:15 b). Ephesians 5:1			v. 36: (a) "Show compassion, just as your Father shows compassion."	a). Matthew 5:48; Ephesians 4:32

Gospel of Mattityahu "Matthew"	OT/NT References	Gospel of Mrk "Mark"	OT/NT References	Gospel of Luk "Luke"	OT/NT References
				Chapter 12 Make Peace with Your Adversary	
				v. 57: "Why don't you decide for yourselves what is the right course to follow?"	
				v. 58: (A) "If someone brings a lawsuit against you, (B) take pains to settle with him first; otherwise he will take the matter to court, and the judge will turn you over to the bailiff, and the bailiff will throw you in jail."	A). Proverbs 25:8; Matthew 5:25–26 B). Psalm 32:6; Isaiah 55:6
				v. 59: "I tell you, you won't get out of there till you have paid the last penny!"	
Chapter 6 Do Good to Please God				**Chapter 6 Yeshua Pronounces Woes**	
v. 1: "Be careful not to parade your acts of *tzedakah* in front of people in order to be seen by them! If you do, you have no reward from your Father in heaven."				v. 25: (A) "Woe to you who are full now, for you will go hungry! (b) "Woe to you who are laughing now, for you will mourn and (c) cry!"	A). Amos 6:1; Luke 12:21; James 5:1–6 b). Luke 12:21 c). Matthew 6:2, 5, 16; Luke 16:25

44 *Just the Words and Teachings of Jesus Christ*

Gospel of Mattityahu "Matthew"	OT/NT References	Gospel of Mrk "Mark"	OT/NT References	Gospel of Luk "Luke"	OT/NT References
Chapter 6 **Do Good to Please God Continued**				**Chapter 6** **Yeshua Pronounces Woes Continued**	
v. 2: "So, when you do (a)*tzedakah, don't announce it with trumpets to win people's praise, like the hypocrites in the synagogues and on the streets. Yes! I tell you, they have their reward already!"	a). Romans 12:8			v. 24: "But (A) woe to you (b) who are rich, for (c) you have already had all the comfort you will get!"	A). Amos 6:1; Luke 12:21; James 5:1–6 b). Luke 12:21 c). Matthew 6:2, 5, 16; Luke 16:25
v. 3: "But you, when you do *tzedakah don't even let your left hand know what your right hand is doing."					
v. 4: "Then your *tzedakah will be in secret; and (a) Your Father, who sees what you do in secret, will reward you."	a). Luke 14:12–14			v. 26: (A) "Woe to you when people speak well of you, for that is just how their fathers treated the false prophets!"	A). Isaiah 65:13
				Chapter 10 **The Parable of the Good Samaritan**	
				v. 26: "But *Yeshua said to him, 'What is written in the *Torah? How do you read it?'"	

Gospel of Mattityahu "Matthew"	OT/NT References	Gospel of Mrk "Mark"	OT/NT References	Gospel of Luk "Luke"	OT/NT References
				Chapter 10 **The Parable of the Good Samaritan Continued**	
				v. 27: "He answered, (A) 'You are to love [the Lord] your God with all your heart, with all your soul, with all your strength and with all your understanding; (B) and your neighbor as yourself.'" I included the Torah expert's answer in v. 27, as this sums up the Torah and the prophets according to Yeshua's teachings.	A). Deuteronomy 6:5 B). Leviticus 19:18; Matthew 19:19
				v. 28: "'That's the right answer.; Yeshua said. 'Do this, (A) and you will have life.'"	A). Leviticus 18:5; Nehemiah 9:29; Ezekiel 20:11, 13, 21; Matthew 19:17; Romans 10:5
				v. 30: "Taking up the question, *Yeshua said: 'A man was going down from *Yerushalayim to *Yericho when he was attacked by robbers. They stripped him naked and beat him up, then went off, leaving him half dead.'"	

Gospel of Mattityahu "Matthew"	OT/NT References	Gospel of Mrk "Mark"	OT/NT References	Gospel of Luk "Luke"	OT/NT References
				Chapter 10 **The Parable of the Good Samaritan Continued**	
				v. 31: "By coincidence, a *cohen* was going down on that road; but when he saw him, (A) he passed by on the other side."	A). Psalm 38:11
				v. 32: "Likewise a *Levi* who reached the place saw him also passed by on the other side."	
				v. 33: "But a man from (a) *Shomron* who was traveling came upon him; and when he saw him, he was moved with (b) compassion."	a). John 4:9 b). Luke 15:20
				v. 34: "So he went up to him, put oil and wine on his wounds and bandaged them. Then he set him on his own donkey, brought him to an inn and took care of him."	
				v. 35: "The next day, he took out (a) two days' wages, gave them to the innkeeper and said, 'Look after him; and if you spend more than this, I'll pay you back when I return.'"	a). Matthew 20:2

Gospel of Mattityahu "Matthew"	OT/NT References	Gospel of Mrk "Mark"	OT/NT References	Gospel of Luk "Luke"	OT/NT References
				Chapter 10 **The Parable of the Good Samaritan Continued**	
				v. 36: "Of these three, which one seems to you to have become the 'neighbor' of the man who fell among robbers?"	
				v. 37: "He answered, 'The one who showed mercy toward him.' *Yeshua* said to him, (A) 'You go and do as he did.'"	A). Proverbs 14:21; Matthew 9:13; 12:7
				Chapter 10 **Mary and Martha Worship and Serve**	
				v. 41: "However, the Lord answered her, '*Marta, Marta,* you are fretting and worrying about so many things!'"	
				v. 42: "But (A) there is only one thing that is essential. *Miryam* has chosen the right thing, and it won't be taken away from her."	A). Psalm 27:4; John 6:27

Gospel of Mattityahu "Matthew"	OT/NT References	Gospel of Mrk "Mark"	OT/NT References	Gospel of Luk "Luke"	OT/NT References
				Chapter 17 **Faith and Duty**	
				v. 6: (a) "The Lord replied, 'If you had *trust* as tiny as a mustard seed, you could say to this fig tree, "Be uprooted and replanted in the sea!" and it would obey you.'" Most manuscripts use the word faith versus trust. Yet in Hebrew trust has a deep sensory meaning. (See "Commentaries.")	a). Matthew 17:20; 21:21; Mark 9:23; 11:23; Luke 13:19
				v. 7: "If one of you has a slave tending the sheep and plowing, when he comes back from the field, will you say to him, 'Come along now, sit down and eat'?"	
				v. 8: "No, you'll say, 'Get my supper ready, dress for work, and (a) serve me until I have finished eating and drinking; after that you may eat and drink.'"	a). Luke 12:37
				v. 9: "Does he thank the slave because he did what he was told to do? No!"	

Gospel of Mattityahu "Matthew"	OT/NT References	Gospel of Mrk "Mark"	OT/NT References	Gospel of Luk "Luke"	OT/NT References
				Chapter 17 **Faith and Duty Continued**	
				v. 10: "It's the same with you—when you have done everything you were told to do, you should be saying, 'We're just (A) ordinary slaves, we have only done our duty.'"	A). Job 22:3; 35:7; Psalm 16:2; Matthew 25:30; Romans 3:12; 11:3–5; 1 Corinthians 9:16–17; Philemon 1:11
				Chapter 11 **A Friend Comes at Midnight**	
				vv. 5–6: "He also said to them, 'Suppose one of you has a friend: and you go to him in the middle of the night and say to him, "Friend, lend me three loaves of bread, because a friend of mine who has been traveling has just arrived at my house, and I have nothing for him to eat."'"	
				v. 7: "Now the one inside may answer, 'Don't bother me! The door is already shut, my children are with me in bed—I can't get up to give you anything!'"	

Gospel of Mattityahu "Matthew"	OT/NT References	Gospel of Mrk "Mark"	OT/NT References	Gospel of Luk "Luke"	OT/NT References
				Chapter 11 **A Friend Comes at Midnight Continued**	
				v. 8: "But I tell you, (a) even if he won't get up because the man is his friend, yet because of the man's *hutzpah* he will get up and give him what he needs."	a). Luke 18:1–5
Chapter 6 **The Model Prayer**					
v. 5: "When you pray, don't be like the hypocrites, who love to pray standing in the synagogues and on street corners, so that people can see them. Yes! I tell you, they have their reward already!"					
v. 6: "But you, when you pray, (A) go into your room, close the door, and pray to your Father in secret. Your Father, who sees what is done in secret, will reward you."	A). 2 Kings 4:33				

Gospel of Mattityahu "Matthew"	OT/NT References	Gospel of Mrk "Mark"	OT/NT References	Gospel of Luk "Luke"	OT/NT References
Chapter 6 The Model Prayer Continued				**Chapter 11 The Model Prayer Continued**	
v. 7: "And when you pray, (A) don't babble on and on like the pagans (B) who think God will hear them better if they talk a lot."	A). Ecclesiastes 5:2 B). 1 Kings 18:26				
v. 8: "Don't be like them, because your Father (a) knows what you need before you ask Him."	a). Romans 8:26–27				
v. 9: "You, therefore, pray (a) like this: (b) 'Our Father in Heaven! May Your (C) Name be kept holy.'"	a). Matthew 6:9–13; Luke 11:2–4; John 16:24; Ephesians 6:18; Jude 1:20 b). Matthew 5:9, 16 C). Malachi 1:11			v. 2: (a) "Father, may your Name be kept holy."	a). Matthew 6:9–13
v. 10: "May Your Kingdom come, (a) Your will be done on earth (B) as in Heaven."	a). Matthew 26:42; Luke 22:42; Acts 21:14 B). Psalm 103:20			v. 2: (a) "May Your Kingdom come."	a). Matthew 6:9–13
v. 11: "Give us (A) the food we need today."	A). Job 23:12; Proverbs 30:8; Isaiah 33:16; Luke 11:3			v. 3: "Give us each day the food we need."	

Gospel of Mattityahu "Matthew"	OT/NT References	Gospel of Mrk "Mark"	OT/NT References	Gospel of Luk "Luke"	OT/NT References
Chapter 6 **The Model Prayer Continued**				**Chapter 11** **The Model Prayer Continued**	
v. 12: (a) "Forgive us what we have done wrong, as we too have forgiven those who have wronged us."	a). Matthew 18:21–22			v. 4: (a) "Forgive us our sins, for we too forgive everyone who has wronged us."	a). Ephesians 4:32
v. 13: (a) "And do not lead us into hard testing, but (b) keep us safe from the Evil One. For Kingship, Power and Glory are Yours forever, Amen."	a). Matthew 26:41; 1 Corinthians 10:31; 2 Peter 2:9; Revelations 3:10 b). John 17:15; 2 Thessalonians 3:13; 2 Timothy 4:8; 1 John 5:18			v. 4: (a) "And do not lead us into hard testing."	a). Ephesians 4:32
v. 14: (a) "For if you forgive others their offenses, your Heavenly Father will also forgive you."	a). Matthew 7:2; Mark 11:25; Ephesians 4:32; Colossians 3:13				
v. 15: But (a) if you do not forgive others their offenses, your heavenly Father will not forgive yours."	a). Matthew 18:35; James 2:13				

Gospel of Mattityahu "Matthew"	OT/NT References	Gospel of Mrk "Mark"	OT/NT References	Gospel of Luk "Luke"	OT/NT References
Chapter 6 Fasting to Be Seen Only by God					
v. 16: "Now (A) when you fast, don't go around looking miserable, like the hypocrites. They make sour faces so that people will know they are fasting. Yes! I tell you, they have their reward already!"	A). Isaiah 58:3–7; Luke 18:12				
v. 17: "But you, when you fast, (A) wash your face and groom yourself."	A). Ruth 3:3; 2 Samuel 12:20; Daniel 10:3				
v. 18: "So that no one will know you are fasting—except your Father, who is with you in secret. Your Father, who sees what is done in secret, will reward you."					
Chapter 6 Layup Treasures in Heaven					
v. 19: (A) "Do not store up for yourselves wealth here on earth, where moths and rust destroy, and burglars break in and steal."	A). Proverbs 23:4; 1 Timothy 6:17; Hebrews 13:5; James 5:1				

Gospel of Mattityahu "Matthew"	OT/NT References	Gospel of Mrk "Mark"	OT/NT References	Gospel of Luk "Luke"	OT/NT References
Chapter 6 Layup Treasures in Heaven Continued				**Chapter 12 Do Not Worry**	
v. 20: (a) "Instead, store up for yourselves wealth in heaven, where neither moth nor rust destroys, and burglars do not break in or steal."	a). Matthew 19:21; Luke 12:33; 18:22; 1 Timothy 6:19; 1 Peter 1:4			v. 33: (a) "Sell what you own and do (b) *tzedakah* (c) make for yourselves purses that don't wear out, riches in heaven that never fail, where no burglar comes near, where no moth destroys."	a). Matthew 9:21; Acts 2:45; 4:34 b). Luke 11:4 c). Matthew 6:20; Luke 16:9; 1 Timothy 6:19
v. 21: "For where your wealth is there your heart will be also."				v. 34: "For where your wealth is, there your heart will be also."	
				Chapter 16 The Rich Man and El'azar (Lazarus)	
				v. 19: "Once there was a rich man who used to dress in the most expensive clothing and spent his days in magnificent luxury."	
				v. 20: "At his gate had been laid a beggar named *El'azar* who was covered with sores."	
				v. 21: "He would have been glad to eat the scraps that fell from the rich man's table; but instead, even the dogs would come and lick sores."	

Gospel of Mattityahu "Matthew"	OT/NT References	Gospel of Mrk "Mark"	OT/NT References	Gospel of Luk "Luke"	OT/NT References
				Chapter 16 **The Rich Man and El'azar (Lazarus) Continued**	
				v. 22: "In time the beggar died and was carried away by the angels to (a) *Avraham's* side; the rich man also died and was buried."	a).Matthew 8:11
				v. 23: "In *Shol*, where he was in torment, the rich man looked up and saw *Avraham* far away with *El'azar* at his side."	
				v. 24: "He called out, 'Father *Avraham*, take pity on me, and send *El'azar* just to dip the tip of his finger in water to (A) cool my tongue, because (B) I'm in agony in this fire!'"	A). Zechariah 14:12 B). Isaiah 66:24; Mark 9:42–48
				v. 25: "However, *Avraham* said, 'Son, (A) remember that when you were alive, you got the good things while he got the bad; but now he gets his consolation here, while you are the one in agony.'"	A). Job 21:13; Luke 6:24; James 5:5

Gospel of Mattityahu "Matthew"	OT/NT References	Gospel of Mrk "Mark"	OT/NT References	Gospel of Luk "Luke"	OT/NT References
				Chapter 16 **The Rich Man and El'azar (Lazarus)** **Continued**	
				v. 26: "Yet that isn't all: between you and us a deep rift has been established, so that those who would like to pass from here to you cannot, nor can anyone cross over from there to us."	
				v. 27: "He answered, 'Then, father, I beg you to send him to my father's house."	
				v. 28: "Where I have five brothers, to warn them; so that they may be spared having to come to this place of torment too."	
				v. 29: "But *Avraham* said, (A) 'They have *Moshe* and the Prophets; they should listen to them.'"	A). Isaiah 8:20; 34:16; John 5:39, 45; Acts 15:21; 17:11; 2 Timothy 3:15
				v. 30: "However, he said, 'No, father *Avraham*, they need more. If someone from the dead goes to them, they'll repent!'"	

Part 4: Subtopic Scriptural Alignment View—Matthew, Mark, and Luke

Gospel of Mattityahu "Matthew"	OT/NT References	Gospel of Mrk "Mark"	OT/NT References	Gospel of Luk "Luke"	OT/NT References
				Chapter 16 **The Rich Man and El'azar (Lazarus) Continued**	
				v. 31: "But he replied, (a) 'If they won't listen to *Moshe* and the Prophets, (b) they won't be convinced even if someone rises from the dead!'"	a). John 5:46 b). John 12:10–11
Chapter 6 **The Lamp of the Body**				**Chapter 11** **Lamp of the Body**	
				33: (a) "No one who has kindled a lamp hides it or places it (b) under a bowl; rather, he puts it on a stand, so that those coming in may see it's light."	a). Matthew 5:15; Mark 4:21; Luke 8:16 b). Matthew 5:15
v. 22: (a) "'The eye is the lamp of the body.' So if you have a *'good eye'* [that is, if you are generous] your whole body will be full of light."	a). Luke 11:34–35			v. 34: (a) "The lamp of your body is the eye. When you have a *'good-eye,'* [that is when you are generous,] your whole body is full of light."	a). Matthew 6:22–23
v. 23: "But if you have an *'evil eye'* [if you are stingy] your whole body will be full of darkness. If, then, the light in you is darkness, how great is that darkness!"				v. 34: "But when you have an *'evil-eye'* [when you are stingy,] your body is full of darkness."	

Gospel of Mattityahu "Matthew"	OT/NT References	Gospel of Mrk "Mark"	OT/NT References	Gospel of Luk "Luke"	OT/NT References
				Chapter 11 **Lamp of the Body Continued**	
				v. 35: "So take care that the light in you is not darkness!"	
				v. 36: "If, then, your whole body is filled with light, with no part dark, it will be wholly lighted, as when a brightly lit lamp shines on you."	
				Chapter 16 **The Parable of the Unjust Servant**	
				v.1: "Speaking to the *talmidim, *Yeshua said: 'There was a wealthy man who employed a general manager. Charges were brought to him that his manager was squandering his resources.'"	
				v. 2: "So he summoned him and asked him, 'What is this I hear about you? (a) Turn in your accounts, for you can no longer be manager.'"	a). Romans 14:12; 2 Corinthians 5:10; 1 Peter 4:5–6
				v. 3: "'What am I to do?' said the manager to himself. 'My boss is firing me, I'm not strong enough to dig ditches, and I'm ashamed to go begging."	

Gospel of Mattityahu "Matthew"	OT/NT References	Gospel of Mrk "Mark"	OT/NT References	Gospel of Luk "Luke"	OT/NT References
				Chapter 16 **The Parable of the Unjust Servant Continued**	
				v. 4: "Aha! I know what I'll do—something that will make people welcome me into their homes after I've lost my job here!"	
				v. 5: "So, after making appointments with each of his employer's debtors, he said to the first, 'How much do you owe my boss?'"	
				v. 6: "'Eight hundred gallons of olive oil.' he replied. 'Take your note back,' he told him. 'Now, quickly! Sit down and write one for four hundred!'"	
				v. 7: "To the next he said, 'And you, how much do you owe?' 'A thousand bushels of wheat,' he replied. 'take your note back and write one for eight hundred.'"	
				v. 8: "And the employer of this dishonest manager applauded him for acting so shrewdly! For the worldly have more *sekhel* (a) than those who have received the light—in dealing with their own kind of people!"	a). John 12:36; Ephesians 5:8; 1 Thessalonians 5:5

60 *Just the Words and Teachings of Jesus Christ*

Gospel of Mattityahu "Matthew"	OT/NT References	Gospel of Mrk "Mark"	OT/NT References	Gospel of Luk "Luke"	OT/NT References
				Chapter 16 **The Parable of the Unjust Servant Continued**	
				v. 9: "Now what I say to you is this: (A) use wordily wealth to make friends for yourselves, so that when it gives out, you may be welcomed into the eternal home."	A). Daniel 4:27; Matthew 6:19; 19:21; Luke 11:41; 1 Timothy 6:17–19
				v. 10: (a) "Someone who is trustworthy in a small matter is also trustworthy in large ones, and someone who is dishonest in a small matter is also dishonest in large ones."	a). Matthew 25:21; Luke 19:17
				v. 11: "So if you haven't been trustworthy in handling worldly wealth, who is going to trust you with the real thing?"	
				v. 12: "And if you haven't been trustworthy with what belongs to someone else, who will give you what ought to belong to (a) you?"	a). 1 Peter 1:3–4

Gospel of Mattityahu "Matthew"	OT/NT References	Gospel of Mrk "Mark"	OT/NT References	Gospel of Luk "Luke"	OT/NT References
Chapter 6 **You Cannot Serve God and Riches**				**Chapter 16** **The Parable of the Unjust Servant Continued**	
v. 24: (a) "No one can be slave to two masters; for he will either hate the first and love the second, or scorn the second and be loyal to the first. (b) You can't be a slave to both God and money."	a). Luke 16:9, 11, 13 b). Galatians 1:10; 1 Timothy 6:17; James 4:4; 1 John 2:15			v. 13: (a) "No servant can be slave to two masters, for he will either hate the first and love the second, or scorn the second and be loyal to the first. You can't be a slave to both God and money."	a). Matthew 6:24; Galatians 1:10
Chapter 6 **Do Not Worry**				**Chapter 12** **Do Not Worry**	
v. 25: "Therefore, I tell you, (A) don't worry about your life—what you will eat or drink; or about your body—what you will wear."	A). Psalm 55:22; Luke 12:22; Philippians 4:6; 1 Peter 5:7			v. 22: "To His *talmidim* *Yeshua* said, 'Because of this I tell you, (a) don't worry about your life—what you will eat or drink; or about your body—what you will wear.'"	a). Matthew 6:25–33
v. 25: "Isn't life more than food and the body, more than clothing?"				v. 23: "For life is more than food, and the body is more than clothing."	
v. 26: (A) "Look at the birds flying about! They neither plant nor harvest, nor do they gather food into barns; yet, your heavenly Father feeds them. Aren't you worth more than they are?"	A). Job 38:41; Psalm 147:9; Matthew 10:29; Luke 12:24			v. 24: "Think about the ravens! They neither plant nor harvest, they have neither storerooms nor barns, yet (A) God feeds then. You are worth much more than the birds!"	A). Job 34:41; Psalm 147:9

Gospel of Mattityahu "Matthew"	OT/NT References	Gospel of Mrk "Mark"	OT/NT References	Gospel of Luk "Luke"	OT/NT References
Chapter 6 **Do Not Worry** **Continued**				**Chapter 12** **Do Not Worry** **Continued**	
v. 27: "Can any of you by worrying add a single hour to his life?"				v. 25: "Can any of you by worrying add an hour to his life?"	
				v. 26: "If you can't do a little thing like that, why worry about the rest?"	
v. 28: "And why be anxious about clothing? Think about the fields of wild irises, and how they grow. They neither work nor spin thread."				v. 27: "Think about the wild irises, and how they grow. They neither work nor spin thread."	
v. 29: "Yet I tell you that not even *Shlomo* in all his glory was clothed as beautifully as one of these."				v. 27: "Yet, I tell not even (A) *Shlomo* in all his glory was clothed as beautifully as one of these."	A). 1 Kings 10:4–7; 2 Chronicles 9:3–6
v. 30: "If this is how God clothes grass in the field—which is here today and gone tomorrow, thrown in an oven—won't He much more clothe you? What little trust you have!"				v. 28: "If this is how God clothes grass, which is alive in the field today and thrown in the oven tomorrow, how much more will He clothe you! (a) What little trust you have!"	a). Matthew 6:30; 8:26; 14:31; 16:8

Part 4: Subtopic Scriptural Alignment View—Matthew, Mark, and Luke

Gospel of Mattityahu "Matthew"	OT/NT References	Gospel of Mrk "Mark"	OT/NT References	Gospel of Luk "Luke"	OT/NT References
Chapter 6 Do Not Worry Continued				**Chapter 12 Do Not Worry Continued**	
v. 31: "So don't be anxious, asking, 'What will we eat?' 'What will we drink?' or 'How will we be clothed?'"				v. 29: "In other words, don't strive after what you will eat and what you will drink—don't be anxious."	
v. 32: "For it is the pagans who set their hearts on all these things. Your heavenly Father knows you need them all."				v. 30: "For all the pagan nations in the world set their hearts on these things. Your Father (a) knows that you need them too."	a). Matthew 6:31–32
v. 33: "But (A) seek first His Kingdom and His righteousness and all these things will be given to you as well."	A). 1 Kings 3:13; Luke 12:31; 1 Timothy 4:8			v. 31: (a) "Rather, seek His Kingdom; and these things will be given to you as well."	a). Matthew 6:33
v. 34: "Don't worry about tomorrow—tomorrow will worry about itself! Today has enough *tusris* already!"				v. 32: "Have no fear, little flock, (A) for your Father has resolved to give you the Kingdom!"	A). Daniel 7:18, 27; Zechariah 13:7; Matthew 11:25–26; Luke 22:29–30

Just the Words and Teachings of Jesus Christ

Gospel of Mattityahu "Matthew"	OT/NT References	Gospel of Mrk "Mark"	OT/NT References	Gospel of Luk "Luke"	OT/NT References
Chapter 7 **Do Not Judge**				**Chapter 6** **Do Not Judge**	
v. 1: (a) "Don't judge, so that you won't be judged."	a). Matthew 7:1–5; Luke 6:37; Romans 14:3; 1 Corinthians 4:3–4			v. 37: (a) "Don't judge, and you wont be judged. Don't condemn and you won't be condemned. (b) Forgive, and you will be forgiven."	a). Matthew 7:1–5; Romans 14:4; 1 Corinthians 4:5 b). Matthew 18:21–35
v. 2: "For the way you judge others is how you will be judged—(a) the measure with which you measure out will be used to measure to you."	a). Mark 4:24; Luke 6:38			v. 36: (a) "Show compassion, just as your Father shows compassion."	a). Matthew 5:48; Ephesians 4:32
				v. 38: (A) "Give, and you will receive gifts—the full measure, compacted, shaken together and overflowing, will be put right in (B) your lap. (c) For the measure with which you measure out will be used to measure back to you!"	A). Proverbs 19:17; 28:27 B). Psalm 79:12; Isaiah 65:6–7; Jeremiah 32:18 c). Matthew 7:2; Mark 4:24; James 2:19
				v. 39: "He also told them a parable: (a) 'Can one blind man lead another blind man? Won't they both fall into a pit.'"	a). Matthew 15:14; 23:16; Romans 2:19

Gospel of Mattityahu "Matthew"	OT/NT References	Gospel of Mrk "Mark"	OT/NT References	Gospel of Luk "Luke"	OT/NT References
Chapter 7 Do Not Judge Continued				**Chapter 6 Do Not Judge Continued**	
				v. 40: (a) "A *talmid* is not above his *rabbi*: but each one, when he is fully trained, will be like his rabbi."	a). Matthew 10:24; John 13:16; 15:20
v. 3: (a) "Why do you see the splinter in your brother's eye but not notice the log in your own eye?"	a). Luke 6:41			v. 41: (a) "So why do you see the splinter in your brother's eye, but not notice the log in your own eye?"	a). Matthew 7:3
v. 4: "How can you say to your brother, 'let me take the splinter out of your eye,' when you have the log in your own eye?"				v. 42: "How can you say to your brother, 'Brother, let me remove the splinter from your eye,' when you yourself don't see the log in your own eye?"	
v. 5: "You hypocrite! First take the log out of your own eye; then you will see clearly, so that you can remove the splinter from your brother's eye!"				v. 42: "Hypocrite! First take the log out of your own eye; then you will see clearly, so that you can remove the splinter from your brother's eye!"	
v. 6: (A) "Don't give to dogs what is holy, and don't throw your pearls to the pigs. If you do, they may trample them under their feet, then turn and attack you."	A). Proverbs 9:7–8; Acts 13:45				

Gospel of Mattityahu "Matthew"	OT/NT References	Gospel of Mrk "Mark"	OT/NT References	Gospel of Luk "Luke"	OT/NT References
Chapter 7 Keep Asking, Seeking, Knocking				**Chapter 11 Keep Asking, Seeking, Knocking**	
v. 7: (a) "Keep asking, and it will be given to you; keep seeking, and you will find: keep knocking, and the door will be given to you."	a). Matt 21:22; Mark 11:24; Luke 11:9–13, 18:1–8; John 15:7; James 1:5,6; 1 John 3:22			v. 9: (A) "Moreover, I myself say to you: keep asking, and it will be given to you; (B) keep seeking, and you will find; keep knocking, and the door will be opened to you."	A). Psalms 50:14,15; Jeremiah 33:3; Matthew 7:7; 21:22; Mark 11:24; John 15:7; James 1:5,6; 1 John 3:22, 5:14,15 B). Isaiah 55:6
v. 8: "For (A) everyone who keeps asking receives; he who keeps seeking finds; and to him who keeps knocking the door will be opened."	A). Proverbs 8:17; Jeremiah 29:12			v. 10: "For everyone who goes on asking receives; and he who goes on seeking finds; and to him who continues knocking, the door will be opened."	
v. 9: (a) "Is there anyone here who, if his son asks him for a loaf of bread, will give him a stone?"	a). Luke 11:11				
v. 10: "Or if he asks for a fish, will give him a snake?"					

Part 4: Subtopic Scriptural Alignment View—Matthew, Mark, and Luke   67

Gospel of Mattityahu "Matthew"	OT/NT References	Gospel of Mrk "Mark"	OT/NT References	Gospel of Luk "Luke"	OT/NT References
Chapter 7 **Keep Asking, Seeking, Knocking Continued**					
v. 11: "So if you, even though (A) you are bad know how to give your children gifts that are good, how much more will your Father in heaven keep giving good things to those who keep asking Him!"	A). Genesis 6:5; 8:21; Psalm 84:11; Isaiah 63:7; Romans 8:32; James 1:17; 1 John 3:1				
v. 12: "Always (a) treat others as you would like them to treat you; that sums up the (b) teaching of the *Torah and the Prophets."	a). Luke 6:31 b). Matthew 22:40; Romans 13:8; Galatians 5:14; 1 Timothy 1:5				
Chapter 7 **The Narrow Way**					
v. 13: (a) "Go in through the narrow gate; for the gate that leads to destruction is wide and the road broad, and many travel it."	a). Luke 13:24				

68 *Just the Words and Teachings of Jesus Christ*

Gospel of Mattityahu "Matthew"	OT/NT References	Gospel of Mrk "Mark"	OT/NT References	Gospel of Luk "Luke"	OT/NT References
Chapter 7 The Narrow Way Continued				**Chapter 13 Key to the Narrow Way**	
v. 14: "But it is a narrow gate and a hard road that leads to life, and only a few find it."				v. 24: "He answered, (a) 'Struggle to get in through the narrow door, because—I'm telling you!—(b) many will be demanding to get in and won't be able to.'"	a). Matthew 7:13 b). John 7:34; 8:21; 13:33; Romans 9:31
Chapter 7 You Will Know Them by Their Fruits				**Chapter 6 A Tree Is Known by Its Fruit**	
v. 15: (A) "Beware of the false prophets! (B) They come to you wearing sheep's clothing, but underneath they are hungry wolves!"	A). Deuteronomy 13:3; Jeremiah 23:16; Ezekiel 22:28; Mark 13:22; Luke 6:26; Romans 16:17; Ephesians 5:6; Colossians 2:8; 2 Peter 2:1; 1 John 4:1–3 B). Micah 3:5				
v. 16: (a) "You will recognize them by their fruit. (b) Can people pick grapes from thorn bushes, or figs from thistles?"	a). Matthew 7:20; 12:33; Luke 6:44; James 3:12 b). Luke 6:43			v. 44: (a) "Each tree is recognized by its own fruit—figs aren't picked from thorn bushes, nor grapes from a briar patch."	a). Matthew 12:33

Gospel of Mattityahu "Matthew"	OT/NT References	Gospel of Mrk "Mark"	OT/NT References	Gospel of Luk "Luke"	OT/NT References
Chapter 7 **You Will Know Them by Their Fruits Continued**				**Chapter 6** **A Tree Is Known by Its Fruit Continued**	
v. 17: "Likewise (A) every healthy tree produces good fruit, but a poor tree produces bad fruit."	A). Jeremiah 11:19; Matthew 12:33			v. 43: (a) "For no good tree produces bad, fruit, nor does a bad tree produce good fruit."	a). Matthew 7:16–18, 20
v. 18: "A healthy tree cannot bear bad fruit, or a poor tree good fruit."					
v. 19: (a) "Any tree that does not produce good fruit is cut down and thrown in the fire!"	a). Matthew 3:10; Luke 3:9; John 15:2, 6			v. 45: (a) "The good person produces good things from the store of good in his heart, while the evil person produces evil things from the store of evil in his heart. For his mouth speaks what overflows from his heart."	a). Matthew 12:35
v. 20: "So you will recognize them by their fruit."				v. 44: (a) "Each tree is recognized by its own fruit—figs aren't picked from thorn bushes, nor grapes from a briar patch."	a). Matthew 12:33

Gospel of Mattityahu "Matthew"	OT/NT References	Gospel of Mrk "Mark"	OT/NT References	Gospel of Luk "Luke"	OT/NT References
				Chapter 13 **Repent or Perish**	
				v. 2: "His answer to them was, 'Do you think that just because they died so horribly, these folks from the *Galil* were worse sinners than all the others from the *Galil*?'"	
				v. 3: "No, I tell you. Rather, unless you turn to God from your sins, you will all die as they did!"	
				v. 4: "Or what about those eighteen people who died when the tower at *Shiloach* fell on them? Do you think they were worse offenders than all the other people living in *Yerushalayim*?"	
				v. 5: "No, I tell you. Rather, unless you turn from your sins, you will all die similarly."	

Gospel of Mattityahu "Matthew"	OT/NT References	Gospel of Mrk "Mark"	OT/NT References	Gospel of Luk "Luke"	OT/NT References
Chapter 7 **I Never Knew You**				**Chapter 13** **The Narrow Way**	
v. 21: (A) "Not everyone who says to me, 'LORD, LORD!' will enter the Kingdom of Heaven, only those who (b) do what my Father wants."	A). Hosea 8:2; Matthew 25:11; Luke 6:46; Acts 19:13 b). Romans 2:13; James 1:22			v. 25: (A) "Once the owner of the house has gotten up and (b) shut the door. You will stand outside, knocking at the door and saying, (c) 'Lord! Open up for us!' But he will answer, (d) 'I don't know you or where you come from!'"	A). Psalm 32:6; Isaiah 55:6 b). Matthew 25:10; Revelation 22:11 c). Luke 6:46 d). Matthew 7:23; 25:41
v. 22: "On that Day, many will say to me, 'Lord, Lord! Didn't we prophesy in Your Name? (A) Didn't we expel demons in Your name? Didn't we perform many	A). Numbers 24:4			v. 26: "Then you will say, 'We ate and drank with you! You taught in our streets!'"	
v. 23: (a) "Then I will tell them to their faces, 'I never knew you! (B) Get away from me, you workers of *lawlessness!'" (See "Commentaries.")	a). Matthew 25:12; Luke 13:25 2 Timothy 2:19 B). Psalm 5:5; 6:8; Matthew 25:41; Luke 13:27			v. 27: (a) "And he will tell you, 'I don't know where you come from. (B) Get away from me, all you workers of wickedness!'"	a). Matthew 7:23; 25:41 B). Psalm 6:8; Matthew 25:41; Titus 1:16

Gospel of Mattityahu "Matthew"	OT/NT References	Gospel of Mrk "Mark"	OT/NT References	Gospel of Luk "Luke"	OT/NT References
				Chapter 13 The Narrow Way Continued	
				v. 28: (a) "You will cry and grind your teeth (b) when you see *Avraham, *Yitz'chak and all the prophets inside the Kingdom of God, but yourselves thrown outside."	a). Matthew 8:12; 13:42; 24:51 b). Matthew 8:11
				v. 29: "Moreover, people will come from the east, the west, the north and the south, to sit at the table in the Kingdom of God."	
				v. 30: (a) "And notice that some who are last will be first, and some who are first will be last."	a). Matthew 19:30; 20:16; Mark 10:31
				v. 32: "He said to them, 'Go tell that fox, "Pay attention: today and tomorrow I am driving out demons and healing people, and on the third day (a) I reach My goal."""	a). Luke 24:46; Acts 10:40; 1 Corinthians 15:4; Hebrews 2:10; 5:9; 7:28
				v. 33: Nevertheless, I must keep traveling today, tomorrow and the next day; because it is unthinkable that a prophet should die anywhere but in *Yerushalayim.	

Gospel of Mattityahu "Matthew"	OT/NT References	Gospel of Mrk "Mark"	OT/NT References	Gospel of Luk "Luke"	OT/NT References
Chapter 7 **Build on the Rock**				**Chapter 6** **Build on the Rock**	
				v. 46: (A) "Why do you call Me, 'Lord! Lord!' But not do what I say?"	A). Malachi 1:6; Matthew 7:21; 25:11; Luke 13:25
v. 24: "So, (a) everyone who hears these words of mine and acts on them will be like a sensible man who built his house on bedrock."	a). Matthew 7:24–27; Luke 6:47–49			v. 47: (a) "Everyone who comes to Me, hears My words and acts on them—I will show you what he is like."	a). Matthew 7:24–27; John 14:21; James 1:22–25
v. 25: "The rain fell, the rivers flooded, the winds blew and beat against that house, but it didn't collapse, because its foundation was on rock."				v. 48: "He is like someone building a house who dug deep and laid the foundation on bedrock. When a flood came, the torrent beat against that house but couldn't shake it, because it was constructed well."	
v. 26: "But everyone who hears these words of mine and does not act on them will be like a stupid man who built his house on sand."				v. 49: "And whoever hears My words but doesn't act on them is like someone who built his house on the ground without any foundation."	
v. 27: "The rain fell, the rivers flooded, the wind blew and beat against that house, and it collapsed—and the collapse was horrendous!"				v. 49: "As soon as the river stuck it, it collapsed and that house became a horrendous wreck!"	

Gospel of Mattityahu "Matthew"	OT/NT References	Gospel of Mrk "Mark"	OT/NT References	Gospel of Luk "Luke"	OT/NT References
Chapter 8 **Yeshua Cleanses a Leper**		**Chapter 1** **Yeshua Cleanses a Leper**		**Chapter 5** **Yeshua Cleanses a Leper**	
v. 3: "*Yeshua* reached out His hand, touched him and said, 'I am willing! Be cleansed!'"		v. 41: "Moved with (a) pity, *Yeshua reached out His hand, touched him and said to him, 'I am willing! Be cleansed!'"	a). Luke 7:13	v. 13: "*Yeshua* reached out His hand and touched him, saying, 'I am willing! Be cleansed!'"	
v. 3: "And at once he (a) was cleansed from his *tzara'at*."	a). Matthew 11:5; Luke 4:27	v. 42: (a) Instantly the *tzara'at* left him, and he was cleansed.	a). Matthew 15:28; Mark 5:29	v. 13: (a) "Immediately the *tzara'at* left him."	a). Matthew 20:34; Luke 8:44; John 5:9
		v. 43: "Yeshua sent him away with this stern warning."			
v. 4: "Then *Yeshua* said to him, (a) 'See that you tell no one; but as a testimony to the people, go and let the *cohen* examine you and offer the sacrifice that (B) *Moshe* (C) commands.'"	a). Matthew 9:30; Mark 5:43; Luke 4:41; 8:56; 9:21 B). Leviticus 14:3–4, 10; Mark 1:44; Luke 5:14 C). Leviticus 14:4–32; Deuteronomy 24:8	v. 44: "See to it that you tell no one; instead, as a testimony to the people, go and let the *cohen* examine you, and offer for your cleansing what (A) *Moshe* commanded."	A). Leviticus 14:1–32	v. 14: (a) "Then *Yeshua* warned him not to tell anyone, 'Instead, as a testimony to the people, go straight to the *cohen* and make an offering for your cleansing, (B) as *Moshe* commanded.'"	a). Matthew 8:4; Luke 17:14 B). Leviticus 13:1–3; 14:2–32

Gospel of Mattityahu "Matthew"	OT/NT References	Gospel of Mrk "Mark"	OT/NT References	Gospel of Luk "Luke"	OT/NT References
				Chapter 17 Ten Lepers Cleansed	
				v. 14: "On seeing them, He said, (A) 'Go and let the *cohanim examine you!' And as they went, they were cleansed."	A). Leviticus 13:1–59; Leviticus 14:1–32; Matthew 8:4; Luke 5:14
				v. 17: "*Yeshua said, 'Weren't ten cleansed? Where are the other nine?'"	
				v. 18: "Was no one found coming back to give glory to God except this foreigner?"	
				v. 19: (a) "And to the man from *Shomron He said, 'Get up, you may go; your trust has saved you.'"	a). Matthew 9:22; Mark 5:34; 10:52; Luke 7:50; 8:48; 18:42
Chapter 8 Yeshua Heals a Centurion's Servant					
v. 7: "*Yeshua said, 'I will go and heal him.'"					

76 *Just the Words and Teachings of Jesus Christ*

Gospel of Mattityahu "Matthew"	OT/NT References	Gospel of Mrk "Mark"	OT/NT References	Gospel of Luk "Luke"	OT/NT References
Chapter 8 Yeshua Heals a Centurion's Servant Continued				**Chapter 7 Yeshua Heals a Centurion's Servant Continued**	
v. 10: "On hearing this *Yeshua was amazed and said to the people following Him, 'Yes! I tell you, I have not found anyone in *Israel with such trust!'"				v. 9: "*Yeshua was astonished at him when He heard this; and He turned and said to the crowd following Him, 'I tell you, not even in *Israel have I found such * trust!'" (See "Commentaries.")	
v. 11: "Moreover, I tell you that (A) many will come from the east and from the west to take their places at the feast in the Kingdom of Heaven with *Avraham, *Yitz'chak and *Ya'akov."	A). Genesis 12:3; Isaiah 2:2–3; 11:10; Malachi 1:11; Luke 13:29; Acts 10:45; 11:18; 14:27; Romans 15:9–13; Ephesians 3:6				
v. 12: "But (a) those born for the Kingdom (b) will be thrown outside in the dark, where people will wail and grind their teeth!"	a). Matthew 21:43 b). Matthew 13:42,50; 22:13; 24:51; 25:30; Luke 13:28; 2 Peter 2:17; Jude 1:13				

Gospel of Mattityahu "Matthew"	OT/NT References	Gospel of Mrk "Mark"	OT/NT References	Gospel of Luk "Luke"	OT/NT References
Chapter 8 **Yeshua Heals a Centurion's Servant Continued**					
v. 13: "Then *Yeshua said to the officer, 'Go; let it be for you as you have trusted.'"					
				Chapter 7 **Yeshua Raises Son of the Widow of Nain**	
				v. 13: "When the Lord saw her, he felt (A) compassion for her and said to her, (b) 'Don't cry.'"	A). Lamentations 3:32; John 11:35; Hebrews 4:15 b).Luke 8:52
				v. 14: "Then He came close and touched the coffin, and the pallbearers halted. He said, 'Young man, I say to you: (a) get up!'"	a). Mark 5:41; Luke 8:54; John 11:43; Acts 9:40; Rom 4:17
Chapter 8 **The Cost of Discipleship**				**Chapter 9** **The Cost of Discipleship**	
v. 20: "*Yeshua said, 'The foxes have holes, and the birds flying about have nests, but the Son of Man has no home of His own.'"				v. 58: "*Yeshua answered him, 'The foxes have holes, and the birds flying about have nests, but the Son of Man (a) has no home of His own.'"	a). Luke 2:7; 8:23

78 *Just the Words and Teachings of Jesus Christ*

Gospel of Mattityahu "Matthew"	OT/NT References	Gospel of Mrk "Mark"	OT/NT References	Gospel of Luk "Luke"	OT/NT References
Chapter 8 **The Cost of Discipleship Continued**				**Chapter 9** **The Cost of Discipleship Continued**	
				v. 59: (a) "To another He said, 'Follow Me!' but the man replied, 'Sir first let me go away and bury my father.'"	a). Matthew 8:21–22
v. 22: "But *Yeshua replied, 'Follow me, and let the dead bury their own dead.'"				v. 60: "*Yeshua said, 'Let the dead bury their own dead; you, go and proclaim the Kingdom of God!'"	
				v. 62: "To him *Yeshua said, 'No one who puts his hand to the plow and keeps looking back is (a) fit to serve in the Kingdom of God.'"	a). 2 Timothy 4:10
		Chapter 4 **Wind and Wave Obey Yeshua**		**Chapter 8** **Wind and Wave Obey Yeshua**	
		v. 35: (a) "That day, when evening had come, *Yeshua said to them, 'Let us cross to the other side of the lake.'"	a). Matthew 8:18; 23–27; Luke 8:22, 25	v. 22: (a) "One day *Yeshua got into a boat with His *talmidim and said to them, 'Let's cross to the other side of the lake.'"	a). Matthew 8:23–27; Mark 4:36–41

Gospel of Mattityahu "Matthew"	OT/NT References	Gospel of Mrk "Mark"	OT/NT References	Gospel of Luk "Luke"	OT/NT References
Chapter 8 **Wind and Wave Obey Yeshua**		**Chapter 4** **Wind and Wave Obey Yeshua Continued**		**Chapter 8** **Wind and Wave Obey Yeshua Continued**	
v. 26: "He said to them, 'Why are you afraid? So little trust you have!' Then (A) He got up and rebuked the winds and the waves, and there was a dead calm."	A). Psalm 65:7; 89:9; 107:29	v. 39: "He awoke, (a) rebuked the wind and said to the waves, (B) 'Quiet! Be Still!' The wind subsided, and there was a dead calm."	a). Mark 9:25; Luke 4:39 B). Psalm 65:7; 89:9; 93:4; 104:6–7; Matthew 8:26; Luke 8:24	v. 24: "They went and woke Him, saying, *Rabbi! Rabbi! We're about to die! He woke up, rebuked the wind and rough water' and they calmed down, so that it was still."	
		v. 40: "Why are you afraid? (a) Have you no trust even now?"	a). Matthew 14:31–32; Luke 8:25	v. 25: "Then He said to His *talmidim, (a) 'Where is your trust?' Awestruck, they marveled, asking one another, (b) 'Who can this be, that He commands even the wind and the water, and they obey Him?'"	a). Luke 9:41 b). Luke 4:36; 5:26
		Chapter 5 **A Demon-Possessed Man Healed**		**Chapter 8** **A Demon-Possessed Man Healed**	
		v. 8: "For *Yeshua had already begun saying to him, (a) 'Unclean spirit, come out of this man!'"	a).Mark 1:25 9:25; Acts 16:18	v. 29: "For *Yeshua had ordered the unclean spirit to come out of the man. It had often taken hold of him—he had been kept under guard, chained hand and foot, but had broken the bonds and been driven by the demon into the desert."	

Gospel of Mattityahu "Matthew"	OT/NT References	Gospel of Mrk "Mark"	OT/NT References	Gospel of Luk "Luke"	OT/NT References
Chapter 8 **Two Demon-Possessed Men Healed**		**Chapter 5** **A Demon-Possessed Man Healed Continued**		**Chapter 8** **A Demon-Possessed Man Healed Continued**	
		v. 9: "*Yeshua* asked him, 'What is your name?' 'My name is Legion,' he answered, 'there are so many of us.'"		v. 30: "*Yeshua* asked him, 'What is your name?' 'Legion,' he said, because many demons had entered him."	
v. 32: "'All right, go!' He told them. So they came out and went into the pigs, whereupon the entire herd rushed down the hillside into the lake and drowned."				v. 32: "Now there was a herd of many (A) pigs, feeding on the hill; and the demons begged Him to let them go into these. So He gave them permission."	A). Leviticus 11:7; Deuteronomy 14:8
				v. 39: "Go back to your home and tell how much God has done for."	
		Chapter 2 **Yeshua Forgives and Heals a Paralytic**			
		v. 2: "And so many people gathered around the house that there was no longer any room, not even in the front of the door. While He was preaching the message to them."			

Gospel of Mattityahu "Matthew"	OT/NT References	Gospel of Mrk "Mark"	OT/NT References	Gospel of Luk "Luke"	OT/NT References
Chapter 9 Yeshua Forgives and Heals a Paralytic Continued		**Chapter 2 Yeshua Forgives and Heals a Paralytic Continued**		**Chapter 5 Yeshua Forgives and Heals a Paralytic Continued**	
v. 2: (a) "Some people brought Him a paralyzed man lying on a mattress. (b) When *Yeshua saw their trust He said to the paralyzed man, 'Courage, son! Your sins are forgiven.'"	a). Mark 2:3–12; Luke 5:18–26 b). Matthew 8:10	v. 5: "Seeing their trust *Yeshua said to the paralyzed man, 'Son, your sons are forgiven.'"		v. 20: "When *Yeshua (a) saw their trust, He said, 'Friend, your sins are forgiven you.'"	
v. 4: "*Yeshua, (A) knowing what they were thinking, said, 'Why are you entertaining evil thoughts in your hearts?'"	A). Psalm 139:2; Matthew 12:25; Mark 12:15; Luke 5:22; 6:8; 9:47; 11:17	v. 8: "But immediately *Yeshua perceiving in His spirit what they were thinking, said to them 'Why are you thinking these things?'"		v. 22: "But *Yeshua, knowing what they were thinking, answered, 'Why are you turning over such thoughts in your hearts?'"	a). Luke 9:47; John 2:25
v. 5: "Tell me, which is easier to say—'Your sins are forgiven' or 'Get up and walk'?"		v. 9: (a) "Which is easier to say to the paralyzed man? 'Your sins are forgiven'? Or 'Get up, pick up your stretcher and walk'?"	a). Matthew 9:5	v. 23: "Which is easier to say? 'Your sins are forgiven you'? Or 'Get up and walk'?"	
v. 6: "But look! I will prove to you that the Son of Man has authority on earth to forgive sins."		v. 10: "But look! I will prove to you that the Son of Man has authority on earth to forgive sins."		v. 24: "But look! I will prove to you that the Son of Man has authority on earth to forgive sins."	

Gospel of Mattityahu "Matthew"	OT/NT References	Gospel of Mrk "Mark"	OT/NT References	Gospel of Luk "Luke"	OT/NT References
Chapter 9 **Yeshua Forgives and Heals a Paralytic Continued**		**Chapter 2** **Yeshua Forgives and Heals a Paralytic Continued**		**Chapter 5** **Yeshua Forgives and Heals a Paralytic Continued**	
v. 6: "He then said to the paralyzed man, 'Get up, pick up your mattress, and go home!'"		v. 11: "I say to you: get up, pick your stretcher up and go home!"		v. 24: "He then said to the paralytic, (a) 'I say to you: get up, pick up your mattress and go home!'"	a). Mark 2:11; 5:41; Luke 7:14
				Chapter 7 **A Sinful Woman Is Forgiven**	
				v. 40: "*Yeshua* answered, '*Shim'on*, I have something to say to you.' 'Say it *Rabbi*,' he replied."	
				v. 41: "A certain creditor had two debtors; the one owed (a) ten times as much as the other."	a). Matthew 18:28; Mark 6:37
				v. 42: "When they were unable to pay him back, he canceled both their debts. Now which of them will love him more?"	
				v. 43: "*Shim'on* answered, 'I suppose the one for whom he canceled the larger debt.' 'Your judgement is right,' *Yeshua* said to him."	

Part 4: Subtopic Scriptural Alignment View—Matthew, Mark, and Luke

Gospel of Mattityahu "Matthew"	OT/NT References	Gospel of Mrk "Mark"	OT/NT References	Gospel of Luk "Luke"	OT/NT References
				Chapter 7 **A Sinful Woman** **Is Forgiven** **Continued**	
				v. 44: "Then, turning to the woman, He said to *Shim'on*, 'Do you see this woman? I came into your house—you didn't give me (A) water for my feet, but this woman has washed My feet with her tears and dried them with her hair!'"	A). Genesis 18:4; 19:2; 43:24; Judges 19:21; 1 Timothy 5:10
				v. 45: "You didn't give Me (a) a kiss; but from the time I arrived, this woman has not stopped kissing My feet!"	a). Romans 16:16
				v. 46: (A) "You didn't put oil on My head, but this woman poured perfume on My feet!"	A). 2 Samuel 12:20
				v. 47: (a) "Because of this, I tell you that her sins—which are many!—have been forgiven, because she loved much. But someone who has been forgiven only a little loves only a little."	a). 1 Timothy 1:14

84 *Just the Words and Teachings of Jesus Christ*

Gospel of Mattityahu "Matthew"	OT/NT References	Gospel of Mrk "Mark"	OT/NT References	Gospel of Luk "Luke"	OT/NT References
				Chapter 7 **A Sinful Woman Is Forgiven Continued**	
				v. 48: "The He said to her, (a) 'Your sins have been forgiven.'"	a). Matthew 9:2; Mark 2:5
				v. 50: "But He said to the woman, (a) 'Your trust has saved you; go in peace.'"	a). Matthew 9:22; Mark 5:34
Chapter 9 **Matthew, the Tax Collector**		**Chapter 2** **Matthew, the Tax Collector**		**Chapter 5** **Matthew, the Tax Collector**	
v. 9: (a) "As *Yeshua* passed on from there He spotted a tax-collector named *Mattiyahu* sitting in his collection booth. He said to him, 'Follow Me!' and he got up and followed Him."	a). Mark 2:14; Luke 5:27	v. 14: (a) "As He passed on from there, He saw *Levi Ben-Halfai* sitting in his tax-collection booth and said to him, (b) 'Follow Me!' And he got up and (c) followed Him."	a). Matthew 9:9–13; Luke 5:27–32 b). Matthew 4:19; 8:22; 19:21; John 1:43; 12:26; 21:22 c). Luke 18:28	v. 27: (a) "Later *Yeshua* went out and saw a tax-collector named *Levi* sitting in his tax-collection booth; and He said to him, (b) 'Follow Me!'"	a). Matthew 9:9–17; Mark 2:13–22 b). Mark 8:34; Luke 9:59; John 12:26; 21:19, 22
Chapter 9 **Who Really Needs a Doctor?**		**Chapter 2** **Who Really Needs a Doctor?**		**Chapter 5** **Who Really Needs a Doctor?**	
v. 12: "But *Yeshua* heard the question and answered, 'The ones who need a doctor aren't the healthy but the sick.'"		v. 17: "But, hearing the question, *Yeshua* answered them, (a) "The ones who need a doctor aren't the healthy but the sick."	a). Matthew 9:12–13; 18:11; Luke 5:31–32; 19:10	v. 31: "It was *Yeshua* who answered them: 'The ones who need a doctor aren't the healthy but the sick.'"	

Gospel of Mattityahu "Matthew"	OT/NT References	Gospel of Mrk "Mark"	OT/NT References	Gospel of Luk "Luke"	OT/NT References
Chapter 9 Who Really Needs a Doctor? Continued		**Chapter 2 Who Really Needs a Doctor? Continued**		**Chapter 5 Who Really Needs a Doctor? Continued**	
v. 13: "As for you, go and learn what this means; (A) 'I want compassion rather than animal-sacrifices.' For I didn't come to call the 'righteous,' (b) but sinners!"	A). Hosea 6:6; Micah 6:6–8; Matthew 12:7 b). Mark 2:17; Luke 5:32; 1 Timothy 1:15	v. 17: "I didn't come to call the 'righteous' but sinners!"		v. 32: "I have not come to call the 'righteous,' but rather to call sinners to turn to God from their sins."	
Chapter 9 Yeshua Is Questioned About Fasting		**Chapter 2 Yeshua Is Questioned About Fasting**		**Chapter 5 Yeshua Is Questioned About Fasting**	
v. 15: "*Yeshua* said to them, 'Can (a) wedding guests mourn while the bridegroom is still with them?'"	a). John 3:29	v. 19: "Can wedding quests fast while the bridegroom is still with them? As long as they have the bridegroom with them, fasting is out of the question.		v. 34: "*Yeshua* said to them, 'Can you make wedding guests fast while the (a) bridegroom is still with them?'"	a). John 3:29
v. 15: "But the time will come when the bridegroom is taken away from them; (b) then they will fast."	b). Acts 13:2–3; 14:23	v. 20: "But the time will come when the bridegroom is (a) taken away from them; and when that day comes, they will fast."	a).Acts 1:9; 13:2–3; 14:23	v. 35: "The time will come when the bridegroom will be taken away from them; and when that time comes, they will fast."	

Just the Words and Teachings of Jesus Christ

Gospel of Mattityahu "Matthew"	OT/NT References	Gospel of Mrk "Mark"	OT/NT References	Gospel of Luk "Luke"	OT/NT References
Chapter 9 **Yeshua Is Questioned About Fasting Continued**		**Chapter 2** **Yeshua Is Questioned About Fasting Continued**		**Chapter 5** **Yeshua Is Questioned About Fasting Continued**	
v. 16: "No one patches an old coat with a piece of unshrunk cloth, because the patch tears away from the coat and leaves a worse hole."		v. 21: "No one sews a piece of unshrunk cloth on an old coat; if he does, the new patch tears away from the old cloth and leaves a worse hole."		v. 36: (a) "Then He gave them an illustration: 'No one tears a piece from a new coat and puts it on an old one; if he does, not only will the new one continue to rip, but the piece from the new will not match the old.'"	a). Matthew 9:16–17; Mark 2:21–22
v. 17: "Nor do people put new wine in old wineskins; if they do, the skins burst, the wine spills and the wineskins are ruined. No, they pour new wine into freshly prepared wineskins, and in this way both are preserved."		v. 22: "And no one puts new wine in old wineskins; if he does, the wine will burst the skins, and both the wine and the skins will be ruined. Rather, new wine is for freshly prepared wineskins."		vv. 37–38: "Also, no one puts new wine into old wineskins; if he does, the new wine will burst the skins and be spilled, and the skins too will be ruined. On the contrary, new wine must be put into freshly prepared wineskins."	
				v. 39: "Besides that, after drinking old wine, people don't want new; because they say, 'The old is good enough.'"	

Gospel of Mattityahu "Matthew"	OT/NT References	Gospel of Mrk "Mark"	OT/NT References	Gospel of Luk "Luke"	OT/NT References
Chapter 9 **A Girl Restored to Life and a Woman Healed**		**Chapter 5** **A Girl Restored to Life and a Woman Healed**		**Chapter 8** **A Girl Restored to Life and a Woman Healed**	
		v. 30: "At the same time, *Yeshua*, aware that (a) power had gone out from him, turned around in the crowd and asked, 'Who touched my clothes?'"	a). Luke 6:19; 8:46	v. 45: "*Yeshua* asked, 'Who touched me?' When they all denied doing it, *Kefa* said, '*Rabbi*' The crowds are hemming you in and jostling you!"	
				v. 46: "But *Yeshua* said, 'Someone did touch Me, because I felt (a) power go out of Me.'"	a). Mark 5:30; Luke 6:19
v. 22: "*Yeshua* turned, saw her and said, 'Courage, daughter! (a) Your trust has healed you.' And she was instantly healed."	a). Matthew 9:29; 15:28; Mark 5:34; 10:52; Luke 7:50; 8:48; 17:19; 18:42	v. 34: "Daughter, (a)…your trust has healed you. (B) Go in peace, and be healed of your disease."	a). Matthew 9:22; Mark 10:52; Acts 14:9 B). 1 Samuel 1:17; 20:42; 2 Kings 5:19; Luke 7:50; 8:48; Acts 16:36; James 2:16	v. 48: "He said to her, 'My daughter, (a) your trust has saved you; (b) go in peace.'"	a). Mark 5:34; Luke 7:50 b). John 8:11
		v. 36: "Ignoring what they had said, *Yeshua* told the synagogue official, 'Don't be afraid, just keep (a) trusting.'"	a). Mark 9:23; John 11:40	v. 50: "But on hearing this, *Yeshua* answered him, 'Don't be afraid! (a) Just go on trusting, and she will be made well.'"	a). Mark 11:22–24

Gospel of Mattityahu "Matthew"	OT/NT References	Gospel of Mrk "Mark"	OT/NT References	Gospel of Luk "Luke"	OT/NT References
Chapter 9 **A Girl Restored to Life and a Woman Healed Continued**		**Chapter 5** **A Girl Restored to Life and a Woman Healed Continued**		**Chapter 8** **A Girl Restored to Life and a Woman Healed Continued**	
vv. 23–24: (a) "When *Yeshua arrived at the official's house and saw the (B) flute-players, and the crowd in an uproar, He said, 'Everybody out! The girl isn't dead, she's only sleeping!' and they jeered at Him."	a). Mark 5:38; Luke 8:51 B). 2 Chronicles 35:25; Jeremiah 9:17; 16:6; Ezekiel 24:17	v. 39: "Why all this commotion and weeping? The child isn't dead, she's just (a) asleep!"	a). John 11:4, 11	v. 52: "All the people were wailing and mourning for her; but He said, (a) 'Don't weep; she hasn't died, (b) she's sleeping.'"	a). Luke 7:13 b). John 11:11, 13
		v. 41: "Taking her by the hand, he said to her, '*Talita, kumi!*' (which means, 'Little girl, I say to you, get up!')."		v. 54: "But He took her by the hand, called out, 'little girl, (a) get up!'"	a). Luke 7:14; John 11:43
				v. 55: "And her spirit returned. She stood up at once, and He directed that something be given her to eat."	
Chapter 9 **Two Blind Men Healed**					
v. 28: "When He entered the house, the blind men came up, and *Yeshua said to them, 'Do you believe that I have the power to do this?' They replied, 'Yes, sir.'"					

Part 4: Subtopic Scriptural Alignment View—Matthew, Mark, and Luke

Gospel of Mattityahu "Matthew"	OT/NT References	Gospel of Mrk "Mark"	OT/NT References	Gospel of Luk "Luke"	OT/NT References
Chapter 9 **Two Blind Men Healed Continued**		**Chapter 8** **Blind Man Healed at Bethsaida**			
v. 29: "Then He touched their eyes and said, 'Let it happen to you according to your trust.'"		v. 23: "Taking the blind man's hand, He led him outside the town. (a) He spit in his eyes, put His hands on him and asked him, 'Do you see anything?'"	a). Mark 7:33		
v. 30: "And their sight was restored. *Yeshua* warned them severely, (a) 'See that no one knows about it.'"	a). Matthew 8:4; Luke 5:14	v. 26: "Yeshua sent him home with the words, (a) 'Don't go into town.'"	a). Matthew 8:4; Mark 5:43; 7:36		
Chapter 9 **The Compassion of Yeshua**					
v. 37: "Then He said to His *talmidim*, (a) 'The harvest is rich, but the workers are few.'"	a). Luke 10:2; Jonh 4:35				
v. 38: (a) "Pray that the Lord of the harvest will send out workers to gather in His harvest."	a). Matthew 28:19–20; Ephesians 4:11–12; 2 Thessalonians 3:1				

Gospel of Mattityahu "Matthew"	OT/NT References	Gospel of Mrk "Mark"	OT/NT References	Gospel of Luk "Luke"	OT/NT References
Chapter 10 Sending Out the Twelve					
v. 5: "These twelve *Yeshua* sent out with the following instructions: (a) 'Don't go in the territory of the *Goyim*, and don't enter any town in (B) *Shomron.'"*	a). Matthew 4:15 B). 2 Kings 17:24; Luke 9:52; 10:33; 17:16; John 4:9				
v. 6: (a) "But go rather to the (B) lost sheep of the house of Israel."	a). Matthew 15:24; Acts 13:46 B). Isaiah 53:6; Jeremiah 50:6				
v. 7: (a) "As you go, proclaim, (b) "The Kingdom of Heaven is near.'"	a). Luke 9:2 b). Matthew 3:2; Luke 10:9				
v. 8: "Heal the sick, raise the dead, cleanse those afflicted with *tzara'at*, and expel demons. (a) You have received without paying, so give without asking payment."	a). Acts 8:18				

Gospel of Mattityahu "Matthew"	OT/NT References	Gospel of Mrk "Mark"	OT/NT References	Gospel of Luk "Luke"	OT/NT References
Chapter 10 Sending Out the Twelve Continued		**Chapter 6 Sending Out the Twelve**		**Chapter 9 Sending Out the Twelve**	
v. 9: (A) "Don't take money in your belts, (b) no gold, no silver, no copper."	A). 1 Samuel 9:7; Mark 6:8 b). Mark 6:8	v. 8: "Take nothing for your trip except a walking stick—no bread, no pack, no money in your belt."		v. 3: (a) "He said to them, 'Take nothing for your trip—neither a walking stick nor a pack, neither bread nor money.'"	a). Matthew 10:9–15; Mark 6:8–11; Luke 10:4–12; 22:35
v. 10: "And for the trip don't take a pack, an extra shirt, shoes, or walking stick—(a) a worker should be given what he needs."	a). Luke 10:7; 1 Corinthians 9:4–14; 1 Timothy 5:18	v. 9: (a) "Wear shoes but not an extra shirt."	a). Ephesians 6:15	v. 3: "And don't have two shirts."	
v. 11: (a) "When you come to a town or village, look for someone trustworthy and stay with him until you leave."	a). Luke 10:8	v. 10: (a) "Whenever you enter a house, stay there until you leave the place."	a). Matthew 10:11; Luke 9:4; 10:7–8	v. 4: (a) "Whatever house your enter, stay there and go out from there."	a). Matthew 10:11; Mark 6:10
v. 12: "When you enter someone's household, say '*Shalom aleikhem!*'"					
v. 13: (a) "If the home deserves it, let your *shalom rest on it; (B) if not, let your *shalom return to you."	a). Luke 10:5 B). Psalm 35:13				

Gospel of Mattityahu "Matthew"	OT/NT References	Gospel of Mrk "Mark"	OT/NT References	Gospel of Luk "Luke"	OT/NT References
Chapter 10 Sending Out the Twelve Continued		**Chapter 6 Sending Out the Twelve Continued**		**Chapter 9 Sending Out the Twelve Continued**	
v. 14: (a) "But if the people of a house or town will not welcome you or listen to you, leave it and (B) shake its dust from your feet!"	a). Mark 6:11; Luke 9:5 B). Nehemiah 5:13; Luke 10:10–11; Acts 13:51	v. 11: (a) "And if the people of some places will not welcome you, and they refuse to hear you, then, as you leave, (b) shake the dust off your feet as a warning to them."	a). Matthew 10:14; Luke 10:10 b). Acts 13:51; 18:6	v. 5: (a) "Wherever they don't welcome you, (b) shake the dust from your feet when you leave that town as a warning to them."	a). Matthew 10:14 b). Luke 10:11; Acts 13:51
v. 15: Yes, I tell you, (a) it will be more tolerable on the Day of Judgment for the people of *S'dom and *Amora than for that town!"	a). Matthew 11:22, 24				
				Chapter 10 The Seventy Sent Out	
				v. 2: "He said to them, 'To be sure, (a) there is a large harvest. But there are few workers. Therefore, (b) plead with the Lord of the Harvest that He [send workers out speedily] to gather in His harvest.'"	a). Matthew 9:37–38; John 4:35 b). 1 Corinthians 3:9; 2 Thessalonians 3:1
				v. 3: "Get going now, (a) but pay attention! I am sending you out like lambs among wolves."	a). Matthew 10:16

Part 4: Subtopic Scriptural Alignment View—Matthew, Mark, and Luke

Gospel of Mattityahu "Matthew"	OT/NT References	Gospel of Mrk "Mark"	OT/NT References	Gospel of Luk "Luke"	OT/NT References
				Chapter 10 **The Seventy Sent Out Continued**	
				v. 4: (a) "Don't carry a money-belt or a pack, and don't stop to (B) *schmooze* with people on the road."	a). Matthew 10:9–14; Mark 6:8–11; Luke 9:3–5 B). 2 Kings 4:29
				v. 5: (A) "Whenever you enter a house, first say, '*Shalom*!' to the household."	A). 1 Samuel 25:6; Matthew 10:12
				v. 6: "If a seeker of *shalom* is there, your '*Shalom*'!' will find rest with him; and if there isn't it will return to you."	
				v. 7: (a) "Stay in that same house, (b) eating and drinking what they offer, (c) for a worker deserves his wages—don't move about from house to house."	a). Matthew 10:11 b). 1 Corinthians 10:27 c). Matthew 10:10; 1 Corinthians 9:4–8; 1 Timothy 5:18
				v. 8: "Whenever you come into a town where they make you welcome, eat what is put in front of you."	

Gospel of Mattityahu "Matthew"	OT/NT References	Gospel of Mrk "Mark"	OT/NT References	Gospel of Luk "Luke"	OT/NT References
				Chapter 10 **The Seventy Sent Out Continued**	
				v. 9: (a) "Heal the sick there, and tell them, (b) 'The Kingdom of God is near you.'"	a). Mark 3:15 b). Matthew 3:2; 10:7; Luke 10:11
				v. 10: "But whenever you enter a town and they don't make you welcome, go out into its streets and say."	
				v. 11: (a) "Even the dust of your town that sticks to our feet we wipe off as a sign against you! But understand this: the Kingdom of God is near!"	a). Matthew 10:14; Mark 6:11; Luke 9:5; Acts 13:51
				v. 12: "I tell you, (A) it will be more tolerable on the Day of Judgement for *S'dom* than for that town."	A). Genesis 19:24-28; Lamentations 4:6; Matthew 10:15; 11:24; Mark 6:11
				Chapter 10 **The Seventy Return with Joy**	
				v. 18: "*Yeshua* said to them, (a) 'I saw *Satan* fall like lightning from heaven.'"	a). John 12:31; Revelations 9:1; 12:8–9

Part 4: Subtopic Scriptural Alignment View—Matthew, Mark, and Luke

Gospel of Mattityahu "Matthew"	OT/NT References	Gospel of Mrk "Mark"	OT/NT References	Gospel of Luk "Luke"	OT/NT References
				Chapter 10 **The Seventy Return with Joy Continued**	
				v. 19: "Remember, (A) I have given you authority; so you can trample down snakes and scorpions, indeed, all the Enemy's forces; and you will remain completely unharmed."	A). Psalm 91:13; Mark 16:18; Acts 28:5
				v. 20: "Nevertheless, don't be glad that the spirits submit to you; be glad that (A) your names have been recorded in heaven."	A). Exodus 32:32–33; Psalm 69:28; Isaiah 4:3; Daniel 12:1; Philippians 4:3; Hebrews 12:23; Revelation 13:8
				v. 21: (a) "At that moment He was filled with joy by the *Ruach HaKodesh* and said, 'Father, Lord of heaven and earth, I thank You because You concealed these things from the sophisticated and educated, yet revealed them to ordinary people. Yes, Father, I thank you that it pleased You to do this.'"	a). Matthew 11:25–27

Gospel of Mattityahu "Matthew"	OT/NT References	Gospel of Mrk "Mark"	OT/NT References	Gospel of Luk "Luke"	OT/NT References
				Chapter 10 **Yeshua Rejoices in the Spirit**	
				v. 22: (a) "My Father has handed over everything to Me. Indeed, (b) no one fully knows who the Son is except the Father, and who the Father is except the Son and those to whom the Son wishes to reveal Him."	a). Matthew 28:18; John 3:35; 5:27; 17:2 b). John 1:18; 6:44, 46
				v. 23: "Then, turning to the *talmidim*, He said, privately, (a) 'How blessed are the eyes that see what you are seeing!'"	a). Matthew 13:16–17
				v. 24: "Indeed, I tell you (a) that many prophets and kings wanted to see the things you are seeing but did not see them, and to hear the things you are hearing but did not hear them."	a). 1 Peter 1:10–11

Gospel of Mattityahu "Matthew"	OT/NT References	Gospel of Mrk "Mark"	OT/NT References	Gospel of Luk "Luke"	OT/NT References
Chapter 10 Persecutions Are Coming					
v. 16: (a) "Pay attention! I am sending you out like sheep among wolves, (b) so be as prudent as snakes and as (c) harmless as doves."	a). Luke 10:3 b). 2 Corinthians 12:16; Ephesians 5:15; Colossians 4:5 c). Philippians 2:14–16				
v. 17: "Be on guard, for (a) there will be people who will hand you over to the local *Sanhedrin's* and (b) flog you in their synagogues."	a). Matthew 23:34; Mark 13:9; Luke 12:11 b). Acts 5:40; 22:19; 26:11				
v. 18: (a) "On My account you will be brought before governors and kings as a testimony to them and to the *Goyim*."	a). Acts 12:1–2; 2 Timothy 4:16				
v. 19: (a) "But when they bring you to trial, do not worry about what to say or how to say it: when the time comes, (B) you will be given what you should say."	a). Mark 13:11; Luke 12:11–12; 21:14–15 B). Exodus 4:12; Jeremiah 1:7				

Gospel of Mattityahu "Matthew"	OT/NT References	Gospel of Mrk "Mark"	OT/NT References	Gospel of Luk "Luke"	OT/NT References
Chapter 10 Persecutions Are Coming Continued				**Chapter 6 Persecutions Are Coming Continued**	
v. 20: (A) "For it will not be just you speaking, but the Spirit of your Heavenly Father speaking through you."	A). 2 Samuel 23:2; 2 Timothy 4:17				
v. 21: (A) "A brother will betray his brother to death, and a father his child; children will turn against their parents and have them put to death."	A). Micah 7:6; Luke 21:16				
v. 22: "Everyone will hate (a) you because of Me, (B) but whoever holds out till the end will be preserved from harm."	a). Matthew 24:9; Luke 21:17; John 15:18 B). Daniel 12:12; Matthew 23:13; Mark 13:13				
v. 23: (a) "When you are persecuted in one town, run away to another. Yes indeed; I tell you, you will not finish (b) going through the towns of *Israel (c) before the Son of Man comes."	a. Matthew 2:13; Acts 8:1 b. Matthew 24:14; Mark 13:10 c. Matthew 16:28				
v. 24: (a) "A *talmid is not greater than his *rabbi, a slave is not greater than his master."	a. Luke 6:40; John 15:2			v. 40: (a) "A *talmid is not above his *rabbi; but each one, when he is fully trained, will be like his *rabbi."	a). Matthew 10:24; John 13:16; 15:20

Gospel of Mattityahu "Matthew"	OT/NT References	Gospel of Mrk "Mark"	OT/NT References	Gospel of Luk "Luke"	OT/NT References
Chapter 10 Persecutions Are Coming Continued					
v. 25: "It is enough for a *talmid* that he become like his *rabbi*, and a slave like his master. Now if (a) people have called the head of the house *Ba'al-Zibbul* how much more will they malign the members of his household!"	a. Mark 3:22; Luke 11:15, 18–19; John 8:48, 52				
v. 26: "So do not fear them; (a) for there is nothing covered that will not be uncovered, or hidden that will not be known."	a. Mark 4:22; Luke 8:17; 12:2–3; 1 Corinthians 4:5				
Chapter 10 Yeshua Teaches the Fear of God					
v. 27: "What I tell you in the dark, (a) speak in the light; what is whispered in your ear, proclaim on the housetops."	a). Luke 12:3; Acts 5:20				

Gospel of Mattityahu "Matthew"	OT/NT References	Gospel of Mrk "Mark"	OT/NT References	Gospel of Luk "Luke"	OT/NT References
Chapter 10 Yeshua Teaches the Fear of God Continued				**Chapter 12 Yeshua Teaches the Fear of God Continued**	
v. 28: (a) "Do not fear those who kill the body but are powerless to kill the soul."	a). Luke 12:14; 1 Peter 3:14			v. 4: (A) "My friends, I tell you: (b) don't fear those who kill the body but then have nothing more they can do."	A). Isaiah 51:7–8, 12–13; Jeremiah 1:8; Matthew 10:28 b). John 15:13–15
v. 28: "Rather (B) fear Him who can destroy both soul and body in *Gei-Hinnom*."	B). Isaiah 8:13; Matthew 5:22; Luke 12:5			v. 5: "I will show you whom to fear: fear Him who after killing you has authority to throw you into *Gei-Hinnom*! Yes, I tell you, this is the (A) One to fear!"	A). Psalm 119:120
v. 29: "Aren't (a) sparrows sold for next to nothing, two for an *assarion* yet not one of them will fall to the ground without your Father's consent."	a). Luke 12:6–7			v. 6: "Aren't sparrows sold for next to nothing, five for two *assarions*? And (a) not one of them has been forgotten by God."	a). Matthew 6:26
v. 30: (A) "As for you, every hair on your head has been counted."	A). 1 Samuel 14:45; 2 Samuel 14:11; 1 Kings 1:52; Luke 21:18; Acts 27:34			v. 7: "Why, every hair on your head has been counted!"	
v. 31: "So do not be afraid, you are worth more than many sparrows."				v. 7: "Don't be afraid, you are worth more than many sparrows."	

Gospel of Mattityahu "Matthew"	OT/NT References	Gospel of Mrk "Mark"	OT/NT References	Gospel of Luk "Luke"	OT/NT References
Chapter 10 Confess Christ before Men				**Chapter 12 Confess Christ before Men**	
v. 32: (A) "Whoever acknowledges Me in the presence of others (b) I will also acknowledge in the presence of My Father in Heaven."	A). Psalm 119:46; Luke 12:8; Romans 10:9 b). Revelation 3:5			v. 8: (A) "Moreover, I tell you, whoever acknowledges Me in the (B) presence of others, the Son of Man will also acknowledge in the presence of God's angels."	A). 1 Samuel 2:30; Matthew 10:32; Mark 8:38; Romans 10:9; 2 Timothy 2:12; 1 John 2:23 B). Psalm 119:46
v. 33: (a) "But whoever disowns Me before others I will disown before My Father in Heaven."	a). Mark 8:38; Luke 9:26; 2 Timothy 2:12			v. 9: "But whoever (a) disowns Me before others will be disowned before God's angels."	a). Matthew 10:33; Mark 8:38; 2 Timothy 2:12
				v. 10: "Also, (a) everyone who says something against the Son of Man will have it forgiven him; but whoever has blasphemed the *Rauch HaKodesh* will not be forgiven."	a). Matthew 12:31–32; Mark 3:28; 1 John 5:16
				v. 11: (a) "When they bring you before the synagogues and the ruling powers and the authorities, don't worry about how you will defend yourself or what you will say."	a). Matthew 6:25; 10:19; Mark 13:11

Gospel of Mattityahu "Matthew"	OT/NT References	Gospel of Mrk "Mark"	OT/NT References	Gospel of Luk "Luke"	OT/NT References
				Chapter 12 Confess Christ before Men	
				v. 11: (a) "When they bring you before the synagogues and the ruling powers and the authorities, don't worry about how you will defend yourself or what you will say."	a). Matthew 6:25; 10:19; Mark 13:11
				v. 12: "Because when the time comes, the *Rauch HaKodesh* will (a) teach you what you need to say."	a). John 14:26
Chapter 10 Christ Brings Division				**Chapter 12 Christ Brings Division**	
v. 34: (a) "Don't suppose that I have come to bring peace to the Land. It is not peace I have cowme to bring, but a *sword!*" (See "Commentaries.")	a). Luke 12:49			v. 49: (a) "I have come to set fire to the earth! And how I wish it were already kindled!"	a). Luke 12:51
v. 35: "For I have come to set."					
				v. 50: (a) "I have an immersion to undergo—how pressured I feel till it's (b) over!"	a). Matthew 20:18, 22, 23; Mark 10:38 b). John 12:27; 19:30

Part 4: Subtopic Scriptural Alignment View—Matthew, Mark, and Luke

Gospel of Mattityahu "Matthew"	OT/NT References	Gospel of Mrk "Mark"	OT/NT References	Gospel of Luk "Luke"	OT/NT References
Chapter 10 Christ Brings Division Continued				**Chapter 12 Christ Brings Division Continued**	
				v. 51: (a) "Do you think that I have come to bring peace in the Land? Not peace, I tell you, (B) but division!"	a). Matthew 10:34–36 B). Micah 7:6; John 7:43; 9:16: 10:19; Acts 14:4
				v. 52: (a) "For from now on, a household of five will be divided, three against two, two against three."	a). Matthew 10:35; Mark 13:12
v. 36: (A) "A man against his father, a daughter against her mother, a daughter-in-law against her mother-in-law, so that a man's (B) enemies will be the members of his own household."	A). Micah 7:6; Matthew 10:21; Luke 12:53 B). Psalm 41:9; 55:13; John 13:18			v. 53: (a) "Father will be divided against son and son against father, mother against daughter and daughter against mother, mother-in-law against her daughter-in-law and daughter-in-law against mother-in-law."	a). Matthew 10:21, 36
v. 37: (A) "Whoever loves his father or mother more than he loves Me is not worthy of Me; anyone who loves his son or daughter more than he loves Me is not worthy of Me."	A). Deuteronomy 33:9; Luke 14:26				

Gospel of Mattityahu "Matthew"	OT/NT References	Gospel of Mrk "Mark"	OT/NT References	Gospel of Luk "Luke"	OT/NT References
Chapter 10 Christ Brings Division Continued					
v. 38: (a) "And anyone who does not take up his *execution-stake* and follow Me is not worthy of Me."	a). Matthew 16:24; Mark 8:34; Luke 9:23; 14:27				
v. 39: (a) "Whoever finds his own life will lose it, but the person who loses his life for My sake will find it."	a). Matthew 16:25; Mark 8:35; Luke 9:24; 17:33; John 12:25				
				Chapter 14 Leaving All to Follow Yeshua	
				v. 26: (A) "If anyone comes to Me (b) and does not hate his father, mother, his wife, his children, his brother and his sisters,(c) yes, and his own life besides, he cannot be My *talmid*."	A). Deuteronomy 13:6; 33:9; Matthew 10:37 b). Romans 9:13 c). Revelation 12:11
				v. 27: (a) "Whoever does not carry his own *execution-stake and come after Me cannot be My *talmid.."	a). Matthew 16:24; Mark 8:34; Luke 9:23; 2 Timothy 3:12

Part 4: Subtopic Scriptural Alignment View—Matthew, Mark, and Luke 105

Gospel of Mattityahu "Matthew"	OT/NT References	Gospel of Mrk "Mark"	OT/NT References	Gospel of Luk "Luke"	OT/NT References
				Chapter 14 Leaving All to Follow Yeshua Continued	
				v. 28: "Suppose (A) one of you wants to build a tower. Don't you sit down and estimate the cost, to see if you have enough capital to complete it?"	A). Proverbs 24:27
				v. 29: "If you don't, then when you have laid the foundation but cant finish, all the onlookers start making fun of you."	
				v. 30: "And say, 'This is the man who began to build, but couldn't finish!'"	
				v. 31: "Or again, suppose one king is going out to wage war with another king. Doesn't he first sit down and consider whether he, with his ten thousand troops, has enough strength to meet the other one, who is coming against him with twenty thousand?"	
				v. 32: "If he hasn't, then while the other is still far away, he sends a delegation to inquire about terms for peace."	

Gospel of Mattityahu "Matthew"	OT/NT References	Gospel of Mrk "Mark"	OT/NT References	Gospel of Luk "Luke"	OT/NT References
				Chapter 14 Leaving All to Follow Yeshua Continued	
				v. 32: "If he hasn't, then while the other is still far away, he sends a delegation to inquire about terms for peace."	
				v. 33: "So every one of you who (a) doesn't renounce all that he has cannot be my *talmid*."	a). Matthew 9:27
Chapter 10 A Cup of Cold Water					
v. 40: (a) "Whoever receives you is receiving Me, and whoever receives Me is receiving the One who sent Me."	a). Mark 9:37; Luke 9:48; John 12:44; Galatians 4:14				
v. 41: (A) "Anyone who receives a prophet because he is a prophet will receive the reward a prophet gets, and anyone who receives a *tzaddik* because he is a *tzaddik* will receive the reward a *tzaddik* gets."	A). 1 Kings 17:10; 2 Kings 4:8				
v. 42: (a) "Indeed, if someone gives just a cup of cold water to one of these little ones because he is My *talmid*—yes!—I tell you, he will certainly not lose his reward!"	a). Matthew 25:40; Mark 9:41; Hebrews 6:10				

Gospel of Mattityahu "Matthew"	OT/NT References	Gospel of Mrk "Mark"	OT/NT References	Gospel of Luk "Luke"	OT/NT References
Chapter 11 Yochanan the Immerser (John the Baptist) Sends Messengers to Yeshua				**Chapter 7 Yochanan the Immerser (John the Baptist) Sends Messengers to Yeshua**	
v. 4: "*Yeshua answered, 'Go and tell *Yochanan what you are hearing and seeing.'"				v. 22: (a) "So He answered them by saying, 'Go, tell *Yochanan what you have been seeing and hearing.'"	a). Matthew 11:4
v. 5: (A) "The blind are seeing again, the lame are walking, people with *tzara'at are being cleansed, the deaf are hearing, the dead are being raised, (B) the Good News is being told to the poor."	A). Isaiah 29:18; 35:4–6; John 2:23 B). Psalm 22:26; Isaiah 61:1; Luke 4:18; James 2:5			v. 22: (B) "The blind are (c) seeing again, the lame are (d) walking, people with *tzara'at are being (e) cleansed, the deaf are (f) hearing, the dead are being raised, the (G) Good News is being told to the poor."	B). Isaiah 35:5 c). John 9:7 d). Matt 15:31 e). Luke 17:12–14 f). Mark 7:37 G). Isaiah 61:1–3; Luke 4:18
v. 6: "And how blessed is anyone not (A) offended by Me!"	A). Isaiah 8:14–15; Romans 9:32; 1 Peter 2:8			v. 23: "And how blessed is anyone not offended by Me!"	
v. 7: (a) "As they were leaving, *Yeshua began speaking about *Yochanan to the crowds; 'What did you go out to the desert to see? (b) Reeds swaying in the breeze?'"	a). Luke 7:24; Ephesians 4:14			v. 24: (a) "When the messengers from *Yochanan had gone, *Yeshua began speaking to the crowds about *Yochanan: 'What did you go out into the desert to see? Reeds swaying in the breeze?'"	a). Matthew 11:7

Gospel of Mattityahu "Matthew"	OT/NT References	Gospel of Mrk "Mark"	OT/NT References	Gospel of Luk "Luke"	OT/NT References
Chapter 11 **Yochanan the Immerser (John the Baptist) Sends Messengers to Yeshua Continued**				**Chapter 7** **Yochanan the Immerser (John the Baptist) Sends Messengers to Yeshua Continued**	
v. 8: "No? Then what did you go out to see? Someone who was well dressed? Well-dressed people live in king's palaces."				v. 25: "No? Then what did you go out to see? Someone who was well dressed? But people who dress beautifully and live in luxury are found in kings' palaces."	
v. 9: "*Nu!* So why did you go out? To see a prophet! Yes! And I tell you he's much (a) more than a prophet."	a). Matthew 14:5; 21:26; Luke 1:76; 20:6			v. 26: "A prophet! Yes, and I tell you he's much more than a prophet."	
v. 10: "This is the one about whom the *Tanakh* says, (A) 'See, I am sending out My messenger ahead of you; He will prepare your way before you.'"	A). Malachi 3:1; Mark 1:2; Luke 1:76			v. 27: "This is the one about whom the *Tanakh* says, (A) 'See, I am sending out My messenger ahead of you; He will prepare your way before you.'"	A). Isaiah 40:3; Malachi 3:1; Matthew 11:10; Mark 1:2
v. 11: "Yes! I tell you that among those born of women there has not arisen anyone greater than *Yochanan the Immerser!* Yet the one who is the least in the Kingdom of Heaven is greater than he!"				v. 28: "I tell you that among those born of women there has not arisen (a) anyone greater than *Yochanan the Immerser!* Yet the one who is least in the Kingdom of Heaven is greater than he!"	a). Luke 1:15

Gospel of Mattityahu "Matthew"	OT/NT References	Gospel of Mrk "Mark"	OT/NT References	Gospel of Luk "Luke"	OT/NT References
Chapter 11 Yochanan the Immerser (John the Baptist) Sends Messengers to Yeshua Continued				**Chapter 7 Yochanan the Immerser (John the Baptist) Sends Messengers to Yeshua Continued**	
v. 12: (a) "From the time of *Yochanan the Immerser* until now, the Kingdom of Heaven has been suffering violence; yes, violent ones are trying to snatch it away."	a). Luke 16:16				
v. 13: (A) "For all the prophets and the *Torah* prophesied until *Yochanan*."	A). Malachi 4:4–6				
v. 14: "Indeed, if you are willing to accept it, he is (A) *Eliyahu* whose coming was predicted."	A). Malachi 4:5; Matthew 17:10–13; Mark 9:11–13; Luke 1:17; John 1:21				
v. 15: (a) "If you have ears, then hear!"	a). Matthew 13:9; Luke 8:8; Revelation 2:7,11, 17, 29; 3:6–13				
v. 16: (a) "Oh, what can I compare this generation with?"	a). Luke 7:31			v. 31: "'Therefore,' said the Lord, (a) 'how can I describe the people of this generation? What are they like?'"	a. Matthew 11:16

110 *Just the Words and Teachings of Jesus Christ*

Gospel of Mattityahu "Matthew"	OT/NT References	Gospel of Mrk "Mark"	OT/NT References	Gospel of Luk "Luke"	OT/NT References
Chapter 11 Yochanan the Immerser (John the Baptist) Sends Messengers to Yeshua Continued				**Chapter 7 Yochanan the Immerser (John the Baptist) Sends Messengers to Yeshua Continued**	
v. 16: "They're like children sitting in the marketplaces, calling out to each other."				v. 32: "They are like children sitting in the marketplaces, calling to one another."	
v. 17: "We made happy music, but you wouldn't dance! We made sad music, but you wouldn't cry!"				v. 32: "We made happy music, but you wouldn't dance! We made sad music, but you wouldn't cry!"	
v. 18: "For *Yochanan came, fasting, not drinking—so they say, 'He has a demon.'"				v. 33: "For (a) *Yochanan has come not (b) eating bread and not drinking wine; and you say 'He has a demon!'"	a). Matthew 3:1 b). Matthew 3:4; Luke 1:15
v. 19: "The Son of Man came, eating freely and drinking wine—so they say, 'Aha! (a) A glutton and a drunkard! A friend of tax-collectors and sinners!'"	a). Matthew 9:10; Luke 7:35; John 2:1–11			v. 34: "The Son of Man has come (a) eating and drinking; and you say, 'Aha! A glutton and a drunkard! A friend of tax-collectors and sinners!'"	a). Luke 15:2
v. 19: "Well, the proof of (b) wisdom is in the actions it produces."	b). Luke 7:35; John 2:1–11			v. 35: (a) "Well, the proof of wisdom is in all the kinds of people it produces."	a). Matthew 11:19

Gospel of Mattityahu "Matthew"	OT/NT References	Gospel of Mrk "Mark"	OT/NT References	Gospel of Luk "Luke"	OT/NT References
Chapter 11 Woe to the Impenitent Cities				**Chapter 10 Woe to the Impenitent Cities**	
v. 20: (a) "Then *Yeshua* began to denounce the towns in which He had done most of His miracles, because the people had not turned from their sins to God."	a). Luke 10:13–15, 18				
v. 21: "Woe to you, *Korazin!* Woe to you, *Beit-Tzaidah!* Why, if the miracles done in you had been done in *Tzor* and *Tzidon*, they would long ago have put on (A) sackcloth and ashes as evidence that they had changed their ways."	A). Jonah 3:6–8			v. 13: (a) "Woe to you, *Korazin!* Woe to you *Beit-Tzaidah!* (B) For if the miracles done in you had been done in *Tzor* and *Tzidon*, they would long ago have put on sackcloth and ashes as evidence that they had changed their ways."	a). Matthew 11:21–23 B). Ezekiel 3:6
v. 22: "But I tell you it will be more (a) bearable for *Tzor* and *Tzidon* than for you on the Day of Judgment!"	a). Matthew 10:15; 11:24			v. 14: "But at the Judgement it will be more bearable for *Tzor* and *Tzidon* than for you!"	
v. 23: "And you, *K'far-Nachum*, will (A) you be exalted to heaven? No, you will be brought down to *Sh'ol!* For if the miracles done in you had been done in *S'dom*, it would still be in existence today."	A). Isaiah 14:13; Lamentations 2:1; Ezekiel 26:20; 31:14; 32:18, 24			v. 15: (a) "And for you, *K'far Nachum*, will you be (B) exalted to heaven? No, you (C) will be brought down to *Sh'ol!*"	a). Matthew 11:23 B. Genesis 11:4; Deuteronomy 1:28; Isaiah 14:13–15; Jeremiah 51:53 C. Ezekiel 26:20

Gospel of Mattityahu "Matthew"	OT/NT References	Gospel of Mrk "Mark"	OT/NT References	Gospel of Luk "Luke"	OT/NT References
Chapter 11 Woe to the Impenitent Cities Continued				**Chapter 10 Woe to the Impenitent Cities Continued**	
v. 24: "But I tell you that on the Day of Judgment (a) it will be more bearable for the land of S'dom than for you!"	a). Matthew 10:15				
				v. 16: (a) "Whoever listens to you listens to Me, also (b) whoever rejects you rejects Me and (c) whoever rejects Me rejects the One who sent Me."	a). Matthew 10:40; Mark 9:37; John 13:20; Galatians 4:14 b). John 12:48; 1 Thessalonians 4:8 c). John 5:23
Chapter 11 Yeshua Gives True Rest					
v.25: (a) "It was at that time that *Yeshua said, "I thank you, Father, Lord of heaven and earth, that (B) you concealed these things from the sophisticated and educated and (c) revealed them to ordinary folks."	a). Luke 10:21–22 B). Psalm 8:2; 1 Corinthians 1:19; 2 Corinthians 3:14 c).Matthew 16:17				
v. 26: "Yes, Father, I thank You that it pleased You to do this."					

Gospel of Mattityahu "Matthew"	OT/NT References	Gospel of Mrk "Mark"	OT/NT References	Gospel of Luk "Luke"	OT/NT References
Chapter 11 Yeshua Gives True Rest Continued					
v. 27: (a) "My Father has handed over everything to Me. Indeed, no one fully knows the Son except the Father, and (b) no one fully knows the Father except the Son and those to whom the Son wishes to reveal him."	a). Matthew 28:18; Luke 10:22; John 3:35; 13:3; 1 Corinthians 15:27 b). John 1:18; 6:46; 10:15				
v. 28: "Come to (a) Me, all of you who are struggling and burdened, and I will give you rest."	a). John 6:35–37				
v. 29: "Take My yoke upon you and (a) learn from Me, because I am (B) gentle and humbled in heart, (C) you will find rest for you souls."	a). John 13:15; Ephesians 4:2; Philippians 2:5; 1 Peter 2:21; 1 John 2:6 b.) Zechariah 9:9; and Philippians 2:7–8 c.) Jeremiah 6:16				
v. 30: (a) "For My yoke is easy, and My burden is light."	a.) 1 John 5:3				

Gospel of Mattityahu "Matthew"	OT/NT References	Gospel of Mrk "Mark"	OT/NT References	Gospel of Luk "Luke"	OT/NT References
Chapter 12 Yeshua Is Lord of the Sabbath		**Chapter 2 Yeshua Is Lord of the Sabbath**		**Chapter 6 Yeshua Is Lord of the Sabbath**	
v. 3: "But He said to them, 'Haven't you ever read (A) what David did when he and those with him were hungry?'"	A). Exodus 31:15; 35:2 1 Samuel 21:6	v. 25: "He said to them, 'Haven't you ever read (A) what David did when he and those with him were hungry and needed food?'"	A). 1 Samuel 21:1–6	v. 3. *Yeshua answered them, "Haven't you ever read (A) what David did when he and his companions were hungry?	A). 1 Sam 21:6
v. 4: "He entered the House of God and (A) ate the Bread of the Presence!—Which was prohibited, both to him and to his companions; it is permitted (B) only to the *cohanim._"	A). Exodus 25:30; Leviticus 24:5 B).Exodus 29:32; Leviticus 8:31; 24:9	v. 26: "'He entered the House of God when *Ebyatar was the *cohen gadol and ate the Bread of the Presence,'— (A) which is forbidden for anyone to eat but the *cohanim_—'and even gave some to his companions.'"	A). Exodus 29:32–33; Leviticus 24:5–9	v. 4. He entered the House of God and took and ate the Bread of Presence—(A) which no one is permitted to eat but the *cohanim._"	A). Lev 24:9
v. 5: "Or haven't you read in the (A) *Torah_ that on *Shabbat_ the *cohanim_ profane *Shabbat_ and yet are blameless?"	A). Numbers 28:9; John 7:22	v. 27: "Then he said to them, '*Shabbat_ was made for mankind, not mankind for the (A) *Shabbat._'"	A). Genesis 2:3; Exodus 23:12; Deuteronomy 5:14; Nehemiah 9:14; Ezekiel 20:12		
v. 6: "I tell you, there is in this place (A) something greater than the Temple!"	A). 2 Chronicles 6:18; John 7:22 Malachi 3:1; Matthew 12:41–42				

Gospel of Mattityahu "Matthew"	OT/NT References	Gospel of Mrk "Mark"	OT/NT References	Gospel of Luk "Luke"	OT/NT References
Chapter 12 **Yeshua Is Lord of the Sabbath Continued**		**Chapter 2** **Yeshua Is Lord of the Sabbath Continued**		**Chapter 6** **Yeshua Is Lord of the Sabbath Continued**	
v. 7: "If you knew what (A) 'I want compassion rather than animal-sacrifice' meant, you would not condemn the innocent."	A). 1 Samuel 15:22; Hosea 6:6; Micah 6:6–8; Matthew 9:13				
v. 8: "For the Son of Man is Lord of *Shabbat!*		v. 28: "So (a) the Son of Man is Lord even of *Shabbat.*"	a). Matt 12:8	v. 5: "'The Son of Man,' He concluded, 'is Lord of *Shabbat.*'"	
Chapter 12 **Healing on the Sabbath**		**Chapter 3** **Healing on the Sabbath**		**Chapter 6** **Healing on the Sabbath**	
v. 11: "But He answered, 'If you have a sheep that falls in a pit on *Shabbat*, which of you won't take hold of it and lift it out?'"		v. 3: "He said to the man with the shriveled hand, 'Come up here where we can see you!'"		v. 8: "But He (a) knew what they were thinking and said to the man with the shriveled hand, 'Come up and stand where we can see you!' He got up and stood there."	a). Matthew 9:4; John 2:24–25
v. 12: "How much more valuable is a man than a sheep! Therefore, what is permitted on *Shabbat* is to do good."		v. 4: "What is permitted on *Shabbat*? Doing good or doing evil? Saving life or killing"		v. 9: "Then *Yeshua* said to them, 'I ask you now: what is (a) permitted on *Shabbat* doing good or doing evil? Saving life or destroying it?'"	a). John 7:23

116 *Just the Words and Teachings of Jesus Christ*

Gospel of Mattityahu "Matthew"	OT/NT References	Gospel of Mrk "Mark"	OT/NT References	Gospel of Luk "Luke"	OT/NT References
Chapter 12 **Healing on the Sabbath Continued**		**Chapter 3** **Healing on the Sabbath Continued**		**Chapter 6** **Healing on the Sabbath Continued**	
v. 13: "Then to the man He said, 'Hold out your hand.' As he held it out, it became restored, as sound as the other one."		v. 5: "Then, looking them over and feeling both anger with them and sympathy for them at the (A) stoniness of their hearts, He said to the man, 'Hold out your hand.' as he held it out, it became restored."	A). Zechariah 7:12	v. 10: "Then, after looking around at all of them, He said to the man, 'Hold out your hand.' As he held it out, his hand was restored."	
				Chapter 13 **A Spirit of Infirmity**	
				v. 12: "On seeing her, *Yeshua* called her and said to her, 'Lady, you have been set free from your (a) weakness!'"	a). Luke 7:21; 8:2
				v. 15: "However, the Lord answered him, 'You hypocrites! Each one of you on *Shabbat*—(a) don't you unloose your ox or donkey from the stall and lead them to drink?'"	a). Matthew 7:5; 23:13; Luke 14:5
				v. 16: "This woman is a (a) daughter of *Avraham*, and the *Adversary* kept her tied up for eighteen years! Shouldn't she be freed from this bondage on *Shabbat?*"	a). Luke 19:9

Part 4: Subtopic Scriptural Alignment View—Matthew, Mark, and Luke

Gospel of Mattityahu "Matthew"	OT/NT References	Gospel of Mrk "Mark"	OT/NT References	Gospel of Luk "Luke"	OT/NT References
				Chapter 13 **A Spirit of Infirmity Continued**	
				v. 17: "By these Words *Yeshua* put to shame the people who opposed Him; but the rest of the crowd were happy about all the wonderful things that were (a) taking place through Him."	a). Mark 5:19–20
				Chapter 14 **A Man with Dropsy Healed on the Sabbath**	
Chapter 12 **Healing on the Sabbath Continued**				v. 3: "*Yeshua* spoke up and asked the *Torah* experts and *P'rushim*, (a) 'Does the *Torah* allow healing on *Shabbat* or not?'"	a). Matthew 12:10
v. 11: "But He answered, 'If you have a sheep that falls in a pit on *Shabbat*, which of you won't take hold of it and lift it out?'"				v. 5: "To them He said, (A) "Which of you, if a son or an ox falls into a well, will hesitate to haul him out on *Shabbat*?"	A). Exodus 23:5; Deuteronomy 22:4; Luke 13:15
v. 12: "How much more valuable is a man than a sheep! Therefore, what is permitted on *Shabbat* is to do good."				*Dropsy is an old term for the swelling of soft tissues due to the accumulation of excess water.*	

Gospel of Mattityahu "Matthew"	OT/NT References	Gospel of Mrk "Mark"	OT/NT References	Gospel of Luk "Luke"	OT/NT References
Chapter 12 A House Divided Cannot Stand		**Chapter 3 A House Divided Cannot Stand**		**Chapter 11 A House Divided Cannot Stand**	
v. 25: "However, (a) knowing what they were thinking, *Yeshua said to them, 'Every kingdom divided against itself will be ruined, and every city or household divided against itself will not survive.'"	a). Matthew 9:4; John 2:25; Revelation 2:23			v. 17: (a) "But (b) He, knowing what they were thinking, said to them, 'Every kingdom divided against itself will be ruined, with one house collapsing on another.'"	a). Matthew 12:25–29; Mark 3:23–27 b). Matthew 9:4; John 2:25
v. 26: "If *Satan drives out *Satan."		v. 23: (a) "But He called them and spoke to them in parables: 'How can *Satan expel *Satan?'"	a). Matthew 12:25–29; Luke 11:17–22		
v. 26: "He is divided against himself; so how can his kingdom survive?"		v. 24: "If a kingdom is divided against itself, that kingdom can't survive."			
		v. 25: "And if a household is divided against itself, that household can't survive."			
		v. 26: "So if *Satan has rebelled against himself and is divided, he can't survive either; and that's the end of him."		v. 18: "So if the *Adversary too is divided against himself, how can his kingdom survive? I'm asking because you claim it is by *Ba'al-Zibbul that I drive out the demons."	

Gospel of Mattityahu "Matthew"	OT/NT References	Gospel of Mrk "Mark"	OT/NT References	Gospel of Luk "Luke"	OT/NT References
Chapter 12 A House Divided Cannot Stand Continued		**Chapter 3 A House Divided Cannot Stand Continued**		**Chapter 11 A House Divided Cannot Stand Continued**	
v. 27: "Besides, if I drive out demons by *Ba'al-Zibbul,* by whom do your people drive them out? So, they will be your judges!"				v. 19: "If I drive out demons by *Ba'al-Zibbul,* by whom do your people drive them out? So, they will be your judges!"	
v. 28: "But if I drive out demons by the Spirit of God, (A) then the Kingdom of God has come upon you!"	A). Daniel 2:44; 7:14; Luke 1:33; 11:20; Luke 17:20–21; 1 John 3:8			v. 20: "But if I drive out demons by the (A) finger of God, then the Kingdom of God has come upon you!"	A). Exodus 8:19
				v. 21: (a) "When a strong man who is fully equipped for battle guards his own house, his possessions are secure."	a). Matthew 12:29; Mark 3:27
v. 29: (A) "Or again, how can someone break into a strong man's house and make off with his possessions unless he first ties up the strong man? After that he can ransack his house."	A). Isaiah 49:24; Luke 11:21–23	v. 27: "Furthermore, (A) no one can break into a strong man's house and make off with his possessions unless he first ties up the strong man. After that, he can ransack his house."	A). Isaiah 49:24–25; Matthew 12:29	v. 22: "But (A) when someone stronger attacks and defeats him, he carries off all the armor and weaponry on which the man was depending, and divides up the soil."	A). Isaiah 53:12; Colossians 2:15
v. 30: "Those who are not with Me are against Me, and those who do not gather with Me are scattering."				v. 23: (a) "Those who are not with Me, are against Me, and those who do not gather with Me are scattering."	a). Matthew 12:30; Mark 9:40

Gospel of Mattityahu "Matthew"	OT/NT References	Gospel of Mrk "Mark"	OT/NT References	Gospel of Luk "Luke"	OT/NT References
Chapter 12 The Unpardonable Sin		**Chapter 3 The Unpardonable Sin**			
v. 31: "Because of this, I tell you that people (a) will be forgiven any sin and blasphemy."	a). Mark 3:28–30; Luke 12:10; Hebrews 6:4–6; 10:26, 29; 1 John 5:16	v. 28: (a) "Yes! I tell you that people will be forgiven all sins and whatever blasphemies they utter."	a). Matthew 12:31–32; Luke 12:10; 1 John 5:16		
v. 31: (b) "But blaspheming the *Ruach HaKodesh* will not be forgiven."	b). Acts 7:51	v. 29: "However, someone who blasphemies against *Rauch HaKodesh* never has forgiveness but is guilty of an eternal sin."			
v. 32: "One can (a) say something against the Son of Man and (b) be forgiven; but whoever keeps on speaking against the *Ruach HaKodesh* will never be forgiven, neither in the *'olam hazeh* [this present age] nor in the *'olam haba* [world to come]."	a). Matthew 11:19; 13:55; John 7:12, 52 b). 1 Timothy 1:13				
Chapter 12 A Tree Known by Its Fruit				**Chapter 6 A Tree Known by Its Fruit**	
v. 33: "If you make a tree good, (a) its fruit will be good; and if you make a tree bad, its fruit will be bad; for a tree is known by its fruit."	a). Matthew 7:16–18; Luke 6:43–44; John 15:4–7			v. 44: (a) "Each tree is recognized by its own fruit—figs aren't picked from thorn bushes, nor grapes from a briar patch."	a). Matthew 12:33

Part 4: Subtopic Scriptural Alignment View—Matthew, Mark, and Luke

Gospel of Mattityahu "Matthew"	OT/NT References	Gospel of Mrk "Mark"	OT/NT References	Gospel of Luk "Luke"	OT/NT References
Chapter 12 A Tree Known by Its Fruit Continued				**Chapter 6 A Tree Known by Its Fruit Continued**	
v. 34: (a) "You snakes! How can you who are evil say anything good? (B) For the mouth speaks what overflows from the heart."	a). Matthew 3:7; 23:33; Luke 3:7 B). 1 Samuel 24:13; Isaiah 32:6; Matthew 15:18; Luke 6:45; Ephesians 4:29; James 3:2–12				
v. 35: "The good person brings forth good things from his store of good and the evil person brings forth evil things from his store of evil."				v. 45: (a) "The good person produces good things from the store of good in his heart, while the evil person produces evil things from the store of evil in his heart."	a). Matthew 12:35
v. 36: "Moreover, I tell you this: on the Day of Judgment people will have to give account for every careless word they have spoken."				v. 45: "For his mouth speaks what (B) overflows from his heart."	B). Proverbs 15:2, 28; 16:23 18:21; Matthew 12:34
v. 37: "For by your own words you will be acquitted, and by your own words you will be condemned."					

122 *Just the Words and Teachings of Jesus Christ*

Gospel of Mattityahu "Matthew"	OT/NT References	Gospel of Mrk "Mark"	OT/NT References	Gospel of Luk "Luke"	OT/NT References
				Chapter 11 **Keeping the Word**	
				v. 28: "But He said, (A) far more blessed are those who hear the Word of God and obey it!"	A). Ps 1:1,2 Ps 112:1 Ps 119:1,2 Is 48:17,18 Matt 7:21 Luke 8:21 James 1:25
Chapter 12 **The Scribes and Pharisees Ask for a Sign**				**Chapter 11** **Seeking a Sign**	
v. 39: "He replied, 'A wicked and (A) adulterous generation asks for a sign? No! None will be given to it but the sign of the prophet *Yonah.*'"	A). Isaiah 57:3; Matthew 16:4; Mark 8:38; Luke 11:29–32; John 4:48			v. 29: (a) "As the people crowded around Him, *Yeshua went on to say, 'This generation is a wicked generation! It asks for a (b) sign, but no sign will be given to it—except the sign of *Yonah.*'"	a). Matthew 12:38–42 b). 1 Corinthians 1:22
v. 40: (A) "For just as *Yonah was three days and three nights in the belly of the sea-monster, so will the Son of Man be three days and three nights in the depths of the earth."	A). Jonah 1:17; Luke 24:46; Acts 10:40; 1 Corinthians 15:4			v. 30: "For just as (A)*Yonah became a sign to the people of *Ninveh, so will the Son of Man be for this generation."	A). Jonah 1:17; 2:10; 3:3–10; Luke 24:46; Acts 10:40; 1 Corinthians 15:4

Gospel of Mattityahu "Matthew"	OT/NT References	Gospel of Mrk "Mark"	OT/NT References	Gospel of Luk "Luke"	OT/NT References
Chapter 12 **The Scribes and Pharisees Ask for a Sign Continued**				**Chapter 11** **Seeking a Sign Continued**	
v. 41: (A) "The people of *Ninveh* will stand up at the judgment with this generation and (B) condemn it, (C) for they turned from their sins to God when *Yonah* preached, but what is here now is greater than *Yonah*."	A. Jonah 3:5; Luke 11:32 B. Jeremiah 3:11; Ezekiel 16:51; Romans 2:27 C. Jonah 3:5			v. 32: "The people of *Ninveh* will stand up at the Judgment with this generation and condemn it, for they (A) turned to God from their sins when *Yonah* preached, and what is here now is greater than *Yonah*."	A). Jonah 3:5
v. 42: (A) "The Queen of the South will stand up at the Judgment with this generation and condemn it, for she came from the ends of the earth to hear the wisdom of *Shalomo*, but what is here now is greater than *Shlomo*."	A). 1 Kings 10:1–13; 2 Chronicles 9:1; Luke 11:31			v. 31: (A) "The Queen of the South will appear at the Judgement with the people of this generation and condemn them; for she came from the ends of the earth to hear the wisdom of *Shlomo*, and what is here now is (B) greater than *Shlomo*."	A). 1 Kings 10:1–9; 2 Chronicles 9:1–8 B). Isaiah 9:6; Romans 9:5
Chapter 12 **An Unclean Spirit Returns**				**Chapter 11** **An Unclean Spirit Returns**	
v. 43: (a) "When an unclean spirit comes out of a person, (B) it travels through dry country seeking rest and does not find it."	a). Luke 11:24–26 B). Job 1:7; 1 Peter 5:8			v. 24: (a) "When an unclean spirit comes out of a person, it travels through dry country seeking rest."	a). Matthew 12:43–45; Mark 1:27; 3:11; 5:13; Acts 5:16; 8:7

124 *Just the Words and Teachings of Jesus Christ*

Gospel of Mattityahu "Matthew"	OT/NT References	Gospel of Mrk "Mark"	OT/NT References	Gospel of Luk "Luke"	OT/NT References
Chapter 12 **An Unclean Spirit Returns Continued**				**Chapter 11** **An Unclean Spirit Returns Continued**	
v. 44: "Then it says to itself, 'I will return to the house I left.'"				v. 24: "On finding none, it says, 'I will return to the house I left.'"	
v. 44: "When it arrives, it finds the house standing empty, swept clean and put in order."				v. 25: "When it arrives, it finds the house swept clean and put in order."	
v. 45: "Then it goes and takes with it seven other spirits more evil than itself, and they come and live there—(a) so that in the end, the person is worse off than he was before. This is how it will be for this wicked generation."	a). Mark 5:9; Luke 11:26; Hebrews 6:4–8; 10:26; 2 Peter 2:20–22			v. 26: "Then it goes and takes seven other spirits more evil than itself, and they come and live there—so that (a) in the end the person is worse off than he was before."	a). John 5:14; Hebrews 6:4–6; 10:26; 2 Peter 2:20
Chapter 12 **Yeshua's Mother and Brothers Send for Him**		**Chapter 3** **Yeshua's Mother and Brothers Send for Him**			
v. 48: "But to the one who informed Him, He replied, 'Who is My mother? Who are My brothers?'"		v. 33: "Who are My mother and brothers?"			
v. 49: "Pointing to His *talmidim*, He said, 'Look! Here are My mother and (a) brothers!'"	a). John 20:17 Rom 8:29	v. 34: "See! Here are My mother and brothers!"			

Part 4: Subtopic Scriptural Alignment View—Matthew, Mark, and Luke

Gospel of Mattityahu "Matthew"	OT/NT References	Gospel of Mrk "Mark"	OT/NT References	Gospel of Luk "Luke"	OT/NT References
Chapter 12 **Yeshua's Mother and Brothers Send for Him Continued**		**Chapter 3** **Yeshua's Mother and Brothers Send for Him Continued**		**Chapter 8** **Yeshua's Mother and Brothers Send for Him**	
v. 50: (a) "Whoever does what My Father in heaven wants, that person is My brother and sister and mother."	a). John 15:14; Galatians 5:6; 6:15; Colossians 3:11; Hebrews 2:11	v. 35: "Whoever does what God (a) wants is My brother, sister and mother!"	a). Ephesians 6:6; Hebrews 10:36	v. 21: "But He gave them this answer: 'My mother and brothers are those who hear God's message and act on it!'"	
Chapter 13 **Parable of the Sower**		**Chapter 4** **Parable of the Sower**		**Chapter 8** **Parable of the Sower**	
v. 3: "He told them many things in parables: (a) 'A farmer went out to sow his seed.'"	a). Luke 8:5	v. 3: "Listen! A farmer went out to sow his seed."		v. 5: "A farmer went out to sow his seed."	
v. 4: "As he sowed, some seed fell alongside the path; and the birds came and ate it up."		v. 4: "As he sowed, some seed fell alongside the path; and the birds came and ate it up."		v. 5: "As he sowed, some fell along the path and was stepped on, and the birds flying around ate it up."	
				v. 12: "The ones along the path are those who hear, but then the *Adversary* comes and takes the message out of their hearts, in order to keep them from being saved by trusting it."	

Gospel of Mattityahu "Matthew"	OT/NT References	Gospel of Mrk "Mark"	OT/NT References	Gospel of Luk "Luke"	OT/NT References
Chapter 13 **Parable of the Sower Continued**		**Chapter 4** **Parable of the Sower Continued**		**Chapter 8** **Parable of the Sower Continued**	
v. 5: "Other seed fell on rocky patches where there was not much soil. It sprouted quickly because the soil was shallow."		v. 5: "Other seed fell on rocky patches where there was not much soil. It sprouted quickly, because the soil was shallow."		v. 6: "Some fell on rock."	
v. 6: "But when the sun had risen, the young plants were scorched; and since their roots were not deep, they dried up."		v. 6: "But when the sun rose, the young plants were scorched; and since their roots were not deep, they dried up."		v. 6: "And after it sprouted, it dried up from lack of moisture."	
				v. 13: "The ones on rock are those who, when they hear the word, accept it with joy; but these have no root—they go on trusting for awhile; but when a time of testing come, they *apostatize*."	
v. 7: "Other seed fell among thorns, which grew up and choked the plants."		v. 7: "Other seed fell among thorns, which grew up and chocked it; so that it yielded no grain."		v. 7: "Some fell in the middle of thorns, and the thorns grew up with it and chocked it."	
				v. 14: "As for what fell in the midst of thorns these are the ones who hear; but as they go along, worries and (a) wealth and life's gratifications crowd in and choke them, so that their fruit never matures."	a). Matthew 19:23; 1 Timothy 6:9–10

Part 4: Subtopic Scriptural Alignment View—Matthew, Mark, and Luke

Gospel of Mattityahu "Matthew"	OT/NT References	Gospel of Mrk "Mark"	OT/NT References	Gospel of Luk "Luke"	OT/NT References
Chapter 13 **Parable of the Sower** **Continued**		**Chapter 4** **Parable of the Sower** **Continued**		**Chapter 8** **Parable of the Sower** **Continued**	
v. 8: "But others fell into rich soil and produced grain."		v. 8: "But other seed fell into rich soil and produced grain."		v. 15: "But what fell in rich soil—these are the ones who, when they hear the message, hold onto it with a good, receptive heart; and by (a) persevering, they bring forth a harvest."	a). Romans 2:7; Hebrews 10:36–39; James 5:7–8
v. 8: (A) "A hundred or sixty or thirty times as much as had been sown."	A). Genesis 26:12; Matthew 13:23	v. 8: "It sprouted, and yielded a crop—thirty, sixty, even a hundred times what was sown."		v. 8: "But some fell into rich soil, and grew, and produced a (a) hundred times as much as had been sown."	a). Matthew 11:15; Mark 7:16; Luke 14:35; Revelation 2:7, 11, 17, 29; 3:6, 13, 22; 13:9
v. 9: (a) "Those who have ears, let them hear!"	a). Matthew 11:15; Mark 4:9; Revelation 2:7, 11, 17, 29; 3:6, 13, 22	v. 9: "Whoever has ears to hear with, let him hear!"		v. 8: "After saying this, He called out, 'Whoever has ears to hear with, let him hear!'"	

Gospel of Mattityahu "Matthew"	OT/NT References	Gospel of Mrk "Mark"	OT/NT References	Gospel of Luk "Luke"	OT/NT References
Chapter 13 **The Purpose of Parables**		**Chapter 4** **The Purpose of Parables**		**Chapter 8** **The Purpose of Parables**	
v. 11: "He answered, 'Because (a) it has been given to you to know the secrets of the Kingdom of Heaven, but it has not been given to them.'"	a). Matthew 11:25; 16:17; Mark 4:10–11; John 6:65; 1 Corinthians 2:10; Colossians 1:27; 1 John 2:20, 27	v. 11: "To you the (a) secret of the Kingdom of God has been given; but to (b) those outside, everything is in parables."	a). Matthew 11:25; 1 Corinthians 2:10–16; 2 Corinthians 4:6 b). 1 Corinthians 5:12–13; Colossians 4:5; 1 Thessalonians 4:12; 1 Timothy 3:7	v. 10: "And He said, 'To you it has been given to know the secrets of the Kingdom of God.'"	
v. 12: (a) "For anyone who has something will be given more, so that he will have plenty; but from anyone who has nothing, even what he does have will be taken away."	a). Matthew 25:29; Mark 4:25; Luke 8:18; 19:26				
v. 13: "Here is why I speak to them in parables; they look without seeing and listen without hearing or understanding."				v. 10: "But the rest are taught in parables, so that they may (A) look but not see, and listen but not understand."	A). Isaiah 6:9; Matthew 13:14; Acts 28:26

Gospel of Mattityahu "Matthew"	OT/NT References	Gospel of Mrk "Mark"	OT/NT References	Gospel of Luk "Luke"	OT/NT References
Chapter 13 The Purpose of Parables Continued		**Chapter 4 The Purpose of Parables Continued**			
v. 14: "That is, in them is fulfilled the prophecy of *Yesha'yahu which says, 'You will keep on (A) hearing but never understand, and keep on seeing but never (b) perceive.'"	A). Isaiah 6:9–10; Ezekiel 12:2; Mark 4:12; Luke 8:10; John 12:40; Acts 28:26–27; Romans 11:8; 2 Corinthians 3:14–15 b). John 3:36	v. 12: "So that they may be always (A) looking but never seeing; always listening but never understanding. Otherwise, they might turn and be forgiven."	A). Isaiah 6:9–10; 43:8; Jeremiah 5:21; Ezekiel 12:2; Matthew 13:14; Luke 8:10; John 12:40; Romans 11:8		
v. 15: "Because the heart of this people has become dull—with their (A) ears they barely hear, and their eyes they have (b) closed, so as not to see with their eyes, hear with their ears, understand with their heart, and do *t'shuvah so that I could (c) heal them."	A). Psalm 119:70; Zechariah 7:11; 2 Timothy 4:4; Hebrews 5:11 b). Luke 19:42 c). Acts 28:26–27				
v. 16: "But you, how (A) blessed are your eyes because they see, and your ears because they hear!"	A). Proverbs 20:12; Matthew 16:17; Luke 10:23–24; John 20:29				

Gospel of Mattityahu "Matthew"	OT/NT References	Gospel of Mrk "Mark"	OT/NT References	Gospel of Luk "Luke"	OT/NT References
Chapter 13 **The Purpose of Parables Continued**		**Chapter 4** **The Purpose of Parables Continued**			
v. 17: "Yes indeed! I tell you (a) that many a prophet and many a *tzaddik* longed to see the things you are seeing but did not see them, and to hear the things you are hearing but did not hear them."	a). John 8:56; Hebrews 11:13; 1 Peter 1:10–11	v. 13: "Don't you understand this parable? How will you be able to understand any parables?"			
Chapter 13 **The Parable of the Sower Explained**		**Chapter 4** **The Parable of the Sower Explained**		**Chapter 8** **The Parable of the Sower Explained**	
v. 18: (a) "So listen to what the parable of the sower means."	a). Mark 4:13–20; Luke 8:11–15	v. 14: (a) "The sower sows the message."	a). Matthew 13:18–23; Luke 8:11–15	v. 11: (a) "The parable is this: the seed is (b) God's message."	a). Matthew 13:18; Mark 4:14; 1 Pet 1:23 b). Luke:5:1; 11:28
v. 19: "Whoever hears the message (a) about the Kingdom, but doesn't understand it, is like the seed sown along the path—the Evil One comes and seizes what was sown in his heart."	A). Matthew 4:23	v. 15: "Those alongside the path where the message is sown are people who no sooner hear it than the *Adversary* comes and takes away the message sown in them."		V. 12: "The ones along the path are those who hear, but then the *Adversary* comes and takes the message out of their hearts, in order to keep them from being saved by trusting it."	
v. 20: "The seed sown on rocky ground is like a person who hears the message and (A) accepts it with joy at once."	A). Isaiah 58:2; Ezekiel 33:31–32; John 5:35	v. 16: "Likewise, those receiving seed on rocky patches are people who hear the message and joyfully accept it at once."		v. 13: "The ones on rock are those who, when they hear the word, accept it with joy."	

Gospel of Mattityahu "Matthew"	OT/NT References	Gospel of Mrk "Mark"	OT/NT References	Gospel of Luk "Luke"	OT/NT References
Chapter 13 **The Parable of the Sower Explained Continued**		**Chapter 4** **The Parable of the Sower Explained Continued**		**Chapter 8** **The Parable of the Sower Explained Continued**	
v. 20: "The seed sown on rocky ground is like a person who hears the message and (A) accepts it with joy at once."	A). Isaiah 58:2; Ezekiel 33:31–32; John 5:35	v. 16: "Likewise, those receiving seed on rocky patches are people who hear the message and joyfully accept it at once."		v. 13: "The ones on rock are those who, when they hear the word, accept it with joy."	
v. 21: "But has no root in himself. So he stays on for a while; but as soon as some (a) trouble or persecution arises on account of the message, (b) he immediately falls away."	a). Acts 14:22 b). Matthew 11:6; 2 Timothy 1:15	v. 17: "But they have no root in themselves. So they hold out for a while, but soon as some trouble or persecution arises on account of the message, they immediately fall away."		v. 13: "The ones on rock are those who, when they hear the word, accept it with joy; but these have no root—they go on trusting for a while; but when a time of testing comes, they *apostatize*."	
v. 22: (a) "Now the seed sown (B) among thorns stands for someone who hears the message."	a). Matthew 19:23; Mark 10:23; Luke 18:24; 1 Timothy 6:9 2 Timothy 4:10 B). Jeremiah 4:3	v. 18: "Others are those sown among thorns—they hear the message."		v. 14: "As for what fell in the midst of thorns these are the ones who hear."	
v. 22: "But it is choked by the worries of the world and the deceitful glamor of wealth, so that it produces nothing."		v. 19: "But the (a) worries of the world, (B) the deceitful glamor of wealth and all the other kinds of desires push in and choke the message; so that it produces nothing."	a). Luke 21:34 B). Proverbs 23:5; Ecclesiastes 5:13; Luke 18:24; 1 Timothy 6:9–10, 17	v. 14: "But as they go along, worries and (a) wealth and life's gratifications crowd in and choke them, so that their fruit never matures."	

132 *Just the Words and Teachings of Jesus Christ*

Gospel of Mattityahu "Matthew"	OT/NT References	Gospel of Mrk "Mark"	OT/NT References	Gospel of Luk "Luke"	OT/NT References
Chapter 13 **The Parable of the Sower Explained Continued**		**Chapter 4** **The Parable of the Sower Explained Continued**		**Chapter 8** **The Parable of the Sower Explained Continued**	
v. 23: "However, what was sown on rich soil is the one who hears the message and understands it; such a person will surely (a) bear fruit, a hundred or sixty or thirty times what was sown."	a). John 15:5; Philippians 1:11; Colossians 1:6	v. 20: "But those sown on rich soil hear the message, accept it and bear (a) fruit—thirty, sixty or a hundredfold."	a). John 15:2, 5; Romans 7:4	v. 15: "But what fell in rich soil—these are the ones who, when they hear the message, hold onto it with a good, receptive heart; and by (a) persevering, they bring forth a harvest."	a). Romans 2:7; Hebrews 10:36–39; James 5:7–8
		Chapter 4 **Light under a Basket**		**Chapter 8** **The Parable of the Revealed Light**	
		v. 21: (a) "A lamp isn't brought in to be put under a bowl or under the bed, is it? Wouldn't you put it on a lampstand?"	a). Matthew 5:15; Luke 8:16; 11:33	v. 16: (a) "No one who has lit a lamp covers it with a bowl or puts it under a bed, no, he puts it on a stand; so that those coming in may see the (b) light."	a). Matthew 5:15; Mark 4:21; Luke 11:33 b). Matthew 5:14
		v. 22: (A) "Indeed, nothing is hidden, except to be disclosed; and nothing is covered up, except to come out in the open."	A). Ecclesiastes 12:14; Matthew 10:26–27; Luke 12:3; 1 Corinthians 4:5	v. 17: (a) "For nothing is hidden that will not be (B) disclosed, not is covered that will not be known and come out into the open."	a). Matthew 10:26; Luke 12:2; 1 Corinthians 4:5 B). Ecclesiastes 12:14; 2 Corinthians 5:10

Gospel of Mattityahu "Matthew"	OT/NT References	Gospel of Mrk "Mark"	OT/NT References	Gospel of Luk "Luke"	OT/NT References
		Chapter 4 **Light Under a Basket Continued**		**Chapter 8** **The Parable of the Revealed Light Continued**	
		v. 23: (a) "Those who have ears to hear with, let them hear!"	a). Matthew 11:15; 13:9,43; Mark 4:9; Luke 8:8; 14:35; Revelation 3:6, 13, 22; 13:9		
		v. 24: "Pay attention to what you are hearing! (a) The measure with which you measure out will be used to measure to you—and more besides!"	a). Matthew 7:2; Luke 6:38; 2 Corinthians 9:6	v.18: "Pay attention, then, to how you hear!"	
		v. 25: (a) "For anyone who has something will be given more; but from anyone who has nothing, even what he does have will be taken away."	a). Matthew 13:12; 25:29; Luke 8:18; 19:26	v. 18: (a) "For anyone who has something will be given more; but from anyone who has nothing, even what he seems to (b) have will be taken away."	a). Matthew 25:29 b). Matthew 13:12
Chapter 13 **The Parable of the Wheat and the Tares**		**Chapter 4** **The Parable of the Growing Seed**			
v. 24: "*Yeshua* put before them another parable. 'The Kingdom of Heaven is like a man who sowed good seed in his field."		v. 26: (a) "The Kingdom of God is like a man who scatters seed on the ground."	a). Matthew 13:24–30, 36–40; Luke 8:1		

134 *Just the Words and Teachings of Jesus Christ*

Gospel of Mattityahu "Matthew"	OT/NT References	Gospel of Mrk "Mark"	OT/NT References	Gospel of Luk "Luke"	OT/NT References
Chapter 13 The Parable of the Wheat and the Tares Continued		**Chapter 4 The Parable of the Growing Seed Continued**			
v. 25: "But while people were sleeping, his enemy came and sowed weeds among the wheat, then went away."					
v. 26: "When the wheat sprouted and formed heads of grain, the weeds also appeared."		v. 27: "Nights he sleeps, days he's awake; and meanwhile the seeds sprout and (a) grow how, he doesn't know."	a). 2 Corinthians 3:18; 2 Peter 3:18		
		v. 28: "By itself the soil (a) produces a crop first the stalk, then the head, and finally the full grain in the head."	a). John 12:24		
v. 27: "The owner's servants came to him and said, 'Sir didn't you sow good seed in your field? Where have the weeds come from?'"					
v. 28: "He answered, 'An enemy has done this.' The servants asked him, 'Then do you want us to go and pull them up?'"					
v. 29: "But he said, 'No, because if you pull up the weeds, you might uproot some of the wheat at the same time.'"					

Gospel of Mattityahu "Matthew"	OT/NT References	Gospel of Mrk "Mark"	OT/NT References	Gospel of Luk "Luke"	OT/NT References
Chapter 13 **The Parable of the Wheat and the Tares Continued**		**Chapter 4** **The Parable of the Growing Seed Continued**			
v. 30: "Let them both grow together until the harvest; and at the harvest-time I will tell the reapers to collect the weeds first and tie them in bundles to be burned, but to (a) gather the wheat into my barn."	a). Matthew 3:12	v. 29: "But as soon as the crop is ready, (a) the man comes with his sickle, because it's harvest-time."	a). Mark 13:30, 39; Revelation 14:15		
Chapter 13 **The Parable of the Mustard Seed**		**Chapter 4** **The Parable of the Mustard Seed**		**Chapter 13** **The Parable of the Mustard Seed**	
v. 31: "*Yeshua* put before them another parable. (A) 'The Kingdom of Heaven is like a mustard seed which a man takes and sows in his field.'"	A). Isaiah 22:3; Micah 4:1; Mark 4:30; Luke 13:18–19	v. 30: (a) "With what can we compare the Kingdom of God? What illustration should we use to describe it?"	a). Matthew 13:31–32; Luke 13:18–19; Acts 2:41; 4:4; 5:14; 19:20	v. 18: (a) "So He went on to say, 'What is the Kingdom of God like? With what will we compare it?'"	a). Matthew 13:31–32; Mark 4:30–32
v. 32: "It is the smallest of all seeds."		v. 31: "It is like a mustard seed, which, when planted, is the smallest of all the seeds in the fields."			
v. 32: "But when it grows up it is larger than any garden plant and becomes a (A) tree, so that the birds flying about come and nest in its branches."	A). Psalm 104:12; Ezekiel 17:22–24; 31:3–9; Daniel 4:12	v. 32: "But after it has been planted, it grows and becomes the largest of all the plants, with such big branches that the birds flying about can build nests in its shade."		v. 19: "It is like a mustard seed that a man took and planted in his own garden and it grew and became a tree, and the birds flying about nested in its branches."	

Gospel of Mattityahu "Matthew"	OT/NT References	Gospel of Mrk "Mark"	OT/NT References	Gospel of Luk "Luke"	OT/NT References
Chapter 13 **The Parable of Leaven**				**Chapter 13** **The Parable of Leaven**	
				v. 20: "Again He said, 'With what will I compare the Kingdom of God?'"	
v. 33: "And He told them yet (a) another parable. 'The Kingdom of Heaven is like yeast that a woman took and mixed with a bushel of flour, then waited (b) until the whole batch of dough rose.'"	a). Luke 13:20–21 b). 1 Corinthians 5:6; Galatians 5:9			v. 21: "It is like (a) yeast that a woman took and mixed with a bushel of flour, then waited until the whole batch of dough rose."	a). Matthew 13:33
Chapter 13 **Prophecy and the Parables**					
v. 34: (a) "All these things *Yeshua said to the crowds in parables; indeed, He said nothing to them without using a parable."	a). Mark 4:33–34; John 10:6; 16:25				
v. 35: "This was to fulfill what had been spoken through the prophet, (a) 'I will open my mouth in parables; (b) I will say what has been hidden since the creation of the universe.'"	a). Psalm 78:2 b). Romans 16:25–26; 1 Corinthians 2:7; Ephesians 3:9; Colossians 1:26				

Part 4: Subtopic Scriptural Alignment View—Matthew, Mark, and Luke 137

Gospel of Mattityahu "Matthew"	OT/NT References	Gospel of Mrk "Mark"	OT/NT References	Gospel of Luk "Luke"	OT/NT References
Chapter 13 **The Parable of the Tares Explained**					
v. 37: "He answered, 'The one who sows the good seed is the Son of Man.'"					
v. 38: (a) "The field is a world. As for the good seed, these are the people who belong to the Kingdom; and the weeds are the (B) people who belong to the Evil One."	a). Matthew 24:14; 28:19; Mark 16:15; Luke 24:47; Romans 10:18; Colossians 1:6 B). Genesis 3:15; John 8:44; Acts 13:10				
v. 39: "The enemy who sows them is the *Adversary*, (A) the harvest is the end of the age, and the harvesters are angels."	A). Joel 3:13; Revelation 14:15				
v. 40: "Just as the weeds are collected and burned up in the fire, so will it be at the end of the age."					
v. 41: "The Son of Man will send forth His angels, (a) and they will collect out of His Kingdom all the things that cause people to sin and all the people who are far from *Torah*."	a). Matthew 18:7; 2 Peter 2:1–2				

Gospel of Mattityahu "Matthew"	OT/NT References	Gospel of Mrk "Mark"	OT/NT References	Gospel of Luk "Luke"	OT/NT References
Chapter 13 **The Parable of the Tares Explained Continued**					
v. 42: (a) "And they will throw them into the fiery furnace, (b) where people will wail and grind their teeth."	a). Matthew 3:12; Revelation 19:20; 20:10 b). Matthew 8:12; 13:50				
v. 43: (A) "Then the righteous will shine forth like the sun in the Kingdom of their Father. (b) Whoever has ears, let him hear!"	A). Daniel 12:3; 1 Corinthians 15:42–43, 58 b). Matthew 13:9				
Chapter 13 **The Parable of Hidden Treasure**					
v. 44: "The Kingdom of Heaven is like a treasure hidden in a field. A man found it, hid it again, then in great joy went and (a) sold everything he owned, and (B) bought that field."	a). Philippians 3:7–8 B). Isaiah 55:1; Revelation 3:18				
Chapter 13 **The Parable of the Pearl of Great Price**					
v. 45: "Again, the Kingdom of Heaven is like a merchant on the lookout for fine pearls."					

Gospel of Mattityahu "Matthew"	OT/NT References	Gospel of Mrk "Mark"	OT/NT References	Gospel of Luk "Luke"	OT/NT References
Chapter 13 **The Parable of the Pearl of Great Price Continued**					
v. 46: "On finding (A) one very valuable pearl he went away, sold everything he owned and bought it."	A). Proverbs 2:4; 3:14–15; 8:10–19				
Chapter 13 **The Parable of the Dragnet**					
v. 47: "Once more, the Kingdom of Heaven is like a net thrown into the lake that (a) caught all kinds of fish."	a). Matthew 22:9–10				
v. 48: "When it was full, the fishermen brought the net up onto the shore, sat down and collected the good fish in baskets, but threw the bad fish away."					
v. 49: "So it will be at the close of this age—the angels will go forth and (a) separate the evil people from among the righteous."	a). Matthew 25:32				
v. 50: "And throw them into the fiery furnace, where they will wail and grind their teeth."					

Gospel of Mattityahu "Matthew"	OT/NT References	Gospel of Mrk "Mark"	OT/NT References	Gospel of Luk "Luke"	OT/NT References
Chapter 13 **The Parable of the Dragnet Continued**					
v. 51: "'Have you understood all these things?' 'Yes,' they answered."					
v. 52: "He said to them, 'So then, every *Torah-teacher who has been made into a *talmid for the Kingdom of Heaven is like the owner of a home who brings out of his storage room both (A) new things and old.'"	A). Song of Solomon 7:13				
Chapter 13 **Yeshua Rejected at Nazareth**		**Chapter 6** **Yeshua Rejected at Nazareth**		**Chapter 9** **A Samaritan Village Rejects the Savior**	
v. 57: "And they (a) took offense at Him. But *Yeshua said to them, 'The only place people don't respect (b) a prophet is in his hometown and in his own house.'"	a). Matthew 11:6; Mark 6:3–4 b). Luke 4:24; John 4:44	v. 4: "The only place people don't respect (a) a prophet is in his home town, among his own relatives, and in his own house."	a). Matthew 13:57; Luke 4:24; John 4:44	v. 54: When the *talmidim (a) *Ya'akov and *Yochanan saw this, they said, "Sir, do you want us to (B) call down fire from heaven to destroy them?"	a). Mark 3:17 B). 2 Kings 1:10, 12
				vv. 55–56: "But He turned and rebuked them. And they went on to another village."	A). Romans 8:15; 2 Timothy 1:7

Gospel of Mattityahu "Matthew"	OT/NT References	Gospel of Mrk "Mark"	OT/NT References	Gospel of Luk "Luke"	OT/NT References
Chapter 14 Feeding the Five Thousand		**Chapter 6 Feeding the Five Thousand**		**Chapter 9 Feeding the Five Thousand**	
		v. 31: (b) "There were so many people coming and going that they couldn't even take time to eat, so He said to them, (a) 'Come with Me by yourselves to a place where we can be alone, and you can get some rest.'"	b). Mark 3:20 a). Matthew 14:13		
v. 16: "But *Yeshua* replied, 'They don't need to go away. Give them something to eat, yourselves!'"		v. 37: "But He answered them, 'Give them something to eat, yourselves!' They replied, (A) 'We are to go and spend thousands on bread, and give it to them to eat?'"	A). Numbers 11:13, 22; 2 Kings 4:43	v. 13: "But He said to them, 'Give them something to eat, yourselves!' They said, 'We have no more than five loaves of bread and two fish—unless we ourselves are supposed to go and buy food for all these people!'"	
v. 18: "He said, 'Bring them here to Me.'"		v. 38: "He asked them, 'How many loaves do you have? Go and check.' When they had found out, they said, (a) 'Five. And two fish.'"	a). Matthew 14:17; Luke 9:13; John 6:9	v. 14: "(For there were about five thousand men.) He said to His *talmidim*, 'Make them sit down in groups of about fifty each.'"	
Chapter 14 Yeshua Walks on the Sea		**Chapter 6 Yeshua Walks on the Sea**			
v. 27: "But at once *Yeshua* spoke to them. (a) 'Courage,' He said, 'It is I. Stop being afraid.'"	a). Acts 23:11; 27:22, 25, 36	v. 50: "For they all seen Him and were terrified. However He spoke to them. (a) 'Courage,' He said, 'it is' I. Stop being afraid!'"	a). Matthew 9:2; John 16:33		

Gospel of Mattityahu "Matthew"	OT/NT References	Gospel of Mrk "Mark"	OT/NT References	Gospel of Luk "Luke"	OT/NT References
Chapter 14 Yeshua Walks on the Sea Continued					
v. 29: "'Come!' He said. So *Kefa got out of the boat and walked on the water toward *Yeshua."					
v. 31: "**Yeshua* immediately stretched out His hand, took hold of him, and said to him, (a) 'Such little trust! Why did you doubt?'"	a). Matthew 6:30; 8:26				
Chapter 15 Defilement Comes from Within		**Chapter 7 Defilement Comes from Within**			
v. 3: "He answered, 'Indeed, why do you break the command of God by your tradition?'"					
v. 4: "For God said, (A) 'Honor your father and mother,' and (B) 'anyone who curses his father or mother must be put to death.'"	A). Exodus 20:1,12; Leviticus 19:3; Deuteronomy 5:16; Proverbs 23:22; Ephesians 6:2–3 B). Exodus 21:17; Leviticus 20:9; Deuteronomy 27:16; Proverbs 20:20; 30:17	v. 10: "For Moshe said, (A) 'Honor your father and your mother,' and (B) 'Anyone who curses his father or mother must be put to death.'"	A). Exodus 20:12; Deuteronomy 5:16; Matthew 15:4 B). Exodus 21:17; Leviticus 20:9; Proverbs 20:20		

Gospel of Mattityahu "Matthew"	OT/NT References	Gospel of Mrk "Mark"	OT/NT References	Gospel of Luk "Luke"	OT/NT References
Chapter 15 Defilement Comes from Within Continued		**Chapter 7 Defilement Comes from Within Continued**			
v. 5: "But you say, 'If anyone says to his father or mother, (a) "I have promised to give to God what I might have used to help you."'"	a). Mark 7:11–12	v. 11: "But you say, 'If some say to his father or mother, (a) "I have promised as a *korban,"' (that is, as a gift to God) '"what I might have used to help you."'"	a). Matthew 15:5; 23:18		
v. 6: "Then he is rid of his duty and honor his father or mother."		v. 12: "Then you no longer let him do anything for his father or mother."			
v. 6: "Thus by your tradition you make null and void the word of God!"		v. 13: "Thus, with your tradition which you had handed down to you, you nullify the Word of God! And you do other things like this."			
		v. 8: "You depart from God's command and hold onto human tradition."			
		v. 9: "'Indeed,' He said to them, 'you have made a fine art (A) of departing from God's command in order to keep your tradition!'"	A). Proverbs 1:25; Isaiah 24:5; Jeremiah 7:23–24		

144 *Just the Words and Teachings of Jesus Christ*

Gospel of Mattityahu "Matthew"	OT/NT References	Gospel of Mrk "Mark"	OT/NT References	Gospel of Luk "Luke"	OT/NT References
Chapter 15 Defilement Comes from Within Continued		**Chapter 7 Defilement Comes from Within Continued**			
v. 7: "You (a) hypocrites! *Yesha'yahu* was right when he prophesied about you."	a). Mark 7:6	v. 6: "*Yeshua* answered them, *Yesha'yahu* was right when he prophesied about you (a) hypocrites—as it is written."	a). Matthew 23:13–29		
v. 8: "These people (A) honor Me with their lips, but their hearts are far away from Me."	A). Psalm 78:36; Isaiah 29:13; Ezekiel 33:13	v. 6: (B) "These people honor Me with their lips, but their hearts are far away from Me."	B). Isaiah 29:13		
v. 9: "Their worship of Me is useless, because they (A) teach man-made rules as if they were doctrines."	A). Isaiah 29:23; Colossians 2:18–22; Titus 1:14	v. 7: "Their worship of Me is useless, because they teach man-made rules as if they were doctrines."			
v. 10: (a) "Then He called the crowd to Him and said, 'Listen and understand this!'"	a). Mark 7:14	v. 14: (a) "Then *Yeshua* called the people to Him again and said, 'Listen to Me, all of you, and understand this!'"	a). Matthew 15:10		
v. 11: "What makes a person unclean is (a) not what goes into his mouth; rather, what comes out of his mouth, that is what makes him unclean!"	a). Acts 10:15 Romans 14:14, 17, 20; 1 Timothy 4:4; Titus 1:15	v. 15: "There is nothing outside a person which, by going into him, can make him unclean, Rather it is the things that come out of a person which (A) make a person unclean!"	A). Isaiah 59:3; Hebrews 5:11–14		

Part 4: Subtopic Scriptural Alignment View—Matthew, Mark, and Luke

Gospel of Mattityahu "Matthew"	OT/NT References	Gospel of Mrk "Mark"	OT/NT References	Gospel of Luk "Luke"	OT/NT References
Chapter 15 Defilement Comes from Within Continued		**Chapter 7 Defilement Comes from Within Continued**			
v. 13: "He replied, (A) 'Every plant that My Father in heaven has not planted will be pulled up by the roots.'"	A). Isaiah 60:21; 61:3; John 15:2; 1 Corinthians 3:12–13	v. 16: (a) "Those who have ears to hear with, let them hear!" (Mark 4:23).	a). Matthew 11:15		
v. 14: "Let them be. (A) They are blind guides. When a blind man guides another blind man, both will fall in a pit." v. 16: "So He said, (a) 'Don't you understand even now?'"	A). Isaiah 9:16; Malachi 2:8; Matthew 23:16, 24; Luke 6:39; Rom 2:19 a). Matt 16;9 Mark 7:18	v. 18: "He replied to them, (A) 'So you too are without understanding? Don't you see that nothing going into a person from outside can make him unclean?'"	A). Isaiah 28:9–11; 1 Corinthians 3:2; Hebrews 5:11–14		
v. 17: "Don't you see that (a) anything that enters the mouth goes into the stomach and passes out into the latrine?"	a). 1 Corinthians 6:13	v. 19: "'For it doesn't go into his heart but into his stomach, and it passes out into the latrine.' (Thus He declared all foods ritually clean.)"			
v. 18: "But (a) what comes out of your mouth is actually coming from your heart, and that is what makes a person unclean."	a). Matthew 12:34; Mark 7:20 James 3:6	v. 20: "'It is (A) what comes out of a person,' He went on, 'that makes him unclean.'"	A). Psalm 39:1; Matthew 12:34–37; James 3:6		

146 *Just the Words and Teachings of Jesus Christ*

Gospel of Mattityahu "Matthew"	OT/NT References	Gospel of Mrk "Mark"	OT/NT References	Gospel of Luk "Luke"	OT/NT References
Chapter 15 Defilement Comes from Within Continued		**Chapter 7 Defilement Comes from Within Continued**			
v. 19: (A) "For out of the heart come forth wicked thoughts, murder, adultery, and other kinds of sexual immorality, theft, lies, slanders…"	A). Genesis 6:5; 8:21; Proverbs 6:14; Jeremiah 17:9; Mark 7:21; Romans 1:29–32; Galatians 5:19–21	v. 21: (A) "For from within, (b) out of a person's heart come forth (c) wicked thoughts, (d) sexual immorality, theft, murder, adultery."	A). Genesis 6:5; 8:21; Proverbs 6:18; Jeremiah 17:9; Matthew 15:19 b). Galatians 5:19–21 c). 2 Peter 2:14 d). 1 Thessalonians 4:3		
		v. 22: (a) "Greed, malice, (b) deceit, (c) indecency, envy, (d) slander (e) arrogance, foolishness."	a). Luke 12:15 b). Romans 1:28–29 c. 1 Peter 4:3 d. Revelation 2:9 e. John 2:16		
v. 20: "These are what really makes a person unclean, but eating without doing *n'ti-lat-yadayim* does not make a person unclean."		v. 23: "All these wicked things come from within, and they make a person unclean."			

Gospel of Mattityahu "Matthew"	OT/NT References	Gospel of Mrk "Mark"	OT/NT References	Gospel of Luk "Luke"	OT/NT References
Chapter 15 **A Gentile Shows Her Faith**					
v. 24: "He said, (a) 'I was sent only to the lost sheep of the house of Israel.'"	a). Matthew 10:5–6; Romans 15:8				
v. 26: "He answered, 'It is not right to take the children's food and toss it to their pet (a) dogs.'"	a). Matthew 7:6; Philippians 3:2	v. 27: "He said, 'Let the children be fed first, for it is not right to take the children's food and toss it to their pet dogs.'"			
v. 28: "Then *Yeshua* answered her, 'Lady, you are a person of (a) great trust. Let your desire be granted.'"	a). Luke 7:9	v. 29: "Then He said to her, 'For such an answer you may go on home; the demon has left your daughter.'"			
Chapter 15 **Feeding the Four Thousand**		**Chapter 8** **Feeding the Four Thousand**			
v. 32: (a) "*Yeshua* called His *talmidim* to Him and said, 'I feel sorry for these people because they have been with Me three days, and now they have nothing to eat.'"	a). Mark 8:1–10	v. 2: "I (a) feel sorry for these people, because they have been with Me three days, and now they have nothing to eat."	a). Matthew 9:36; 14:14; Mark 1:41; 6:34		
v. 32: "I don't want to send them away hungry, because they might collapse on the way home."		v. 3: "If I send them off to their homes hungry, they will collapse on the way; some of them have come a long distance."			

148 *Just the Words and Teachings of Jesus Christ*

Gospel of Mattityahu "Matthew"	OT/NT References	Gospel of Mrk "Mark"	OT/NT References	Gospel of Luk "Luke"	OT/NT References
Chapter 15 Feeding the Four Thousand Continued		**Chapter 8 Feeding the Four Thousand Continued**			
v. 34: "*Yeshua asked them, 'How many loaves do you have?' They said, 'Seven, and a few fish.'"		v. 5: (a) "'How many loaves do you have?' He asked them. They answered, 'seven.'"	a. Matthew 15:34; Mark 6:38; John 6:9		
Chapter 16 The Pharisees and Sadducees Seek a Sign				**Chapter 12 The Pharisees and Sadducees Seek a Sign**	
v. 2: "But His response was, 'When it is evening, you say, "Fair weather ahead, because the sky is red."'"				v. 54: "Then to the crowds *Yeshua said, (a) 'When you see a cloud-bank rising in the west, at once you say that a rainstorm is coming.'"	a). Matthew 16:2–3
v. 3: "And in the morning you say, 'Storm today!' because the sky is red and overcast."				v. 55: "And when then (A) wind is from the south, you say there will be a heat wave, and there is."	A). Job 37:17
v. 3: "You know how to read the appearance of the sky, but you can't read the signs of the times!"				v. 56: "Hypocrites! You know how to interpret the appearance of the earth and the sky—how is it that you don't know how to interpret this (a) present Time."	a). Luke 19:41–44

Gospel of Mattityahu "Matthew"	OT/NT References	Gospel of Mrk "Mark"	OT/NT References	Gospel of Luk "Luke"	OT/NT References
Chapter 16 The Pharisees and Sadducees Seek a Sign Continued		**Chapter 8 The Pharisees and Sadducees Seek a Sign Continued**			
v. 4: (A) "'A wicked and adulterous generation is asking for a sign? It will certainly not be given a sign—except the sigh of *Yonah!* With that He left them and went off."	A). Proverbs 30:12; Matthew 12:39; Luke 11:29; 24:46	v. 12: "With a (a) sigh that came straight from His heart, He said, 'Why does this generation want a sign? Yes! I tell you, (b) no sign will be given to this generation!'"	a). Mark 7:34 b). Matthew 12:39		
Chapter 16 The Levan of the Pharisees and Sadducees		**Chapter 8 Beware the Levan of the Pharisees and Herod**		**Chapter 12 Beware of Hypocrisy**	
v. 6: "So when *Yeshua* said to them, (a) 'Watch out! Guard yourselves against the *hametz* of the *P'rushim* and *Tz'dukim*.'"	a). Mark 8:15; Luke 12:1	v. 15: (a) "So when *Yeshua* said to them, 'Watch out! Guard yourselves from the *hametz* of the *P'rushim* and the *hametz* of Herod.'"	a). Matthew 16:6; Luke 12:1	v. 1: (a) "Meanwhile, as a crowd in the tens of thousands gathered so closely as to trample each other down, *Yeshua* began to say to His *talmidim* first, (b) "Guard yourselves from the *hametz* of the *P'rushim*, by which I mean their hypocrisy.'"	a). Matthew 16:6; Mark 8:15 b). Matthew 16:12; Luke 11:39
v. 8: "But *Yeshua*, aware of this, said, 'Such little trust you have! Why are you talking with each other about not having bread?'"		v. 17: "But, aware of this, He said, 'Why are you talking with each other about having no bread? (a) Don't you see or understand yet? Have your hearts been made like stone?'"	a). Mark 6:52; 16:14		

Gospel of Mattityahu "Matthew"	OT/NT References	Gospel of Mrk "Mark"	OT/NT References	Gospel of Luk "Luke"	OT/NT References
Chapter 16 The Levan of the Pharisees and Sadducees Continued		**Chapter 8 Beware the Levan of the Pharisees and Herod Continued**		**Chapter 12 Beware of Hypocrisy Continued**	
		v. 18: "You have eyes—don't you see? You have ears—don't you hear? And don't you remember?"			
v. 9: (a) "Don't you understand yet? Don't you remember the five loaves of the five thousand and how many baskets you filled?"	a). Matthew 14:15–21; Mark 6:30–44; Luke 9:10–17; John 6:1–14	v. 19: (a) "When I broke the five loaves for the five thousand, how many baskets full of broken pieces did you collect?"	a). Matthew 14:20; Mark 6:43; Luke 9:17; John 6:13		
v. 10: (a) "Or the seven loaves of the four thousand and how many you filled?"	a). Matthew 15:32–38	v. 20: "And (a) when I broke the seven loaves for the four thousand, how many baskets full of broken pieces did you collect?"	a). Matthew 15:37		
v. 11: "How can you possibly think I was talking to you about bread? Guard yourselves from the *hametz of the *P'rushim and *Tz'dukim!"		v. 21: "He said to them, 'And (a) you still don't understand?'"	a). Mark 6:52		
				v. 2: (a) "There is nothing covered up that will not be uncovered, or hidden that will not become known."	a). Matthew 10:26; Mark 4:22; Luke 8:17; 1 Corinthians 4:5

Gospel of Mattityahu "Matthew"	OT/NT References	Gospel of Mrk "Mark"	OT/NT References	Gospel of Luk "Luke"	OT/NT References
				Chapter 12 Beware of Hypocrisy Continued	
				v. 3: "What you have spoken in the dark will be heard in the light, and what you have whispered behind closed doors will be proclaimed on the housetops."	
Chapter 16 Peter Confesses Yeshua as the Christ (the Son of the Living God)		**Chapter 8 Peter Confesses Yeshua as the Christ (the Son of the Living God)**		**Chapter 9 Peter Confesses Yeshua as the Christ (the Son of the Living God)**	
v. 13: "When *Yeshua came into the territory around *Caesarea Philippi, He asked His *talmidim, (a) 'Who are people saying the Son of Man is?'"	a). Mark 8:27; Luke 9:18	v. 27: (a) "*Yeshua and his *talmidim went on to the towns of *Caesarea Philippi. On the way, He asked His *talmidim, 'Who are people saying I am?'"	a). Matthew 16:13–16; Luke 9:18–20	v. 18: (a) "Once when *Yeshua was praying in private, His *talmidim were with Him; and He asked them, 'Who are the crowds saying I am?'"	a). Matthew 16:13–16; Mark 8:27–29
v. 15: "'But you,' He said to them, 'who do (a) you say that I am?'"	a). John 6:67	v. 29: "'But you,' He asked, 'who do you say I am?' *Kefa answered, (a) 'You are the *Mashiach.'"	a). John 1:41; 4:42; 6:69; 11:27; Acts 2:3; 8:37; 9:20	v. 20: "'But you,' He said to them, 'who do you say I am?' (a) *Kefa answered. 'The *Mashiach of God!'"	a). Matthew 16:16; John 6:68–69
v. 17: "'*Shim'on Bar-Yochanan,' *Yeshua said to him, 'How blessed you are! (a) For no human being revealed this to you, no, it was (b) My Father in heaven.'"	a). Ephesians 2:8 b). Matthew 11:27; 1 Corinthians 2:10; Galatians 1:16				

Gospel of Mattityahu "Matthew"	OT/NT References	Gospel of Mrk "Mark"	OT/NT References	Gospel of Luk "Luke"	OT/NT References
Chapter 16 Peter Confesses Yeshua as the Christ (the Son of the Living God) Continued				**Chapter 9 Peter Confesses Yeshua as the Christ (the Son of the Living God) Continued**	
v. 18: "I also tell you this: (a) you are *Kefa*, [which means 'rock,'] and (b) on this rock I will build My Community and (C) the gates of *Sh'ol* will not overcome it."	a). John 1:42 b). Acts 2:41; Ephesians 2:20; Revelation 21:14 C). Job 33:17; Psalm 9:13; 107:18; Isaiah 38:10				
v. 19: (a) "I will give you the keys of the Kingdom of Heaven. Whatever you prohibit on earth will be prohibited in heaven, and whatever you permit on earth will be permitted in heaven."	a). Matthew 18:18; John 20:23				
v. 20: (a) "Then He warned the *talmidim* not to tell anyone that He was the *Messiah*."	a). Matthew 17:9; Mark 8:30; Luke 9:21			v. 21: (a) "However, He, warning them, ordered them to tell this to no one."	a). Matthew 8:4; 16:20; Mark 8:30
				v. 22: "Adding, (a) 'The Son of Man has to endure much suffering and be rejected by the elders, the head *cohanim* and *Torah-teachers;* and He has to be put to death; but on the third day, He has to be raised to life.'"	a). Matthew 16:21; 17:22; Luke 18:31–33; 23:46; 24:46

Gospel of Mattityahu "Matthew"	OT/NT References	Gospel of Mrk "Mark"	OT/NT References	Gospel of Luk "Luke"	OT/NT References
Chapter 16 **Yeshua Predicts His Death and Resurrection**					
v. 23: "But *Yeshua* turned his back on *Kefa* saying, 'Get behind me, (a) *Satan!* (b) You are an obstacle in My path, because your thinking is from a human perspective, not from God's perspective!'"	a). Matthew 4:10 b). Romans 8:7				
Chapter 16 **Take up the Execution Stake (*Cross*) and Follow Him**		**Chapter 8** **Take up the Execution Stake (*Cross*) and Follow Him**		**Chapter 9** **Take up the Execution Stake (*Cross*) and Follow Him**	
v. 24: (a) "Then *Yeshua* told His *talmidim*, 'If anyone wants to come after Me, let him say "No" to himself, take up his *execution-stake*, and keep (b) following Me.'"	a). Mark 8:34; Luke 9:23; Acts 14:22; 2 Corinthians 4:10–11; 1 Thessalonians 3:3; 2 Timothy 3:12 b). 1 Peter 2:21	v. 34: "Then *Yeshua* called the crowd and His *talmidim* to Him and told them, (a) 'If anyone wants to come after Me, let him say "No" to himself, take up his *execution-stake*, and keep following Me.'"	a). Matthew 10:38; Luke 14:27	v. 23: (a) "Then to everyone He said, 'If anyone wants to come after Me, let him say "No" to himself, take up his *execution-stake* daily and keep following me.'"	a). Matthew 10:38; 16:24; Mark 8:34; Luke 14:27
v. 25: "For (a) whoever wants to save his own life will destroy it, but whoever destroys his life for My sake will find it."	a). Luke 17:33; John 12:25	v. 35: "For (a) whoever wants to save his own life will destroy it, but whoever destroys his life for My sake and for the sake of the Good News will save it."	a). Matthew 10:39; Luke 17:33; John 12:25	v. 24: (a) "For whoever tries to save his own life will destroy it, but whoever destroys his life on My account will save it."	a). Matthew 10:39; Luke 17:33; John 12:25

Gospel of Mattityahu "Matthew"	OT/NT References	Gospel of Mrk "Mark"	OT/NT References	Gospel of Luk "Luke"	OT/NT References
Chapter 16 **Take up the Execution Stake (*Cross*) and Follow Him**		**Chapter 8** **Take up the Execution Stake (*Cross*) and Follow Him**		**Chapter 9** **Take up the Execution Stake (*Cross*) and Follow Him**	
v. 26: "What (a) good will it do someone if he gains the whole world but forfeits his life?"	a). Luke 12:20–21	v. 36: "Indeed, what will it benefit a person if he gains the whole world but forfeits his life?"		v. 25: (a) "What will it benefit a person if he gains the whole world but destroys or forfeits his own life?"	a. Matthew 16:26; Mark 8:36; Luke 16:19–31; Acts 1:18, 25
v. 26: "Or, (B) what can a person give in exchange for his life!"	B). Psalm 49:7–8	v. 37: "What could a person give in exchange for his life?"			
v. 27: "For the (a) Son of Man will come in His Father's Glory, (B) with His angels; (C) and then He will repay everyone according to His conduct."	a). Matthew 26:64; Mark 8:38; Luke 9:26 B). Daniel 7:10; Zechariah 14:5 C). Job 34:11; Psalm 62:12; Proverbs 24:12; Romans 2:6; 2 Corinthians 5:10; 1 Peter 1:17; Revelation 2:23	v. 38: (a) "For if someone (b) is ashamed of Me and of what I say in this adulterous and sinful generation, the Son of Man also will be ashamed of him when he comes in His Father's glory with the holy angels."	a). Matthew 10:33; Luke 9:26; 12:9 b). Romans 1:16; 2 Timothy 1:8–9; 2:12	v. 26: (a) "For if someone is ashamed of Me and of what I say, the Son of Man will be (b) ashamed of him when He comes in His glory and that of the Father and of the holy angels."	a). Romans 1:16 b). Matthew 10:33; Mark 8:38; Luke 12:9; 2 Timothy 2:12
v. 28: "Yes! I tell you that (a) there are some people standing here who will not experience death until they see the Son of Man coming in His Kingdom!"	a). Mark 9:1; Luke 9:27; Acts 7:55–56; Revelation 19:11	9:1: "'Yes!' He went on, (a) 'I tell you that there are some people standing here who will not experience death until they see (b) the Kingdom of God come in a powerful way!"	a). Matthew 16:28; Mark 13:26; Luke 9:27; Acts 7:55–56; Revelation 20:4 b). Matthew 24:30	v. 27: (a) "I tell you the truth, there are some people standing here who will not experience death until they see the Kingdom of God."	a). Matthew 16:28; Mark 9:1; Acts 7:55–56; Revelation 20:4

Gospel of Mattityahu "Matthew"	OT/NT References	Gospel of Mrk "Mark"	OT/NT References	Gospel of Luk "Luke"	OT/NT References
				Chapter 14 **Leaving All to Follow Yeshua**	
				v. 27: (a) "Whoever does not carry his own *execution-stake* and come after Me cannot be My *talmid*."	a). Matthew 16:24; Mark 8:34; Luke 9:23; 2 Timothy 3:12
Chapter 17 **Yeshua Transfigured on the Mount**		**Chapter 9** **Yeshua Transfigured on the Mount**		**Chapter 9** **Yeshua Transfigured on the Mount**	
		v. 7: "Then a (A) cloud enveloped them; and a *voice came out of the cloud, 'This is (B) My Son, whom I love. (c) Listen to Him!'" (See "Commentaries.")	A). Exodus 40:34; 1 Kings 8:10; Acts 1:9; Revelation 1:7 B). Psalm 2:7; Isaiah 42:1; Matthew 3:17; Mark 1:11; Luke 1:35; 3:22; 2 Peter 1:17 c). Acts 3:22	v. 35: "And a voice came out of the cloud, saying, 'This is My Son, who, I have chosen. Listen to Him!'"	
v. 7: "But *Yeshua* came and (A) touched them. 'Get up!' He said, 'Don't be afraid.'"	A). Daniel 8:18				
v. 9: "As they came down the mountain, *Yeshua* ordered them, 'Don't tell anyone what you have seen until the Son of Man has been raised from the dead.'"					

156 *Just the Words and Teachings of Jesus Christ*

Gospel of Mattityahu "Matthew"	OT/NT References	Gospel of Mrk "Mark"	OT/NT References	Gospel of Luk "Luke"	OT/NT References
Chapter 17 **Yeshua Transfigured on the Mount Continued**		**Chapter 9** **Yeshua Transfigured on the Mount Continued**			
v. 11: "He answered, 'On the one hand, *Eliyahu* is coming and will (A) restore all things.'"	A). Malachi 4:6; Luke 1:17	v. 12: "'*Eliyahu* will indeed come first,' He answered, 'and he will restore everything. Nevertheless, why is it (A) written in the *Tanakh* that the Son of Man must suffer much and (b) be rejected?'"	A). Psalm 22:6; Isaiah 53:3; Daniel 9:26 b). Luke 23:11; Philippians 2:7		
v. 12: "On the other hand, (a) I tell you that *Eliyahu* has come already, and people (b) did not recognize him but did whatever they pleased to him. In the same way, (c) the Son of Man too is about to suffer at their hands."	a). Matthew 11:14; Mark 9:12–13 b). Matthew 14:3, 10 c). Matthew 16:21	v. 13: "There's more to it: I tell you that (A)*Eliyahu* has come, and they did whatever they please to him, just as the *Tanakh* says about him."	A). Malachi 4:5; Matthew 11:14; 17:12; Luke 1:17		
Chapter 17 **A Boy Is Healed**		**Chapter 9** **A Boy Is Healed**		**Chapter 9** **A Boy Is Healed**	
		v. 16: "He asked them, 'What's the discussion about?'"			
v. 17: "*Yeshua* answered, (A) 'Perverted people, without any trust! How long will I be with you? How long must I put up with you? Bring him here to Me!'"	A). Deuteronomy 32:5; Philippians 2:15	v. 19: (a) "'People without any trust!' He responded. 'How long will I have to be with you? How long must I put up with you? Bring him to Me!'"	a). John 4:48	v. 41: "'Perverted people, without any trust!' *Yeshua* answered, 'How long do I have to be with you and put up with you? Bring your son here.'"	

Part 4: Subtopic Scriptural Alignment View—Matthew, Mark, and Luke   157

Gospel of Mattityahu "Matthew"	OT/NT References	Gospel of Mrk "Mark"	OT/NT References	Gospel of Luk "Luke"	OT/NT References
Chapter 17 A Boy Is Healed Continued		**Chapter 9 A Boy Is Healed Continued**		**Chapter 9 A Boy Is Healed Continued**	
v. 18: "*Yeshua* (a) rebuked sharply the demon, and it came out of the boy, so that from that moment he was healed."	a. Luke 4:41			4:41: (a) "Also demons came out of many, crying, (b) 'You are the Son of God!' But, (c) rebuking them, he did not permit them to say that they knew He was the *Messiah*."	a. Mark 1:34; 3:11; Acts 8:7 b. Mark 8:29 c). Mark 1:25, 34 3:11; Luke 4:34–35
v. 20: "He said to them, 'Because you have such little trust! Yes! I tell you that (a) if you have trust as tiny as a mustard seed, you will be able to say to this mountain, "Move from here to there!" and it will move; indeed, nothing will be impossible for you!'"	a). Matthew 21:21; Mark 11:23; Luke 17:6; 1 Corinthians 12:9				
		v. 21: "*Yeshua* asked the boy's father, 'How long has this been happening to him?'"			
		v. 23: "*Yeshua* said to him, 'What do you mean, (a) "if you can"? Everything is possible to someone who has trust!'"	a). Matthew 17:20; Mark 11:23; Luke 17:6; John 11:40		

158 *Just the Words and Teachings of Jesus Christ*

Gospel of Mattityahu "Matthew"	OT/NT References	Gospel of Mrk "Mark"	OT/NT References	Gospel of Luk "Luke"	OT/NT References
		Chapter 9 **A Boy Is Healed Continued**		**Chapter 9** **A Boy Is Healed Continued**	
		v. 25: "When *Yeshua saw that the crowd was closing in on them, He (a) rebuked the unclean spirit, saying to it, 'You deaf and dumb spirit! I command you; come out of him, and never go back into him again!'"	a). Mark 1:25	v. 42: "Even as the boy was coming, the demon dashed him to the ground and threw him into a fit. But *Yeshua rebuked the unclean spirit, healed the boy and gave him back to his father."	
		v. 29: "He said to them, 'This is the kind of spirit that can be driven out (a) only by prayer.'" (Some manuscripts say prayer and fasting.)	a). James 5:16		
Chapter 17 **Yeshua Again Predicts His Death and Resurrection**		**Chapter 9** **Yeshua Again Predicts His Death and Resurrection**		**Chapter 9** **Yeshua Again Predicts His Death and Resurrection**	
v. 22: (a) "As they were going about together in the *Galil, *Yeshua said to them, 'The Son of Man is about to be betrayed into the hands of people.'"	a). Matthew 16:21; 26:57; Mark 8:31; Luke 9:22, 44; John 18:12	v. 31: "Because (a) He was teaching His *talmidim. He told them, 'The Son of Man will be betrayed into the hands of men who will (b) put Him to death; but after He has been killed, (c) three days later He will rise.'"	a). Matthew 17:22; Luke 9:44 b). Matthew 16:21; 27:50; Luke 18:33; 23:46; Acts 2:23 c). Matthew 20:19; Luke 24:46; Acts 10:40; 1 Corinthians 15:4	v. 44: (a) "Listen very carefully to what I'm going to say. The Son of Man is about to be betrayed into the hands of men."	a). Matthew 9:4; John 2:24–25

Gospel of Mattityahu "Matthew"	OT/NT References	Gospel of Mrk "Mark"	OT/NT References	Gospel of Luk "Luke"	OT/NT References
Chapter 17 Yeshua Again Predicts His Death and Resurrection Continued					
v. 23: "'Who will put Him to death, and on the third day He will be raised.' And they were filled with (a) sadness."	a). Matthew 26:22; 27:50; Luke 23:46; 24:46; John 16:6; 19:30; Acts 10:40				
Chapter 18 Who Is the Greatest?		**Chapter 9 Greatness Is Serving**			
		v. 33: (a) "They arrived at *K'far-Nachum*. When *Yeshua* was inside the house, He asked them, 'What were you discussing as we were traveling?'"	a). Matthew 18:1–5 Mark 14:53, 64; Luke 9:46–48; 22:24; John 18:12; 19:7		
		v. 35: "He sat down, summoned the Twelve and said to them, (a) 'if anyone wants to be first, he must make himself last of all and servant of all.'"	a). Matthew 20:26–27; 23:11; Mark 10:43–44; Luke 22:26–27		
v. 3: "And said, 'Yes! I tell you that (A) unless you change and become like little children, you won't even enter the Kingdom of Heaven!'"	A). Psalm 131:2; Matthew 19:14; Mark 10:15; Luke 18:16; 1 Corinthians 14:20; 1 Peter 2:2				

Just the Words and Teachings of Jesus Christ

Gospel of Mattityahu "Matthew"	OT/NT References	Gospel of Mrk "Mark"	OT/NT References	Gospel of Luk "Luke"	OT/NT References
Chapter 18 Who Is the Greatest? Continued		**Chapter 9 Greatness Is Serving Continued**		**Chapter 9 Who Is the Greatest?**	
v. 4: (a) "So the greatest in the Kingdom is whoever makes himself as humble as this child."	a). Matthew 20:27; 23:11				
v. 5: (a) "Whoever welcomes one such child in My name welcomes Me."	a). Matthew 10:42; Luke 9:48	v. 37: "Whoever welcomes one such child in My Name welcomes Me, and (a) whoever welcomes Me welcomes not Me but the One who sent Me."	a). Matthew 10:40; Luke 10:16; John 13:20	v. 48: "And said to them, (a) 'Whoever welcomes this child in My Name welcomes Me, and (b) whoever welcomes Me (c) welcomes the One who sent Me. In other words, (d) the one who is least among you all—this is the one who is great.'"	a). Matthew 18:5 b). Matthew 10:40; Mark 9:37; John 12:44 c). John 13:20 d). Matthew 23:11–12; 1 Corinthians 15:9; Ephesians 3:8
Chapter 18 Yeshua Warns of Offenses		**Chapter 9 Yeshua Warns of Offenses**		**Chapter 17 Yeshua Warns of Offenses**	
v. 6: "And (a) whoever ensnares one of these little ones who trust Me, it would be better for him to have a millstone hung around his neck and be drowned in the open sea!"	a). Mark 9:42; Luke 17:2; 1 Corinthians 8:12	v. 42: "Whoever ensnares one of these little ones who trust Me—it would be better for him to have a millstone hung around his neck and be thrown in the sea."		v. 2: "It would be to his advantage that he have a millstone hung around his neck and he be thrown into the sea, rather than that he ensnare one of these little ones."	

Gospel of Mattityahu "Matthew"	OT/NT References	Gospel of Mrk "Mark"	OT/NT References	Gospel of Luk "Luke"	OT/NT References
Chapter 18 Yeshua Warns of Offenses Continued		**Chapter 9 Yeshua Warns of Offenses Continued**		**Chapter 17 Yeshua Warns of Offenses Continued**	
v. 7: "Woe to the world because of snares! For (a) there must be snares, but (b) woe to the person who sets the snare!"	a). Luke 17:1; 1 Corinthians 11:19; 1 Timothy 4:1 b). Matthew 26:24; 27:4–5			v. 1: "*Yeshua said to his *talmidim, (a) 'It is impossible that snares will not be set. But (b) woe to the person who sets them!'"	a). 1 Corinthians 11:19 b). Matthew 18:6–7; 26:24; Mark 9:42; 2 Thessalonians 1:6; Jude 1:11
v. 8: (a) "So if your hand or foot becomes a snare for you, cut it off and throw it away! Better that you should be maimed or crippled and obtain eternal life than keep both hands or both feet and be thrown into everlasting fire!"	a). Matthew 5:29–30; Mark 9:43, 45	v. 43: (A) "If your hand makes you sin, cut it off! Better that you should be maimed but obtain eternal life, rather than keep both hands and go to *Gei-Hinnom*, to unquenchable fire!"	A). Deuteronomy 13:6; Matthew 5:29–30; 18:8–9		
		v. 44–45: "And if your foot makes you sin, cut it off! Better that you should be lame but obtain eternal life, rather than keep both feet and be thrown into *Gei-Hinnom!*"			
v. 9: "And if your eye is a snare for you, gouge it out and fling it away! Better that you should be one-eyed and obtain eternal life than keep both eyes and be thrown into the fire of *Gei-Hinnom.*"		v. 46–47: "And if your eye makes you sin, pluck it out! Better that you should be one-eyed but enter the Kingdom of God, rather than keep both eyes and be thrown into *Gei-Hinnom.*"			

Just the Words and Teachings of Jesus Christ

Gospel of Mattityahu "Matthew"	OT/NT References	Gospel of Mrk "Mark"	OT/NT References	Gospel of Luk "Luke"	OT/NT References
		Chapter 9 **Yeshua Warns of Offenses Continued**			
		v. 48: (A) "Where their worm does not die, and the (B) fire is not quenched."	A). Isaiah 66:24 B). Jeremiah 7:20; Revelation 21:8		
		v. 49: "Indeed, everyone is going to be (a) salted with fire."	a. Matthew 3:11		
		v. 50: (a) "Salt is excellent, but if it loses its saltiness, how will you season it? So (b) have salt in yourselves—that is, (c) be at peace with each other."	a). Matthew 5:13; Luke 14:34 b). Ephesians 4:29; Colossians 4:6 c). Romans 12:18; 14:19; 2 Corinthians 13:11; 1 Thessalonians 5:13; Hebrews 12:14		
				Chapter 22 **The Disciples Argue about Greatness**	
				v. 25: (a) "But *Yeshua said to them, 'The kings of the *Goyim lord it over them; and those in authority over them are given the tile, "Benefactor."'"	a). Matthew 20:25–28; Mark 10:42–45

Gospel of Mattityahu "Matthew"	OT/NT References	Gospel of Mrk "Mark"	OT/NT References	Gospel of Luk "Luke"	OT/NT References
				Chapter 22 The Disciples Argue about Greatness Continued	
				v. 26: (a) "But not so with you! On the contrary, let the (b) greater among you become like the younger, and one who rules like one who serves."	a). Matthew 20:26; 1 Peter 5:3
				v. 27: (a) "For who is greater? The one reclining at the table? Or the one who serves? It's the one reclining at the table, isn't it? But (b) I myself am among you like one who serves."	a). Luke 12:37 b). Matthew 20:28; John 13:13–14; Philippians 2:7
				v. 28: "You are the ones who have stayed with Me throughout (a) My trials."	a). Hebrews 2:18; 4:15
				v. 29: "Just as My Father gave Me the right to rule, so (a) I give you an appointment."	a). Matthew 24:47
				v. 30: "Namely, (a) to eat and drink at my table in My Kingdom and to (B) sit on thrones judging the twelve tribes of *Isra'el."	a). Matthew 8:11; Revelation 19:9 B). Psalm 49:14

Gospel of Mattityahu "Matthew"	OT/NT References	Gospel of Mrk "Mark"	OT/NT References	Gospel of Luk "Luke"	OT/NT References
		Chapter 9 **Yeshua Forbids Sectarianism**		**Chapter 9** **Yeshua Forbids Sectarianism**	
		v. 39: "But *Yeshua* said,'Don't stop him, (a) because no one who works a miracle in My Name will soon after be able to say something bad about Me.'"	a). 1 Corinthians 12:3	v. 50: "Yeshua said to him, 'Don't stop such people.'"	
		v. 40: "For (a) whoever is not against us is for us."	a). Matthew 12:30; Luke 11:23	v. 50: "Because (a) whoever isn't against you is for you."	a). Matthew 12:30; Luke 11:23
		v. 41: "Indeed, (a) whoever gives you even a cup of water to drink because you come in the Name of the *Messiah*—yes! I tell you that he will certainly not lose his reward."	a). Matthew 10:42		
Chapter 18 **The Parable of the Lost Sheep**					
v. 10: "See that you never despise one of these little ones, for I tell you that (A) their angels in heaven are continually (B) seeing the face of My Father in heaven."	A). Psalm 34:7; Zechariah 13:7; Hebrews 1:14 B). Esther 1:14; Luke 1:19; Acts 12:15; Revelation 8:2				

Gospel of Mattityahu "Matthew"	OT/NT References	Gospel of Mrk "Mark"	OT/NT References	Gospel of Luk "Luke"	OT/NT References
Chapter 18 The Parable of the Lost Sheep Continued				**Chapter 15 The Parable of the Lost Sheep Continued**	
v. 11: (a) "For the Son of Man came to save the lost!"	a). Luke 9:56; John 3:17				
v. 12: (a) "What's your opinion? What will somebody do who has a hundred sheep, and one of them wanders away? Won't he leave the ninety-nine on the hillsides and go off to find the stray?"	a). Matthew 18:12–14; Luke 15:4–7			v. 4: (a) "If one of you has a hundred sheep and loses one of them, doesn't he leave the other ninety-nine in the desert and go after the lost one until he finds it?"	a). Matthew 18:12–14; 1 Peter 2:25
v. 13: "And if he happens to find it?"				v. 5: "When he does find it, he joyfully hoists it onto his shoulders."	
v. 13: "Yes! I tell you he is happier over it than the ninety-nine that never strayed!"				v. 6: "And when he gets home, he calls his friends and neighbors together and says, 'Come, (a) celebrate with me, because I have found my (b) lost sheep!'"	a). Romans 12:15 b). Luke 19:10; 1 Peter 2:10, 25
v. 14: "Thus your Father in heaven (a) does not want even one of these little ones to be lost."	a). 1 Timothy 2:4			v. 7: "I tell you that in the same way, there will be more joy in heaven over one sinner who (a) turns to God from sin than over ninety-nine righteous people who (b) have no need to repent."	a. Luke 5:32 b. Mark 2:17

Gospel of Mattityahu "Matthew"	OT/NT References	Gospel of Mrk "Mark"	OT/NT References	Gospel of Luk "Luke"	OT/NT References
				Chapter 15 **The Parable of the Lost Son**	
				v. 11: "Again *Yeshua* said, 'A man had two sons.'"	
				v. 12: "The younger of them said to his father. 'Father, give me the share of the estate that will be mine.' So the father divided (a) the property between them."	a). Mark 2:17
				v. 13: "As soon as he could convert his share into cash, the younger son left home and went off to a distant country, where he squandered his money in reckless living."	
				v. 14: "But after he had spent it all a severe famine arose throughout the country, and he began to feel the pinch."	
				v. 15: "So he went and attached himself to one of the citizens of that country, who sent him into his fields to feed pigs."	
				v. 16: "He longed to fill his stomach with the carob pods the pigs were eating, but no one gave him any."	

Gospel of Mattityahu "Matthew"	OT/NT References	Gospel of Mrk "Mark"	OT/NT References	Gospel of Luk "Luke"	OT/NT References
				Chapter 15 **The Parable of the Lost Son Continued**	
				v. 17: "At last he came to his senses and said, 'Any number of my father's hired workers have food to spare; and here I am, starving to death!'"	
				v. 18: "I'm going to get up and go back to my father and say to him, 'Father, (A) I have sinned against Heaven and against you.'"	A). Exodus 9:27; 10:16; Numbers 22:34; Josh 7:20; 1 Samuel 15:24, 30; 26:21; 2 Samuel 12:13; 24:10, 17; Psalm 51:4; Matthew 27:4
				v. 19: "I am no longer worthy to be called your son; treat me like one of your hired workers."	
				v. 20: "So he got up and started back to his father. But (A) while he was still a long way off, his father saw him and was moved with pity. He ran and threw his arms around him and kissed him warmly."	A).Jeremiah 3:12; Matthew 9:36; Acts 2:39; Ephesians 2:13, 17

Gospel of Mattityahu "Matthew"	OT/NT References	Gospel of Mrk "Mark"	OT/NT References	Gospel of Luk "Luke"	OT/NT References
				Chapter 15 **The Parable of the Lost Son Continued**	
				v. 21: "His son said to him, 'Father, I have sinned against Heaven (A) and against you.; I am no longer worthy to be called your son.'"	A). Psalm 51:4
				v. 22: "But his father said to his slaves, 'Quick, bring out at robe, the best one, and put it on him; and put a ring on his finger and shoes on his feet.'"	
				v. 23: "And bring the calf that has been fattened up, and kill it. Let's eat and have a celebration!"	
				v. 24: (a) "'For this son of mine was dead, but now he's alive again! He was lost, but now he has been found!' And they began celebrating."	a). Matthew 8:22; Luke 9:60; 15:32; Romans 11:15; Ephesians 2:1, 5; 5:14; Colossians 2:13; 1 Timothy 5:6
				v. 25: "Now his older son was in the field. As he came close to the house, he heard music and dancing."	

Gospel of Mattityahu "Matthew"	OT/NT References	Gospel of Mrk "Mark"	OT/NT References	Gospel of Luk "Luke"	OT/NT References
				Chapter 15 **The Parable of the Lost Son Continued**	
				v. 26: "So he called one of the servants and asked, 'What's going on?'"	
				v. 27: "The servant told him, 'Your brother has come back, and your father has slaughtered the calf that was fattened up, because he has gotten him back safe and sound.'"	
				v. 28: "But the older son became angry and refused to go inside. So his father came out and pleaded with him."	
				v. 29: "'Look,' the son answered, 'I have worked for you all these years, and I have never disobeyed your orders. But you have never even given me a young goat, so that I could celebrate with my friends.'"	
				v. 30: "Yet this son of yours comes, who squandered your property with prostitutes, and for him you slaughter the fattened calf!"	

Gospel of Mattityahu "Matthew"	OT/NT References	Gospel of Mrk "Mark"	OT/NT References	Gospel of Luk "Luke"	OT/NT References
				Chapter 15 The Parable of the Lost Son Continued	
				v. 31: "'Son you are always with me,' said the father, 'and everything I have is yours.'"	
				v. 32: 'We had to celebrate and rejoice, (a) because this brother of yours was dead but has come back to life—he was lost but he's been found."	a). Luke 15:24
				Chapter 17 Dealing with a Sinning Brother	
Chapter 18 Dealing with a Sinning Brother					
v. 15: "Moreover, (A) if your brother commits a sin against you, go and show him his fault—but privately, just between the two of you. If he listens to you, (b) you have won back your brother."	A). Leviticus 19:17; Luke 17:3–4 Galatians 6:1; 2 Thessalonians 3:15; James 5:19 b). James 5:20; 1 Peter 3:1			v. 3: "Watch yourselves! (a) If your brother sins, (B) rebuke him; and if he repents, forgive him."	a). Matthew 18:15, 21 B). Leviticus 19:17; Proverbs 17:10; Galatians 6:1; James 5:19–20
v. 16: "If he doesn't listen, take one or two others with you so that every accusation can be supported by the (A) testimony of two or three witnesses."	A). Deuteronomy 17:6; 19:15; John 8:17; 2 Corinthians 13:1; 1 Timothy 5:19; Hebrews 10:28				

Gospel of Mattityahu "Matthew"	OT/NT References	Gospel of Mrk "Mark"	OT/NT References	Gospel of Luk "Luke"	OT/NT References
Chapter 18 Dealing with a Sinning Brother Continued					
v. 17: "If he refuses to hear them, tell the congregation; and if he refuses to listen to the congregation, treat him as you would a (a) pagan or tax-collector."	a). Romans 16:17; 1 Corinthians 5:9; 2 Thessalonians 3:6, 14; 2 John 1:10				
v. 18: "Yes! I tell you people that (a) whatever you prohibit on earth will be prohibited in heaven, and you people that whatever you permit on earth will be permitted in heaven."	a). Matthew 16:19; John 20:22–23; 1 Corinthians 5:4				
v. 19: (a) "To repeat, I tell you that if two of you here on earth agree about anything people ask, (b) it will be for them from My Father in heaven."	a). 1 Corinthians 1:10 b). 1 John 3:22; 5:14				
v. 20: "For wherever two or three are (a) assembled in My Name, I am there with them?"	a). Acts 20:7; 1 Corinthians 14:26				

Gospel of Mattityahu "Matthew"	OT/NT References	Gospel of Mrk "Mark"	OT/NT References	Gospel of Luk "Luke"	OT/NT References
Chapter 18 **The Parable of the Unforgiving Servant**				**Chapter 17** **The Parable of the Unforgiving Servant**	
v. 22: "'No, not seven times,' answered *Yeshua*, (a) 'but seventy times seven!'"	a). Matthew 6:14; Mark 11:25; Colossians 3:13			v. 4: "Also, if seven times in one day he sins against you, and seven times he comes to and says, 'I repent,' you are to forgive him."	
v. 23: "Because of this, the Kingdom of Heaven may be compared with a king who decided to settle accounts with his deputies."					
v. 24: "Right away they brought forward a man who owed him many millions."					
v. 25: "And since he couldn't pay, his master ordered that he, his wife, his children and all his possessions (A) be sold to pay the debt."	A). Exodus 21:2; Leviticus 25:39; 2 Kings 4:1; Nehemiah 5:5, 8				
v. 26: "But the servant fell down before him. 'Be patient with me,' he begged, 'and I will pay back everything.'"					
v. 27: "So out of pity for him, the master let him go and forgave the debt."					

Gospel of Mattityahu "Matthew"	OT/NT References	Gospel of Mrk "Mark"	OT/NT References	Gospel of Luk "Luke"	OT/NT References
Chapter 18 **The Parable of the Unforgiving Servant**					
v. 28 "But as that servant was leaving, he came upon one of his fellow servants who owed him some tiny sum. He grabbed him and began to choke him, crying, 'Pay back what you owe me!'"					
v. 29: "His fellow servant fell before him and begged, 'Be patient with me and I will pay you back.'"					
v. 30: "But he refused; instead, he had him thrown in jail until he should repay the debt."					
v. 31: "When the other servants saw what had happened, they were extremely distressed; and they went and told their master everything that had taken place."					
v. 32: "Then the master summoned his servant and said, 'You wicked servant! I forgave you (a) all that debt because you begged me to do it.'"	a). Luke 7:41–43				

Gospel of Mattityahu "Matthew"	OT/NT References	Gospel of Mrk "Mark"	OT/NT References	Gospel of Luk "Luke"	OT/NT References
Chapter 18 **The Parable of the Unforgiving Servant Continued**					
v. 33: "Shouldn't you have had pity on you fellow servant, just as I had pity on you?"					
v. 34: "And in anger his master turned him over to the jailers for punishment until he paid back everything he owed."					
v. 35: (A) "This is how My heavenly Father will treat you unless you each forgive your brother from your hearts."	A). Proverbs 21:13; Matthew 6:12; Mark 11:26; James 2:13				
		Chapter 10 **Marriage and Divorce**			
		v. 3: "He replied, 'What did *Moshe* command you?'"			
		v. 5: "But *Yeshua* said to them, 'He wrote this commandment for you because of your hardheartedness.'"			
v. 4: "He replied, 'Haven't you read that at the beginning the Creator (A) made them male and female.'"	A). Genesis 1:27; 5:2; Malachi 2:15	v. 6: "However, at the beginning of creation, God (A) made them male and female."	A). Genesis 1:27; 5:2		

Part 4: Subtopic Scriptural Alignment View—Matthew, Mark, and Luke

Gospel of Mattityahu "Matthew"	OT/NT References	Gospel of Mrk "Mark"	OT/NT References	Gospel of Luk "Luke"	OT/NT References
Chapter 19 Marriage and Divorce Continued		**Chapter 10 Marriage and Divorce Continued**			
v. 5: "And that He said. (A) 'For this reason a man should leave his father and mother and be united with his wife, and (b) the two are to become one flesh'?"	A). Genesis 2:24; Mark 10:5–9; Ephesians 5:31 b). 1 Corinthians 6:16; 7:2	v. 7: (A) "For this reason, a man should leave his father and mother and be united with his wife."	A). Genesis 2:24; 1 Corinthians 6:16; Ephesians 5:31		
v. 6: "Thus they are no longer two, but one. So then, no one should split apart what God has joined together."		v. 8: "And the two are to become one flesh. Thus they are no longer two, but one."			
v. 8: "He answered, '*Moshe* allowed you to divorce your (B) wives because your (a) hearts are so hardened. But this is not how it was at the beginning.'"	a). Hebrews 3:15 B). Malachi 2:16	v. 9: "So then, no one should break apart what God has joined together."			
v. 9: (a) "Now what I say to you is that whoever divorces his wife, except on the ground of sexual immorality, and marries another woman commits adultery!"	a). Matthew 5:32; Mark 10:11; Luke 16:18; 1 Corinthians 7:10	v. 11: "He said to them, (A) 'Whoever divorces his wife and marries another woman commits adultery against his wife.'"	A). Exodus 20:14; Matthew 5:32; 19:9; Luke 16:18; Romans 7:3; 1 Corinthians 7:10–11		
		v. 12: "And if a wife divorces her husband and marries another man, she too commits adultery."			

Gospel of Mattityahu "Matthew"	OT/NT References	Gospel of Mrk "Mark"	OT/NT References	Gospel of Luk "Luke"	OT/NT References
Chapter 19 Yeshua Teaches on Celibacy					
v. 11: "He said to them, (a) 'Not everyone grasps this teaching, only those for whom it is meant.'"	a). 1 Corinthians 7:2, 7, 9, 17				
v. 12: "For there are different reasons why men do not marry—some because they were born without the desire, (a) some because they have been castrated, and some because they have renounced marriage for the sake of the Kingdom of Heaven. Whoever can grasp this, let him do so."	a). 1 Corinthians 7:32				
Chapter 19 Yeshua Blesses Little Children		**Chapter 10 Yeshua Blesses Little Children**		**Chapter 18 Yeshua Blesses Little Children**	
v. 14: "However, *Yeshua said, 'Let the children come to Me, don't stop them, for the Kingdom of Heaven belongs to (a) such as these.'"	a). Matthew 8:3–4; Mark 10:15; Luke 18:17; 1 Corinthians 14:20; 1 Peter 2:2	v. 14: "However, when *Yeshua saw it, He became indignant and said to them, 'Let the children come to Me, don't stop them, for the (a) Kingdom of God belongs to such as these.'"	a). 1 Corinthians 14:20; 1 Peter 2:2	v. 16: "However, *Yeshua called the children to Him and said, 'Let the children come to me, and stop hindering them, (a) because the Kingdom of God belongs to such as these.'"	a). Matthew 18:3; 1 Corinthians 14:20; 1 Peter 2:2

Gospel of Mattityahu "Matthew"	OT/NT References	Gospel of Mrk "Mark"	OT/NT References	Gospel of Luk "Luke"	OT/NT References
		Chapter 10 Yeshua Blesses Little Children Continued		**Chapter 18 Yeshua Blesses Little Children Continued**	
		v. 15: "Yes! I tell you, (a) whoever does not receive the Kingdom of God like a child will (b) not enter it!"	a). Matthew 18:3–4; 19:14; Luke 18:17 b). Luke 13:28	v. 17: (a) "Yes! I tell you that whoever does not receive the Kingdom of God like a little child will not enter it at all!"	a). Matthew 18:3; 19:14; Mark 10:15
Chapter 19 Yeshua Counsels the Rich Young Ruler		**Chapter 10 Yeshua Counsels the Rich Young Ruler**		**Chapter 18 Yeshua Counsels the Rich Young Ruler**	
v. 16: (a) "A man approached *Yeshua* and said, '*Rabbi*, what good thing should I do in order to have eternal life?' He said to him."	a). Matthew 19:16–29; Mark 10:17–30; Luke 18:18–30 b). Luke 10:25				
v. 17: "Why are you asking Me about good? There is (A) One who is good! But if you want to obtain eternal life, (B) observe the *mitzvoth*."	A). Psalm 25:8; 34:8; Nahum 1:7; Romans 2:4 B). Leviticus 18:5; Deuteronomy 4:40; 6:17; 7:11; 11:22; 28:9; Nehemiah 9:29; Ezekiel 20:21; Galatians 3:10	v. 18: "So *Yeshua* said to him, 'Why are you calling Me good? No one is good except God!'"		v. 19: "*Yeshua* said to him, 'Why are you calling Me good? No one is good but God!'"	
v. 18: "The man asked Him, 'Which ones?' and *Yeshua* said, (A) 'Don't murder, don't commit adultery, don't steal, don't give false testimony.'"	A). Exodus 20:13; Deuteronomy 5:17	v. 19: "You know the *mitzvot* (A) 'Don't murder, don't commit adultery, don't steal, don't give false testimony, don't defraud.'"	A). Exodus 20:13; Deuteronomy 5:17; Romans 13:9; James 2:10–11	v. 20: "You know the *mitzvot*— (A) 'Don't commit adultery, don't murder, don't steal, don't give false testimony.'"	A). Exodus 20:13; Deuteronomy 5:17; Mark 10:19; Romans 13:9

Gospel of Mattityahu "Matthew"	OT/NT References	Gospel of Mrk "Mark"	OT/NT References	Gospel of Luk "Luke"	OT/NT References
Chapter 19 Yeshua Counsels the Rich Young Ruler Continued		**Chapter 10 Yeshua Counsels the Rich Young Ruler Continued**		**Chapter 18 Yeshua Counsels the Rich Young Ruler Continued**	
v. 19: (A) "Honor father and mother and (B) love your neighbor as yourself."	A). Exodus 20:12; Deuteronomy 5:16; Matthew 15:4 B). Leviticus 19:18; Matthew 22:39; Romans 13:9; Galatians 5:14; James 2:8	v. 19:(A) "Honor your father and mother,…"	A). Exodus 20:12; Deuteronomy 5:16	v. 20: (A) "Honor your father and mother."	A). Exodus 20:12; Deuteronomy 5:16
v. 21: "*Yeshua said to him, 'If you are serious about reaching the goal, (a) go and sell your possessions, give to the poor, and you will have riches in heaven. Then come, follow Me!'"	a). Matthew 6:20; Luke 12:33; Acts 2:45; 4:34–35; 1 Timothy 6:18–19	v. 21: "*Yeshua, looking at him, felt love for him and said to him, 'You're missing one thing. Go, (a) sell whatever you own, give to the poor, and you will have (b) riches in heaven. (c) Then come follow Me!'"	a). Luke 12:33; 16:9 b). Matthew 6:19,20; 19:21 c). Mark 8:34	v. 22: "On hearing this *Yeshua said to him, 'There is one thing you still lack. (a) Sell whatever you have, distribute the proceeds to the poor, and you will have riches in heaven. Then come, follow Me!'"	a). Matthew 6:19,20–21; 1 Timothy 6:19
				Chapter 12 The Parable of the Rich Fool	
				v. 14: "But Yeshua answered him, (a) 'My friend, who appointed Me judge or arbitrator over you?'"	a). John 18:36

Gospel of Mattityahu "Matthew"	OT/NT References	Gospel of Mrk "Mark"	OT/NT References	Gospel of Luk "Luke"	OT/NT References
				Chapter 12 **The Parable of the Rich Fool Continued**	
				v. 15: "Then to the people He said, (a) 'Be careful to guard against all forms of greed, because even if someone is rich; his life does not consist in what he owns.'"	a). 1 Timothy 6:6–10
				v. 16: "And He gave them this illustration: 'There was a man whose land was very productive.'"	
				v. 17: "He debated with himself, 'What should I do? I haven't enough room for all my crops.'"	
				v. 18: "Then he said, 'This is what I will do; I'll tear down my barns and build bigger ones, and I'll store all my wheat and other goods there.'"	
				v. 19: "Then I'll say to myself, (A) 'You're a lucky man! You have a big supply of goods laid up that will last many years. Start taking it easy! (B) Eat! Drink! Enjoy yourself!'"	A). Ecclesiastes 11:9; 1 Corinthians 15:32; James 5:5 B). Ecclesiastes 2:24; 3:13; 5:18; 8:15

Gospel of Mattityahu "Matthew"	OT/NT References	Gospel of Mrk "Mark"	OT/NT References	Gospel of Luk "Luke"	OT/NT References
				Chapter 12 **The Parable of the Rich Fool Continued**	
				v. 20: "But God said to him, 'You fool! This very night (A) you will die! (B) And the things you prepared—whose will they be?'"	A). Job 27:8; Psalm 52:7; Jame 4:14 B). Psalm 39:6; Jeremiah 17:11
				v. 21: "That's how it is with anyone who stores up wealth for himself (a) without being rich toward God."	a). Matthew 6:20; Luke 12:33; 1 Timothy 6:18–19; James 2:5; 5:1–5
Chapter 19 **With God All Things Are Possible**		**Chapter 10** **With God All Things Are Possible**		**Chapter 18** **With God All Things Are Possible**	
v. 23: "Then *Yeshua* said to His *talmidim*, "Yes, I tell you that (a) it will be very hard for a rich man to enter the Kingdom of Heaven.'"	a). Matthew 13:22; Mark 10:24; 1 Corinthians 1:26; 1 Timothy 6:9	v. 23: (a) "*Yeshua* looked around and said to His *talmidim*, 'How hard it is going to be for people with wealth to enter the Kingdom of God!'"	a). Matthew 19:23; Mark 4:19; Luke 18:24	v. 24: "*Yeshua* looked at him and said, (A) 'How hard it is for people with wealth to enter the Kingdom of God!'"	A). Proverbs 11:28; Matthew 19:23; Mark 10:23
		v. 24: "The *talmidim* were astounded at these words; but *Yeshua* said to them again, 'My friends, (A) how hard it is to enter the Kingdom of God!'"	A). Job 31:24; Psalm 52:7; 62:10; Proverbs 11:28; 1 Timothy 6:17		

Gospel of Mattityahu "Matthew"	OT/NT References	Gospel of Mrk "Mark"	OT/NT References	Gospel of Luk "Luke"	OT/NT References
Chapter 19 With God All Things Are Possible Continued		**Chapter 10 With God All Things Are Possible Continued**		**Chapter 18 With God All Things Are Possible Continued**	
v. 24: "Furthermore, I tell you that is it easier for a *camel to pass through a needle's eye than for a rich man to enter the Kingdom of God." (See "Commentaries.")		v. 25: "It's easier for a camel to pass through a needle's eye than for a (a) rich man to enter the Kingdom of God."	a). Matthew 13:22; 19:24	v. 25: "It's easier for a camel to pass through a needle's eye than for a rich man to enter the Kingdom of God!"	
v. 26: "*Yeshua looked at them and said, 'Humanly, this is impossible but (A) with God everything is possible.'"	A). Genesis 18:14; Numbers 11:23; Job:42:2; Isaiah 59:1; Jeremiah 32:17; Zechariah 8:6; Luke 1:37	v. 27: "*Yeshua looked at them and said, 'Humanly, it is impossible, but not (A) with God; with God, everything is possible.'"	A). Job 42:2; Jeremiah 32:17; Matthew 19:26; Luke 1:37	v. 27: "He said, (A) 'What is impossible humanly is possible with God.'"	A). Job 42:2; Jeremiah 32:17; Zechariah 8:6; Matthew 19:26; Luke 1:37
v. 28: "*Yeshua said to them, 'Yes, I tell you that in the regenerated world, when the Son of Man sits on His glorious throne, (a) you who have followed Me will also sit on twelve thrones and judge the twelve tribes of *Israel.'"	a). Matthew 20:21; Luke 22:28–30; 1 Corinthians 6:2l; Revelation 2:26				
v. 29: (a) "Everyone who has left houses, brothers, sisters, father, mother, children or fields for My sake."	a). Matthew 6:33; Mark 10:29–30; Luke 18:29–30	v. 29: "*Yeshua said, 'Yes! I tell you that there is no one who has left house, brothers, sisters, mother, father, children or fields, for My sake and for the sake of the Good News.'"		v. 29: "*Yeshua answered them, 'Yes! I tell you that (A) everyone who has left house, wife, brothers, parents and children, for the sake of the Kingdom of God.'"	A). Deuteronomy 33:9

182 *Just the Words and Teachings of Jesus Christ*

Gospel of Mattityahu "Matthew"	OT/NT References	Gospel of Mrk "Mark"	OT/NT References	Gospel of Luk "Luke"	OT/NT References
Chapter 19 With God All Things Are Possible Continued		**Chapter 10 With God All Things Are Possible Continued**		**Chapter 18 With God All Things Are Possible Continued**	
v. 29: "Will receive a hundred times more, and he will obtain eternal life."		v. 30: (A) "Who will not receive a hundred times over, now, in the *'olam hazeh [this world] homes, brothers, sisters, mothers, children and lands—with (b) persecutions!—and in the *'olam haba [world to come], eternal life."	A). 2 Chronicles 25:9; Luke 18:29–30 b). 1 Thessalonians 3:3; 2 Timothy 3:12; 1 Peter 4:12–13	v. 30: (A) "Will receive many times as much in the *'olam hazeh [this world], and in the *'olam haba [world to come] eternal life."	A). Job 42:10
v. 30: (a) "But many who are first will be last, and many who are last will be first."	a). Matthew 20:16; 21:31–32; Mark 10:31; Luke 13:30	v. 31: (a) "But many who are first will be last, and many who are last will be first!"	a). Matthew 19:30; 20:16; Luke 13:30		
Chapter 20 The Parable of the Workers in the Vineyard					
v. 1: "The Kingdom of Heaven is like a farmer who went out at daybreak to hire workers for his vineyard."					
v. 2: "After agreeing with the workers on a wage of one *denarius, he sent them off to his vineyard."					

Gospel of Mattityahu "Matthew"	OT/NT References	Gospel of Mrk "Mark"	OT/NT References	Gospel of Luk "Luke"	OT/NT References
Chapter 20 The Parable of the Workers in the Vineyard Continued					
v. 3: "Then, going out at about nine in the morning, he saw more men standing around in the market-square doing nothing."					
v. 4: "And he said to them, 'You go to the vineyard too—I'll pay you a fair wage.' So they went."					
v. 5: "At noon, and again around three in the afternoon, he did the same thing."					
v. 6: "About an hour before sundown, he went out, found still others standing around, and asked then, 'Why have you been standing here all day, doing nothing?'"					
v. 7: "They said to him, 'Because no one hired us.' 'You too,' he told them, 'go to the vineyard.'"					

Gospel of Mattityahu "Matthew"	OT/NT References	Gospel of Mrk "Mark"	OT/NT References	Gospel of Luk "Luke"	OT/NT References
Chapter 20 The Parable of the Workers in the Vineyard Continued					
v. 8: "When evening came, the owner of the vineyard said to his foreman, 'Call the workers and pay them their wages, starting with the last ones hired and ending with the first."					
v. 9: "The workers who came an hour before sunset each received a *denarius.*"					
v. 10: "So the workers who came first expected they would get more, but each of them also received just a denarius."					
v. 11: "On receiving their wages, they began grumbling to the farmer."					
v. 12: "These latecomers have worked only one hour, while we have borne the brunt of the day's work in the hot sun, yet you have put them on an equal footing with us!"					
v. 13: "But he answered one of them, 'Look, friend, I'm not being unfair with you. Didn't you agree to work today for a *denarius?*'"					

Gospel of Mattityahu "Matthew"	OT/NT References	Gospel of Mrk "Mark"	OT/NT References	Gospel of Luk "Luke"	OT/NT References
Chapter 20 The Parable of the Workers in the Vineyard Continued					
v. 14: "Now take your pay and go! I choose to give the last worker as much as I'm giving you."					
v. 15: (a) "Haven't I the right to do what I want with what belongs to me? (B) Or do you begrudge my generosity?"	a). Romans 9:20–21 B). Deuteronomy 15:9; Proverbs 23:6; Matthew 6:23; Mark 7:22				
v. 16: (a) "Thus the last ones will be first and the first last."	a). Matthew 19:30; Mark 10:31; Luke 13:30				
Chapter 20 Yeshua a Third Time Predicts His Death and Resurrection		**Chapter 10 Yeshua a Third Time Predicts His Death and Resurrection**		**Chapter 18 Yeshua a Third Time Predicts His Death and Resurrection**	
v. 18: (a) "We are now going up to *Yerushalayim, where the Son of Man will be handed over to the head *cohanim and *Torah-teachers. They will sentence Him to death."	a). Matthew 16:21; 26:47–57; Mark 14:42, 64; John 18:5; 19:7	v. 33: "We are now going up to *Yerushalayim, where the Son of Man will be handed over to the head *cohanim. They will sentence Him to death and turn Him over to the *Goyim."		v. 31: (a) "Then, taking the Twelve, *Yeshua said to them, 'We are now going up to *Yerushalayim, where (B) everything written through the prophets about the Son of Man will come true.'"	a). Matthew 16:21; 17:22; 20:17; Mark 10:32; Luke 9:51 B). Psalm 22; Isaiah 5:3

186 *Just the Words and Teachings of Jesus Christ*

Gospel of Mattityahu "Matthew"	OT/NT References	Gospel of Mrk "Mark"	OT/NT References	Gospel of Luk "Luke"	OT/NT References
Chapter 20 Yeshua a Third Time Predicts His Death and Resurrection Continued		**Chapter 10 Yeshua a Third Time Predicts His Death and Resurrection Continued**		**Chapter 18 Yeshua a Third Time Predicts His Death and Resurrection Continued**	
v. 19: (a) "And turn Him over to the *Goyim, who will (b) jeer at Him, (c) beat Him and (d) execute Him on a stake as a criminal.	a). Matthew 27:2; Mark 15:1,16; Luke 23:1; John 18:28; Acts 3:13 b). Matthew 26:67–68; 27:29, 41; Mark 15:20, 31 c). Matthew 27:26; Mark 15:15; John 19:1 d). Matthew 27:35; Luke 23:33; Acts 3:13–15	v. 34: "Who will jeer at Him, spit on him."		v. 32: "For (a) He will be handed over to the *Goyim and be ridiculed, insulted and spat upon."	a). Matthew 26:27; 27:2,29, 41; Mark 14:65; 15:1, 19–20, 31; Luke 23:1; John 18:28; Acts 3:13
v. 19: "But on the third day, (e) He will be raised."	e). Matthew 28:5–6; Mark 16:6, 9; Luke 24:5–8, 46; Acts 10:40; 1 Corinthians 15:4	v. 34: "But after three days, He will rise."		v. 33: "Then, after they have beaten Him, they will kill Him. But on the third day He will rise."	

Gospel of Mattityahu "Matthew"	OT/NT References	Gospel of Mrk "Mark"	OT/NT References	Gospel of Luk "Luke"	OT/NT References
Chapter 20 Greatness Is Serving		**Chapter 10 Greatness Is Serving**			
v. 21: "He said to her, 'What do you want?' She replied, 'Promise that when you become king, these two sons of mine (a) may sit, one on your right and the other on your left.'"	a). Matthew 19:28	v. 36: "He said to them, 'What do you want Me to do for you?'"			
v. 22: "But *Yeshua* answered, 'You people don't know what you are asking. (A) Can you drink the cup that (b) I am about to drink?'"	A). Isaiah 51:17, 22; Jeremiah 49:12; Matthew 26:39, 42; Mark 14:36; Luke 22:42; John 18:11 b). Luke 12:50	v. 38: "But *Yeshua* answered, 'You don't know what you are asking! Can you drink the (a) cup that I am drinking? Or be immersed with the (b) immersion that I must undergo?'"	a). Matthew 26:39, 42; Mark 14:36; Luke 22:42; John 18:11 b). Luke 12:50		
v. 22: "They said to Him, 'We can.'"		v. 39: "They said to Him, 'We can.'"			
v. 23: "He said to them, (a) 'Yes, you will drink my cup.'"	a). Acts 12:2; Romans 8:17; 2 Corinthians 1:7; Revelation 1:9	v. 39. "*Yeshua* replied, (a) 'The cup that I am drinking, you will drink; and the immersion I am being immersed with, you will undergo.'"	a). Matthew 10:17–18, 21–22; 24:9; John 16:33; Acts 12:2; Revelation 1:9		

Gospel of Mattityahu "Matthew"	OT/NT References	Gospel of Mrk "Mark"	OT/NT References	Gospel of Luk "Luke"	OT/NT References
Chapter 20 Greatness Is Serving Continued		**Chapter 10 Greatness Is Serving Continued**			
v. 23: "But to sit on My right and on My left is not Mine to give, it is for those for whom My Father has prepared it."		v. 40: "But to sit on My right and on My left is not Mine to give, Rather, it is for those for (a) whom it has been prepared."	a). Matthew 25:34; John 17:2, 6, 24; Romans 8:30; Hebrews 11:16		
v. 25: "But *Yeshua* called them and said, 'You know that among the *Goyim*, those who are supposed to rule them become tyrants, and their superiors become dictators.'"		v. 42: "But *Yeshua* called them to Him and said to them, (a) 'You know that among the *Goyim*, those who are supposed to rule them become tyrants, and their superiors become dictators.'"	a). Luke 22:25		
v. 26: "Among you, (a) it must not be like that. On the contrary, whoever among you (b) wants to be a leader must become your servant."	a). 1 Peter 5:3 b). Matthew 23:11; Mark 9:35; 10:43; Luke 22:26	v. 43: "But among you, (a) it must not be like that! On the contrary, whoever among you wants to be a leader must be your servant."	a). Matthew 20:26, 28; Mark 9:35; Luke 9:48		
v. 27: (a) "And whoever wants to be first must be your slave!"	a). Matthew 18:4	v. 44. "And whoever wants to be first among you must become everyone's slave!"			

Part 4: Subtopic Scriptural Alignment View—Matthew, Mark, and Luke

Gospel of Mattityahu "Matthew"	OT/NT References	Gospel of Mrk "Mark"	OT/NT References	Gospel of Luk "Luke"	OT/NT References
Chapter 20 **Greatness Is Serving Continued**		**Chapter 10** **Greatness Is Serving Continued**			
v. 28: (a) "For the (b) Son of Man did not come to be served, (c) but to serve—and (D) to give His life as a ransom (e) for many."	a). John 3:4 b). Matthew 26:28; John 13:13; 2 Corinthians 8:9; Philippians 2:6–7; 1 Timothy 2:5–6; Titus 2:14; Hebrews 9:28; Revelation 1:5 c). Luke 22:27; John 13:14 D). Isaiah 53:10–11; Daniel 9:24,26; John 11:51–52; 1 Peter 1:18–19 e). Romans 5:15, 19; Hebrews 9:28	v. 45: "For the (a) Son of Man did not come to be served, but to serve—and (b) to give His life as a ransom for many."	a). Luke 22:27; John 13:14; Philippians 2:7–8 b). Matthew 20:28; 2 Corinthians 5:21; 1 Timothy 2:5–6; Titus 2:14		
		Chapter 10 **Yeshua Heals Blind Bartimaeus**		**Chapter 18** **A Blind Man Receives His Sight**	
		v. 49: "*Yeshua stopped and said, 'Call him over!' They called to the blind man, 'Courage! Get up! He's calling you!'"		v. 40: "*Yeshua stopped and ordered the man to be brought to Him. When he had come, *Yeshua asked him."	

190 *Just the Words and Teachings of Jesus Christ*

Gospel of Mattityahu "Matthew"	OT/NT References	Gospel of Mrk "Mark"	OT/NT References	Gospel of Luk "Luke"	OT/NT References
Chapter 20 **Two Blind Men Receive Their Sight** v. 32: "**Yeshua* stopped, called them and said, "What do you want Me to do for you?" v. 33: "They said to Him, 'Lord, open our eyes.'"		**Chapter 10** **Yeshua Heals Blind Bartimaeus Continued** v. 51: "'What do you want Me to do for you?' asked *Yeshua.*"		**Chapter 18** **A Blind Man Receives His Sight Continued** v. 41: "What do you want Me to do for you?" v. 41: "The blind man said, 'Lord, let me be able to see.'"	
		v. 52: "*Yeshua* said to him, 'Go! (a) Your trust has healed you.' Instantly he received his sight and followed Him on the road."	a). Matthew 9:22; Mark 5:34	v. 42: "*Yeshua* said to him, 'See again! (a) Your trust has healed you!'"	a). Luke 17:19
				Chapter 19 **Yeshua Comes to Zakkai (Zacharia) House** v. 5: "When He came to the place, He looked up and said to him, 'Zakkai! Hurry! Come down, because I have to stay at your house today!'"	
				v. 9: "*Yeshua* said to him, 'Today, salvation has come to this house, inasmuch as (a) this man too is (b) a son of *Avraham.*'"	a). Luke 3:8; 13;16; Romans 4:16; Galatians 3:7 b). Luke 13:16

Gospel of Mattityahu "Matthew"	OT/NT References	Gospel of Mrk "Mark"	OT/NT References	Gospel of Luk "Luke"	OT/NT References
				Chapter 19 **Yeshua Comes to Zakkai (Zacharia) House Continued**	
				v. 10: (a) "For the Son of Man came to seek and save what was lost."	a). Matthew 18:11; Luke 5:32; Romans 5:8
Chapter 21 **The Triumphal Entry of Yeshua**		**Chapter 11** **The Triumphal Entry of Yeshua**		**Chapter 19** **The Triumphal Entry of Yeshua**	
v. 1: (a) "As they were approaching *Yerushalayim*, they came to *Beit-Pagei* on the (B) Mount of Olives. *Yeshua* sent two *talmidim*."	a). Mark 11:1–10; Luke 19:29–38 B). Zechariah 14:4				
v. 2: "With these instructions: 'Go into the village ahead of you, and you will immediately find a donkey tethered there with its colt. Untie them and bring them to me.'"		v. 2: "With these instructions: 'Go into the village ahead of you; and as soon as you enter it, you will find a colt tied there that has never been ridden. Untie it, and bring it here.'"		v. 30: "Instructing them, 'Go into the village ahead; on entering it, you will find a colt tied up that has never been ridden. Untie it and bring it here.'"	
v. 3: "If anyone says anything to you, tell him, 'The Lord needs them'; and he will let them go at once."		v. 3: "If anyone asks you, 'Why are you doing this?' Tell him, 'The Lord needs it.' and he will send it here right away."		v. 31 "If anyone asks you why you are untying it, tell him, 'The Lord needs it.'"	
v. 4: "This happened in order to fulfill what had been spoken through the prophet."					

Gospel of Mattityahu "Matthew"	OT/NT References	Gospel of Mrk "Mark"	OT/NT References	Gospel of Luk "Luke"	OT/NT References
Chapter 21 The Triumphal Entry of Yeshua Continued				**Chapter 19 The Triumphal Entry of Yeshua Continued**	
v. 5: "Say to the (A) daughter of *Tziyon* [Zion], 'Look! Your King is coming to you, riding humbly on a donkey, and on a colt, the offspring of a beast of burden!'"	A). Isaiah 62:11; Zechariah 9:9; John 12:15				
				v. 40: "But He answered them, 'I tell you that if they keep quiet, (A) the stones will shout!'"	A). Habakkuk 2:11
Chapter 21 Yeshua Cleanses the Temple		**Chapter 11 Yeshua Cleanses the Temple**		**Chapter 19 Yeshua Cleanses the Temple**	
v. 13: "He said to them, 'It has been written, (A) "My house will be a house of prayer." But you are making it into a (B) den of robbers!'"	A). Isaiah 56:7 B). Jeremiah 7:11	v. 17: "Then, as He taught them He said, 'Isn't it written in the *Tanakh*, (A) "My house will be called a house of prayer for all the *Goyim*. But you have made it into a (B) den of robbers!"'"	A). Isaiah 56:7 B). Jeremiah 7:11	v. 46: "Saying too them, "The *Tanakh* says, (A) 'My House is to be a house of prayer, but you have made it into a (B) den of robbers!'"	A). Isaiah 56:7 B). Jeremiah 7:11
v. 16: "They said to him, 'Do you hear what they're saying?' *Yeshua* replied, 'Of course! Haven't you ever read, (A) "From the mouths of children and infants you have prepared praise for yourself"?'"	A). Psalm 8:2; Matthew 11:25				

Part 4: Subtopic Scriptural Alignment View—Matthew, Mark, and Luke

Gospel of Mattityahu "Matthew"	OT/NT References	Gospel of Mrk "Mark"	OT/NT References	Gospel of Luk "Luke"	OT/NT References
Chapter 21 **The Fig Tree Withered** v. 19: (a) "Spotting a fig tree by the road, He went up to it but found nothing on it except leaves. So He said to it, 'May you never again bear fruit!' and immediately the fig tree dried up.	a). Mark 11:13	**Chapter 11** **Yeshua Cursed the Fig Tree** v. 14: "He said to it, 'May no one ever eat fruit from you again!' And his *talmidim* heard what He said."			
				Chapter 13 **The Parable of the Barren Fig Tree** v. 6: "Then *Yeshua* gave this illustration: (A) 'A man had a fig tree planted in his vineyard, and he came looking for fruit but didn't find any.'"	A). Isaiah 5:2; Matthew 21:19
				v. 7: "So he said to the man who took care of the vineyard, 'Here, I've come looking for fruit on this fig tree for three years now without finding any. Cut it down—why let it go on using up the soil?'"	
				v. 8: "But he answered, 'Sir, leave it alone one more year. I'll dig around it and put manure on it.'"	

Gospel of Mattityahu "Matthew"	OT/NT References	Gospel of Mrk "Mark"	OT/NT References	Gospel of Luk "Luke"	OT/NT References
				Chapter 13 **The Parable of the Barren Fig Tree Continued**	
				v. 9: "If it bears fruit next year, well and good; if not, you will have it (a) cut down then."	a. John 15:2
Chapter 21 **The Lesson of the Withered Fig Tree**		**Chapter 11** **The Lesson of the Withered Fig Tree**			
		v. 22: "He responded, 'Have the kind of trust that comes from God!'"			
v. 21: "*Yeshua* answered them, 'Yes! I tell you, (a) if you have trust and (b) don't doubt, you will not only do what was done to this fig tree; (c) but even if you say to this mountain, "Go and throw yourself into the sea!" it will be done.'"	a). Matthew 17:20 b). James 1:6 c). 1 Corinthians 13:2	v. 23: (a) "Yes! I tell you that whoever does not doubt in his heart but trusts that what he says will happen can say to this mountain, 'Go and throw yourself into the sea!' and it will be done for him."	a). Matthew 17:20; 21:21; Luke 17:6		
v. 22: "In other words, you will receive (a) everything you ask for in prayer, no matter what it is, provided you have trust."	a). Matthew 7:7–11; Mark 11:24; Luke 11:9; John 15:7; James 5:16; 1 John 3:22; 5:14	v. 24: "Therefore, I tell you, (a) whatever you ask for in prayer, trust that you are receiving it, and it will be yours."	a). Matthew 7:7; Luke 11:9; John 14:13; 15:7; John 16:24; James 1:5–6		

Part 4: Subtopic Scriptural Alignment View—Matthew, Mark, and Luke

Gospel of Mattityahu "Matthew"	OT/NT References	Gospel of Mrk "Mark"	OT/NT References	Gospel of Luk "Luke"	OT/NT References
		Chapter 11 The Lesson of the Withered Fig Tree Continued			
		v. 25: "And when you stand praying, (a) if you have anything against someone, forgive him; so that your Father in Heaven may also forgive your offenses."	a). Matthew 6:14; 18:23–35; Ephesians 4:32; Colossians 3:13		
Chapter 21 Yeshua's Authority Questioned		**Chapter 11 Yeshua's Authority Questioned**		**Chapter 20 Yeshua's Authority Questioned**	
v. 24: "*Yeshua answered, 'I too will ask you a question. If you answer it, then I will tell you by what *s'mikhah I do these things.'"		v. 29: "*Yeshua said to them, 'I will ask you just one question: answer Me, and I will tell you by what *s'mikhah I do these things.'"			
v. 25: "The (a) immersion of (b) *Yochanan—where did it come from? From Heaven or from a human source?"	a). John 1:29–34 b). John 1:15–28	v. 30: "The (a) immersion of *Yochanan—was it from Heaven or from a human source? Answer Me."	a). Mark 1:4–5, 8	v. 3: "He answered, 'I to will ask you a question. Tell me, the immersion of *Yochanan—was it from Heaven or from a human source.'"	
v. 27: "So they answered *Yeshua, 'We don't know.' And He replied, 'Then I won't tell you by what *s'mikah I do these things.'"		v. 33: "So they answered *Yeshua, 'We don't know.' 'Then,' He replied, 'I won't tell you by what *s'mikhah I do these things.'"		v. 8: "*Yeshua said to them, 'Then I won't tell you by what *s'mikhah I do these things.'"	

Gospel of Mattityahu "Matthew"	OT/NT References	Gospel of Mrk "Mark"	OT/NT References	Gospel of Luk "Luke"	OT/NT References
Chapter 21 The Parable of the Two Sons					
v. 28: "But give Me your opinion: a man had two sons. He went to the first and said, 'Son, go and work today in the (a) vineyard.'"	a). Matthew 20:1; 21:33				
v. 29: "He answered, 'I don't want to'; but later he changed his mind and went."					
v. 30: "The father went to his other son and said the same thing. This one answered, 'I will go sir'; but he didn't go."					
v. 31: "'Which of the two did what has father wanted?' 'The first,' they replied. 'That's right!' *Yeshua said to them. (a) 'I tell you that the tax-collectors and prostitutes are going into the kingdom of God ahead of you!'"	a). Luke 7:29, 37–50				
v. 32: "For (a) *Yochanan came to you showing the path to righteousness, and you wouldn't trust him. (b) The tax-collectors and prostitutes trusted him; but you, even after you saw this, didn't change your minds later and trust him."	a). Luke 3:1–12, 7:29 b). Luke 3:12–13				

Gospel of Mattityahu "Matthew"	OT/NT References	Gospel of Mrk "Mark"	OT/NT References	Gospel of Luk "Luke"	OT/NT References
Chapter 21 **The Parable of the Wicked Vinedressers**		**Chapter 12** **The Parable of the Wicked Vinedressers**		**Chapter 20** **The Parable of the Wicked Vinedressers**	
v. 33: "Now listen to another parable. There was a farmer (A) who planted a vineyard. He put a wall around it, dug a pit for the winepress and built a tower; then he rented it to tenants and (b) left."	A). Psalm 80:9; Mark 12:1–12; Luke 20:9–19 b). Matthew 25:14	v. 1: (a) "*Yeshua began speaking to them in parables. 'A man planted a vineyard. He put a wall around it, dug a pit for the wine press and built a tower: then he rented it to tenant-farmers and left.'"	a). Matthew 21:33–46; Luke 20:9–19	v. 9: "Next *Yeshua told the people this parable: (A) 'A man planted a vineyard, rented it to tenant-farmers and went away for a long time.'"	A). Psalm 80:8; Matthew 21:33–46; Mark 12:1–12
v. 34: "When harvest-time came, he sent his servants to the tenants to collect his share of the crop."		v. 2: "When harvest time came, he sent a servant to the tenants to collect his share of the crop from the vineyard."		v. 10: "When the time came, (A) he sent a servant to the tenants to receive his share of the crop from the vineyard."	A). 2 Kings 17:13–14; 2 Chronicles 36:15–16; Acts 7:52; 1 Thessalonians 2:15
v. 35: (A) "But the tenants seized his servants—this one they beat up, that one killed, another they stoned."	A). 2 Chronicles 24:21; 36:16; Matthew 23:34; Acts 7:52; 1 Thessalonians 2:15; Hebrews 11:36–37	v. 3: "But they took him, beat him up and sent him away empty-handed."		v. 10: "But the tenants beat him up and sent him away empty-handed."	
v. 36: "So he sent some other servants, more than the first group, and they did the same to them."		v. 4: "So he sent another servant; this one they punched in the head and insulted."		v. 11: "He sent another servant; they beat him too, insulted him and sent him away empty-handed."	

Gospel of Mattityahu "Matthew"	OT/NT References	Gospel of Mrk "Mark"	OT/NT References	Gospel of Luk "Luke"	OT/NT References
Chapter 21 **The Parable of the Wicked Vinedressers Continued**		**Chapter 12** **The Parable of the Wicked Vinedressers Continued**		**Chapter 20** **The Parable of the Wicked Vinedressers Continued**	
		v. 5: 'He sent another one, and him they killed; and so with many others (A) some they beat up, others they killed."	A). 2 Chronicles 36:16	v. 12: "He sent yet a third; this one they wounded and threw out."	
v. 37: "Finally, he sent them (a) his son, saying, 'My Son they will respect.'"	a). John 3:16	v. 6: "He had still one person left, a son whom he loved; in the end, he sent him to them saying, 'My son they will respect.'"		v. 13: "Then the owner of the vineyard said, 'What am I to do? I will send my son, whom I love; maybe they will respect him.'"	
v. 38: "But when the tenants saw the son, they said to each other, (A) 'This is the heir. (B) Come, let's kill him and take his inheritance!'"	A). Psalm 2:8; Hebrews 1:2 B). Psalm 2:2; John 11:53; Acts 4:27	v. 7: "But the tenants said to each other, 'This is the heir. Come, let's kill him, and the inheritance will be ours!'"		v. 14: "But when the tenants saw him, they discussed it among themselves and said, 'This is the (a) heir; (b) let's kill him, so that the inheritance will be (c) ours!'"	a). Hebrews 1:1–3 b). Matthew 27:21–23 c). John 11:47–48
v. 39: (a) "So they grabbed him, threw him out of the vineyard and killed him."	a). Matthew 26:50; Mark 14:46; Luke 22:54; John 18:12; Acts 2:23	v. 8: 'So they seized him, (a) killed him and threw him out of the vineyard."	a). Acts 2:23	v. 15: "And they threw him out of the vineyard and (a) killed him."	a). Luke 23:33; Acts 2:22–23; 3:15
v. 40: "Now when the owner of the property comes, what will he do to those tenants?"		v. 9: "What will the owner of the vineyard do?"		v. 15: "Now what will the owner of the vineyard do to them?"	

Part 4: Subtopic Scriptural Alignment View—Matthew, Mark, and Luke

Gospel of Mattityahu "Matthew"	OT/NT References	Gospel of Mrk "Mark"	OT/NT References	Gospel of Luk "Luke"	OT/NT References
Chapter 21 **The Parable of the Wicked Vinedressers Continued**		**Chapter 12** **The Parable of the Wicked Vinedressers Continued**		**Chapter 20** **The Parable of the Wicked Vinedressers Continued**	
v. 41: (a) "They answered Him, (b) 'He will viciously destroy those vicious men and (c) rent out the vineyard to other tenants who will give him share of the crop when it's due.'"	a). Luke 20:16 b). Luke 21:24 c). Matthew 8:11; Acts 13:46; Romans 9:10	v.9: "He will come, destroy those tenants and give the vineyard to others!"		v. 16: "'He will come and put an end to those tenants and give the vineyard to (a) others!' When the people heard this, they said, 'Heaven forbid!'"	a). John 1:11–13; Romans 11:1, 11; 1 Corinthians 6:15; Galatians 2:17; 3:21; 6:14
v. 42: "*Yeshua said to them, 'Haven't you ever read in the *Tanakh, (A) "The very rock which the builders rejected has become the cornerstone! This has come from *Adonai, and in our eyes it is amazing"?'"	A). Psalm 118:22–23; Isaiah 23:16; Mark 12:10; Luke 20:17; Acts 4:11; Romans 9:33; Ephesians 2:20	vv. 10–11: "Haven't you read the passage in the *Tanakh that says, (A) 'The very rock which the builders rejected has become the cornerstone! This has come from *Adonai, and in our eyes it is amazing'?"	A). Psalm 118:22–23	v. 17: "But *Yeshua looked searchingly at them and said, 'Then what is this which is written in the *Tanakh, (A) "The very rock which the builders rejected has become the cornerstone"?'"	A). Psalm 118:22; Matthew 21:42; 1 Peter 2:7–8
v. 43: "Therefore I tell you the (a) Kingdom of God will be taken away from you and given to the kind of people that will produce its fruit!"	a). Matthew 8:12; Acts 13:46				
v. 44: (A) "Whoever falls on this stone will be broken in pieces; but if it falls on him, (B) he will be crushed to pieces!"	A). Isaiah 8:14–15; Zechariah 12:3; Luke 20:18; Romans 9:33; 1 Peter 2:8 B). Isaiah 60:12; Daniel 2:44			v. 18: "Whoever falls on that stone will be (A) broken in pieces; but if it falls (B) on him, he will be crushed to powder!"	A). Isaiah 8:14–15 B). Daniel 2:34–35, 44–45; Matthew 21:44

Gospel of Mattityahu "Matthew"	OT/NT References	Gospel of Mrk "Mark"	OT/NT References	Gospel of Luk "Luke"	OT/NT References
Chapter 22 **The Parable of the Wedding Feast**				**Chapter 14** **The Parable of the Great Supper**	
v. 1: "*Yeshua* again used (a) parables in speaking to them."	a). Luke 14:16; Revelation 19:7–9				
v. 2: "The Kingdom of Heaven is like a king who prepared a wedding feast for his son."				v. 16: "But He replied, (a) "Once a man gave a banquet and invited many people."	a). Matthew 22:2–14
v. 3: "But when he sent his slaves to summon the invited guests to the wedding, they refused to come."				v. 18: "But they responded with a chorus of excuses. The first said to him, 'I've just bought a field, and I have to go out and see it. Please accept my apologies.'"	
v. 4: "So he sent some more slaves, instructing them to tell the guests, 'Look, I've prepared my banquet, I've slaughtered (A) my bulls and my fattened cattle, and everything is ready. Come to the wedding!'"	A). Proverbs 9:2			v. 17: "When the time came for the banquet, he (A) sent his slave to tell those who had been invited, 'Come! Everything is ready!'"	A). Proverbs 9:2, 5
v. 5: "But they weren't interested and went off, one to his farm, another to his business."				v. 19: "Another said, 'I've just bought five yoke of oxen, and I'm on my way to test them out. Please accept my apologies.'"	

Part 4: Subtopic Scriptural Alignment View—Matthew, Mark, and Luke

Gospel of Mattityahu "Matthew"	OT/NT References	Gospel of Mrk "Mark"	OT/NT References	Gospel of Luk "Luke"	OT/NT References
Chapter 22 **The Parable of the Wedding Feast Continued**				**Chapter 14** **The Parable of the Great Supper Continued**	
				v. 20: "Still another said, 'I have just gotten married, so I can't come.'"	
v. 6: "And the rest grabbed his slaves, mistreated them and killed them."					
v. 7: "The king was furious and (A) sent his soldiers, who killed those murderers and burned down their city."	A). Daniel 9:26				
v. 8: "Then he said to his slaves, 'Well, the wedding feast is ready; but the ones who were invited (a) didn't deserve it.'"	a). Matthew 10:11				
v. 9: "So go out to the street-corner and invite to the banquet as many as you can find."				v. 21: "The slave came and reported these things to his master. Then the owner of the house, in a rage, told his slave, 'Quick, go out into the streets and alleys of the city; and bring in the poor, the disfigured, the blind and the crippled!'"	

Gospel of Mattityahu "Matthew"	OT/NT References	Gospel of Mrk "Mark"	OT/NT References	Gospel of Luk "Luke"	OT/NT References
Chapter 22 The Parable of the Wedding Feast Continued				**Chapter 14 The Parable of the Great Supper Continued**	
v. 10: "The slaves went out into the streets, (a) gathered all the people they could find, the bad along with the good; and the wedding hall was filled with guests."	a). Matthew 13:38, 47–48; Acts 28:28			v. 22: "The slave said, 'Sir, what you ordered has been done, and there is still room.'"	
				v. 23: "The master said to the slave, 'Go out to the country roads and boundary walls, and insistently persuade people to come in, so that my house will be full.'"	
v. 11: "Now when the king came in to look at the guests, he saw there a man (a) who wasn't dressed for a wedding; so he asked him."	a). 2 Corinthians 5:3; Ephesians 4:24; Colossians 3:10, 12; Revelation 3:4; 16:15; 19:8				
v. 12: "'Friend, how did you get in here without wedding clothes?' The man was (a) speechless."	a). Romans 3:19				
v. 13: "Then the king said to the servants, 'Bind him hand and foot, and throw him (a) outside in the dark!' In that place people will wail and grind their teeth."	a). Matthew 8:12; 25:30; Luke 13:28				

Gospel of Mattityahu "Matthew"	OT/NT References	Gospel of Mrk "Mark"	OT/NT References	Gospel of Luk "Luke"	OT/NT References
Chapter 22 **The Parable of the Wedding Feast Continued**				**Chapter 14** **The Parable of the Great Supper Continued**	
v. 14: (a) "For many are invited, but few are chosen."	a). Matthew 20:16			v. 24: "I tell you, (a) not one of those who were invited will get a taste of my banquet!"	a). Matthew 21:43; 22:8; Acts 13:46
				Chapter 14 **Take the Lowly Place**	
				v. 7: "When *Yeshua noticed how the guests were choosing for themselves the best seats at the table, He told them this parable."	
				v. 8: "When you are invited by someone to a wedding feast, don't sit down in the best seat: because if there is someone more important than you who has been invited."	
				v. 9: "The person who invited both of you might come and say to you, 'Give this man your place.' Then you will be humiliated as you go take the least important place."	

Gospel of Mattityahu "Matthew"	OT/NT References	Gospel of Mrk "Mark"	OT/NT References	Gospel of Luk "Luke"	OT/NT References
				Chapter 14 Take the Lowly Place Continued	
				v. 10: (A) "Instead, when you are invited, go and sit in the least important place; so that when the one who invited you comes, he will say to you, 'Go on up to a better seat.' Then you will be honored in front of everyone sitting with you."	A). Proverbs 25:6–7
				v. 11: (A) "Because everyone who exalts himself will be humbled, but everyone who humbles himself will be exalted."	A). Job 22:29; Psalm 18:27; Proverbs 29:23; Matthew 23:12; Luke 18:14; James 4:6; 1 Peter 5:5
				v. 12: "*Yeshua also said to the one who had invited Him, 'When you give a lunch or a dinner, don't invite your friends, brothers, relatives or rich neighbors; for they may well invite you in return, and that will be your repayment.'"	
				v. 13: "Instead, when you have a party, (A) invite poor people, disfigured people, the crippled, the blind!"	A). Nehemiah 8:10, 12

Gospel of Mattityahu "Matthew"	OT/NT References	Gospel of Mrk "Mark"	OT/NT References	Gospel of Luk "Luke"	OT/NT References
				Chapter 14 **Take the Lowly Place Continued**	
				v. 14: "How (a) blessed you will be that they have nothing with which to repay you! *For you will be repaid at the resurrection of the righteous." (*See "Commentaries.")	a). Matthew 25:34–40
				Chapter 18 **The Parable of the Persistent Widow**	
				v. 1: "Then *Yeshua told His *talmidim a parable, in order to impress on them that they must (a) always keep praying and not lose heart."	a). Luke 11:5–10; Romans 12:12; Ephesians 6:18; Colossians 4:2
				v. 2: "In a certain town, there was a judge who neither feared God nor respected other people."	
				v. 3: "There was also in that town a widow who kept coming to him and saying, 'Give me a judgment against the man who is trying to ruin me.'"	
				v. 4: "For a long time he refused; but after awhile, he said to himself, 'I don't fear God, and I don't respect other people.'"	

Gospel of Mattityahu "Matthew"	OT/NT References	Gospel of Mrk "Mark"	OT/NT References	Gospel of Luk "Luke"	OT/NT References
				Chapter 18 **The Parable of the Persistent Widow Continued**	
				v. 5: (a) "But because this widow is such a *nudnik*, I will see to it that she gets justice—otherwise, she'll keep coming and pestering me till she wears me out!"	a). Luke 11:8
				v. 6: "Then the Lord commented, 'Notice what this corrupt judge says.'"	
				v. 7: (a) "Now won't God grant justice to His chosen people who cry out to Him day and night? Is He delaying long over them?"	a). Revelation 6:10
				v. 8: "I tell you (a) that He will judge in their favor, and quickly! But when Son of Man comes, will He find this trust on the earth at all?"	
				Chapter 18 **The Parable of the Pharisee and the Tax Collector**	
				v. 9: "Also, to some (A) who were relying on their own righteousness and looking down on everyone else, He told this parable."	A). Proverbs 30:12; Luke 10:29; 16:15

Gospel of Mattityahu "Matthew"	OT/NT References	Gospel of Mrk "Mark"	OT/NT References	Gospel of Luk "Luke"	OT/NT References
				Chapter 18 **The Parable of the Pharisee and the Tax Collector Continued**	
				v. 10: "Two men went up to the Temple to pray, one a *Parush and the other a tax-collector."	
				v. 11: "The *Parush (A) stood and prayed to himself, (B) 'O God! I thank you that I am not like the rest of humanity—greedy, dishonest, immoral, or like this tax-collector!'"	A). Psalm 135:2 B). Isaiah 1:15; 58:2; Revelation 3:17
				v. 12: "I fast twice a week, I pay tithes on my entire income."	
				v. 13: "But the tax-collector standing far off, would not even raise his eyes toward heaven, but beat his breast and said, 'God! Have mercy on me, sinner that I am!'"	
				v. 14: "I tell you, this man went down to his home right with God rather than the other. (A) For everyone who exalts himself will be humbled, but everyone who humbles himself will be exalted."	A). Job 22:29; Matthew 23:12; Luke: 14:11; James 4:6; 1 Peter 5:5

Gospel of Mattityahu "Matthew"	OT/NT References	Gospel of Mrk "Mark"	OT/NT References	Gospel of Luk "Luke"	OT/NT References
Chapter 17 Peter and His Master Pay Their Taxes				**Chapter 18 The Parable of the Pharisee and the Tax Collector Continued**	
v. 25: "'Of course He does,' said *Kefa*. When he arrived home, *Yeshua* spoke first. '*Shim'on*, what's your opinion? The kings of the earth—from whom do they collect duties and taxes? From their sons or from (A) others?'"	A). Isaiah 60:10–17			v. 9: Also, to some (A) who were relying on their own righteousness and looking down on everyone else, He told this parable;	A). Proverbs 30:12; Luke 10:29, 16:15
v. 26 "'From others,' he answered. 'Then,' said *Yeshua*, 'The sons are exempt.'"				v. 10: "Two men went up to the Temple to pray, one a *Parush* and the other a tax-collector.	
v. 27: "But to avoid offending them—go to the lake, throw out a line, and take the first fish you catch. Open its mouth, and you will find a *shekel*. Take it and give it to them for me and you."				v. 11: The *Parush* (A) stood and prayed to himself, (B) "O God! I thank you that I am not like the rest of humanity — greedy, dishonest, immoral, or like this tax collector!	A). Psalm 135:2 B). Isaiah 1:15; 58:2; Revelation 3:17
				v. 12: I fast twice a week, I pay tithes on my entire income,…'	

Part 4: Subtopic Scriptural Alignment View—Matthew, Mark, and Luke

Gospel of Mattityahu "Matthew"	OT/NT References	Gospel of Mrk "Mark"	OT/NT References	Gospel of Luk "Luke"	OT/NT References
				Chapter 18 The Parable of the Pharisee and the Tax Collector Continued	
				vs. 13: But the tax-collector standing far off, would not even raise his eyes toward heaven, but beat his breast and said, 'God! Have mercy on me, sinner that I am!'	
				vs. 14: I tell you, this man went down to his home right with God rather than the other. (A) For everyone who exalts himself will be humbled, but everyone who humbles himself will be exalted."	A). Job 22:29; Matthew 23:12; Luke 14:11; James 4:6; 1 Peter 5:5
Chapter 22 The Pharisees: Is It Lawful to Pay Taxes to Caesar?		**Chapter 12 The Pharisees: Is It Lawful to Pay Taxes to Caesar?**		**Chapter 20 The Pharisees: Is It Lawful to Pay Taxes to Caesar?**	
v. 18: "*Yeshua*, however, knowing their malicious intent, said, 'You hypocrites! Why are you trying to trap Me?'"		v. 15: "But He, knowing their (a) hypocrisy, said to them, 'Why are you trying to trap Me?'"	a). Matthew 23:28; Luke 12:1	v. 23: "But He, spotted their craftiness, said to them."	
v. 19: "'Show Me the coin used to pay the tax!' They brought Him a *denarius*."		v. 15: "Bring Me a *denarius* so I can look at it."		v. 24: "Show Me a *denarius!*"	

Gospel of Mattityahu "Matthew"	OT/NT References	Gospel of Mrk "Mark"	OT/NT References	Gospel of Luk "Luke"	OT/NT References
Chapter 22 **The Pharisees: Is It Lawful to Pay Taxes to Caesar? Continued** v. 20: "And He asked them, 'Whose name and picture are these?'"		**Chapter 12** **The Pharisees: Is It Lawful to Pay Taxes to Caesar? Continued** v. 16: "They brought one; and He asked them, 'Whose name and picture are these?' 'The Emperor's,' they replied."		**Chapter 20** **The Pharisees: Is It Lawful to Pay Taxes to Caesar? Continued** v. 24: "Whose name and picture does it have?"	
v. 21: "'The Emperor's,' they replied. *Yeshua said to them, (a) '*Nu, give the Emperor what belongs to the (b) Emperor. And give to God what belongs to (c) God!'"	a). Matthew 17:25 b). Romans 13:1–7; 1 Peter 2:13–15 c). 1 Corinthians 3:23; 6:19–20; 12:27	v. 17: "*Yeshua said, 'Give the Emperor what belongs to the Emperor. And give to (A) God what belongs to God!' And they were amazed at Him."	A). Ecclesiastes 5:4–5	v. 25: "'Then,' He said to them, (a) 'give the Emperor what belongs to the Emperor. And give God what belongs to God!'"	a). Matthew 17:24–27; Romans 13:7; 1 Peter 2:13–17
Chapter 22 **The Sadducees: What about the Resurrection?** v. 29: "*Yeshua answered them, 'The reason you go astray is that you are ignorant both of the (a) *Tanakh and the power of God.'"	a). John 20:9	**Chapter 12** **The Sadducees: What about the Resurrection?** v. 24: "*Yeshua said to them, 'Isn't this the reason that you go astray? Because you are ignorant both of the *Tanakh and the power of God?'"		**Chapter 20** **The Sadducees: What about the Resurrection?** v. 34: "*Yeshua said to them, "In this age, men and woman marry.'"	

Gospel of Mattityahu "Matthew"	OT/NT References	Gospel of Mrk "Mark"	OT/NT References	Gospel of Luk "Luke"	OT/NT References
Chapter 22 The Sadducees: What about the Resurrection? Continued		**Chapter 12 The Sadducees: What about the Resurrection? Continued**		**Chapter 20 The Sadducees: What about the Resurrection? Continued**	
v. 30: "For in the Resurrection, neither men nor women will marry."		v. 25: "For when people rise from the dead, neither men nor women marry."		v. 35: "But those judged worthy of the age to come, and of resurrection from the dead, do not get married."	
v. 30: "Rather, they will be (a) like angels in heaven."	a). 1 John 3:2	v. 25: (a) "They are like angels in heaven."	a). 1 Corinthians 15:42, 49, 52	v. 36: "Because they can no longer die. (a) Being children of the Resurrection, they are like angels; indeed, they are children of God."	a). Philippians 3:11
v. 31: "And as for whether the dead are resurrected, haven't you read what God said to you."		v. 26: "And as for the dead (a) being raised, haven't you read in the book of *Moshe*, in the passage about the bush, how God said to him."	a). John 5:25, 28–29; Acts 26:8; Romans 4:17; Revelation 20:12–13	v. 37: "But even *Moshe* showed that the dead are raised; for in the passage about the bush."	
v. 32: (A) "'I am the God of *Avraham*, the God of *Yitz'chak* and the God of *Ya'akov*'! He is God not of the dead but of the living!"	A). Genesis 17:7; 26:24; 28:21; Exodus 3:6, 15; Mark 12:26; Luke 20:37; Acts 7:32; Hebrews 11:16	v. 26: "'I am the God of *Avraham*, the God of *Yit'chak* and the God of *Ya'akov*?'"		v. 37: (A) "He calls *Adonai* the God of *Avraham*, the God of *Yitz'chak* and the God of *Ya'akov*."	A). Exodus 3:1–6, 15; Acts 7:30–32
v. 32: "He is God not of the dead but of the living!"		v. 27: "He is God not of the dead, but of the living! You are going far astray!"		v. 38: "Now he is not God of the dead, but of the living—(a) to him all are alive."	a). Romans 6:10,11; 14:8–9; Hebrews 11:16

Gospel of Mattityahu "Matthew"	OT/NT References	Gospel of Mrk "Mark"	OT/NT References	Gospel of Luk "Luke"	OT/NT References
Chapter 22 The Scribes: Which Is the First Commandment of All?		**Chapter 12 The Scribes: Which Is the First Commandment of All?**			
v. 37: "He told him, (A) 'You are to love *Adonai your God with all your heart with all your soul and with all your strength.'"	A). Deuteronomy 6:5; 10:12; 30:6	v. 29: "*Yeshua answered, 'The most important is, (A) "*Sh'ma Yisra'el, Adonai Eloheinu, Adonai echad [Hear, O Isra'el, the Lord our God, the Lord is ONE]."'" (See "Commentaries.")	A). Deuteronomy 6:4–5; Isaiah 44:8; 45:22; 46:9; 1 Corinthians 8:6		
		v. 30: "And you are to (A) love *Adonai your God with all your heart, with all your soul, with all your understanding and with all your strength."	A). Deuteronomy 10:12; 30:6; Luke 0:27		
v. 38: "This is the greatest and most important *mitzvah."					
v. 39: "And a second is similar to it, (A) 'You are to love your neighbor as yourself.'"	A). Leviticus 19:18; Matthew 19:19; Mark 12:31; Luke 10:27; Romans 13:9; Galatians 5:14; James 2:8	v. 31: "The second is this: (A) 'You are to love your neighbor as yourself.'"	A). Leviticus 19:18; Matthew 22:39; Galatians 5:14; James 2:8		

Part 4: Subtopic Scriptural Alignment View—Matthew, Mark, and Luke

Gospel of Mattityahu "Matthew"	OT/NT References	Gospel of Mrk "Mark"	OT/NT References	Gospel of Luk "Luke"	OT/NT References
Chapter 22 The Scribes: Which Is the First Commandment of All? Continued		**Chapter 12 The Scribes: Which Is the First Commandment of All? Continued**			
v. 40: (a) "All of the *Torah* and the Prophets are dependent on these two *mitzvoth*."	a). Matthew 7:12; Romans 13:10; 1 Timothy 1:5	v. 31: "There is no other *mitzvah* greater than (b) these."	b). Romans 13:9		
		v. 34: "When *Yeshua* saw that he responded sensibly, He said to him, 'You are not far from the Kingdom of God.' (a) And after that, no one dared put to Him another *sh'eilah*."	a). Matthew 22:46		
Chapter 22 Yeshua: How Can David Call His Descendant Lord?		**Chapter 12 Yeshua: How Can David Call His Descendant Lord?**		**Chapter 20 Yeshua: How Can David Call His Descendant Lord?**	
v. 41: (a) "Then, turning to the assembled *P'rushim*, *Yeshua* put a *sh'eilah* to them."	a). Mark 12:35–37; Luke 20:41–44			v. 41: "But He said to them, (a) 'How is it that people say the Messiah is David's son?'"	a). Matthew 22:41–46; Mark 12:35–37
v. 42: "'Tell Me your view concerning the *Messiah*: (a) whose Son is He?' They said to Him, 'David's.'"	a). Matthew 1:1; 21:9	v. 35: (a) "As *Yeshua* was teaching in the Temple, He asked, 'How is it that the *Torah-teachers* say the *Messiah* is the Son of David?'"	a). Matthew 22:41–46; Luke 20:41–44	v. 42: "For David himself says in the book of Psalms.'"	

214 *Just the Words and Teachings of Jesus Christ*

Gospel of Mattityahu "Matthew"	OT/NT References	Gospel of Mrk "Mark"	OT/NT References	Gospel of Luk "Luke"	OT/NT References
Chapter 22 Yeshua: How Can David Call His Descendant Lord? Continued		**Chapter 12 Yeshua: How Can David Call His Descendant Lord? Continued**		**Chapter 20 Yeshua: How Can David Call His Descendant Lord? Continued**	
v. 43: "'Then how is it,' He asked them, 'that David, inspired by the Spirit calls Him "Lord" when he says.'"		v. 36: "David himself, inspired by the (A) *Rauch HaKodesh said."	A). 2 Samuel 23:2		
v. 44: (A) "*Adonai said to my Lord, 'Sit here at My right hand until I put your enemies under Your feet'?"	A). Psalm 110:1; Matthew 26:64; Mark 16:19; Acts 2:34; 1 Corinthians 15:25; Hebrews 1:13; 10:13	v. 36: "'*Adonai said to the Lord, "Sit here at my right hand until I put your enemies under your feet."'"	B). Psalm 110:1	v. 43: (A) "'*Adonai said to my Lord, 'Sit at my right hand until I make your enemies your footstool.'"	A). Psalm 110:1; Acts 2:34–35
v. 45: "If David thus calls Him 'Lord,' how is He his son?"		v. 37: "David himself calls Him 'Lord'; so how is He His (a) Son?"	a). Acts 2:29–31	v. 44: "David thus calls him, 'Lord.' (a) So how, can he be David's son."	a). Acts 13:22, 23; Romans 1:3; 9:4–5
		Chapter 12 Beware of the Scribes		**Chapter 20 Woe to the Pharisees and Lawyers**	
		v. 38: (a) "As He taught them, (b) He said, 'Watch out for the kind of *Torah-teachers who (c) like to walk around in robes and be greeted deferentially in the marketplaces.'"	a). Mark 4:2 b). Matthew 23:1–7; Luke 20:45–47 c). Matthew 23:7; Luke 11:43	v. 46: (a) "Watch out for the kind of *Torah-teachers that like to walk around in robes and be (b) greeted deferentially in the marketplaces."	a). Matthew 23:5 b). Luke 11:43; 14:7

Part 4: Subtopic Scriptural Alignment View—Matthew, Mark, and Luke

Gospel of Mattityahu "Matthew"	OT/NT References	Gospel of Mrk "Mark"	OT/NT References	Gospel of Luk "Luke"	OT/NT References
Chapter 23 Beware of the Scribes Continued		**Chapter 12 Beware of the Scribes Continued**		**Chapter 20 Woe to the Pharisees and Lawyers Continued**	
		v. 39: "Who like to have the (a) best seats in the *synagogues* and take the places of honor at banquets."	a). Luke 14:7	v.46: "The kind that like to have the best seats in the *synagogues* and the places of honor at banquets."	
v. 14: "Woe to you, scribes and *Pharisees*, hypocrites! (a) For you devour widows' houses, and for a pretense make long prayers. Therefore you will receive-greater condemnation."	a). Mark 12:40; Luke 20:47; 2 Timothy 3:6; Titus 1:10–11	v. 40: (a) "Who like to swallow up widows' houses while making a show of *davening* at great length. Their punishment will be all the worse!"	a). Matthew 23:14	v. 47: "The kind that (a) swallow up widows' houses while making a (b) show of *davening* at great length. Their punishment will be all the worse!"	a). Matthew 23:14 b). Matthew 6:5–6
Chapter 23 Woe to the Scribes and Pharisees					
v. 2: (A) "'The *Torah-teachers* and the *P'rushim*,' He said, 'sit in the seat of *Moshe.*'"	A). Deuteronomy 33:3; Ezra 7:6, 25; Nehemiah 8:4, 8; Malachi 2:7; Mark 12:38; Luke 20:45				
v. 3: "So whatever they tell you take care to do it. But don't do what they do, because they (a) talk but don't act!"	a). Romans 2:19				

Gospel of Mattityahu "Matthew"	OT/NT References	Gospel of Mrk "Mark"	OT/NT References	Gospel of Luk "Luke"	OT/NT References
Chapter 23 Woe to the Scribes and Pharisees Continued				**Chapter 11 Woe to the Scribes and Pharisees**	
v. 4: (a) "They tie heavy loads onto people's shoulders but won't lift a finger to help carry them."	a). Matthew 11:29–30; Luke 11:46; Acts 15:10; Romans 2:17–24; Galatians 5:1; 6:13; Colossians 2:16–17			v. 46: "*Yeshua* said, 'Woe to you *Torah* experts too! (a) You load people down with burdens they can hardly bear, and you won't lift a finger to help them!'"	a). Matthew 23:4
v. 5: "Everything they do is done to be (a) seen by others; for they make their *t'fillin* broad and their *tzitziyot* long."	a). Matthew 6:1–6,16–18				
v. 6: (a) "They love the place of honor at banquets and the best seats in the *synagogues*."	a). Mark 12:38–39; Luke 11:43; 20:46; 3 John 1:9			v. 43: (a) "Woe to your *P'rushim*, because you love the best seat in the *synagogues*."	a). Matthew 23:6; Mark 12:38–39; Luke 14:7; 20:46
v. 7: "And they love being greeted deferentially in the marketplaces and being called '*Rabbi*.'"				v. 43: "And being greeted deferentially in the marketplace!"	
v. 8: (a) "But you are not to let yourselves be called '*Rabbi*'; because you have one *Rabbi [Holy Spirit]*, and you are all each other's brothers."	a). 2 Corinthians 1:24; James 3:1; 1 Peter 5:3				

Gospel of Mattityahu "Matthew"	OT/NT References	Gospel of Mrk "Mark"	OT/NT References	Gospel of Luk "Luke"	OT/NT References
Chapter 23 Woe to the Scribes and Pharisees Continued				**Chapter 11 Woe to the Pharisees and Lawyers Continued**	
v. 9: "And do not call anyone on earth 'Father' because you have (A) one Father [God], and He is in Heaven."	A). Malachi 1:6; Matthew 5:16, 48; 6:1, 9, 14, 26, 32; 7:11				
v. 10: "Nor are you to let yourselves be called 'leaders,' because you have one Leader, and He is the *Messiah [Yeshua]!"*					
v. 11: "The (a) greatest among you must be your servant."	a). Matthew 20:26–27				
v. 12: (A) "For whoever promotes himself will be humbled, and whoever humbles himself will be promoted."	A). Job 22:29; Proverbs 15:33; 29:23; Luke 14:11; 18:14; James 4:6; 1 Peter 5:5				
v. 13: "But (a) woe to you hypocritical *Torah-teachers* and *P'rushim!* For you are shutting the Kingdom of Heaven in people's faces, neither entering yourselves nor allowing those who wish to enter to do so."	a). Luke 11:52			v. 52: (a) "Woe to you *Torah* experts! For you have taken away the key of knowledge! Not only did you yourselves not go in, you also stopped those who were trying to enter!"	a). Matthew 23:13

218 *Just the Words and Teachings of Jesus Christ*

Gospel of Mattityahu "Matthew"	OT/NT References	Gospel of Mrk "Mark"	OT/NT References	Gospel of Luk "Luke"	OT/NT References
Chapter 23 Woe to the Scribes and Pharisees Continued					
v. 15: "Woe to you hypocritical *Torah-teachers* and *P'rushim!* You go about over land and sea to make one proselyte; and when you succeed, you make him twice as fit for *Gei-Hinnom* as you are!"					
v. 16: "Woe to you, you (a) blind guides! You say, 'If (b) someone swears by the Temple, he is not bound by his oath; but if he swears by the gold in the Temple, he is bound.'"	a). Matthew 15:14, 23:24 b). Matthew 5:33–34				
v. 17: "You blind fools! Which is more important? The gold? Or the (A) Temple which makes the gold holy?"	A). Exodus 30:29				
v. 18: "And you say, 'If someone swears by the altar, he is not bound by his oath; but if he swears by the offering at the altar, he is bound!'"					

Gospel of Mattityahu "Matthew"	OT/NT References	Gospel of Mrk "Mark"	OT/NT References	Gospel of Luk "Luke"	OT/NT References
Chapter 23 Woe to the Scribes and Pharisees Continued				**Chapter 11 Woe to the Pharisees and Lawyers Continued**	
v. 19: "Blind men! Which is more important? The sacrifice? Or the (A) altar which makes the sacrifice holy?"	A). Exodus 29:37				
v. 20: "So someone who swears by the altar swears by it and everything on it."					
v. 21: "And someone who swears by the Temple swears by it and the (A) One who lives in it."	A). 1 Kings 8:13; 2 Chronicles 6:2; Psalm 26:8; 132:14				
v. 22: "And someone who swears by Heaven swears by God's (A) Throne and the One who sits on it."	A). Psalm 11:4; Isaiah 66:1; Matthew 5:34; Acts 7:49				
v. 23: "Woe to you hypocritical *Torah-teachers and *P'rushim! (a) You pay your tithes of mint, dill, and cumin; but you have (B) neglected the weightier matters of the *Torah—justice, mercy, trust. These are the things you should have tended to—without neglecting the others!"	a). Matthew 23:13; Luke 11:42; 18:12 B). 1 Samuel 15:22; Hosea 6:6; Micah 6:8; Matthew 9:13; 12:7			v. 42: (a) "But woe to your *P'rushim! You pay your tithes of mint and rue and every garden herb, but you (B) ignore justice and the (c) love of God. You have an obligation to do these things—but without disregarding the others!"	a). Matthew 23:23 B). Micah 6:7–8 c). John 5:42

Gospel of Mattityahu "Matthew"	OT/NT References	Gospel of Mrk "Mark"	OT/NT References	Gospel of Luk "Luke"	OT/NT References
Chapter 23 Woe to the Scribes and Pharisees Continued				**Chapter 11 Woe to the Pharisees and Lawyers Continued**	
v. 24: "Blind guides!—straining out a gnat, meanwhile swallowing a camel!"					
v. 25: "Woe to you hypocritical *Torah-teachers* and *P'rushim!* (a) You clean the outside of the cup and the dish, but inside they are full of robbery, and self-indulgence."	a). Mark 7:4; Luke 11:39			v. 39: (a) "However, the Lord said to him, 'Now then, you *P'rushim*, you clean the outside of the cup and plate; but (B) inside, you are full of robbery and wickedness.'"	a). Matthew 23:25 B). Genesis 6:5; Titus 1:15
v. 26: "Blind *Parush!* First clean the inside of the cup, so that the outside may be clean too."				v. 40: "Fools! Didn't the (A) One who made the outside make the inside too?"	A). Genesis 1:26–27
				v. 41: (A) "Rather, give as alms what is inside, and then everything will be clean for you!"	A). Isaiah 58:7; Daniel 4:27; Luke 12:33; 16:9
v. 27: "Woe to you hypocritical *Torah-teachers* and *P'rushim!* (a) You are like whitewashed tombs, which look fine on the outside but inside are full of dead people's homes and all kinds of rottenness."	a). Luke 11:44; Acts 23:3			v. 44: (a) "Woe to you, (B) because you are like unmarked graves, which people walk over without knowing it."	a). Mattheew 23:27 B). Psalm 5:9

Gospel of Mattityahu "Matthew"	OT/NT References	Gospel of Mrk "Mark"	OT/NT References	Gospel of Luk "Luke"	OT/NT References
Chapter 23 **Woe to the Scribes and Pharisees Continued**				**Chapter 11** **Woe to the Pharisees and Lawyers Continued**	
v. 28: "Likewise, you appear to people to be good and honest, but inwardly you are full of hypocrisy and far from *Torah.'*					
v. 29: (a) "Woe to you hypocritical *Torah-teachers* and *P'rushim!* You build tombs for the prophets and decorate the graves of the *tzaddikim.*"	a). Luke 11:47–48			v. 47: (a) "Woe to you! You build tombs in memory of the prophets, but your fathers murdered them!"	a). Matthew 23:29; Acts 7:52
v. 30: "And you say, 'Had we lived when our fathers did, we would never have taken part in killing the prophets.'"				v. 48: "Thus you testify that you completely approved of what your fathers did—they did the killing, you do the building!"	
v. 31: "In this you testify against yourselves that (a) you are worthy descendants of those who murdered the prophets."	a). Matthew 23:34, 37; Acts 7:51–52; 1 Thessalonians 2:15				
v. 32: (A) "Go ahead then, finish what your father's started!"	A). Genesis 15:16; 1 Thessalonians 2:16				
v. 33: "You snakes! (a) Sons of snakes! How can you escape being condemned to *Gei-Hinnom?*"	a). Matthew 3:7; 12:34; Luke 3:7				

Gospel of Mattityahu "Matthew"	OT/NT References	Gospel of Mrk "Mark"	OT/NT References	Gospel of Luk "Luke"	OT/NT References
Chapter 23 Woe to the Scribes and Pharisees Continued				**Chapter 11 Woe to the Pharisees and Lawyers Continued**	
v. 34: (a) "Therefore I am sending you prophets and sages and *Torah-teachers*—(b) some of them you will kill, indeed, you will have them executed on stakes as criminals; (c) some you will flog in your *synagogues* and pursue from town to town."	a). Matthew 21:34–35; Luke 11:49 b). John 16:2; Acts 7:54–60; 22:19 c). Matthew 10:17; Acts 5:40; 2 Corinthians 11:24–25			v. 49: "Therefore the Wisdom of God said, (A) 'I will send them prophets and emissaries; they will kill some and persecute others.'"	A). Proverbs 1:20; Matthew 23:24
v. 35: "And so, (a) on you will fall the guilt for all the innocent blood that has ever been shed on earth, from the (B) blood of innocent *Hevel* to the (C) blood of *Z'kharyah Ben-Berekyah*, whom you murdered between the Temple and the altar."	a). Revelation 18:24 B). Genesis 4:8 Hebrews 11:4; 1 John 3:12 C). 2 Chronicles 24:20–21			v. 51: (A) "From the blood of *Hevel* to (B) the blood of *Z'kaharyah*, who was killed between the altar and the Holy Place, Yes, I tell you, the responsibility for it will fall on this generation!"	A). Genesis 4:8; 2 Chronicles 36:16 B). 2 Chronicles 24:20–21
v. 36: "Yes! I tell you that all this will fall on this generation!"				v. 50: "So that on this generation will fall the responsibility for all the prophets' blood that has been shed since the world was established."	

Gospel of Mattityahu "Matthew"	OT/NT References	Gospel of Mrk "Mark"	OT/NT References	Gospel of Luk "Luke"	OT/NT References
		Chapter 12 The Widow's Two Mites		**Chapter 21 The Widow's Two Mites**	
		v. 43: "He called *talmidim* to Him and said to them, 'Yes! I tell you, (a) this poor widow has put more in the offering-box than all the others making donations.'"	a). 2 Corinthians 8:12	v. 3: "He said, 'I tell you the truth, (a) this poor widow has put in more than all the others.'"	a). 2 Corinthians 8:12
		v. 44: "For all of them, out of their wealth, have contributed money they can easily spare; but she, out of her poverty, has given everything (A) she had to live on."	A). Deuteronomy 24:6	v. 4: "For they, out of their wealth, have contributed money they could easily spare; but she, out of her poverty, (a) has given all she had to live on."	a). 2 Corinthians 8:12
Chapter 23 Yeshua Laments over Jerusalem				**Chapter 13 Yeshua Laments over Jerusalem**	
v. 37: (a) "*Yerushalayim*! Yerushalayim! You kill the prophets! You (B) stone those who are sent to you! How often (C) I wanted to gather your children, just as a hen gathers her chickens (D) under her wings, but you refused!"	a). Luke 13:34–35 B). 2 Chronicles 24:20–21; 36:15–16; Nehemiah 9:26; Matthew 21:35–36 C). Deuteronomy 32:11–12; Matthew 11:28–30 D). Psalm 17:8; 91:4; Isaiah 49:5			v. 34: (A) "*Yerushalayim! Yerushalayim!* You killed the prophets! You stone those who are sent to you! How often I wanted to gather your children, just as a hen gathers her chickens under her wings, but you refused!"	A). 2 Chronicles 24:20–21; 36:15–16; Matthew 23:37–39

224 *Just the Words and Teachings of Jesus Christ*

Gospel of Mattityahu "Matthew"	OT/NT References	Gospel of Mrk "Mark"	OT/NT References	Gospel of Luk "Luke"	OT/NT References
Chapter 23 Yeshua Laments over Jerusalem Continued				**Chapter 13 Yeshua Laments over Jerusalem Continued**	
v. 38: "Look! God is abandoning your house to you, leaving it desolate."				v. 35: "Look! God is (A) abandoning your house to you!"	A). Leviticus 26:31–32; Psalm 69:25; Isaiah 1:17; Jeremiah 22:5; Daniel 9:27; Micah 3:12
v. 39: "For I tell you, from now on, you will not see Me again until you say, (A) 'Blessed is He who comes in the Name of *Adonai.'"	A). Psalm 118:26; Matthew 21:9			v. 35: "I tell you, you will not see Me again until you say, (B) 'Blessed is He who comes in the Name of *Adonai!'"	B). Psalm 118:26; Matthew 21:9; Mark 11:10; Luke 19:38; John 12:13
Chapter 24 Yeshua Predicts the Destruction of the Temple		**Chapter 13 Yeshua Predicts the Destruction of the Temple**		**Chapter 21 Yeshua Predicts the Destruction of the Temple**	
v. 2: "But He answered them, 'You see all these? Yes! I tell you, they will be totally destroyed—(A) not a single stone will be left standing!'"	A). 1 Kings 9:7; Micah 3:12; Luke 19:44	v. 2: "'You see all these great buildings?' *Yeshua said to him, 'They will be totally destroyed (a) not a single stone will be left standing!'"	a). Luke 19:44	v. 6: "The time is coming when what you see here will be totally destroyed—(A) not a single stone will be left standing!"	A). Isaiah 64:10–11; Lamentations 2:6–9; Micah 3:12; Luke 19:41–44

Part 4: Subtopic Scriptural Alignment View—Matthew, Mark, and Luke

Gospel of Mattityahu "Matthew"	OT/NT References	Gospel of Mrk "Mark"	OT/NT References	Gospel of Luk "Luke"	OT/NT References
Chapter 24 **The Signs of the Times and the End of the Age**		**Chapter 13** **The Signs of the Times and the End of the Age**		**Chapter 21** **The Signs of the Times and the End of the Age**	
v. 4: "*Yeshua* replied: (a) 'Watch out! Don't let anyone fool you!'"	a). Ephesians 5:6; Colossians 2:8, 18; 2 Thessalonians 2:3; 1 John 4:1–3	v. 5: "*Yeshua* began speaking to them: (A) 'Watch out! Don't let anyone fool you!'"	A). Jeremiah 29:8; Ephesians 5:6; Colossians 2:8; 1 Thessalonians 2:3; 2 Thessalonians 2:3	v. 8: "He answered, (a) 'Watch out! Don't be fooled!'"	a). Matthew 24:4; Mark 13:5; Ephesians 5:6; 2 Thessalonians 2:3; 1 John 4:1
v. 5: "For (A) many will come in My Name, saying, 'I am the *Messiah!*' and they will lead many astray."	A). Jeremiah 14:14; John 5:43; Acts 5:36; 1 John 2:18; 4:3	v. 6: "Many will come in My Name, saying, 'I am He!' And they will fool many people."		v. 8: "For many will come in My Name, saying, 'I am He!' and, 'The time has come! Don't go after them.'"	
v. 6: "You will hear the noise of (a) wars nearby and the news of wars far off; see to it that you don't become frightened. Such things must happen, but the end is yet to come."	a). Revelatioon 6:2–4	v. 7: "When you hear the noise of wars nearby and the news of wars far off, don't become frightened. Such things must happen, but the end is yet to come."		v. 9: "And when you hear of (a) wars and revolutions, don't panic. For these things must happen first, but the end will not follow immediately."	a). Revelation 6:4
v. 7: "For peoples will fight each other, (A) nations will fight each other."	A). 2 Chronicles 15:6; Isaiah 19:2; Haggai 2:22; Zechariah 14:13	v. 8: "For peoples will fight each other, and (A) nations will fight each other."	A). Haggai 2:22	v. 10: (a) "Then He told them, 'Peoples will fight each other, nations will fight each other.'"	a). Matthew 24:7

Gospel of Mattityahu "Matthew"	OT/NT References	Gospel of Mrk "Mark"	OT/NT References	Gospel of Luk "Luke"	OT/NT References
Chapter 24 **The Signs of the Times and the End of the Age Continued**		**Chapter 13** **The Signs of the Times and the End of the Age Continued**		**Chapter 21** **The Signs of the Times and the End of the Age Continued**	
v. 7: "And there will be (b) famines and earthquakes in various parts of the world."	b). Acts 11:28; Revelation 6:5–6	v. 8: "There will be earthquakes in various places, their will be famines."		v. 11: "There will be great (a) earthquakes, there will be epidemics and famines in various places, and there will be fearful sights and great signs from Heaven."	a). Revelation 6:12
v. 8: "All this is but the beginning of the 'birth-pains.'"		v. 8: (b) "This is the beginning of the 'birth pains.'"	b). Matthew 24:8		
v. 9: "At that (a) time you will be arrested and handed over to be punished and put to death, and all peoples will hate you because of Me."	a). Matthew 10:17; Luke 21:2; John 16:2; Acts 4:2–3; Revelation 2:10	v. 9: "But you, (a) watch yourselves! They will hand you over to the local *Sanhedrins*, you will be beaten up in synagogues, and on My account you will stand before governors and kings as witnesses to them."	a). Matthew 10:17–18; 24:9; Acts 12:4; Revelation 2:10	v. 12: (a) "But before all this, they will arrest you and persecute you, handing you over to the synagogues and (b) prisons; and (c) you will be brought before kings and governors. This will all be on (d) account of Me."	a). Mark 13:9; John 16:2; Revelation 2:10 b). Acts 4:3; 5:18; 12:4; 16:24 c). Acts 25:23 d). 1 Peter 2:13
		v. 10: "Indeed, the (a) Good News has to be proclaimed first to the *Goyim*."	a). Matthew 24:14	v. 13: "But (a) it will prove an opportunity for you to bear witness."	a). Philippians 1:12–14, 28; 2 Thessalonians 1:5

Gospel of Mattityahu "Matthew"	OT/NT References	Gospel of Mrk "Mark"	OT/NT References	Gospel of Luk "Luke"	OT/NT References
Chapter 24 The Signs of the Times and the End of the Age Continued		**Chapter 13 The Signs of the Times and the End of the Age Continued**		**Chapter 21 The Signs of the Times and the End of the Age Continued**	
		v. 11: (a) "Now when they arrest you and bring you to trial, don't worry beforehand what to say. Rather, say whatever is given you when the time comes for it will not be just you speaking, but (b) the *Rauch HaKodesh."*	a). Matt 10:19–22; Luke 12:11; 21:12–17 b). Acts 2:4; 4:8,31	v. 14: (a) "So make up your minds not to worry, rehearsing your defense beforehand."	a). Matt 10:19, Mark 13:11, Luke 12:11
				v. 15: "For I Myself will give you an eloquence and a wisdom (a) that no adversary will be able to resist or refute."	a). Acts 6:10
v. 10: "At that time many will be trapped into betraying and hating each other."		v. 12: (A) "Brother will betray brother to death, and a father his child; children will turn against their parents and have them put to death."	A). Micah 7:6; Matthew 10:21; 24:10; Luke 21:16	v. 16: (A) "You will be betrayed even by parents, brothers, relatives and friends; (b) some of you they will have put to death."	A). Micah 7:6; Mark 13:12 b). Acts 7:59; 12:2
v. 11: (a) "Many false prophets will appear and (b) fool many peoples."	a).Acts 20:29; 2 Peter 2:1; Revelation 13:11; 19:20 b). 1 Timothy 3:1–3				

Gospel of Mattityahu "Matthew"	OT/NT References	Gospel of Mrk "Mark"	OT/NT References	Gospel of Luk "Luke"	OT/NT References
Chapter 24 **The Signs of the Times and the End of the Age Continued**		**Chapter 13** **The Signs of the Times and the End of the Age Continued**		**Chapter 21** **The Signs of the Times and the End of the Age Continued**	
v. 12: "And many people's love will grow (a) cold because of increased distance from *Torah.*"	a). 2 Thessalonianss 2:3; 2 Timothy 3:1–3	v. 13: "And (a) everyone will hate you because of Me."	a). Matthew 24:9; Luke 21:17; John 15:21	v. 17: "And everyone will hate (a) you because of Me."	a). Matthew 10:22
v. 13: (a) "But whoever holds out till the end will be delivered."	a). Matthew 10:22; Mark 13:13	v. 13: "But (B) whoever holds out till the end will be delivered."	B). Daniel 12:12; Matthew 10:22; 24:13; Revelation 2:10	v. 19: "By standing firm you will save your lives."	
				v. 18: (a) "But not a hair on your head will be lost."	a). Matt 10:30, Luke 12:7
v. 14: "And this (a) Good News about the Kingdom will be (b) announced throughout the whole world as a witness to all the *Goyim.* It is then that the end will come."	a). Matthew 4:23 b). Romans 10:18; Colossians 1:6, 23				
v. 15: (a) "'So when you see the (B) abomination that causes desolation spoken about through the prophet Dani'el standing in the Holy Place' (C) *[let the reader understand the allusion].*"	a). Luke 21:20; John 11:48; Acts 6:13; 21:28 B). Daniel 9:27; 11:31; 12:11 C). Daniel 9:23	v. 14: (a) "'Now when you see the (B) abomination that causes devastation standing where it ought not to be' *[let the reader understand this allusion].*"	a). Matthew 24:15 B). Daniel 9:27; 11:31; 12:11	v. 20: (a) "However, when you see *Yerushalayim* surrounded by armies, then you are to understand that she is about to be destroyed."	a). Matthew 24:15; Mark 13:14

Gospel of Mattityahu "Matthew"	OT/NT References	Gospel of Mrk "Mark"	OT/NT References	Gospel of Luk "Luke"	OT/NT References
Chapter 24 **The Great Tribulation**		**Chapter 13** **The Great Tribulation**		**Chapter 21** **The Destruction of Yerushalayim**	
v. 16: "That will be the time for those in *Y'hudah to escape to the hills."		v. 14: "That will be the time (c) for those in *Y'hudah to escape to the hills."	c). Luke 21:21	v. 21: "Those in *Y'hudah must escape to the hills, those inside the city must get out, and those in the country must not enter it."	
v. 17: "If someone is on the roof, he must not go down to gather his belongings from his house."		v. 15: "If someone is on the roof, he must not go down and enter his house to take any of his belongings."			
v. 18: "If someone is in the field, he must not turn back to get his coat."		v. 16: 'If someone is in the field, he must not turn back to get his coat."			
				v. 22: "For these are the days of vengeance, when (A) everything that has been written in the *Tanakh will come true."	A). Isaiah 63:4; Daniel 9:24–27; Hosea 9:7; Zechariah 11:1
v. 19: (a) "What a terrible time it will be for pregnant women and nursing mothers!"	a). Luke 23:29	v. 17: (a) "What a terrible time it will be for pregnant women and nursing mothers!"	a). Luke 21:23	v. 23: (a) "What a terrible time it will be for pregnant women and nursing mothers! For there will be great distress in the Land and judgment on the people."	a). Matthew 24:19

230 *Just the Words and Teachings of Jesus Christ*

Gospel of Mattityahu "Matthew"	OT/NT References	Gospel of Mrk "Mark"	OT/NT References	Gospel of Luk "Luke"	OT/NT References
Chapter 24 **The Great Tribulation Continued**		**Chapter 13** **The Great Tribulation Continued**		**Chapter 21** **The Destruction of Yerushalayim Continued**	
				v. 24: "Some will fall by the edge of the sword, others will be carried into all the countries of the *Goyim,* and *Yerushalayim* will be trampled down by the *Goyim* (A) until the age of the *Goyim* has run its course."	A). Daniel 9:27; 12:7
v. 20: "Pray that you will not have to escape in winter or on *Shabbat.*"		v. 18: "Pray that it may not happen in winter."			
v. 21: "For (A) there will be trouble then worse than there has ever been from the beginning of the world until now, and there will be nothing like it again!"	A). Daniel 9:26	v. 19: (A) "For there will be worse trouble at that time than there has ever been from the beginning, when God created the universe, until now; and there will be nothing like it again."	A). Daniel 9:26; 12:1; Joel 2:2 Matthew 24:21; Mark 10:6		
v. 22: "Indeed, if the length of this time had not been limited, no one would survive; (A) but for the sake of those who have been chosen, its length will be limited."	A). Isaiah 65:8–9; Zechariah 14:2	v. 20: "Indeed, if God had not limited the duration of the trouble, no one would survive; but for the sake of the elect, those whom He has chosen, He has limited it."			

Gospel of Mattityahu "Matthew"	OT/NT References	Gospel of Mrk "Mark"	OT/NT References	Gospel of Luk "Luke"	OT/NT References
Chapter 24 **The Great Tribulation Continued**		**Chapter 13** **The Great Tribulation Continued**			
v. 23: (a) "At that time, if someone says to you, 'Look! Here's the *Messiah!*' or, 'There He is!' don't believe him."	a). Mark 13:21; Luke 17:23	v. 21: (a) "At that time, if anyone says to you, 'Look! Here's the *Messiah!*' or 'See, there He is!'—don't believe him!"	a). Matthew 24:23; Luke 17:23; 21:8		
v. 24: "For there will appear (A) false Messiahs and false prophets performing great miracles—amazing things!—So as to fool (b) even the chosen, if possible."	A). Deuteronomy 13:1; John 4:48; 2 Thessalonians 2:9; Revelation 13:13 b). John 6:37; Romans 8:28; 2 Timothy 2:19	v. 22: "There will appear false Messiahs and false prophets performing signs and (A) wonders for the purpose, if possible, of misleading the chosen."	A). Deuteronomy 13:1–3; Revelation 13:13–14		
v. 25: "There! I have told you in advance!"		v. 23: "But you, (a) watch out! I have told you everything in advance!"	a). John 16:1–4; 2 Peter 3:17		
Chapter 24 **The Great Tribulation Continued**					
v. 26: "So if people say to you, 'Listen He's out in the desert! Don't go'; or, 'Look! He's hidden away in a secret room!' don't believe it."					

232 *Just the Words and Teachings of Jesus Christ*

Gospel of Mattityahu "Matthew"	OT/NT References	Gospel of Mrk "Mark"	OT/NT References	Gospel of Luk "Luke"	OT/NT References
Chapter 24 **The Great Tribulation Continued**				**Chapter 17** **The Coming of the Kingdom**	
v. 27: (a) "For when the Son of Man does come, it will be like lighting that flashes out of the east and fills the sky to the western horizon."	a). Luke 17:24				
v. 28: (A) "Whenever there's a dead body, that's where you will find vultures."	A). Job 39:30; Ezekiel 39:17; Habakkuk 1:8; Luke 17:37			v. 37: "They asked Him, (A) 'Where, Lord?' He answered, 'Wherever there's a dead body, that's where the vultures gather.'"	A). Job 39:30; Matthew 24:28
Chapter 24 **The Coming of the Son of Man**		**Chapter 13** **The Coming of the Son of Man**		**Chapter 21** **The Coming of the Son of Man**	
v. 29: "But (A) immediately following the trouble of those times."	A). Daniel 7:11	v. 24: (A) "In those days, after that trouble."	A). Zephaniah 1:15; Matthew 24:29	v. 25: (A) "There will appear signs in the sun, moon and stars; and on earth, nations will be in anxiety and bewilderment at the sound and surge of the sea."	A). Isaiah 13:9–10, 13; Matthew 24:29; Mark 13:24; 2 Peter 3:10–12
v. 29: (B) "The sun will grow dark, the moon will stop shinning."	B). Isaiah 13:10; 24:23; Ezekiel 32:7; Joel 2:10, 31; 3:15; Amos 5:20; 8:9; Zephaniah 1:15	v. 24: (A) "The sun will grow dark, the moon will stop shinning."	A). Zephaniah 1:15; Matthew 24:29	v. 26: "As people faint with fear at the prospect of what is overtaking the world; (a) for the powers in Heaven will be shaken."	a). Matthew 24:29

Gospel of Mattityahu "Matthew"	OT/NT References	Gospel of Mrk "Mark"	OT/NT References	Gospel of Luk "Luke"	OT/NT References
Chapter 24 **The Coming of the Son of Man Continued**		**Chapter 13** **The Coming of the Son of Man Continued**		**Chapter 21** **The Coming of the Son of Man Continued**	
v. 29: (b) "The stars will fall from the sky, and the powers in Heaven will be shaken."	b). Matthew 24:29–35; Acts 2:20; Revelation 6:12–17; 8:12	v. 25: "The stars will fall from the sky, and the powers in Heaven will be (A) shaken."	A). Isaiah 13:10; 34:4; Hebrews 12:26; Revelation 6:13	v. 27: "And then they will see the Son of Man (A) coming in a cloud with tremendous power and glory."	A). Daniel 7:13; Matthew 16:27; 24:30; 26:64; Mark 13:26; Revelation 1:7; 14:14
v. 30: (A) "Then the sign of the Son of Man will appear in the sky, all the tribes of the Land will mourn, (B) and they will see the Son of Man coming on the clouds of Heaven with tremendous power and glory."	A). Daniel 7:13–14; Matthew 16:27; 24:3, 37, 39 B). Zechariah 12:12	v. 26: (A) "Then they will see the Son of Man coming in clouds with tremendous power and glory."	A). Isaiah 13:10; 34:4; Hebrews 12:26; Revelation 6:13		
v. 31: (A) "He will send out His angels with a great *shofar;* and they will gather together His chosen people from the four winds, from one end of Heaven to the other."	A). Exodus 19:16; Deuteronomy 30:4; Isaiah 27:13; Zechariah 9:14; 1 Corinthians 15:52; 1 Thessalonians 4:16; Hebrews 12:19; Revelation 8:2; 11:15	v. 27: "He will send out His angels and gather together His chosen people from the four winds, from the ends of the earth to the ends of Heaven."	A). Daniel 7:13–14; Matthew 16:27; 24:30; Mark 14:62; Acts 1:11; 1 Thessalonians 4:16; 2 Thessalonians 1:7, 10; Revelation 1:7	v. 28: "When these things start to happen, stand up and hold your heads high; because (a) you are about to be liberated!"	a). Romans 8:19, 23

Gospel of Mattityahu "Matthew"	OT/NT References	Gospel of Mrk "Mark"	OT/NT References	Gospel of Luk "Luke"	OT/NT References
Chapter 24 **The Parable of the Fig Tree**		**Chapter 13** **The Parable of the Fig Tree**		**Chapter 21** **The Parable of the Fig Tree**	
v. 32: "Now let the (a) fig tree teach you its lesson."	a). Luke 21:29	v. 28: (a) "Now let the fig tree teach you its lesson."	a). Matthew 24:33	v. 29: "Then [the Lord] told them a parable: 'Look at the fig tree, indeed, all the trees.'"	
v. 32: "When its branches begin to sprout and leaves appear, you know that summer is approaching."		v. 28: "When its branches begin to sprout and leaves appear, you know that summer is approaching."		v. 30: "As soon as they sprout leaves, you can see for yourselves that summer is near."	
v. 33: "In the same way, when you see all these things, you are to know (a) that the time is near, right at the door."	a). James 5:9; Revelation 3:20	v. 29: "In the same way, when you see all these things happening, you are to know that the time is near, right at the door."		v. 31: "In the same way, when you see these things taking place, you are to know that the Kingdom of God is near!"	
v. 34: "Yes! I tell you that this (a) people will certainly not pass away before all these things happen."	a). Matthew 10:23; 16:28	v. 30: "Yes! I tell you that this people will certainly not pass away before all these things happen."		v. 32: "Yes! I tell you that this people will certainly not pass away before it has all happened."	
v. 35: (A) "Heaven and earth will pass away, but My words will never pass away."	A). Psalm 102:25–26; Isaiah 51:6; Mark 13:31; Luke 21:33; 1 Peter 1:23–25; 2 Peter 3:10	v. 31: "Heaven and earth will pass away, but (A) My words will certainly not pass away."	A). Isaiah 40:8; 2 Peter 3:7, 10, 12	v. 33: (A) "Heaven and earth will pass away, but (B) My words will certainly not pass away."	A). Isaiah 51:6; Matthew 24:35; Hebrews 1:10–11; 2 Peter 3:7, 10, 12 B). Isaiah 40:8; Luke 16:17; 1 Peter 1:24–25

Gospel of Mattityahu "Matthew"	OT/NT References	Gospel of Mrk "Mark"	OT/NT References	Gospel of Luk "Luke"	OT/NT References
				Chapter 21 **The Importance of Watching**	
				v. 34: (a) "But keep watch on yourselves, or your ears will become dulled by carousing, drunkenness and the (b) worries of everyday living, and that Day will be sprung upon you suddenly like a trap!"	a). Matthew 24:42–44; Mark 4:19; Luke 12:40, 45; Romans 13:13; 1 Thessalonians 5:6; 1 Peter 4:7 b). Luke 8:14
				v. 35: "For (a) it will close in on everyone, no matter where they live, throughout the whole world."	a). 1 Thessalonians 5:2; 2 Peter 3:10; Revelation 3:3; 16:15
				v. 36: (a) "Stay alert, always (b) praying that you will have the (c) strength to escape all the things that will happen and to (D) stand in the presence of the Son of Man."	a). Matthew 24:42; 25:13; Mark 13:33; Luke 12:40 b). Luke 18:1; Ephesians 6:18; Colossians 4:2; 1 Thessalonians 5:17 c). Luke 20:35 D). Psalm 1:5; Ephesians 6:13

Just the Words and Teachings of Jesus Christ

Gospel of Mattityahu "Matthew"	OT/NT References	Gospel of Mrk "Mark"	OT/NT References	Gospel of Luk "Luke"	OT/NT References
Chapter 24 **No One Knows the Day and Hour**		**Chapter 13** **No One Knows the Day and Hour**		**Chapter 17** **The Coming of the Kingdom**	
v. 36: (a) "But when that day and hour come, no one knows—not the angels in heaven, not the Son, (B) only the Father."	a). Mark 13:32; Acts 1:7; 1 Thessalonians 5:2; 2 Peter 3:10 B). Zechariah 14:7	v. 32: "However, when that day and hour will come, (a) no one knows—not the angels in heaven, not the Son, just the (b) Father."	a). Matthew 25:13 b). Matthew 24:36; Acts 1:7	v. 20: "The *P'rushim* asked *Yeshua* when the Kingdom of God would come. 'The Kingdom of God,' He answered, 'does not come with visible signs.'"	
				v. 21: (a) "Nor will people be able to say, 'Look! Here it is!' or, 'Over there!' Because, you see, (b) the Kingdom of God is among you."	a). Luke 17:23 b). Romans 14:17
				v. 22: "Then He said to His *talmidim,* (a) 'The time is coming when you will long to see even one of the days of the Son of Man, but you will not see it.'"	a). Matthew 9:15; Mark 2:20; Luke 5:35; John 17:12
				v. 23: (a) "People will say to you, 'Look! Right here!' or, 'See! Over there!' Don't run off, don't follow them."	a). Matthew 24:23; Mark 13:21; Luke 21:8
				v. 24: "Because the Son of Man in His day (a) will be like lightening that flashes and lights up the sky from one horizon to the other."	a). Matthew 24:27

Gospel of Mattityahu "Matthew"	OT/NT References	Gospel of Mrk "Mark"	OT/NT References	Gospel of Luk "Luke"	OT/NT References
Chapter 24 No One Knows the Day and Hour Continued				**Chapter 17 The Coming of the Kingdom Continued**	
				v. 25: (a) "But first He must endure horrible suffering and be (b) rejected by this generation."	a). Matthew 26:67; 27:29–31; Mark 8:31; 9:31; 10:33 b). Luke 9:22
v. 37: "For the Son of Man's coming will be just as it was in the days of *Noach.*				v. 26: (a) "Also, at the time of the Son of Man, (B) it will be just as it was (C) at the time of (d)*Noach.*"	a). Matthew 24:37–39 B). Genesis 6:5–7 C). Genesis 6:8–13
v. 38: (A) "Back then, before the Flood, people went on eating and drinking, taking wives and becoming wives, right up till the day *Noach* entered the ark."	A). Genesis 6:3–5; Luke 17:26; 1 Peter 3:20			v. 27: "People ate and drank, and men and women married, right up until the (A) day *Noach* entered the ark; then the flood came and (B) destroyed them all."	A). Genesis 7:1–16 B). Genesis 7:19–23
v. 39: "And they didn't know what was happening until the Flood came and swept them all away. It will be just like that when the Son of Man comes."					

Gospel of Mattityahu "Matthew"	OT/NT References	Gospel of Mrk "Mark"	OT/NT References	Gospel of Luk "Luke"	OT/NT References
				Chapter 17 The Coming of the Kingdom Continued	
				v. 28: (A) "Likewise, as it was in the time of *Lot*—people ate and drank, bought and sold, planted and built."	A). Genesis 19
				v. 29: "But (A) the day *Lot* left *S'dom,* fire and sulfur rained down from heaven and destroyed them all."	A). Genesis 19:16, 24, 29; 2 Peter 2:6–7
				v. 30: "That is how it will be on the day the Son of Man (a) is revealed."	a). Matthew 16:27; 1 Corinthians 1:8; Colossians 3:4; 2 Thessalonians 1:7; 1 Peter 1:7; 4:13; 1 John 2:28
				v. 31: "On that day, if (a) someone is on the roof with his belongings in his house, he must not go down to take them away. Similarly, if someone is in the field, he must not turn back."	a). Matthew 24:17–18; Mark 13:15
				v. 32: "Remember *Lot's wife!*"	

Gospel of Mattityahu "Matthew"	OT/NT References	Gospel of Mrk "Mark"	OT/NT References	Gospel of Luk "Luke"	OT/NT References
Chapter 24 No One Knows the Day and Hour Continued		**Chapter 13 No One Knows the Day and Hour Continued**		**Chapter 17 The Coming of the Kingdom Continued**	
				v. 33: (a) "Whoever aims at preserving his own life will lose it, but whoever loses his life will stay alive."	a). Matt 10:39; 16:25, Mark 8:35, Luke 9:24 John 12;25
v. 40: (a) "Then there will be two men in a field—one will be taken and the other left behind."	a). Luke 17:34	v. 34: (a) "It's like a man who travels away from home, puts his servants in (b) charge, each with his own task, and tells the doorkeeper to stay alert."	a). Matthew 24:45; 25:14 b). Matthew 16:19	v. 34: (a) "I tell you, on that night there will be two people in one bed—one will be taken and the other left behind."	a). Matthew 24:40–41; 1 Thessalonians 4:17
v. 41: "There will two women grinding flour at the mill—one will be taken and the other left behind."				v. 35: "There will be (a) two women grinding grain together—one will be taken and the other left behind."	a). Matthew 24:40–41
v. 42: (a) "So stay alert, because you don't know on what day your Lord will come."	a). Matthew 25:13; Luke 21:36; 1 Thessalonians 5:6	v. 35: (a) "So stay alert! For you don't know when the owner of the house will come."	a). Matthew 24:42, 44		
v. 43: (a) "But you do know this: had the owner of the house known when the thief was coming, he would have stayed awake and not allowed his house to be broken into."	a).Luke 12:39; 1 Thessalonians 5:2; Revelation 3:3	v. 36: "Whether it will be evening, midnight, cockcrow or morning—you don't want him to come suddenly and find you sleeping!"		12:39: (a) "But notice this; no house-owner would let his house be broken into if he knew when the thief was coming."	a). Matthew 24:43; 1 Thessalonians 5:2; 2 Peter 3:10; Revelation 3:3; 16:15

Gospel of Mattityahu "Matthew"	OT/NT References	Gospel of Mrk "Mark"	OT/NT References	Gospel of Luk "Luke"	OT/NT References
Chapter 24 **No One Knows the Day and Hour Continued**		**Chapter 13** **No One Knows the Day and Hour Continued**		**Chapter 17** **The Coming of the Kingdom Continued**	
v. 44: (a) "Therefore you too must always be ready, for the Son of Man will come when you are not expecting Him."	a). Luke 12:35–40	v. 37: "And what I say to you, I say to everyone: stay alert!"		12:40: (a) "You too, be ready! For the Son of Man will come when you are least expecting Him."	a). Matthew 24:44; 25:13; Mark 13:33; Luke 21:34, 36; 1 Thessalonians 5:6; 2 Peter 3:12
				Chapter 12 **The Faithful Servant and the Evil Servant**	
				v. 35: (a) "Be dressed for action and have (b) your lamps lit."	a). 1 Peter 1:13 b). Matthew 25:1–13
				v. 36: "Like people waiting for their master's return after a wedding feast; so that when he comes and knocks, they will open the door for him without delay."	
				v. 37: (a) "Happy the slaves whom the master finds alert when he comes! Yes! I tell you he will put on his work clothes, seat them at the table, and come serve them himself!"	a). Matthew 24:46

Gospel of Mattityahu "Matthew"	OT/NT References	Gospel of Mrk "Mark"	OT/NT References	Gospel of Luk "Luke"	OT/NT References
Chapter 24 The Faithful Servant and the Evil Servant Continued				**Chapter 12 The Faithful Servant and the Evil Servant Continued**	
v. 45: (a) "Who is the faithful and sensible servant whose master puts him in charge of the household staff, to give them their food at the proper time?"	a). Luke 12:42–46			v. 42: "The Lord replied, '*Nu, (a) who is the faithful and sensible manager whose master puts him in charge of the household staff to give them their share of food at the proper time?'"	a). Matthew 24:45–46; 25:21; 1 Corinthians 4:2
v. 46: (a) "It will go well with that servant if he is found doing his job when his master comes."	a). Revelation 16:15			v. 43: "It will go well with that servant if he is found doing his job when his master comes."	
				v. 38: "Whether it is late at night or early in the morning if this is how he finds them, those slaves are happy."	
v. 47: "Yes, I tell you that (a) he will put him in charge of all he owns."	a). Matthew 25:21, 23; Luke 22:29			v. 44: (a) "Yes, I tell you he will put him in charge of all he owns."	a). Matthew 24:47; 25:21; Revelation 3:21
v. 48: "But if that servant is wicked and says to himself, 'My master (a) is taking his time.'"	a). 2 Peter 3:4–9			v. 45: (a) "But if that servant says to himself, 'My master is taking his time coming,'"	a). Matthew 24:48 2 Peter 3:3–4
v. 49: "And he starts beating up his fellow servants and spends his time eating and drinking with drunkards."				v. 45: "And starts bullying the men and women servants and eating and drinking, getting drunk."	

242 *Just the Words and Teachings of Jesus Christ*

Gospel of Mattityahu "Matthew"	OT/NT References	Gospel of Mrk "Mark"	OT/NT References	Gospel of Luk "Luke"	OT/NT References
Chapter 24 The Faithful Servant and the Evil Servant Continued				**Chapter 12 The Faithful Servant and the Evil Servant Continued**	
v. 50: "Then his master will come on a day the servant does not expect, at a time he (a) doesn't know."	a). Mark 13:32			v. 46: "Then his master will come on a (a) day when the servant isn't expecting him, at a time he doesn't know in advance."	a). 1 Thessalonians 5:3
v. 51: "And he will cut him in two and put him with the hypocrites, (a) where people will wail and grind their teeth!"	a). Matthew 8:12; 25:30			v. 46: "His master will cut him in two and put him with the disloyal."	
				v. 47: "Now the (A) servant who (b) knew what his master wanted but didn't prepare or act according to his will, will be whipped with many lashes."	A). Numbers 15:30; Deuteronomy 25:2; John 9:41; 15:22; Acts 17:30 b). James: 4:17
				v. 48: (A) "However, the one who did what deserves a beating, but didn't know, will receive few lashes. From him who has been given much, much will be demanded—from someone to whom people entrust much, they ask still more."	A). Leviticus 5:17; Numbers 15:29; 1 Timothy 1:13

Gospel of Mattityahu "Matthew"	OT/NT References	Gospel of Mrk "Mark"	OT/NT References	Gospel of Luk "Luke"	OT/NT References
Chapter 25 **The Parable of the Wise and Foolish Virgins**					
v. 1: "The Kingdom of Heaven at that time will be like ten bridesmaids who took their lamps and went out to meet (a) the groom."	A). Ephesians 5:29–30; Revelation 19:7; 21:2, 9				
v. 2: (a) "Five of them were foolish and five were sensible."	a). Matthew 13:47; 22:10				
v. 3: "The foolish ones took lamps with them but no oil."					
v. 4: "Whereas the others took flasks of oil with their lamps."					
v. 5: "Now the bridegroom was late, (a) so they all went to sleep."	a). 1 Thessalonians 4:16				
v. 6: "It was the middle of the night when the (a) cry rang out, 'The bridegroom is here! Go out to meet him!'"	a). Matthew 24:31; 1 Thessalonians 4:16				
v. 7: "The girls all woke up and (a) prepared their lamps."	a). Luke 12:35				
v. 8: "The foolish ones said to the sensible ones, 'Give us some of you oil, because our lamps are going out!'"					

Gospel of Mattityahu "Matthew"	OT/NT References	Gospel of Mrk "Mark"	OT/NT References	Gospel of Luk "Luke"	OT/NT References
Chapter 25 The Parable of the Wise and Foolish Virgins Continued					
v. 9: "'No,' they replied, 'there may not be enough for both you and us. Go to the oil dealers and buy some for yourself.'"					
v. 10: "But as they were going off to buy, the bridegroom came. Those who were ready went with him to the wedding feast, and the (a) door was shut."	a). Matthew 7:21; Luke 13:25				
v. 11: "Later, the other bridesmaids came. (a) 'Sir! Sir!' They cried. 'Let us in!'"	a). Matthew 7:21–23; Luke 13:25–30				
v. 12: "But he answered, 'Indeed! I tell you, (A) I don't know you!'"	A). Psalm 5:5; Habakkuk 1:13; John 9:31				
v. 13: (a) "So stay alert, because you (b) know neither the day nor the hour."	a). Mark 13:35; Luke 21:36; 1 Thessalonians 5:6 b). Matthew 24:36, 42				

Part 4: Subtopic Scriptural Alignment View—Matthew, Mark, and Luke

Gospel of Mattityahu "Matthew"	OT/NT References	Gospel of Mrk "Mark"	OT/NT References	Gospel of Luk "Luke"	OT/NT References
Chapter 25 **The Parable of the Talents**				**Chapter 19** **The Parable of the Minas**	
v. 14: (b) "For it will be like a man about to leave (a) home for a while, who entrusted his possessions to his servants."	a). Luke 19:12–27 b). Matthew 21:33			v. 12: (a) "Therefore He said, 'A nobleman went to a country far away to have himself crowned king and then return.'"	a). Matthew 25:14–30; Mark 13:34
				v. 13: "Calling ten of his servants, he gave them ten *manim* [a maneh is about three months' wages] and said to them, 'Do business with this while I'm away.'"	
v. 15: "To one he gave five *talents* [equivalent to a hundred years' wages]: to another, two talents, and to another, one talent—(a) to each according to his ability. Then he left."	a). Romans 12:6; 1 Corinthians 12:7, 11, 29; Ephesians 4:11				
v. 16: "The one who had received five talents immediately went out, invested it and earned another five."				v. 16: "The first one came in and said, 'Sir, your *maneh* has earned ten more *manim.*'"	
				v. 17: (a) "'Excellent!' He said to him. 'You are a good servant. Because you have been (b) trustworthy in a small matter, I am putting in charge of ten towns.'"	a). Matthew 25:21,23 b). Luke 16:10

246 *Just the Words and Teachings of Jesus Christ*

Gospel of Mattityahu "Matthew"	OT/NT References	Gospel of Mrk "Mark"	OT/NT References	Gospel of Luk "Luke"	OT/NT References
Chapter 25 **The Parable of the Talents Continued**				**Chapter 19** **The Parable of the Minas Continued**	
v. 17: "Similarly, the one given two earned another two."					
v. 18: "But the one given one talent went off, dug a hole in the ground and hid his master's money."					
				v. 14: (a) "But his countrymen hated him, and they sent a delegation after him to say, 'We don't want this man to rule over us.'"	a). John 1:11
v. 19: "After a long time, the master of those servants returned to settle accounts with them."				v. 15: "However, he returned, having been made king, and sent for the servants to whom he had given the money, to find out what each one had earned in his business dealings."	
v. 20: "The one who had received five talents came forward brining the other five and said, 'Sir, you gave me five talents; here, I have made five more.'"				v. 18: "The second one came and said, 'Sir, your *maneh* has earned five more *manim*.'"	

Part 4: Subtopic Scriptural Alignment View—Matthew, Mark, and Luke

Gospel of Mattityahu "Matthew"	OT/NT References	Gospel of Mrk "Mark"	OT/NT References	Gospel of Luk "Luke"	OT/NT References
Chapter 25 **The Parable of the Talents Continued**				**Chapter 19** **The Parable of the Minas Continued**	
v. 21: "His master said to him, 'Excellent! You are a good and trustworthy servant. You have been (a) faithful, with a small amount so (b) I will put you in charge of a large amount. Come and join in your master's (c) happiness!'"	a). Luke 16:10; 1 Corinthians 4:2; 2 Timothy 4:7–8 b). Matthew 24:47; 25:34, 46; Luke 12:44; 22:29–30; Revelation 3:21: 21:7 c). 2 Timothy 2:12; Hebrews 12:2; 1 Peter 1:8			v. 19: "And to this one he said, 'You be charge of five towns.'"	
v. 22: "Also the one who had received two came forward and said, 'Sir, you gave me two talents; here I have made two more.'"					
v. 23: "His master said to him, (a) 'Excellent! You are a good and trustworthy servant. You have been faithful with a small amount, so I will put you in charge of a large amount. Come and join in your master's (B) happiness!'"	a). Matthew 24:45, 47; 25:21 B). Psalm 16:11; John 15:10–11				

Gospel of Mattityahu "Matthew"	OT/NT References	Gospel of Mrk "Mark"	OT/NT References	Gospel of Luk "Luke"	OT/NT References
Chapter 25 **The Parable of the Talents Continued**				**Chapter 19** **The Parable of the Minas Continued**	
v. 24: "Now the one who had received one talent came forward and said, 'I knew you were a hard man. You harvest where you didn't plant and gather where you didn't sow seed.'"				v. 21: (a) "Because I was afraid of you—you take out what you didn't put in, and you harvest what you didn't plant."	
v. 25: "I was afraid, so I went and hid your talent in the ground. Here! Take what belongs to you!"				v. 20: "Then another one came and said, 'Sir, here is your *maneh. I kept it hidden in a piece of cloth.'"	
v. 26: "'You (a) wicked, lazy servant!' said his master, 'So you knew, did you, that I harvest where I haven't planted? And that I gather where I don't sow seed?'"	a). Matthew 18:32; Luke 19:22			v. 22: "To him the master said, 'You wicked servant! I will judge you by (A) your own words! So you knew, did you, (b) that I was a severe man taking out what I didn't put in and harvesting what I didn't plant.'"	A). 2 Samuel 1:16; Job 15:6; Matthew 12:37 b). Matthew 25:26
v. 27: "Then you should have deposited my money with the bankers, so that when I returned, I would at least have gotten back interest with my capital!"				v. 23: "Then why didn't you put my money in the bank Then, when I returned, I would have gotten it back with interest!"	
v. 28: "Take the *talent from him and give it to the one who has ten."				v. 24: "To those standing by, he said, 'Take the *maneh from him and give it to the one with ten *manim.'"	

Gospel of Mattityahu "Matthew"	OT/NT References	Gospel of Mrk "Mark"	OT/NT References	Gospel of Luk "Luke"	OT/NT References
Chapter 25 **The Parable of the Talents Continued**				**Chapter 19** **The Parable of the Minas Continued**	
v. 29: (a) "For everyone who has something will be given more, so that he will have more than enough; but from anyone who has nothing; even what he does have will be taken away."	a). Matthew 13:12; Mark 4:25; Luke 8:18; John 15:2			v. 26: "But the master answered, 'I tell you, (a) everyone who has something will be given more; but from anyone who has nothing, even what he does have will be taken away.'"	a). Matthew 13:12; 25:29; Mark 4:25; Luke 8:18
v. 30: "As for this worthless servant, (a) throw him out in the dark, (b) where people will wail and (C) grind their teeth!"	a). Matthew 8:12; 22:13; Luke 13:28 b). Matthew 7:23; 8:12; 24:51 C). Psalm 112:10			v. 27: "However, as for these enemies of mine who did not want me to be their king, bring them here and execute them in my presence!"	
				Chapter 19 **Yeshua Weeps over Jerusalem**	
				v. 41: "When *Yeshua had come closer and could see the city, (A) He wept over it."	A). Isaiah 53:3; John 11:35
				v. 42: "Saying, 'If you only knew (A) today (b) what is needed for (c) *shalom! But for now it is hidden from your sight.'"	A). Psalm 95:7–8; Hebrews 3:13 b). Luke 1:77–79; Acts 10:36 c). Romans 5:1

250 *Just the Words and Teachings of Jesus Christ*

Gospel of Mattityahu "Matthew"	OT/NT References	Gospel of Mrk "Mark"	OT/NT References	Gospel of Luk "Luke"	OT/NT References
				Chapter 19 Yeshua Weeps over Jerusalem Continued	
				v. 43: "For the days are coming upon you when your enemies will (A) set up a barricade around you, encircle you, hem you in on every side."	A). Isaiah 29:3–4; Jeremiah 6:3, 6; Luke 21:20
				v. 44: (A) "And dash you to the ground, you and your children within your walls, (b) leaving not one stone standing on another—and all (C) because you did not recognize your opportunity when God offered it!"	A). 1 Kings 9:7–8; Micah 3:12 b). Matthew 24:2; Mark 13:2; Luke 21:6 C). Daniel 9:24; Luke 1:68, 78; 1 Peter 2:12
Chapter 25 The Son of Man Will Judge the Nations					
v. 31: (A) "When the Son of Man comes in His glory, accompanied by all the angels, He will sit on His glorious throne."	A). Zechariah 14:5; Matthew 16:27; Mark 8:38; Acts 1:11; 1 Thessalonians 4:16; 2 Thessalonians 1:7; Jude 1:14; Revelation 1:7				

Gospel of Mattityahu "Matthew"	OT/NT References	Gospel of Mrk "Mark"	OT/NT References	Gospel of Luk "Luke"	OT/NT References
Chapter 25 The Son of Man Will Judge the Nations Continued					
v. 32: (a) "All of the nations will be assembled before Him, and (B) He will separate people one from another as a shepherd separates sheep from goats."	a). Romans 14:10; 2 Corinthians 5:10; Revelation 20:12 B). Ezekiel 20:38				
v. 33: "The (A) 'sheep' He will place at His right hand and the 'goats' at His left."	A). Psalm 79:13; 100:3; John 10:11; 27–28				
v. 34: "Then the King will say to those on His right, 'Come, you whom My Father has blessed, take your (a) inheritance, the Kingdom (b) prepared for you from the beginning of the world.'"	a). Romans 8:17; 1 Peter 1:4, 9; Revelation 21:7 b). Matthew 20:23; Mark 10:40; 1 Corinthians 2:9; Hebrews 11:16				
v. 35: (A) "For I was hungry and you gave Me food, I was thirsty and you gave Me something to drink, (B) I was a stranger and you made Me your guest."	A). Isaiah 58:7; Ezekiel 18:7, 16; James 1:27; 2:15–16 B). Job 31:32; Hebrews 13:2; 3 John 1:5				

Gospel of Mattityahu "Matthew"	OT/NT References	Gospel of Mrk "Mark"	OT/NT References	Gospel of Luk "Luke"	OT/NT References
Chapter 25 The Son of Man Will Judge the Nations Continued					
v. 36: "I (A) needed clothes and you provided them, I was sick and you took care of Me, (b) I was in prison and you visited Me."	A). Isaiah 58:7; Ezekiel 18:7, 16 b). 2 Timothy 1:16				
v. 37: "Then the people who have done what God wants will reply, 'Lord when did we see You hungry and feed You, or thirsty and give You something to drink?'"					
v. 38: "When did we see You a stranger and make You our guest, or needing clothes and provide them?"					
v. 39: "When did we see You sick or in prison, and visit You?"					
v. 40: "The King will say to them, 'Yes! I tell you that (A) whenever you did these things for one of the least important of these brothers of Mine, you did them to Me!'"	A). Proverbs 14:31; Matthew 10:42; Mark 9:41; Hebrews 6:10				

Part 4: Subtopic Scriptural Alignment View—Matthew, Mark, and Luke

Gospel of Mattityahu "Matthew"	OT/NT References	Gospel of Mrk "Mark"	OT/NT References	Gospel of Luk "Luke"	OT/NT References
Chapter 25 The Son of Man Will Judge the Nations Continued					
v. 41: "Then He will also speak to those on His left, saying, (A) 'Get away from Me, you the cursed! Go off (b) into the fire prepared for the (c) *Adversary* and his angels!'"	A). Psalm 6:8; Matthew 7:23; Luke 13:27 b). Matthew 13:40, 42 c). 2 Peter 2:4; Jude 1:6				
v. 42: "For I was hungry and you gave Me no food, thirsty and you gave Me nothing to drink."					
v. 43: "A stranger and you did not welcome Me, needing clothes and you did not give them to Me, sick and in prison and you did not visit Me."					
v. 44: "Then they too will reply, 'Lord, when did we see You hungry, thirsty, a stranger needing clothes, sick or in prison, and not take care of you?'"					
v. 45: "And He will answer them, 'Yes! I tell you that (A) whenever you refused to do it for the least important of these people, you refused to do it for Me!'"	A). Proverbs 14:31; Zechariah 2:8; Acts :5				

254 *Just the Words and Teachings of Jesus Christ*

Gospel of Mattityahu "Matthew"	OT/NT References	Gospel of Mrk "Mark"	OT/NT References	Gospel of Luk "Luke"	OT/NT References
Chapter 25 **The Son of Man Will Judge the Nations Continued**					
v. 46: (A) "They will go off to eternal punishment, but those who have done what God wants will go to eternal life."	A). Daniel 12:2; John 5:29; Acts 24:15; Romans 2:7				
Chapter 26 **The Plot to Kill Yeshua**					
v. 2: (a) "As you know, *Pesach* is two days away, and the Son of Man will be handed over to be nailed to the *execution stake*."	a). Matthew 27:35; Mark 14:1–2; Luke 22:1–2; John 13:1; 19:18				
Chapter 26 **Anointing at Bethany**		**Chapter 14** **Anointing at Bethany**			
v. 10: "But *Yeshua, aware of what was going on, said to them, 'Why are you bothering this woman? She has done a beautiful thing for Me.'"		v. 6: "But He said, 'Let her be. Why are you bothering her? She has done a beautiful thing for Me.'"			
v. 11: (A) "The poor you will always have with you, (b) but you will not always have Me."	A). Deuteronomy 15:11; Mark 14:7; John 12:8 b). Matthew 18:20; 28:20; John 13:33; 14:19; 16:5, 28; 17:11	v. 7: (A) "For you will always have the poor with you; and whenever you want to, you can help them. (b) But you will not always have Me."	A). Deuteronomy 15:11; Matthew 26:11; John 12:8 b). John 7:33; 8:21; 14:2, 12; 16:10, 17, 28		

Gospel of Mattityahu "Matthew"	OT/NT References	Gospel of Mrk "Mark"	OT/NT References	Gospel of Luk "Luke"	OT/NT References
Chapter 26 Anointing at Bethany Continued		**Chapter 14 Anointing at Bethany Continued**			
v. 12: "She poured this perfume on Me to prepare My body for (a) burial."	a). Matthew 27:60; Luke 23:53; John 19:38–42	v. 8: "What she could do, she did do—in advance she poured perfume on My body to prepare it for burial."			
v. 13: "Yes! I tell you that throughout the whole world, wherever this Good News is proclaimed, *what she had done will be told in her memory." (See "Commentaries.")		v. 9: "Yes! I tell you that wherever in the whole world this Good News is (a) proclaimed, what she has done will be told in her memory."	a). Matthew 28:19–20; Mark 16:15; Luke 24:47		
Chapter 26 Yeshua Celebrates Pesach (*Passover*) with His Disciples and Foretells of His Betrayer		**Chapter 14 Yeshua Celebrates Pesach (*Passover*) with His Disciples and Foretells of His Betrayer**		**Chapter 22 Yeshua Celebrates Pesach (*Passover*) with His Disciples and Foretells of His Betrayer**	
v. 18: "'Go into the city, to so-and-so,' he replied, 'and tell him that the *Rabbi* says, (a) "My time is near, My *talmidim* and I are celebrating *Pesach* at your house."'"	a). Luke 9:51; John 12:23; 13:1; 17:1	v. 13: "He sent two of His *talmidim* with these instructions; 'Go into the city.'"		v. 8: "*Yeshua* sent *Kefa* and *Yochanan*, instructing them, Go and prepare our *Seder*, so we can eat."	
		v. 13: "And a man carrying a jar of water will meet you. Follow him."		v. 10: "He told them, 'As you're going into the city, a man carrying a jar of water will meet you. Follow him into the house he enters.'"	

Gospel of Mattityahu "Matthew"	OT/NT References	Gospel of Mrk "Mark"	OT/NT References	Gospel of Luk "Luke"	OT/NT References
Chapter 26 Yeshua Celebrates Pesach (*Passover*) with His Disciples and Foretells of His Betrayer Continued		**Chapter 14 Yeshua Celebrates Pesach (*Passover*) with His Disciples and Foretells of His Betrayer Continued**		**Chapter 22 Yeshua Celebrates Pesach (*Passover*) with His Disciples and Foretells of His Betrayer Continued**	
		v. 14: "And whichever house he enters, tell the owner that the *Rabbi* says, 'Where is the guest room for Me, where I am to eat the *Pesach* meal with My *talmidim*?'"		v. 11: "And say to its owner, 'The *Rabbi* says to you, "Where is the guest room, where I am to eat the *Pesach* meal with my *talmidim*?"'"	
		v. 15: "He will show you a large room upstairs, furnished and ready, make the preparations there."		v. 12: "He will show you a large room upstairs already furnished; make the preparations there."	
v. 21: "And as they were eating, He said, 'Yes, I tell you that one of you is going to (a) betray Me.'"	a). Matthew 26:46; Mark 14:42; Luke 22:21–23; John 6:70–71; 13:21	v. 18: "As they were eating, Yeshua said, 'Yes! I tell you that (A) one of you is going to betray Me.'"	A). Psalm 41:9; Matthew 26:46; Mark 14:42; John 6:70–71; 13:18	v. 21: (A) "But look! The person who is betraying Me is here at the table with Me!"	A). Psalm 41:9; Matthew 26:21, 23; Mark 14:18; Luke 22:48; John 13:21, 26–27
v. 23: "He answered, (A) 'The one who dips his *matzah* in the dish with Me is the one who will betray Me.'"	A).Psalm 41:9; Luke 22:21; John 13:18	v. 20: "'It's one of the Twelve,' He said to them, 'someone dipping *matzah* in the dish with Me.'"			

Part 4: Subtopic Scriptural Alignment View—Matthew, Mark, and Luke

Gospel of Mattityahu "Matthew"	OT/NT References	Gospel of Mrk "Mark"	OT/NT References	Gospel of Luk "Luke"	OT/NT References
Chapter 26 Yeshua Celebrates Pesach (*Passover*) with His Disciples and Foretells of His Betrayer Continued		**Chapter 14 Yeshua Celebrates Pesach (*Passover*) with His Disciples and Foretells of His Betrayer Continued**		**Chapter 22 Yeshua Celebrates Pesach (*Passover*) with His Disciples and Foretells of His Betrayer Continued**	
v. 24: "The Son of Man will die just as the (A) *Tanakh* says He will; but (b) woe to that man by whom the Son of Man is betrayed! (c) It would have been better for him had he never been born!"	A). Psalm 22; Daniel 9:26; Mark 9:12; Luke 24:25–26, 46; Acts:17:2–3; 26:22–23; 1 Corinthians 15:3 b). Matthew 27:3–5; Luke 17:1; Acts:1:16–20 c). John 17:12; Acts:1:25	v. 21: (a) "For the Son of Man will die, just as the *Tanakh* says He will; but woe to that man by whom the Son of Man is betrayed! It would have been better for him had he never been born!"	A). Matthew 26:24; Luke 22:22; Acts 1:16–20	v. 22: (a) "The Son of Man is going to His death (b) according to God's plan, but woe to that man by whom He is being betrayed!"	a). Matthew 26:24 b). John 17:12; Acts 2:23
v. 25: "*Y'hudah* the one who was betraying Him, then asked, 'Surely, *Rabbi*, you don't mean me?' He answered. 'The words are yours.'"					

258 *Just the Words and Teachings of Jesus Christ*

Gospel of Mattityahu "Matthew"	OT/NT References	Gospel of Mrk "Mark"	OT/NT References	Gospel of Luk "Luke"	OT/NT References
Chapter 26 Yeshua Institutes the Lord's Supper (Seder)		**Chapter 14 Yeshua Institutes the Lord's Supper (Seder)**		**Chapter 22 Yeshua Institutes the Lord's Supper (Seder)**	
v. 24: "The Son of Man will die just as the (A) *Tanakh* says He will; but (b) woe to that man by whom the Son of Man is betrayed! (c) It would have been better for him had he never been born!"	A). Psalm 22; Daniel 9:26; Mark 9:12; Luke 24:25–26, 46; Acts 17:2–3; 26:22–23; 1 Corinthians 15:3　b). Matthew 273–5; Luke 17:1; Acts 1:16–20　c). John 17:12; Acts 1:25	v. 21. (a) "For the Son of Man will die, just as the *Tanakh* says He will; but woe to that man by whom the Son of Man is betrayed! It would have been better for him had he never been born!"	a). Matthew 26:24; Luke 22:22; Acts 1:16–20	v. 22: (a) "The Son of Man is going to His death (b) according to God's plan, but woe to that man by whom He is being betrayed!"	a). Matthew 26:24　b). John 17:12; Acts 2:23
v. 25: "*Y'hudah* the one who was betraying Him, then asked, 'Surely, *Rabbi*, you don't mean me?' He answered. 'The words are yours.'"					
				v. 15: "And He said to them, 'I have really wanted so much to celebrate this *Seder* with you before I die!'"	
				v. 16: "For I tell you, it is certain that I will not celebrate it again (a) until it is given its full meaning in the Kingdom of God."	a). Luke 14:15; Acts 10:41; Revelation 19:9

Part 4: Subtopic Scriptural Alignment View—Matthew, Mark, and Luke

Gospel of Mattityahu "Matthew"	OT/NT References	Gospel of Mrk "Mark"	OT/NT References	Gospel of Luk "Luke"	OT/NT References
Chapter 26 Yeshua Institutes the Lord's Supper (Seder) Continued		**Chapter 14 Yeshua Institutes the Lord's Supper (Seder) Continued**		**Chapter 22 Yeshua Institutes the Lord's Supper (Seder) Continued**	
v. 26: (a) "While they were eating, (b) *Yeshua took a piece of *matzah, made the *b'rakhah, broke it, gave it to the *talmidim and said, 'Take! Eat! (c) This is my body!'"	a). Mark 14:22–25; Luke 22:17–20 b). 1 Corinthians 11:23–25 c).1 Peter 2:24	v. 22: (a) "While they were eating, *Yeshua took a piece of *matzah, made the *b'rakhah, broke it, gave it to them and said, 'Take it! This is My (b) body.'"	a). Matthew 26:26–29; Luke 22:17–20; 1 Cointhians 11:23–25 b). 1 Peter 2:24	v. 19: (a) "Also, taking a piece of *matzah, He made the *b'rakhah, broke it, gave it to them and said, 'This is My (b) body, which is being given to you; (c) do this in memory of Me.'"	a). Matthew 26:26; Mark 14:22 b).1 Peter 2:24 c).1 Corinthians 11:23–26
v. 27: 'Also He took a cup of wine, made the *b'rakhah, and gave it to them, saying, 'All of you, (a) drink from it!'"	a). Mark 14:23			v. 17: "Then, taking a cup of wine, he made a *b'rakhah and said, 'Take this and share it among yourselves.'"	
v. 28: "For (A) this is My blood, which ratifies the (B) New Covenant, My blood shed on behalf (c) of many, so that they may have their sins forgiven."	A). Exodus 24:8; Leviticus 17:11; Hebrews 9:20 B). Jeremiah 31:31 c). Matthew 20:28; Romans 5:15; Hebrews 9:22	v. 24: 'He said to them, 'This is My blood, which ratifies the New Covenant, My blood shed on behalf of many people.'"		v. 20: "He did the same with the cup after the meal, saying, (a) 'This cup is the New Covenant, ratified by My blood, which is being poured out for you.'"	a). 1 Corinthians 10:16
v. 29: (a) "I tell you, I will not drink from this 'fruit of the vine' again (b) until the day I drink new wine with you in My Father's Kingdom."	a). Mark 14:25; Luke 22:18 b). Acts 10:41	v. 25: "Yes! I tell you. I will not drink this 'fruit of the vine' again until the day I drink new wine in the Kingdom of God."		v. 18: "For (a) I tell you that from now on, I will not drink the 'fruit of the vine' until the Kingdom of God comes."	a). Matthew 26:29; Mark 14:25

Gospel of Mattityahu "Matthew"	OT/NT References	Gospel of Mrk "Mark"	OT/NT References	Gospel of Luk "Luke"	OT/NT References
Chapter 26 Yeshua Predicts Peter's Denial		**Chapter 14 Yeshua Predicts Peter's Denial**		**Chapter 22 Yeshua Predicts Peter's Denial**	
				v. 31: "*Shim'on, Shim'on, listen! The (a) *Adversary demanded to have you people for himself, to (B) sift you like wheat!"	a). 1 Peter 5:8 B). Amos 9:9
				v. 32: "But (a) I prayed for you, *Shim'on, that your trust might not fail. And you, once you have turned back in repentance, (b) strengthen your brothers!"	a). John 17:9, 11, 15 b). John 21:15–17; Acts 1:15; 2:14; 2 Peter 1:10–15
v. 31: "*Yeshua then said to them, 'Tonight you will (a) all lose (b) faith in Me, as the *Tanakh says, (C) "I will strike the shepherd dead, and the sheep of the flock will be scattered."'"	a). Matthew 26:56; Mark 14:27; John 16:32 b). Matthew 11:6 C). Zechariah 13:7	v. 27: (a) "*Yeshua said to them, 'You will all lose faith in Me, for the *Tanakh says, (B) "I will strike the shepherd dead, and the sheep will be scattered."'"	a). Matthew 26:31–35; Mark 14:50; John 16:32 B). Isaiah 53:5, 10; Zechariah 13:7		
v. 34: "*Yeshua said to him, (a) 'Yes! I tell you that tonight before the rooster crows, you will disown Me three times!'"	a). Matthew 26:47, 75; Mark 14:30; Luke 22:34; John 13:38	v. 30: "*Yeshua replied, 'Yes! I tell you *Kefa that this very night, before the rooster crows twice, you will disown Me three times!'"		v. 34: (a) "*Yeshua replied, 'I tell you, *Kefa, the rooster will not crow today until you have denied three times that you know Me.'"	a). Matthew 26:33–35; Mark 14:29–31; Luke 22:61; John 13:37–38

Gospel of Mattityahu "Matthew"	OT/NT References	Gospel of Mrk "Mark"	OT/NT References	Gospel of Luk "Luke"	OT/NT References
				Chapter 22 Supplies for the Road	
				v. 35: (a) "He said to them, 'When I sent you out without wallet, pack or shoes, were you ever short of anything?' 'Not a thing,' they answered."	a). Matthew 10:9; Mark 6:8; Luke 9:3; 10:4
				v. 36: "'But now,' He said, 'if you have a wallet or a pack, take it; and if you don't have a sword, sell your robe to buy one.'"	
				v. 37: "For I tell you this: the passage from the *Tanakh that says, (A) 'He was counted with transgressors,' has to be fulfilled in Me; since what is happening to Me has a purpose."	A). Isaiah 53:12; Matthew 27:38; Mark 15:28; Luke 22:32
				v. 38: "They said, 'Look, Lord, there are two swords right here!' 'Enough!' He replied."	

Gospel of Mattityahu "Matthew"	OT/NT References	Gospel of Mrk "Mark"	OT/NT References	Gospel of Luk "Luke"	OT/NT References
Chapter 26 **The Prayer in the Garden**		**Chapter 14** **The Prayer in the Garden**		**Chapter 22** **The Prayer in the Garden**	
v. 36: (a) "Then *Yeshua went with His *talmidim to a place called *Gat-Sh'manim and said to them, 'Sit here while I go over there and pray.'"	a). Mark 14:32–35; Luke 2:39–40; John 18:1	v. 32: (a) "They went to a place called *Gat Sh'manim; and *Yeshua said to His *talmidim 'Sit here while I pray.'"	a). Matthew 26:36–46; Luke 22:40–46; John 18:1	v. 40: (a) "When He arrived, He said to them, 'Pray you won't be put to the test.'"	a). Matthew 26:36–46; Mark 14:32–42
v. 37: "He took with him *Kefa and *Zavdai's (a) two sons. Grief and anguish came over Him."	a). Matthew 4:21; 17:1; Mark 5:37				
v. 38: "And He said to them, (a) 'My heart is so filled with sadness that I could die! Remain here and stay awake with Me.'"	a). John 12:27	v. 34: "And He said to them, (A) 'My heart is so filled with sadness that I could die! Remain here and stay awake.'"	A). Isaiah 53:3; Matthew 26:38; John 12:27		
v. 39: "Going on a little farther, He fell on His face, (a) praying, (b) 'My Father, if possible, (c) let this cup pass from Me! Yet—(D) not what I want, but what you want!'"	a). Mark 14:36; Luke 22:42; Hebrews 5:7–9 b). John 12:27 c). Matthew 20:22 D). Psalm 40:8; Isaiah 50:5; John 5:30; 6:38; Philippians 2:8	v. 36: (a) "'*Abba!'…(b) 'All things are possible for You. Take this cup away from me! (C) Still, not what I want, but what You want.'"	a). Romans 8:15; Galatians 4:6 b). Hebrews 5:7 C). Isaiah 50:5; John 5:30; 6:38	v. 42: "Father, if you are willing, take this cup away from Me; still, let (A) not My will but Yours be done."	A). Isaiah 50:5; John 4:34; 5:30; 6:38; 8:29

Part 4: Subtopic Scriptural Alignment View—Matthew, Mark, and Luke

Gospel of Mattityahu "Matthew"	OT/NT References	Gospel of Mrk "Mark"	OT/NT References	Gospel of Luk "Luke"	OT/NT References
Chapter 26 **The Prayer in the Garden Continued**		**Chapter 14** **The Prayer in the Garden Continued**		**Chapter 22** **The Prayer in the Garden Continued**	
v. 40: "He returned to the *talmidim* and found them sleeping. He said to *Kefa*, 'Were you so weak that you couldn't stay awake with Me for even an hour?'"		v. 37: "He came and found them sleeping; and He said to *Kefa*, 'Shim'on, are you asleep? Couldn't you stay awake one hour?'"		v. 46: "He said to them, (a) 'Why are you sleeping?'"	a). Luke 9:32
v. 41: (a) "Stay awake, and pray that you will not be put to the test—(B) the spirit indeed is eager, but human nature is weak."	a). Mark 13:33; 14:38; Luke 22:40, 46; Ephesians 6:18 B). Psalm 103:14–16; Romans 7:15; 8:23; Galatians 5:17	v. 38: (a) "Stay awake, and pray that you will not be put to the test—(b) the spirit indeed is eager, but human nature is weak."	a). Luke 21:36 b). Romans 7:18, 21–24; Galatians 5:17	v. 46: "Get up and (B) pray that you won't be put to the test!"	B). 1 Chronicles 16:11; Luke 2:40; Ephesians 6:18; 1 Thessalonians 5:17
v. 42: "A second time He went off and prayed. 'My Father, if this cup cannot pass away unless I drink it, let what You want be done.'"					
v. 45: "Then He came to the *talmidim* and said, 'For now, go on sleeping, take your rest....Look! The time has come for the Son of Man to be (a) betrayed into the hands of sinners.'"	a). Matthew 17:22–23; 20:18–19	v. 41: "The third time, He came and said to them, 'For now, go on sleeping, take your rest... There, that's enough! (a) The time has come! Look! The Son of Man is being betrayed into the hands of sinners!'"	a). John 13:1; 17:1		

Gospel of Mattityahu "Matthew"	OT/NT References	Gospel of Mrk "Mark"	OT/NT References	Gospel of Luk "Luke"	OT/NT References
Chapter 26 **The Prayer in the Garden Continued** v. 46: "Get up! Let's go! Here comes My betrayer!"		**Chapter 14** **The Prayer in the Garden Continued** v. 42: (a) "Get up! Let's go! Here comes My betrayer!"	a). Matthew 26:46; Mark 14:18; Luke 9:44; John 13:21; 18:1–2		
Chapter 26 **Betrayal and Arrest in the Garden of Gethsemane**				**Chapter 22** **Betrayal and Arrest in the Garden of Gethsemane**	
v. 50: "*Yeshua* said to him, (A) 'Friend, do what you came to do.' Then they moved forward; laid hold of *Yeshua* and arrested Him."	A). Psalm 41:9; 55:13			v. 48: "But *Yeshua* said to him, '*Y'hudah,* are you betraying the Son of Man with a (A) kiss?'"	A). Proverbs 27:6
v. 52: "Yeshua said to him, 'Put your sword back where it belongs, for (A) everyone who uses the sword will die by the sword.'"	A). Genesis 9:6; Revelation 13:10			v. 51: "But *Yeshua* answered, 'Just let Me do this,' and, touching the man's ear, He healed him."	
v. 53: "Don't you know that I can ask My Father, and He will instantly provide (A) more than a dozen armies of angels to help Me?"	A). 2 Kings 6:17; Daniel 7:10				

Part 4: Subtopic Scriptural Alignment View—Matthew, Mark, and Luke

Gospel of Mattityahu "Matthew"	OT/NT References	Gospel of Mrk "Mark"	OT/NT References	Gospel of Luk "Luke"	OT/NT References
Chapter 26 Betrayal and Arrest in the Garden of Gethsemane Continued		**Chapter 26 Betrayal and Arrest in the Garden of Gethsemane Continued**		**Chapter 22 Betrayal and Arrest in the Garden of Gethsemane Continued**	
v. 54: "But if I did that, how could the passages in the *Tanakh* be fulfilled that say it (A) has to happen this way?"	A). Isaiah 50:6; 53:2–11; Luke 24:25–27, 44–46; John 19:28; Acts 13:29; 17:3; 26:23				
v. 55: "Then *Yeshua* addressed the crowd: 'So you came out to take Me with swords and clubs, the way you would the leader of a rebellion?'"		v. 48: (a) "*Yeshua* addressed them: 'So you came out to take Me with swords and clubs, the way you would the leader of a rebellion?'"	a). Matthew 26:55; Luke 22:52	v. 52: (a) "Then *Yeshua* said to the head *cohanim*, the officers of the Temple guard and the elders who had come to seize Him, 'So you came out just as you would to the leaders of a (b) rebellion, with swords and clubs?'"	a). Matthew 26:55 b). Luke 23:32
v. 55: "Every day I sat in the Temple court, teaching; and you didn't seize Me then."		v. 49: (a) "Every day I was with you in the Temple court teaching, and you didn't seize Me then!"	a). Matthew 21:23	v. 53: "Everyday I was there with you in the (a) Temple court, yet you didn't arrest Me."	a). Luke 19:47–48
v. 56: "'But all this has to happen so that what the (A) prophets wrote may be fulfilled.' Then the (B) *talmidim* all deserted Him and ran away."	A). Lamentations 4:20 B). Zechariah 13:7; Matthew 26:31; Mark 14:27; John 18:15	v. 49: "But let the (B) Tanakh be fulfilled."	B). Psalm 22:6; Isaiah 53:7; Luke 22:37; 24:44	v. 53: "But this is your hour—the (b) hour when darkness rules."	b). John 12:27

Gospel of Mattityahu "Matthew"	OT/NT References	Gospel of Mrk "Mark"	OT/NT References	Gospel of Luk "Luke"	OT/NT References
				Chapter 22 **Peter Denies Yeshua and Weeps Bitterly**	
				v. 61: "The Lord turned and looked straight at *Kefa;* and (a) *Kefa* remembered what the Lord had said, (b) 'Before the rooster crows today, you will deny Me three times.'"	a). Matthew 26:75; Mark 14:72 b). Matthew 26:34, 75; Mark 14:30; Luke 22:34; John 13:38
				v. 62: "And *he went outside and cried bitterly." (See "Commentaries.")	
				Chapter 22 **Yeshua Faces the Sanhedrin**	
				v. 67: "Where they said, (a) 'If you are the *Mashiach,* tell us.' He answered. 'If I tell you, you (b) won't believe Me.'"	a). Matthew 26:63–66; Mark 14:61–63; Luke 22:67–71; John 18:19–21 b). Luke 20:5–7
				v. 68: "And if I ask you, you won't answer."	

Gospel of Mattityahu "Matthew"	OT/NT References	Gospel of Mrk "Mark"	OT/NT References	Gospel of Luk "Luke"	OT/NT References
Chapter 26 Yeshua Faces the Sanhedrin Continued		**Chapter 14 Yeshua Faces the Sanhedrin Continued**		**Chapter 22 Yeshua Faces the Sanhedrin Continued**	
v. 64: "*Yeshua said to him, 'The words are your own. But I tell you that one day you will see the Son of Man sitting at the right hand of *HaG'vurah and coming on the clouds of heaven.'"		v. 62: "'I AM' answered *Yeshua. 'Moreover, you will see the Son of Man sitting at the right hand of *HaG'uvrah and coming on the clouds of heaven.'"		v. 69: (A) "But from now on, the Son of Man will be sitting at the right hand of *HaG'vurah."	A). Psalm 110:1; Matthew 26:64; Mark 14:62; 16:19; Acts 2:33; 7:55; Ephesians 1:20; Colossians 3:1; Hebrews 1:3; 8:1
				v. 70: "They all said, 'Does this mean, then, that you are the Son of God?' And He answered them, (a) 'You say I am.'"	a). Matthew 26:64; 27:11; Mark 14:62; Luke 1:35
Chapter 27 Yeshua Faces Pontius Pilate		**Chapter 15 Yeshua Faces Pontius Pilate**		**Chapter 23 Yeshua Handed Over to Pontius Pilate**	
v. 11: "Meanwhile, *Yeshua was brought before the governor, and the (a) governor put this question to Him: 'Are you the King of the Jews?' *Yeshua answered, (b) 'The words are yours.'"	a). Mark 15:2–5; Luke 23:2–3; John 18:29–38 b). John 18:37; 1 Timothy 6:13	v. 2: (a) "Pilate put this question to Him: 'Are You the King of the Jews?' He answered him, 'The words are yours.'"	a). Matthew 27:11–14; Luke 23:2–3; John 18:29–38	v. 3: (a) "Pilate asked Him, 'Are you king of the Jews?' And He answered him, 'The words are yours.'"	a). Matthew 27:11; 1 Timothy 6:13

Gospel of Mattityahu "Matthew"	OT/NT References	Gospel of Mrk "Mark"	OT/NT References	Gospel of Luk "Luke"	OT/NT References
				Chapter 23 **The King on a Cross**	
				v. 28: "*Yeshua turned to them and said, 'Daughters of *Yerushalayim, don't cry for Me; cry for yourselves and your children!'"	
				v. 29: "For the time is coming when people will say, "The childless women are the lucky ones—those whose wombs have never borne a child, whose breasts have never nursed a baby!'"	
				v. 30: "Then they will begin to say (A) to the mountains, 'Fall on us!' and to the hills, 'Cover us!'"	A). Isaiah 2:19; Hosea 10:8; Revelation 6:16–17; 9:6
				v. 31: (A) "For if they do these things when the wood is green, what is going to happen when it's dry?"	A). Proverbs 11:31; Jeremiah 25:29; Ezekiel 20:47; 21:3–4
				v. 34: "*Yeshua said, 'Father, (A) forgive them; (b) they don't understand what they are doing.' They (C) divided up His clothes by throwing dice."	A). Psalm 109:4; Matthew 5:44; Acts 7:60; 1 Corinthians 4:12 b). Acts 3:17 C). Psalm 22:18; Matthew 27:35; Mark 15:24; John 19:23

Gospel of Mattityahu "Matthew"	OT/NT References	Gospel of Mrk "Mark"	OT/NT References	Gospel of Luk "Luke"	OT/NT References
				Chapter 23 The King on a Cross Continued	
				v. 43: "*Yeshua said to him, 'Yes! I promise that you will be with me today, in (a) *Gan-'Eden.'"	a). 2 Corinthians 12:4; Ephesians 4:8–10; Revelation 2:7
Chapter 27 Yeshua Dies on the Cross (*Execution Stake*)		**Chapter 15 Yeshua Dies on the Cross (*Execution Stake*)**		**Chapter 23 Yeshua Dies on the Cross (Execution Stake)**	
v. 46: "At about three, (a) *Yeshua uttered a loud cry, '*Eli! Eli! L'mah sh'vaktani?' (B) (My God! My God! Why have you deserted Me?)." (See "Commentaries.")	a). Hebrews 5:7 B). Psalm 22:1	v. 34: "At three, He uttered a loud cry, '*Elohi! Elohi! L'mah sh'vaktani?' (A) ('My God! My God! Why have You deserted Me?)." (See "Commentaries.")	A). Psalm 22:1; Matthew 27:46		
v. 50: "But *Yeshua, again (a) crying out in a loud voice, (B) yielded up His Spirit."	a). Mark 15:37; Luke 23:46; John 19:30 B). Daniel 9:26; Zechariah 11:10–11; Matthew 17:23; John:10:18; 1 Corinthians 15:3	v. 37: (A) "But *Yeshua let out a loud cry and gave up His Spirit."	A). Daniel 9:26; Zechariah 11:10–11; Matthew 27:50; Mark 8:31; Luke 23:46; John 19:30	v. 46: "Crying out in a loud voice, *Yeshua said, 'Father! (A) Into Your hands, I commit My spirit.' (B) With these words He gave up His spirit."	A). Psalm 31:5; 1 Peter 2:23 B). Daniel 9:26;; Zechariah 11:10–11; Matthew 27:50; Mark 15:37; Luke 9:22; 18:33

Gospel of Mattityahu "Matthew"	OT/NT References	Gospel of Mrk "Mark"	OT/NT References	Gospel of Luk "Luke"	OT/NT References
Chapter 28 The Women Worship the Risen Lord					
v. 9: "Suddenly, (a) *Yeshua* met them and said, '*Shalom!*' They came up and took hold of His feet as they fell down in front of Him."	a). Mark 16:9; John 20:14				
v. 10: "Then *Yeshua* said to them, 'Don't be afraid! Go and tell My (A) brothers to go to the *Galil*, and they will see Me there.'"	A). Psalm 22:22; John 20:17; Romans 8:29; Hebrews 2:11				
				Chapter 24 The Road to Emmaus	
				v. 17: "He asked them, 'What are you talking about with each other as you walk along?' They stopped short, their faces downcast."	
				v. 19: "'What things' He asked them. They said to him,'The things about *Yeshua* from *Natzeret*. (a) He was a prophet and proved it by the (b) things He did and said before God and all the people.'"	a). Matthew 21:11; Luke 7:16; John 3:2; Acts 2:22 b). Acts 7:22

Part 4: Subtopic Scriptural Alignment View—Matthew, Mark, and Luke

Gospel of Mattityahu "Matthew"	OT/NT References	Gospel of Mrk "Mark"	OT/NT References	Gospel of Luk "Luke"	OT/NT References
				Chapter 24 The Road to Emmaus Continued	
				v. 25: "He said to them, 'Foolish people! So unwilling to put your trust in everything the prophets spoke!'"	
				v. 26: (a) "Didn't the *Messiah* have to die like this before entering His (b) glory?"	a). Acts 17:2–3; Hebrews 2:9–10 b). 1 Peter 1:10–12
				v. 27: "Then starting with (A) *Moshe* and (B) all the prophets, He explained to them the things that can be found throughout the *Tanakh* concerning Himself."	A). Genesis 3:15; 12:3; Numbers 21:9; Deuteronomy 8:15; John 5:46 B). Psalm 16:9; 10:22; 132:11; Isaiah 7:14; 9:6; Jeremiah 23:5; 33:14–15; Ezekiel 34:23; 37:25; Daniel 9:24; Micah 7:20; Malachi 3:1; 4:2; John 1:45; 5:39; Romans 1:1–6

Gospel of Mattityahu "Matthew"	OT/NT References	Gospel of Mrk "Mark"	OT/NT References	Gospel of Luk "Luke"	OT/NT References
				Chapter 24 **The Disciples' Eyes Opened**	
				v. 30: As He was *reclining* with them at the table, He took the *matzah*, made the *b'rakhah*, broke it and handed it to them. (See "Commentaries.")	
				v. 31: Then their eyes were opened, and they recognized Him. But He became invisible to them. (See "Commentaries.")	
				v. 32: They said to each other, "*Didn't our hearts burn inside us as He spoke to us on the road, opening up the *Tanakh* to us?" (See "Commentaries.")	
				Chapter 24 **Yeshua Appears to His Disciples**	
				v. 38: "But He said to them, 'Why are you so upset? Why are these doubts welling up inside you?'"	
				v. 39: "Look at My hands and feet—it is, I, Myself! (a) Touch Me and see—a (b) ghost doesn't have flesh and bones, as you can see I do."	a). John 20:20, 27; 1 John 1:1 b). 1 Corinthians 15:50

Gospel of Mattityahu "Matthew"	OT/NT References	Gospel of Mrk "Mark"	OT/NT References	Gospel of Luk "Luke"	OT/NT References
				Chapter 24 **Yeshua Appears to His Disciples**	
				v. 41: "While they were still unable to believe it (A) for joy and stood there dumbfounded, He said to them, (b) 'Have you something to eat?'"	A). Genesis 45:26 b). John 21:5
				Chapter 24 **The Scriptures Opened to Their Minds**	
				v. 44: "*Yeshua* said to them, (a) 'This is what I meant when I was still with you and told you that everything written about Me in the *Torah* of *Moshe*, the Prophets and the *Psalms* had to be fulfilled.'"	a). Matthew 16:21; 17:22; 20:18; Mark 8:31; Luke 9:22; 18:31
				v. 45: * *"Then He opened their minds, so that they could understand the *Tanakh*."* (See "Commentaries.")	a). Acts 16:14; 1 John 5:20
				v. 46: "Telling them, (A) 'Here is what it says: the *Messiah* is to suffer and to rise from the dead on the third day.'"	A). Psalm 1:22; Hosea 6:2; Luke 11:29–30; Acts 17:3

Gospel of Mattityahu "Matthew"	OT/NT References	Gospel of Mrk "Mark"	OT/NT References	Gospel of Luk "Luke"	OT/NT References
				Chapter 24 The Scriptures Opened to Their Minds Continued	
				v. 47: "And in His Name (A) repentance leading to forgiveness of sins is to be proclaimed to people from (B) all nations, starting with *Yerushalayim*."	A. Daniel 9:24; Acts 5:31; 10:43; 13:38; 26:18 B. Psalm 22:27; Jeremiah 31:34; Micah 4:2
				v. 48: (a) "You are witnesses of these things."	a). Acts 1:8; 1 Peter 5:1
				v. 49: (A) ""Now I am sending forth upon you what My Father promised, so stay here in the city until you have been equipped with power from above."	A). Isaiah 44:3; Joel 2:28; Acts 2:4
				v. 50: "He led them out (a) toward *Beit-Anyah*; then, raising His hands, He said a *b'rakhah* over them."	a). Matthew 21:17; Acts 1:12
				v. 51: (A) "As He was blessing them, He withdrew from them and was carried up into Heaven."	A). Psalm 68:18; 110:1; Mark 16:19; Acts 1:9–11

Gospel of Mattityahu "Matthew"	OT/NT References	Gospel of Mrk "Mark"	OT/NT References	Gospel of Luk "Luke"	OT/NT References
Chapter 28 The Great Commission		**Chapter 16 The Great Commission**			
v. 18: "*Yeshua came and talked with them. He said, (A) 'All authority in Heaven and on earth has been given to Me.'"	A). Daniel 7:13–14; Matthew 11:27; Luke 1:32; 10:22; John 3:35; Acts 2:36; Romans 14:9; 1 Corinthians 15:27; Ephesians 1:10, 21; Philippians 2:9–10; Hebrews 1:2; 1 Peter 3:22				
v. 19: "Therefore, (a) go and (B) make people from all nations into *talmidim, immersing them into the reality of the Father, the Son and the *Ruach HaKodesh."	a). Mark 16:15 B). Isaiah 52:10; Luke 24:47; Acts 2:38–39; Romans 10:18; Colossians 1:23	v. 15: (a) "Then He said to them, 'As you go throughout the world, (b) proclaim the Good News to all creation.'"	a). Matthew 28:19; John 15:16; Acts 1:8; Colossians 1:6 b). Colossians ll:23		
		v. 16: (a) "Whoever trusts and is immersed will be saved; (b) whoever does not trust will be condemned."	a). John 3:18, 36; Act 2:38; 16:30–1; Romans 10:8–10 b). John 12:48		

276 *Just the Words and Teachings of Jesus Christ*

Gospel of Mattityahu "Matthew"	OT/NT References	Gospel of Mrk "Mark"	OT/NT References	Gospel of Luk "Luke"	OT/NT References
Chapter 28 The Great Commission Continued		**Chapter 16 The Great Commission Continued**			
		v. 17: "And these (a) signs will accompany those who do trust; (b) in My Name they will drive out demons, (c) speak with new tongues."	a). Acts 5:12 b). Mark 9:38; Luke 10:17; Acts 5:16; 8:7; 16:18; 19:12 c). Acts 2:4; 1 Corinthians 12:10		
		v. 18: (a) "Not be injured if they handle snakes or drink poison, and (b) heal the sick by laying hands on them."	a). Luke 10:19; Acts 28:3–6 b). Acts 5:15; James 5:14		
v. 20: "And (a) teaching them to obey everything that I have commanded you. And remember! (b) I will be with you always, yes, even until the end of the age."	a).Acts 2:42 b).Acts 4:31; 18:10; 23:11				

PART 5:

"75" SUBTOPIC TEACHINGS—GOSPEL OF JOHN

Starting on Page 284:

The First Disciples: 1:38–39, 42

Philip and Nathanael: 1:43, 47, 48, 50–51

Water Turned to Wine: 2:4, 7–8

Starting on Page 285:

Yeshua Cleanses the Temple: 2:16, 19

The New Birth: 3:3, 5–8, 10–21

Starting on Page 286:

Samaritan Woman Meets Her Messiah: 4:7, 10, 13–14, 16, 17–18, 21–24, 26

Starting on Page 287:

The Whitened Harvest: 4:32, 34–38

Starting on Page 288:

Welcome at Galilee: 4:44

A Nobleman's Son Healed: 4:48, 50

A Man Healed at the Pool of Bethesda: 5:6, 8, 14

Starting on Page 289:

Honor the Father and the Son: 5:17, 19, 20–23

Life and Judgment Are through the Son: 5:24–30

Starting on Page 290:

The Fourfold Witness: 5:31–47

Starting on Page 292:

Feeding the Five Thousand: 6:5, 10, 12

Yeshua Walks on the Sea: 6:20

The Bread from Heaven: 6:26–27, 29, 32–33, 35–40

Starting on Page 293:

Rejected by His Own: 6:41, 43–51, 53–58

Starting on Page 294:

Many Disciples Turn Away: 6:61–65, 67–71

Starting on Page 295:

Yeshua's Brothers Disbelieve: 7:6–8

Starting on Page 296:

The Heavenly Scholar: 7:16–19, 21–24

Could This Be the Christ?: 7:28–29

Starting on Page 297:

Yeshua and the Religious Leaders: 7:33–34

The Promise of the Holy Spirit: 7:37–39

An Adulteress Faces the Light of the World 8:7, 10–12

Starting on Page 298:

Yeshua Defends His Self-Witness: 8:14–20

Yeshua Predicts His Departure: 8:21, 23–26, 28–29

Starting on Page 299:

The Truth Shall Make You Free: 8:31–32, 34–35

Abraham's Seed and Satan's: 8:36–47

Starting on Page 300:

Before Abraham Was, I Am: 8:49–51, 54–58

Starting on Page 301:

Man Born Blind Receives Sight: 9:3–5, 7

Starting on Page 302:

True Vision and True Blindness: 9:35, 37, 39, 41

Yeshua the True Shepherd: 10:1–6

Starting on Page 303:

Yeshua the Good Shepherd: 10:7–18

Starting on Page 304:

The Shepherd Knows His Sheep: 10:25–30

Renewed Efforts to Stone Yeshua: 10:32, 34–38

Starting on Page 305:

The Death of Lazarus: 11:4, 7, 9–11, 14–15

Starting on Page 306:

I Am the Resurrection and the Life: 11:23, 25–26

Yeshua and Death, the Last Enemy: 11:34

Lazarus Raised from the Dead: 11:39–44

Starting on Page 307:

The Anointing at Bethany: 12:7–8

The Fruitful Grain of Wheat: 12:23–26

Yeshua Predicts His Death on the Cross: 12:27–28, 30–32, 35–36

Starting on Page 308:

Walk in the Light: 12:44–50

Starting on Page 309:

Yeshua Washes the Disciples' Feet: 13:7–8, 10–17

Starting on Page 310:

Yeshua Identifies His Betrayer: 13:18–21, 26–27

The New Commandment: 13:31–35

Starting on Page 311:

Yeshua Predicts Peter's Denial: 13:36, 38

The Way, the Truth, and the Life: 14:1–4, 6

The Father Revealed: 14:7, 9–11

Starting on Page 312:

The Answered Prayer 14:12–14

Starting on Page 312:

Yeshua Promises Another Helper: 14:15–18

Starting on Page 313:

Indwelling of the Father and the Son: 14:19–21, 23–24

The Gift of His Peace: 14:25–31

Starting on Page 314:

The True Vine: 15:1–8

Starting on Page 315:

Love and Joy Perfected: 15:9–17

The World's Hatred: 15:18–25

Starting on Page 316:

The Coming Rejection: 15:26–27, 16:1–4

Starting on Page 317:

The Work of the Holy Spirit: 16:5–15

Starting on Page 318:

Sorrow Will Turn to Joy: 16:16, 19–24

Christ Yeshua Has Overcome the World: 16:25–28, 31–33

Starting on Page 319:

Yeshua Prays for Himself: 17:1–5

Starting on Page 320:

Yeshua Prays for His Disciples: 17:6–19

Starting on Page 321:

Yeshua Prays for All Believers: 17:20–26

Starting on Page 322:

Betrayal and Arrest in Gethsemane: 18:4–8, 11

Yeshua Questioned by the High Priest: 18:20–21, 23

Starting on Page 323:

In Pilate's Court: 18:34, 36–37

Pilate's Decision: 19:11

Behold Your Mother: 19:26–28, 30

Starting on Page 324:

Mary Magdalene Sees the Risen Lord: 20:15–17

The Apostles Commissioned: 20:19, 21–23

Starting on Page 325:

Seeing and Believing: 20:26–27, 29

Breakfast by the Sea: 21:5–6, 10, 12

Yeshua Restores Peter (Kefa): 21:15–19

Starting on Page 326:

The Beloved Disciple and His Book: 21:22

PART 6:
SUBTOPIC SCRIPTURES—GOSPEL OF JOHN

Not in Alignment with the First Three Gospels

(OT/Tanakh and NT/B'rit Hadashah References Included)

John 1:1–5

In the beginning was the Word, and the Word was with God, and the Word was God. He was with God in the beginning. All things came to be through Him, and without Him nothing made had being. In Him was life, and the life was the light of the mankind. The light shines in the darkness, and the darkness has not suppressed it.

~ Within Yeshua's Resurrected Life you to are a new beginning ~

Gospel of Yochanan (John)	OT/NT References
Chapter 1 **The First Disciples**	
v. 38: "*Yeshua* turned and saw them following Him, and He asked them, 'What are you looking for?' They said to Him, '*Rabbi!*' (which means 'Teacher!') 'Where are You staying?'"	
v. 39: "He said to them, 'Come and see.' So they went and saw where He was staying, and remained with Him the rest of the day—it was about four o'clock in the afternoon."	
v. 42: "He took him to *Yeshua*. Looking at him, *Yeshua* said, 'You are *Shim'on Bar-Yochanan*; (a) you will be known as *Kefa.*' (The name means 'rock.')"	a).Matthew 16:19
Chapter 1 **Philip and Nathanael**	
v. 43: "The next day, having decided to leave for the *Galil,* *Yeshua* found (a) Philip and said, 'Follow Me!'"	a).Matthew 10:3; John 5; 12:21–22; 14:8–9
v. 47: "*Yeshua* saw *Natan'el* coming toward Him, (A) 'Here's a true son of *Is'rael*—nothing false in him!'"	A).Psalm 32:2; 73:1
v. 48: "*Natan'el* said to Him, 'How do you know me?' *Yeshua* answered him, 'Before Philip called you, when you were under the fig tree, I saw you.'"	
v. 50: "*Yeshua* answered him, 'you believe all this just because I told you I saw you under the fig tree? You will see greater things than that!'"	
v. 51: "Then He said to him, 'Yes indeed! I tell you that (A) you will see heaven open up and the angels of God going up coming down on the Son of Man!'"	A).Genesis 28:12; Luke 2:9, 13; Acts 1:10; 7:55–56
Chapter 2 **Water turned Into Wine**	
v. 4: "*Yeshua* replied, '(a) Mother, (B) why should that concern Me?—or you? (c) My time hasn't come yet.'"	a).John 19:26 B).2 Samuel 16:10 c).John 7:6, 8, 30; 8:20
v. 7: "*Yeshua* told them, 'Fill the jars with water,' and they filled them to the brim."	
v. 8: "He said, 'Now draw some out, and take it to the man in charge of the banquet'; and they took it."	

Gospel of Yochanan (John)	OT/NT References
Chapter 2 **Yeshua Cleanses the Temple**	
v. 16: "And to the pigeon-sellers He said, 'Get these things out of here! How dare you turn (a) My Father's house into a market!'"	a).Luke 2:49
v. 19: "*Yeshua answered them, (a) 'Destroy this temple, and in three days I will raise it up again.'"	a).Matthew 26:61; 27:40; Mark 14:58; 15:29; Luke 24:46; Acts 6:14; 10:40; 1 Corinthians 15:4
Chapter 3 **The New Birth**	
v. 3: "'Yes indeed,' *Yeshua answered him, 'I tell you that (a) unless a person is born again from above, he cannot see the Kingdom of God.'"	a).John 1:13; Galatians 6:15; Titus 3:5; James 1:18; 1 Peter 1:23; 1 John 3:9
v. 5: "*Yeshua answered, 'Yes, indeed, I tell you that (a) unless a person is born from water and the Spirit, he cannot enter the Kingdom of God.'"	a).Mark 16:16; Acts 2:38
v. 6: "What is born from the flesh is (a) flesh, and what is born from the Spirit is spirit."	a).John 1:13; 1 Corinthians 15:50
v. 7: "Stop being amazed at My telling you that you must be born again from above!"	
v. 8: (A) "The wind blows, where it wants to, and you hear its sound, but you don't know where it comes from or where it's going. That's how it is with everyone who has been born from the Spirit."	A).Psalm 135:7; Ecclesiastes 11:5; Ezekiel 37:9; 1 Corinthians 2:11
v. 10: "*Yeshua answered him, 'You hold the office of teacher in *Isra'el, and you don't know this?'"	
v. 11: (a) "Yes indeed! I tell you that what we speak about, we know; and what we give evidence of, we have seen; but (b) you people don't accept our evidence!"	a).Matthew 11:27 b).John 3:28; 8:14
v. 12: "If you people don't believe Me when I tell you about the things of the world, how will you believe Me when I tell you about the things of heaven?"	
v. 13: (A) "No one has gone up into heaven; there is only the One who has come down from heaven, the Son of Man."	A).Deuteronomy 30:1; 2 Proverbs 30:4; Acts 2:34; Romans 10:6; 1 Corinthians 15:47; Ephesians 9

Gospel of Yochanan (John)	OT/NT References
Chapter 3 **The New Birth Continued**	
v. 14: (A) "Just as *Moshe* lifted up the serpent in the desert, so must the (b) Son of Man be lifted up."	A).Numbers 21:9 b).Matthew 27:35; Mark 15:24; Luke 23:33; John 8:28; 12:34; 19:18
v. 15: "So that everyone who (a) trusts in Him may (b) have eternal life."	a).John 6:47 b).John 3:36
v. 16: (a) "For God so loved the world that He gave His only and unique (B) Son, so that everyone who trusts in Him may have eternal life, instead of being utterly destroyed."	a).Romans 5:8; Ephesians 2:4; 2 Thessalonians 2:16; 1 John 4:9–10; Revelation 1:5 B).Isaiah 9:6
v. 17: (a) "For God did not send the Son into the world to judge the world, but rather so that through Him, the world might be saved."	a).Matthew 1:21; Luke 9:56; 1 John 4:14
v. 18: (a) "Those who trust in Him are not judged; those who do not trust have been judged already, in that they have not trusted in the One who is God's only and unique Son."	a).John 5:24; 6:40, 47; 20:31; Romans 8:1
v. 19: "Now this is the judgement: (a) the light has come into the world, but people loved the darkness rather than the light. Why? Because their actions were wicked."	a). John 1:4, 9–11
v. 20: "For (A) everyone who does evil things hates the light and avoids it, so that his actions won't be exposed."	A). Job 24:13; Ephesians 5:11, 13
v. 21: "But everyone who does what is true comes to the light, so that all may see that his actions are accomplished (a) through God."	a). John 15:4–5 1 Corinthians 15:10
Chapter 4 **Samaritan Woman Meets Her Messiah**	
v. 7: "A woman from *Shomron* came to draw some water; and *Yeshua* said to her, 'Give Me a drink of water.'"	
v. 10: "*Yeshua* answered her, 'If you knew God's (a) gift, that is, Who it is saying to you, "Give Me a drink of water," then you would have asked Him; and He would have given you (B) living water.'"	a). Romans 5:15 B).Isaiah 12:3; 44:3; Jeremiah 2:13; Zechariah 13:1; 14:8; John 7:38
v. 13: "*Yeshua* answered, 'Everyone who drinks this water will get thirsty again.'"	

Gospel of Yochanan (John)	OT/NT References
Chapter 4 **Samaritan Woman Meets Her Messiah Continued**	
v. 14: "But (a) whoever drinks the water I will give him will never be thirsty again! On the contrary, the water I give him (b) will become a spring of water inside him, welling up into eternal life!"	a). John 6:35, 58 b). John 7:37–38
v. 16: "He said to her, 'Go, call your husband, and come back.'"	
v. 17: "She answered, 'I don't have a husband.' *Yeshua* said to her, 'You're right, you don't have a husband!'"	
v. 18: "You've had five husbands in the past, and you're not married to the man you're living with now! You've spoken the truth!"	
v. 21: "*Yeshua* said, 'Lady, believe Me, the time is coming when you will worship the Father (A) neither on this mountain nor in *Yerushalayim*.'"	A). Malachi 1:11; 1 Timothy 2:8
v. 22: "You people don't know (A) what you are worshipping; we worship what we do know, because (B) salvation comes from the Jews."	A). 2 Kings 17: 28–41 B). Isaiah 2:3; Luke 4:47; Romans 3:1; 9:4–5
v. 23: "But the time is coming—indeed, it's here now—when the true worshippers will (a) worship the Father (b) spiritually and (c) truly, for these are the kind of people the Father wants worshipping Him."	a). Matthew 18:29; Hebrews 13:10–14 b). Philippians 3:3 c). John 1:17
v. 24: (a) "God is spirit; and worshippers must worship Him spiritually and truly."	a). 2 Corinthians 3:17
v. 26: "*Yeshua* said to her, '(A) I, the person speaking to you, am He.'"	A). Daniel 9:25; Matthew 26:63–64; Mark 14:61–62
Chapter 4 **The Whitened Harvest**	
v. 32: "But He answered, 'I have food to eat that you don't know about.'"	
v. 34: "*Yeshua* said to them, '(A) My food is to do what the One who sent Me wants and to (B) bring His work to completion.'"	A). Psalm 40:7–8; Hebrews 10:9 B). Job 23:12; John 6:38; 17:4; 19:30

Gospel of Yochanan (John)	OT/NT References
Chapter 4 **The Whitened Harvest Continued**	
v. 35: "Don't you have a saying, 'Four more months and then (A) the harvest'? Well, what I say to you is: open your eyes and look at the fields! They're already (b) ripe for harvest!"	A).Genesis 8:22 b).Matthew 9:37; Luke 10:2
v. 36: (A) "The one who reaps receives his wages and gathers fruit for eternal life, (b) so that the reaper and the sower many be glad together."	A).Daniel 12:3; Romans 6:22 b).1 Thessalonians 2:1, 9
v. 37: "For in this matter, the proverb, (a) 'One sows and another reaps,' holds true."	a).1 Corinthians 3:5–9
v. 38: "I sent you to reap what you haven't worked for. (A) Others have done the hard labor, and you have benefited from their work."	A).Jeremiah 44:4; 1 Peter 1:12
Chapter 4 **Welcome at Galilee**	
v. 44: "Now(a) *Yeshua* Himself said, 'A prophet is not respected in his own country.'"	a).Matthew 13:57; Mark 6:4; Luke 4:24
Chapter 4 **A Nobleman's Son Healed**	
v. 48: "*Yeshua* answered, (a) 'Unless you people see signs and miracles, you simply will not trust!'"	a).John 6:30; Romans 15:19; 1 Corinthians 1:22; 2 Corinthians 12:12; 2 Thessalonians 2:9; Hebrews 2:4
v. 50: "*Yeshua* replied, 'You may go, your son is alive.' The man believed what *Yeshua* said and left."	
Chapter 5 **A Man Healed at the Pool of Bethesda**	
v. 6: "*Yeshua*, seeing this man and knowing that he had been there a long time, said to him, 'Do you want to be healed?'"	
v. 8: "*Yeshua* said to him, (a) 'Get up, pick up your mat and walk!'"	a).Matthew 9:6; Mark 2:11; Luke 5:24

Gospel of Yochanan (John)	OT/NT References
Chapter 5 **A Man Healed at the Pool of Bethesda Continued**	
v. 14: "Afterwards *Yeshua* found him in the Temple court and said to him, 'See, you are well! (a) Now stop sinning, or something worse may happen to you!'"	a).Matthew 12:45; Mark 2:5; John 8:11
Chapter 5 **Honor the Father and the Son**	
v. 17: "But He answered then, (a) 'My Father has been working until now, and I too am working.'"	a).John 9:4; 17:4
v. 19: "Therefore, *Yeshua* said this to them; 'Yes indeed! I tell you that the (a) Son cannot do anything on His own, but only what He sees the Father doing; whatever the Father does, the Son does too.'"	a).Matthew 26:39; John 5:30; 6:38; 8:28; 12:49; 14:10
v. 20: "For the (a) Father loves the Son and (b) shows Him everything He does; and He will show Him even greater things than these, so that you will be amazed."	a).Matthew 3:17; John 3:35; 2 Peter 1:17 b).Matthew 11:27
v. 21: "Just as the Father raises the dead and makes them alive, (a) so too the Son makes alive anyone He wants."	a).Luke 7:14; 8:54; John 11:25
v. 22: "The Father does not judge anyone but (a) has entrusted all judgement to the Son."	a).Matthew 11:27; 28:18; John 3:35; 17:2; Acts 17:31; 1 Peter 4:5
v. 23: "So that all may honor the Son as they honor the Father. (a) Whoever fails to honor the Son is not honoring the Father who sent Him."	a).Luke 10:16; 1 John 2:23
Chapter 5 **Life and Judgment Are through the Son**	
v. 24: "Yes, indeed! I tell you that (a) whoever hears what I am saying and trusts the One who sent Me has eternal life—that is, he will not come up for judgment (b) but has already crossed over from death to life!"	a).John 3:16, 18; 6:47 b).1 John 3:14
v. 25: "Yes, indeed! I tell you that there is coming a time—in fact, it's already here—when (a) the dead will hear the voice of the Son of God, and those who listen will come to life."	a).Ephesians 2:1, 5; Colossians 2:13

Part 6: Subtopic Scriptures—Gospel of John

Gospel of Yochanan (John)	OT/NT References
Chapter 5 **Life and Judgment Are through the Son Continued**	
v. 26: "For just (A) as the Father has life in Himself, so He has given the Son (b) life to have in Himself."	A).Psalm 36:9 b).John 1:4; 14:6; 1 Corinthians 15:45
v. 27: "Also He (a) has given Him authority to execute judgment, (B) because He is the Son of Man."	a). John 9:39; Acts 10:42; 17:31 B).Daniel 7:13
v. 28: "Don't be surprised at this; because the time is coming when all who are in the grave will (a) hear His voice."	a).1 Thessalonians 4:15 17
v. 29: (A) "And come out—(B) those who have done good to a resurrection of life, and those who have done evil to a resurrection of judgment."	A).Isaiah 26:19; 1 Corinthians 15:52 B).Daniel 12:2; Matthew 25:46; Acts 24:15
v. 30: (a) "I can't do a thing on My own. As I hear, I judge; and My judgment is right; because (b) I don't seek My own desire, but the desire of the One who sent Me."	a).John 5:19 b).Matthew 26:39; John 4:34; 6:38
Chapter 5 **The Fourfold Witness**	
v. 31: (a) "If I testify on My own behalf, My testimony is not valid."	a).John 8:14; Revelation 3:14
v. 32: (a) "But there is someone else testifying on My behalf, and I know that the testimony He is making is valid."	a).Matthew 3:17; John 8:18; 1 John 5:6
v. 33: "You have sent *Yochanan*, and (a) he has testified to the truth."	a).John 1:15; 19:27, 32
v. 34: "Not that I collect human testimony; rather, I say these things so that you might be saved."	
v. 35: "He was a lamp burning and (A) shining, and for a little while (b) you were willing to bask in his light."	A).2 Samuel 21:17; 2 Peter 1:19 b).Matthew 13:20; Mark 6:20
v. 36: "But (a) I have a testimony that is greater than *Yohanan's*. For the (b) things the Father has given Me to do, the very (c) things I am doing now, testify on My behalf that the Father has sent Me."	a).1 John:5:9 b).John 3:2; 10:25; 17:4 c).John 9:16; 10:38

Gospel of Yochanan (John)	OT/NT References
Chapter 5 **The Fourfold Witness Continued**	
v. 37: "In addition, the Father who sent Me (a) has Himself testified on My behalf. But you have (B) never heard His voice or seen His shape."	a).Matthew 3:17; John 6:27; 8:18 B) Deuteronomy 4:12; John 1:18; 1 Timothy 1:17; 1 John 4:12
v. 38: "Moreover, His word does not stay in you, because you don't trust the One He sent."	
v. 39: (A) "You keep examining the *Tanakh* because you think that in it you have eternal life. (B) Those very Scriptures bear witness to Me."	A).Isaiah 8:20; 34:16; Luke 16:29; Acts 17:11 B).Deuteronomy 18:15, 18; Luke 24:27
v. 40: (a) "But you won't come to Me in order to have life!"	a).John 1:11; 3:19
v. 41: (a) "I don't collect praise from men."	a).John 5:44; 7:18; 1 Thessalonians 2:6
v. 42: "But I do know you people—I know you have no love for God in you!"	
v. 43: "I have come in My Father's name, and you don't accept Me; if someone else comes in His own name, him you will accept."	
v. 44: (a) "How can you trust? You're busy collecting praise from each other, instead of (b) seeking praise from God only."	a).John 12:43 b).Romans 2:29
v. 45: "But don't think that it is I who will be your accuser before the Father. (a) Do you know who will accuse you? *Moshe,* the very one you have counted on!"	a).Romans 2:12
v. 46: "For if you really believed *Moshe,* you would believe Me; because (A) it was about Me that he wrote."	A).Genesis 3:15; Deuteronomy 18:15, 18; John 1:45; Acts 26:22
v. 47: "But if you (a) don't believe what he wrote, how are you going to believe what I say?"	a).Luke 16:29, 31

Gospel of Yochanan (John)	OT/NT References
Chapter 6 **Feeding the Five Thousand**	
v. 5: (a) "So when *Yeshua looked up and saw that a large crowd was approaching, (b) He said to Philip, 'Where will we be able to buy bread, so that these people can eat?'"	a). Matthew 14:14; Mark 6:35; Luke 9:12 b). John 1:43
v. 10: "*Yeshua said, 'Have the people sit down.' There was a lot of grass there, so they sat down. The number of men was about five thousand."	
v. 12: "After they had eaten their fill, He told His *talmidim, 'Gather the leftover pieces, so that nothing gets wasted.'"	
Chapter 6 **Yeshua Walks on the Sea**	
v. 20: "But He said to them, 'Stop being afraid, (A) it is I.'"	A). Isaiah 43:1–2
Chapter 6 **The Bread from Heaven**	
v. 26: "*Yeshua answered, 'Yes, indeed! I tell you, you're not looking for Me because you saw miraculous signs, but because you ate the bread and had all you wanted!'"	
v. 27: (a) "Don't work for the food which passes away but (b) for the food that stays on into eternal life, which the Son of Man will give you. (C) For this is the One on whom God the Father has put His seal."	a). Matthew 6:19 b). John 4:14; Ephesians 2:8–9 C). Psalm 2:7; Isaiah 42:1; Mathew 3:17; 17:5; Mark 1:11; 9:7; Luke 3:22; 9:35; John 3:22; 9:35; John 5:37; Acts 2:22; 2 Peter 1:17
v. 29: "*Yeshua answered, (a) 'Here's what the work of God is: to trust in the One He sent!'"	a). 1 Thessalonians 1:3; James 2:22; 1 John 3:23; Revelation 2:26
v. 32: "*Yeshua said to them, 'Yes, indeed! I tell you it wasn't *Moshe who gave you the bread from heaven. But (a) My Father is giving you the genuine bread from heaven.'"	a). John 3:13, 16
v. 33: "For God's bread is the One who comes down out of heaven and gives life to the world."	

Gospel of Yochanan (John)	OT/NT References
Chapter 6 **The Bread from Heaven Continued**	
v. 35: "*Yeshua* answered, (a) 'I am the bread which is life! (b) Whoever comes to Me will never go hungry, and (C) whoever trusts in Me will never be thirsty.'"	a).John 6:48, 58 b).John 4:14; 7:37; Revelation 7:16 C).Isaiah 55:1–2
v. 36: (a) "I told you that you have seen but still (b) don't trust."	a).John 6:26, 64; 15:24 b).John 10:26
v. 37: (a) "Everyone the Father gives Me will come to Me, and (b) whoever comes to Me I will certainly not turn away."	a).John 6:45 b).Matthew 24:24; John 10:28–29; 2 Timothy 2:19; 1 John 2:19
v. 38: "For I have come down from heaven to (a) do not My own will (b) but the will of the One who sent Me."	a).Matthew 26:39; John 5:30 b).John 4:34
v. 39: "And this is the will of the One who sent Me; (a) that I should not lose any of all those He has given Me but should raise then up on the Last Day."	a).John 10:28; 17:12; 18:9
v. 40: "Yes, this is the will of My Father: (a) that all who see the Son and trust in Him should have eternal life, and that I should raise them up on the Last Day."	a).John 3:15–16; 4:14; 6:27, 47, 54
Chapter 6 **Rejected by His Own**	
v. 41: "At this the *Judeans* began grumbling about Him because He said, 'I am the bread which has come down from heaven.'"	
v. 43: "*Yeshua* answered them, 'Stop grumbling to each other!'"	
v. 44: (A) "No one can come to Me unless the Father—the One who sent Me—(b) draws him. And I will raise him up on the Last Day."	A).Song of Solomon 1:4 b).Ephesians 2:8–9; Philippians 1:29; 2:12–13
v. 45: "It is written in the Prophets, (A) 'They will all be taught by *Adonai.*' (b) Everyone who listens to the Father and learns from Him comes to Me."	A).Isaiah 54:13; Jeremiah 31:34; Micah 4:2; Hebrews 8:10 b).John 6:37
v. 46: (a) "Not that anyone has seen the Father (b) except the One who is from God—He has seen the Father."	a).John 1:18 b).Matthew 11:27; Luke 10:22; John 7:29

Gospel of Yochanan (John)	OT/NT References
Chapter 6 **Rejected by His Own Continued**	
v. 47: "Yes, indeed! I tell you, (a) whoever trusts has eternal life."	a). John 3:16, 18
v. 48: (a) "I am the bread which is life."	a). John 6:33, 35; Galatians 2:20; Colossians 3:3–4
v. 49: (a) "Your fathers ate the *man* in the desert; they died."	a). John 6:31, 58
v. 50: (a) "But the bread that comes down from heaven is such that a person may eat it and not die."	a). John 6:51, 58
v. 51: "I am the living bread (a) that has come down from heaven; if anyone eats this bread, he will life forever. Furthermore, (b) the bread that I will give is My own flesh; and I will give it for the life of the world."	a). John 3:13 b). Hebrews 10:5
v. 53: "Then *Yeshua* said to them, 'Yes, indeed! I tell you that unless (a) you eat the flesh of the Son of Man and drink His blood, you do not have life in yourselves.'"	a). Matthew 26: 26
v. 54: (a) "Whoever eats My flesh and drinks My blood has eternal life—that is, I will raise him up on the Last Day."	a). John 4:14; 6:27, 40
v. 55: "For My flesh is true food, and My blood is true drink."	
v. 56: "Whoever easts My flesh and drinks My blood (a) lives in Me, and I live in him."	a). 1 John 3:24; 4:15–16
v. 57: "Just as the living Father sent Me, and I live through the Father, so also whoever eats Me will live through Me."	
v. 58: (a) "So this is the bread that has come down from heaven—it is not like the bread (B) the fathers ate; they're dead, but whoever eats this bread will live forever!"	a). John 6:49–51 B). Exodus 16:14–35
Chapter 6 **Many Disciples Turn Away**	
v. 61: "But *Yeshua*, aware that His *talmidim* were grumbling about this, said to them, 'This is a trap for you?'"	

Gospel of Yochanan (John)	OT/NT References
Chapter 6 **Many Disciples Turn Away Continued**	
v. 62: (a) "Suppose you were to see the Son of Man going back up to where He was before?"	a).Mark 16:19; John 3:13; Acts 1:9; 2:32–33; Ephesians 4:8
v. 63: (A) "It is the Spirit who gives life, the (b) flesh is no help. The (c) words I have spoken to you are Spirit and life."	A).Genesis 2:7; 2 Corinthians 3:6 b).John 3:6 c). John 6:68; 14:24
v. 64: (a) "'Yet some among you do not trust.' (b) (For *Yeshua* knew from the outset which ones would not trust Him, also which one would betray Him.)"	a).John 6:36 b).John 2:24–25; 13:11
v. 65: "'This,' He said, 'is why (a) I told you that no one can come to Me unless the Father has made it possible for him.'"	a).John 6:37, 44–45
v. 67: "So *Yeshua* said to the Twelve, 'Don't you want to leave too?'"	
v. 68: "*Shim'on Kefa* answered Him, 'Lord, to whom would we go? You have (a) the word of eternal life.'"	a).Acts 5:20
v. 69: (a) "We have trusted, and we know that you are the Holy One of God."	a).Matthew 16:16; Mark 8:29; Luke 9:20; John 1:49; 11:27
v. 70: "*Yeshua* answered them, (a) 'Didn't I choose you, the Twelve? Yet (b) one of you is an adversary.'"	a).Luke 6:13 b).John 13:27
v. 71: "He was speaking of (a) *Y'hudah Ben-Shim'on*, from *K'riot*; for this man—one of the Twelve!—was soon to (b) betray Him."	a).John 12:4; 13:2, 26 b).Matthew 26:14–16
Chapter 7 **Yeshua's Brothers Disbelieve**	
v. 6: "*Yeshua* said to them, (a) 'My time has not yet come; but for you, anytime is right.'"	a).John 2:4; 8:20
v. 7: (a) "The world can't hate you, but it does hate Me, (b) because I keep telling it how wicked its ways are."	a).John 15:19 b).John 3:19
v. 8: "You, go on up to the festival; as for Me, I am not going up to this festival now, (a) because the right time has not yet come."	a).John 8:20

Part 6: Subtopic Scriptures—Gospel of John

Gospel of Yochanan (John)	OT/NT References
Chapter 7 **The Heavenly Scholar**	
v. 16: "So *Yeshua* gave them an answer; (A) 'My teaching is not My own, it comes from the One who sent Me.'"	A).Deuteronomy 18:15, 19; John 3:11
v. 17: (A) "If anyone wants to do His will, he will know whether My teaching is from God or I speak on My own."	A).Psalm 25:9, 14; Proverbs 3:32; Daniel 12:10; John 3:21; 8:43
v. 18: (a) "A person who speaks on his own is trying to win praise for himself; but a Person who (b) tries to win praise for the One who sent Him is honest, (c) there is nothing false about Him."	a).John 5:41 b).John 8:50 c).John 8:46; 2 Corinthians 5:21; Hebrews 4:15; 7:26; 1 Peter 1:19; 2:22
v. 19: (A) "Didn't *Moshe* give you the *Torah*? Yet not one of you obeys the *Torah*! (b) Why are you out to kill Me?"	A).Exodus 24:3; Deuteronomy 33:4; Acts 7:38 b).Matthew 12:14
v. 21: "*Yeshua* answered them, 'I did one thing; and because of this, all of you are amazed.'"	
v. 22: (A) "*Moshe* gave you *b'rit-milah* not that it came from *Moshe* but from the (B) *Patriarchs*—and you do a boy's *b'rit-milah* on *Shabbat*."	A).Leviticus 12:3 B).Genesis 19:9–14; Acts 7:8
v. 23: "If a boy is circumcised on *Shabbat* so that the *Torah* of *Moshe* will not be broken, why are you angry at Me because (a) I made a man's whole body well on *Shabbat*?"	a).John 5:8, 9, 16
v. 24: (A) "Stop judging by surface appearances, and judge the right way!"	A).Deuteronomy 1:16; Proverbs 24:23; John 8:15; James 2:1
Chapter 7 **Could This Be the Christ?**	
v. 28: "Whereupon *Yeshua*, continuing to teach in the Temple courts, cried out, (a) 'Indeed you do know Me! (b) And I have not come on My own! The One who sent Me (c) is real. (d) But Him you don't know!'"	a).John 8:14 b).John 5:43 c).Romans 3:4 d).John 1:18; 8:55
v. 29: (a) "I do know Him, because I am with Him, and He sent Me!"	a).Matthew 11:27; John 8:55; 17:25

Gospel of Yochanan (John)	OT/NT References
Chapter 7 **Yeshua and the Religious Leaders**	
v. 33: "*Yeshua* said, (a) 'I will be with you only a little while longer; then I will (b) go away to the One who sent Me.'"	a).John 13:33 b).Mark 16:18; Luke 24:51; Acts 1:9; Hebrews 9:24; 1 Peter 3:22
v. 34: "You (A) will look for Me and not find Me; indeed where I am, you (b) cannot come."	A).Hosea 5:6 b).Matthew 5:20; 1 Corinthians 6:9; 15:50; Revelation 21:27
Chapter 7 **The Promise of the Holy Spirit**	
v. 37: (A) "Now on the last day of the festival, *Hoshana Rabbah,* *Yeshua* stood and cried out, (B) 'If anyone is thirsty, let him keep coming to Me and drinking!'"	A).Leviticus 23:36; Numbers 29:35; Nehemiah 8:18 B).Isaiah 55:1
v. 38: (A) "Whoever puts his trust in Me, as the Scripture says, (B) rivers of living water will flow from his inmost being!"	A).Deuteronomy 18:15 B).Isaiah 12:3; 43:20; 44:3; 55:1; John 6:35; Revelation 21:6; 22:17
v. 39: (A) "Now He said this about the Spirit, whom those who trusted in Him were to receive later—the Spirit had not yet been given, because *Yeshua* had not yet been glorified."	A).Isaiah 44:3; Joe 2:28; John 1:33
Chapter 8 **An Adulteress Faces the Light of the World**	
v. 7: "When they kept questioning Him, He straighten up and said to them, (A) 'The one of you who is without sin, let him be the first to throw a stone at her.'"	A).Deuteronomy 17:7; Romans 2:1
v. 10: "Standing up, *Yeshua* said to her, 'Where are they? Has no one condemned you?'"	
v. 11: "She said, 'No one sir.' *Yeshua* said, (a) 'Neither do I condemn you. Now go, and (b) don't sin any more.'"	a).Luke 9:56; 12:14; John 3:17 b).John 5:14
v. 12: "*Yeshua* spoke to them again: (A) 'I am the light of the world; whoever (b) follows Me will never walk in darkness but will have the light which gives life.'"	A).Is 9:2; Mal 4:2; John 1:4; 9:5; 12:35; 2 Tim 1:10 b).1 Thess:5:5

Gospel of Yochanan (John)	OT/NT References
Chapter 8 **Yeshua Defends His Self-Witness**	
v. 14: "*Yeshua* answered them, 'Even if I do testify on My own behalf, My testimony is indeed valid; because I know where I come from and where I'm going; but (a) you do not know where I came from or where I'm going.'"	a).John 7:28; 9:29
v. 15: (A) "You judge by merely human standards. As for Me, (b) I pass judgment on no one."	A).1 Samuel 16:7 John 7:24 b).John 3:17; 12:47; 18:36
v. 16: "But if I were indeed to pass judgement, My judgement would be valid; because it is (a) not I alone who judge, but I and the One who sent Me."	a).John 16:32
v. 17: (A) "And even in your *Torah* it is written that the testimony of two people is valid."	A).Deuteronomy 17:6; 19:15; Matthew 18:16; 2 Corinthians 13:1; Hebrews 10:28
v. 18: "I Myself testify on My own behalf, and so does (a) the Father who sent Me."	a).John 5:37; 1 John 5:9
v. 19: "They said to Him, 'Where is this "Father" of Yours?' *Yeshua* answered, (a) 'You know neither Me nor My Father; (b) if you knew Me, you would know My Father too.'"	a).John 16:3 b).John 14:7
v. 20: "He said these things when He was in the (a) Temple treasury room; yet (b) no one arrested Him, because (c) His time had not yet come."	a).Mark 12:41, 43; Luke 21:1 b).John 2:4; 7:30 c).John 7:8
Chapter 8 **Yeshua Predicts His Departure**	
v. 21: "Again He told them, 'I am going away, and (a) you will look for Me, but you (b) will die in your sin—where I am going to, you cannot come.'"	a).John 7:34; 13:33 b).John 15:19; 17:16; 1 John 4:5
v. 23: "*Yeshua* said to them, (a) 'You are from below, I am from above; (b) you are of this world, I am not of this world.'"	a).John 3:31 b).John 15:19; 17:16; 1 John 4:5
v. 24: (a) "This is why I said to you that you will die in your sins; for if (b) you do not trust that I AM [who I say I AM], you will die in your sins."	a).John 8:21 b).Mark 16:16
v. 25: "At this, they said to Him, 'You? Who are you?' *Yeshua* answered, (a) 'Just what I've been telling you from the start.'"	a).John 4:26

Gospel of Yochanan (John)	OT/NT References
Chapter 8 **Yeshua Predicts His Departure Continued**	
v. 26: "There are many things I could say about you, and many judgments I could make. However, the (a) One who sent Me is true; so (b) I say in the world only what I have heard from Him."	a).John 7:28 b).John 3:32; 15:15
v. 28: "So *Yeshua* said, 'When you (a) lift up the Son of Man, (b) then you will know that I AM [who I say I AM], and (c) that of Myself I do nothing, (D) but say only what the Father has taught Me.'"	a).Matthew 27:35; Mark 15:24; Luke 23:13; John 3:14; 12:32; 19:18 b).Romans 1:4 c).John 5:19, 30 D).Deuteronomy 18:15, 18–19; John 3:11
v. 29: "Also, the (a) One who sent Me is still with Me; (b) He did not leave Me to Myself, (c) because I always do what pleases Him."	a).John 14:10 b).John 8:16; 16:32 c).John 4:34; 5:30; 6:38
Chapter 8 **The Truth Shall Make You Free**	
v. 31: "So *Yeshua* said to the Judeans who had trusted Him, 'If you (a) obey what I say, then you are really My *talmidim*.'"	a).John 14:15, 23
v. 32: "You will know the (a) truth and (b) the truth will set you free."	a).John 1:14, 17; 14:6 b).Romans 6:14; 18:22; James 1:25; 2:12
v. 34: "*Yeshua* answered them, 'Yes, indeed! I tell you that (A) everyone who practices sin is a slave of sin.'"	A).Proverbs 5:22; Romans 6:16; 2 Peter 2:19
v. 35: "Now (A) a slave does not remain with a family forever, but a son does remain with it forever."	A).Genesis 2110; Galatians 4:30
Chapter 8 **Abraham's Seed and Satan's**	
v. 36: (a) "So if the Son frees you, you will really be free!"	a).Romans 8:2; 2 Corinthians 3:17; Galatians 5:1
v. 37: "I know you are the seed of *Avraham*. Yet (a) you are out to kill Me, because what I am saying makes no headway in you."	a).John 7:19

Gospel of Yochanan (John)	OT/NT References
Chapter 8 **Abraham's Seed and Satan's Continued**	
v. 38: (a) "I say what My Father has shown Me; you do what your father has told you!"	a).John 3:32; 5:19, 30; 14:10, 24
v. 39: "They answered Him, (a) 'Our father is *Avraham.*' *Yeshua* replied, (b) 'If you are children of *Avraham*, then do the things *Avraham* did!'"	a).Matthew 3:9; John 8:37 b).Romans 2:28; Galatians 3:7, 29
v. 40: (a) "As it is, you are out to kill Me, a man who has told you the truth (b) which I heard from God. *Avraham* did nothing like that!"	a).John 8:37 b).John 8:26
v. 41: "'You are doing the things your father does.' 'We're not illegitimate children!' they said to Him. (A) 'We have only one Father—God!'"	A).Deuteronomy 32:6; Isaiah 63:16; Malachi 1:6
v. 42: "*Yeshua* replied to them, (a) 'If God were your Father, you would love Me; because (b) I came out from God; and now I have arrived here. (c) I did not come on My own; He sent Me.'"	a).1 John 5:1 b).John 16:27; 17:8, 25 c).John 5:43; Galatians 4:4
v. 43: (a) "Why don't you understand what I'm saying? Because you can't bear to listen to My message."	a).John 7:17
v. 44: (a) "You belong to your father, Satan, and (c) you want to carry out (b) your father's desires. From the start he was a murderer, and he has (D) never stood by the truth, because there is no truth in him. When he tells a lie, he is in character; because he is a liar—indeed, the inventor of the lie!"	a).Matthew 13:38; 1 John 3:8 b).1 John 2:26, 17 c).1 John 3:8–10, 15 D).Jude 1:6
v. 45: "But as for Me, because I tell the truth you don't believe me."	
v. 46: "Which one of you can show Me where I'm wrong? If I'm telling the truth, why don't you believe Me?"	
v. 47: (a) "Whoever belongs to God listens to what God says; the reason you don't listen is that you don't belong to God!"	a).Luke 8:15; John 10:26; 1 John 4:6
Chapter 8 **Before Abraham Was, I Am**	
v. 49: "*Yeshua* replied, 'Me? I have no demon. I am honoring My Father. But you (a) dishonor Me.'"	a).John 5:41

Gospel of Yochanan (John)	OT/NT References
Chapter 8 **Before Abraham Was, I Am Continued**	
v. 50: (a) "I am not seeking praise for Myself. There is One who is seeking it, and He is the judge."	a).John 5:41; 7:18; Philippians 2:6–8
v. 51: "Yes, indeed! I tell you that (a) whoever obeys My teaching will never see death."	a).John 5:24; 11:26
v. 54: "*Yeshua* answered, (a) 'If I praise Myself, My praise counts for nothing. The (b) One who is praising Me is My Father, the very One about whom you keep saying, "He is our God."'"	a).John 5:31–32 b).John 5:41; Acts 3:13
v. 55: "Now (a) you have not known Him, but I do know Him; indeed, if I were to say that I don't know Him, I would be a liar like you! But I do know Him, and (b) I obey His word."	a).John 5:31–32 b).John 5:41; Acts 3:13
v. 56: "*Avraham,* your father, was (a) glad that he would see My day; (b) then he saw it and was overjoyed."	a).Luke 10:24 b).Matthew 13:17; Hebrews 11:13
v. 57: "'Why, you're not yet fifty years old,' the Judeans replied, 'and You have seen *Avraham?*'"	
v. 58: "*Yeshua* said to them, 'Yes, indeed! Before (A) *Avraham* came into being, (B) I AM!'"	A).Micah 5:2; John 17:5; Hebrews 7:3; Revelation 22:13 B).Exodus 3:14; Isaiah 43:13; John 17:5, 24; Colossians 1:17; Revelation 1:8
Chapter 9 **Man Born Blind Receives Sight**	
v. 3: "*Yeshua* answered, 'His blindness is due neither to his sin nor to that of his parents; (a) it happened so that God's power might be seen at work in him.'"	a).John 11:4
v. 4: (b) "As long as it is day, (a) we must keep doing the work of the One who sent Me; the night is coming, when no one can work."	a).John 4:34; 5:19, 36; 17:4 b).John 11:9–10; 12:25; Galatians 6:10
v. 5: "While I am in the world, (a) I am the light of the world."	a).John 1:5, 9; 3:19; 8:12; 12:35, 46

Gospel of Yochanan (John)	OT/NT References
Chapter 9 **Man Born Blind Receives Sight Continued**	
v. 7: "And said to him, 'Go, wash off (A) in the Pool of *Shiloach!*' (The name means 'sent.') So (B) he went and washed and came away seeing."	A).Nehemiah 3:15; Isaiah 8:6; Luke 13:4; John 9:11 B).2 Kings 5:14
Chapter 9 **True Vision and True Blindness**	
v. 35: "*Yeshua* heard that they had thrown the man out. (a) He found him and said, 'Do you (b) trust in (c) the Son of Man?'"	a).John 5:14 b).John 1:7; 16:31 c).Matthew 14:33; 16:16; Mark 1:1; John 10:36; 1 John 5:13
v. 37: "*Yeshua* said to him, 'You have seen Him. In fact, (a) He's the one speaking with you now.'"	a).John 4:26
v. 39: "*Yeshua* said, 'It is to (a) judge that I came into this world, so (b) that those who do not see might see, and those who do see might become blind.'"	a).John 3:17; 5:22, 27; 12:47 b).Matthew 13:13; 15:14
v. 41: "*Yeshua* answered them, (a) 'If you were blind, you would not be guilty of sin. But since you still say, "We see," your guilt remains.'"	a).John 15:22, 24
Chapter 10 **Yeshua the True Shepard**	
v. 1: "Yes, indeed! I tell you, the person who doesn't enter the sheep-pen through the door, but climbs in some other way, is a thief and a robber."	
v. 2: "But the one who goes in through the gate is the sheep's own shepherd."	
v. 3: "This is the one the gate-keeper admits, and the sheep hears his voice. He calls his own sheep, each one (a) by name, and leads them out."	a).John 20:16
v. 4: "After taking out all that are his own, he goes on ahead of them; and the sheep follow him because they recognize his voice."	
v. 5: "They never follow (a) a stranger but will run away from him, because strangers' voices are unfamiliar to them."	a).2 Corinthians 11:13–15

Gospel of Yochanan (John)	OT/NT References
Chapter 10 **Yeshua the True Shepard Continued**	
v. 6: "*Yeshua* used this indirect manner of speaking with them, but they didn't understand what He was talking to them about."	
Chapter 10 **Yeshua the Good Shepard**	
v. 7: "So *Yeshua* said to them again, 'Yes, indeed! I tell you that I am the gate for the sheep.'"	
v. 8: "All those who have come before Me have been thieves and robbers, but the sheep didn't listen to them."	
v. 9: (a) "I am the gate; if someone enters through Me, he will be safe and will go in and out and find pasture."	a).John 4:6; Ephesians 2:18
v. 10: "The thief comes only in order to steal, kill and destroy; I have come so that they may have life, life in its fullest measure."	
v. 11: (A) "I am the good shepherd. The good shepherd lays down His life for the sheep."	A).Genesis 49: 24; Isaiah 40:11; Ezekiel 34:23; Hebrews 13:20; 1 Peter 2:25; 5:4; Revelation 7:17
v. 12: "The hired hand, since he isn't a shepherd and the sheep aren't his own, sees the wolf coming, (A) abandons the sheep and runs away. Then the wolf drags them off and scatters them."	A).Zechariah 11: 16–17
v. 13: "The hired worker behaves like this because that's all he is, a hired worker; so it doesn't matter to him what happens to the sheep."	
v. 14: "I am the good shepherd; (A) I know My own, and (b) My own know Me."	A).Isaiah 40:11; Nahum 1:7; Zechariah 13:7; John 6:64; 2 Timothy 2:19 b).2 Timothy 1:12
v. 15: (a) "Just as the Father knows Me, and I know the Father—(b) and I lay down My life on behalf of the sheep."	a).Matthew 11:27 b).Matthew 27:50; Mark 15:37; Luke 23:46; John:15:13; 19:30; 1 John 3:16

Gospel of Yochanan (John)	OT/NT References
Chapter 10 **Yeshua the Good Shepard Continued**	
v. 16: "Also I have (A) other sheep which are not from this pen; I need to bring them, and they will hear My voice; and (B) there will be one flock, one shepherd."	A).Isaiah 42:6; 56:8; Acts 10:45; 11:18; 13:46 B).Ezekiel 37:22; John:11:52; 17:20; Ephesians 2:13–18; 1 Peter 2:25
v. 17: "This is why the Father (a) loves Me; (B) because I lay down My life—in order to take it up again!"	a).John 5:20 B).Isaiah 53:7–8, 12; Hebrews 2:9
v. 18: "No one takes it away from Me; on the contrary, I lay it down of My own free will. (a) I have the power to lay it down, and I have the power to take it up again. This is what My Father (b) commanded Me to do."	a).Matthew 26:53; John 2:19; 5:26 b).John 6:38; 14:31; 17:4; Acts 2:24, 32
Chapter 10 **The Shepard Knows His Sheep**	
v. 25: "*Yeshua* answered them, 'I have already told you, and you don't trust Me. (a) The works I do in My Father's name (b) testify on My behalf.'"	a).John 5:36; 10:38 b).Matthew 11:4; John 2:11; 20:30
v. 26: "But the reason (a) you don't trust is that you are not included among My sheep."	a).John 8:47
v. 27: "My sheep listen to My voice, I recognize them, they follow Me."	
v. 28: "And I give them eternal life. They will absolutely never be destroyed, and no one will snatch them from My hands."	
v. 29: (a) "My Father, (b) who gave them to Me, is greater than all; and no one can snatch them from the Father's hands."	a).John 14:28 b).John 17:2, 6, 12, 24
v. 30: (a) "I and the Father are one."	a).John 17:11, 21–24
Chapter 10 **Renewed Efforts to Stone Yeshua**	
v. 32: *Yeshua* answered them, "You have seen Me do many good deeds that reflect the Father's power; for which one of these deeds are you stoning Me?"	

304 *Just the Words and Teachings of Jesus Christ*

Gospel of Yochanan (John)	OT/NT References
Chapter 10 **Renewed Efforts to Stone Yeshua**	
v. 34: "*Yeshua answered them, 'Isn't it written in your *Torah, "I have said, (A) 'You people are *Elohim'"?'"	A).Psalm 82:6
v. 35: "If He called *'elohim' the people (a) to whom the word *Elohim was addressed (and the *Tanakh (b) cannot be broken)."	a).Mathew 5:17–18 b).1 Peter 1:25
v. 36: "Then are you telling the One (a) whom the Father set apart as holy and (b) sent into this world, 'You are committing blasphemy,' just (c) because I said, 'I am a (d) Son of *Elohim'?"	a).John 6:27 b).John 3:17 c).John 5:17–18 d).Luke 1:35
v. 37: (a) "If I am not doing deeds that reflect My Father's power, don't trust Me."	a).John 10:25; 15:24
v. 38: "But if I am, then, even if you don't trust Me,(a) trust the deeds; so that you may understand once and for all (b) that the Father is united with Me, and I am united with the Father."	a).John 5:36 b).John 14:10–11
Chapter 11 **The Death of Lazarus**	
v. 4: "On hearing it, He said, 'This sickness will not end in death. No, it is for God's glory, so that the Son of God may receive glory through it.'"	
v. 7: "Then, after this, He said to the *talmidim, 'Let's go back to *Y'hudah.'"	
v. 9: "*Yeshua answered, 'Aren't there twelve hours of daylight? (a) If a person walks during daylight, he doesn't stumble; because he sees the (B) light of this world.'"	a).Luke 13:33; John 9:4; 12:35 B).Isaiah 9:2
v. 10: "But (a) if a person walks at night, he does stumble; because he has no light with him."	a).John 12:35
v. 11: "*Yeshua said these things, and afterwards He said to the *talmidim, 'Our friend *El'azar has gone to (A) sleep; but I am going in order to wake him up.'"	A).Deuteronomy 31:16; Daniel 12:2; Matthew 9:24; Acts 7:60; 1 Corinthians 15:18, 51
v. 14: "So *Yeshua told them in plain language, '*El'azar has died.'"	

Part 6: Subtopic Scriptures—Gospel of John

Gospel of Yochanan (John)	OT/NT References
Chapter 11 **The Death of Lazarus Continued**	
v. 15: "And for your sakes, I am glad that I wasn't there, so that you may come to trust. But let's go to him."	
Chapter 11 **I Am the Resurrection and the Life**	
v. 23: "*Yeshua said to her, 'Your brother will rise again.'"	
v. 25: "*Yeshua said to her, '(a) I AM the Resurrection and the Life! (b) Whoever puts his trust in me will live, even if he (c) dies.'"	a).John 5:21; 6:39–40, 44; Revelation 1:18 b).John 3:16, 36; 1 John 5:10 c).1 Corinthians 15:22; Hebrews 9:27
v. 26: "And everyone living and trusting in me will never die. Do you believe this?"	
Chapter 11 **Yeshua and Death, the Last Enemy**	
v. 34: "He said, 'Where have you buried him?' They said, 'Lord, come and see.'"	
Chapter 11 **Lazarus Raised from the Dead**	
v. 39: "*Yeshua said, 'Take the stone away!' *Marta, the sister of the dead man, said to *Yeshua, 'By now his body must smell, for it has been four days since he died!'"	
v. 40: "*Yeshua said to her, 'Didn't I tell you that if you keep trusting, you will (a) see the glory of God?'"	a).John 11:4, 23
v. 41: "So they removed the stone. *Yeshua looked upward and said, 'Father, I thank you that you have heard Me.'"	
v. 42: "I Myself know that You always hear Me, but I say this (a) because of the crowd standing around, so that they may believe that You have sent Me."	a).John 12:30; 17:21

Gospel of Yochanan (John)	OT/NT References
Chapter 11 **Lazarus Raised from the Dead Continue**	
v. 43: "Having said this, He shouted, '*El'azar!* Come out!'"	
v. 44: "The man who had been dead came out, his hands and feet (a) wrapped in strips of linen and (b) his face covered with a cloth. *Yeshua said to them, 'Unwrap him, and let him go!'"	a).John 19:40 b).John 20:7
Chapter 12 **The Anointing at Bethany**	
v. 7: "*Yeshua, said, 'Leave her alone! She kept this for the day of My burial.'"	
v. 8: "You always have the (A) poor among you, but you will not always have Me."	A).Deuteronomy 15:11; Matthew 26:11; Mark 14:7; John 17:11
Chapter 12 **The Fruitful Grain of Wheat**	
v. 23: "*Yeshua gave them this answer: (a) 'The time has come for the Son of Man to be glorified.'"	a).Matthew 26:18, 45; John 13:32; Acts 3:13
v. 24: "Yes, indeed! I tell you that (a) unless a grain of wheat that falls to the ground dies, it stays just a grain; but if it dies, it produces a big harvest."	a).Romans 14:9; 1 Corinthians 15:36
v. 25: (a) "He who loves his life loses it, but he who hates his life in this world will keep it safe right on into eternal life!"	a).Matthew 10:39; Mark 8:35; Luke 9:24
v. 26: "If someone is serving Me, let him (a) follow Me; (b) wherever I am, My servant will be there too. My Father will honor anyone who serves Me."	a).Matthew 16:24 b).John 14:3; 17:24; 1 Thessalonians 4:17
Chapter 12 **Yeshua Predicts His Death on the Cross**	
v. 27: (a) "Now I am in turmoil. What can I say—'Father, save me from this hour'? No, it was for this very (b) reason that I have come to this hour. I will say this."	a).Matthew 26:38–39; Mark 14:34; Luke 12:50; John 11:33 b).Luke 22:53; John 18:37
v. 28: "'Father, glorify Your name!' At this a (a) *bat-kol* came out of heaven, 'I have glorified it before, and I will glorify it again!'"	a).Matthew 3:17; 17:5; Mark 1:11; 9:7; Luke 3:22; 9:35

Gospel of Yochanan (John)	OT/NT References
Chapter 12 **Yeshua Predicts His Death on the Cross Continued**	
v. 30: "*Yeshua* answered, 'This (a) *bat-kol* did not come for My sake but for yours.'"	a).John 11:42
v. 31: "Now is the time for this world to be judged, now the ruler of this world will be expelled."	
v. 32: "As for Me, when I am lifted up from the earth, I will draw everyone to Myself."	
v. 35: "*Yeshua* said to them, '(a) The light will be with you only a little while longer. (B) Walk while you have the light, or the dark will overtake you; (c) he who walks in the dark doesn't know where he's going.'"	a).John 1:9; 7:33; 8:12 B).Jeremiah 13:16; Galatians 6:10; Ephesians 5:8 c).John 11:10; 1John 2:9–11
v. 36: "'While you have light, put your trust in the light, so that you may become (a) people of light.' *Yeshua* said these things, then went off and kept Himself (b) hidden from them."	a).Luke 16:8; John 8:12 b).John 8:59
Chapter 12 **Walk in the Light**	
v. 44: "*Yeshua* declared publicly, (a) 'Those who put their (b) trust in Me are trusting not merely in Me, (c) but in the One who sent Me.'"	a).Mark 9:37 b).John 3:16, 18, 36; 11:25–26 c).John 14:9
v. 45: "Also (a) those who see Me see the One who sent Me."	a).John 14:9
v. 46: (a) "I have come as a light into the world, so that everyone who trusts in Me might not remain in the dark."	a).John 1:4–5; 8:12; 12:35–36
v. 47: "If anyone hears what I am saying and does not observe it, (a) I don't judge him; for (b) I did not come to judge the world, but to save the world."	a).John 5:45 b).John 3:17
v. 48: (a) "Those who reject Me and don't accept what I say have a judge—(B) the word which I have spoken will judge them on the Last Day."	a).Luke 10:16 B).Deuteronomy 18:18–19; John 5:45; 8:47
v. 49: "For (a) I have not spoken on My own initiative, but the Father who sent Me has given Me a command, namely, (B) what to say and how to say it."	a).John 8:38 B).Deuteronomy 18:18

Gospel of Yochanan (John)	OT/NT References
Chapter 12 **Walk in the Light Continued**	
v. 50: "And I know that His command is eternal life. So (a) what I say is simply what the Father has told Me to say."	a).John 5:19; 8:28
Chapter 13 **Yeshua Washes the Disciples' Feet**	
v. 7: "*Yeshua answered him, '(a) You don't understand yet what I am doing, (b) but in time you will understand.'"	a).John 12:16; 16:12 b).John 13:19
v. 8: "'No!' said *Kefa, 'You will never wash my feet!' *Yeshua answered him, '(A) If I don't wash you, you have no share with Me.'"	A).Psalm 51:2, 7; Ezekiel 36:25; Acts 22:16; 1 Corinthians 6:11; Ephesians 5:26;; Titus 3:5; Hebrews 10:22
v. 10: "*Yeshua said to him, 'A man who has had a bath doesn't need to wash, except his feet—(a) his body is already clean, but not all of you.'"	a).John 15:3; Ephesians 5:26
v. 11: (a) "He knew who was betraying Him; this is why He said, 'Not all of you are clean.'"	a).John 6:64; 18:4
v. 12: "After He had washed their feet, taken back His clothes and returned to the table, He said to them, 'Do you understand what I have done to you?'"	
v. 13: (a) "You call Me '*Rabbi' and 'Lord,' and you are right, because I am."	a).Matthew 23:8, 10; Luke 6:46; 1 Corinthians 8:6; 12:3; Ephesians 6:9; Philippians 2:11
v. 14: (a) "Now if I, the Lord and *Rabbi, have washed your feet, (b) you also should wash each other's feet."	a).Luke 22:27 b).Romans 12:10 Galatians 6:1–2; 1 Peter 5:5
v. 15: "For (a) I have set you an example, so that you may do as I have done to you."	a).Matthew 11:29; Philippians 2:5; 1 Peter 2:21–24; 1 John 2:6
v. 16: (a) "Yes, indeed! I tell you, a slave is not greater than his master, nor is an emissary greater than the one who sent him."	a).Matthew 10:24; Luke 6:40; John 15:20
v. 17: (a) "If you know these things, you will be blessed if you do them."	a).Matthew 7:24; Luke 11:28; James 1:25

Gospel of Yochanan (John)	OT/NT References
Chapter 13 **Yeshua Identifies His Betrayer**	
v. 18: "I'm not talking to all of you—I know which ones I have chosen. But the words of the (a) *Tanakh* must be fulfilled that say, (B) 'The one eating My bread has turned against Me.'"	a).John 15:25; 17:12 B).Psalm 41:9; Matthew 26:23
v. 19: (a) "I'm telling you now, before it happens; so that when it does happen, you may believe that I AM [who I say I AM]."	a).John 14:29; 16:4
v. 20: (a) "Yes, indeed! I tell you that a person who receives someone I send receives Me, and that anyone who receives Me receives the One who sent Me."	a).Matthew 10:40; Mark 9:37; Luke 9:48; 10:16; Galatians 4:14
v. 21: (a) "After saying this, (b) *Yeshua* in deep anguish of spirit, declared, 'Yes, indeed! I tell you that (C) one of you will betray Me.'"	a).Matthew 26:21; Mark 14:18; Luke 22:21 b).John 12:27 C).Psalm 41:9; Matthew 26:46; Mark 14:42; Luke 22:48; Joh 6:64; 18:5; Acts 1:17; 1 John 2:19
v. 26: "*Yeshua* answered, 'It's the one to whom I give this piece of *matzah* after I dip it in the dish.' So He dipped the piece of *matzah*, and gave it to (a) *Y'hudah Ben-Shim'on* from *K'riot*."	a).Matthew 10:4; John 6:70–71; 12:4; Acts:1:16
v. 27: (a) "As soon as *Y'hudah* took the piece of *matzah*, the Adversary went into him. 'What you are doing, do quickly!' *Yeshua* said to him."	a).Luke 22:3
Chapter 13 **The New Commandment**	
v. 31: "After *Y'hudah* had left, *Yeshua* said, (a) 'Now the Son of Man has been glorified in Him.'"	a).John 12:23; Acts 3:13 b).John 14:13; 17:4; 1 Peter 4:11
v. 32: "If the Son has glorified God, God will Himself glorify the Son, and (a) will do so without delay."	a).John 12:23
v. 33: "Little children, I will be with you only (a) a little longer. You will look for Me; (b) and, as I said to the *Judeans*, 'Where I am going, you cannot come,' now I say it to you as well."	a).John 12:35; 14:19; 16:16–19 b).Mark 16:19; John 1:34; 8:21; Acts 1:9
v. 34: (A) "I am giving you a new command: that you keep on loving each other. In the same way that I have loved you, you are also to keep on loving each other."	A).Leviticus 19:18; Ephesians 5:2; 1 Thessalonians 4:9; James 2:8; 1 Peter 1:22; 1 John 2:7

Gospel of Yochanan (John)	OT/NT References
Chapter 13 **The New Commandment Continued**	
v. 35: (a) "Everyone will know that you are My *talmidim* by the fact that you have love for each other."	a).John 2:5
Chapter 13 **Yeshua Predicts Peter's Denial**	
v. 36: "*Shim'on Kefa* said to Him, 'Lord, where are you going?' *Yeshua* answered, 'Where I (a) am going, you cannot follow Me now; (b) but you will follow later.'"	a).John 13:33; 14:2; 16:5 b).John 21:17; 2 Peter 1:14
v. 38: "*Yeshua* answered, 'You will lay down your life for Me? Yes, indeed! I tell you, before the rooster (a) crows you will disown Me three times.'"	a).Matthew 26:74; Mark 14:30; Luke 22:61; John 18:25–27
Chapter 14 **The Way, the Truth, and the Life**	
v. 1: (a) "Don't let yourselves be disturbed. Trust in God and trust in Me."	a).John 14:27; 16:22, 24
v. 2: "In My Father's house are many places to live. If there weren't, I would have told you; because (a) I am going there to prepare a place for you."	a).Matthew 25:34; John 13:33, 36; Hebrews 1:16
v. 3: "Since I am going and preparing a place for you, (a) I will return to take you with Me; so that (b) where I am; you may be also."	a).Acts 1:11 b).John 12:26; 1 Thessalonians 4:17
v. 4: "Furthermore, you know where I'm going; and you know the way there."	
v. 6: "*Yeshua* said, 'I AM (a) the Way—and (b) the Truth and (c) the Life; (d) no one comes to the Father (e) except through Me.'"	a).John 10:9 Romans 5:2; Ephesians 2:18; Hebrews 9:8; 10:19–20 b).John 1:14, 17; 8:32; 18:37 c).John 11:25 d).1 Timothy 2:5 e).John 10:7–9; Acts 4:12
Chapter 14 **The Father Revealed**	
v. 7: (a) "Because you have known Me, you will also know My Father; from now on, you do know Him—in fact, you have seen Him."	a).John 8:19

Gospel of Yochanan (John)	OT/NT References
Chapter 14 **The Father Revealed Continued**	
v. 9: "*Yeshua* replied to him, 'Have I been with you so long without your knowing Me, Philip? (a) Whoever has seen Me has seen the Father; so how can you say, "Show us the Father"?'"	a).John 12:45; Colossians 1:15; Hebrews 1:3
v. 10: "Don't you believe that (a) I am united with the Father, and the Father united with Me? What I am telling you, (B) I am not saying on My own initiative; the Father living in Me is doing His own works."	a).John 10:38; 14:11, 20 B).Deuteronomy 18:18; John 5:19; 14:24
v. 11: "Trust Me, that I am united with the Father, and the Father united with Me. But if you can't, (a) then trust because of the works themselves."	a).John 5:36; 10:38
Chapter 14 **The Answered Prayer**	
v. 12: (a) "Yes, indeed! I tell you that whoever trusts in Me will also do the works I do! Indeed, he will do greater ones, because I am going to the Father."	a).Matthew 21:21; Mark 16:17; Luke 10:17
v. 13: (a) "In fact, whatever you ask for in My name, I will do; so that the Father may be (b) glorified in the Son."	a).Matthew 7:7; Mark 11:24; Luke 11:9; John 15:16; 16:23–24; James 1:5–7; 1 John 3:22 b).John 3:22
v. 14: "If you ask Me for something in My name, I will do it."	
Chapter 14 **Yeshua Promises Another Helper**	
v. 15: (a) "If you love Me, you will keep My commands."	a).1 John 5:3
v. 16: "And I will ask the Father, and (a) He will give you another comforting Counselor like Me, the Spirit of Truth, to be with you forever."	a).John 15:26; 20:24; Acts 2:4, 33; Romans 8:15
v. 17: (b) "The world cannot receive (a) Him, because it neither sees nor knows Him. You know Him, because He is staying with you and (c) will be united with you."	a).John 15:26; 16:13; 1 John 4:6; 5:7 b).1 Corinthians 2:14 c).1 John 2:27
v. 18: (a) "I will not leave you orphans—(b) I am coming to you."	a).Matthew 28:20 b).John 14:3, 28

Gospel of Yochanan (John)	OT/NT References
Chapter 14 **Indwelling of the Father and the Son**	
v. 19: "In just a little while, the world will no longer see Me; but (a) you will see Me. (b) Because I live, you too will live."	a. John 16:16, 22 b). Romans 5:10; 1 Corinthians 15:20; 2 Corinthians 4:10
v. 20: "When that day comes, you will know that (a) I am united with My Father, and you with Me, and I with you."	a). John:10:38; 14:11
v. 21: (a) "Whoever has My commands and Keeps them is the one who loves Me, and the one who loves Me will be loved by My Father, and I will love him and reveal Myself to him."	a). 1 John 2:5
v. 23: "*Yeshua* answered him, 'If someone loves Me, he will keep My word; and My Father will love Him, (a) and We will come to him and make Our home with him.'"	a). 2 Corinthians 6:16; Ephesians 3:17; 1 John 2:24; Revelation 3:20; 21:3
v. 24: "Someone who doesn't love Me doesn't keep My words—and (a) the word you are hearing is not My own but that of the Father who sent Me."	a). John 5:19
Chapter 14 **The Gift of His Peace**	
v. 25: "I have told you these things while I am still with you."	
v. 26: "But (a) the Counselor, the *Ruach HaKodesh,* whom the Father will (b) send in My name, (c) will teach you everything; that is, He will (d) remind you of everything I have said to you."	a). Luke 24:49 b). John 15:26 c). 1 Corinthians 2:13 d). John 2:22; 12:16; 1 John 2:20
v. 27: (a) "What I am leaving with you is *Shalom*—I am giving you My *Shalom*. I don't give the way the world gives. Don't let yourselves be upset or frightened."	a). Luke 1:79; John 16:33; 20:19; Philippians 4:7; Colossians 3:15
v. 28: "You heard Me (a) tell you, 'I am leaving, and I will come back to you.' If you loved Me, you would have been glad that (b) I am going to the Father; (c) because the Father is greater than I."	a). John 14:3, 18 b). John 16:16 c). John 5:18; Philippians 2:6
v. 29: "Also, (a) I have said it to you now, before it happens; so that when it does happen, you will trust."	a). John 13:19

Part 6: Subtopic Scriptures—Gospel of John

Gospel of Yochanan (John)	OT/NT References
Chapter 14 **The Gift of His Peace Continued**	
v. 30: "I won't be talking with you much longer, because (a) the ruler of this world is coming. He has (b) no claim on Me."	a).John 12:31 b).John 8:46; 2 Corinthians 5:21; Hebrews 4:15; 1 Peter 1:19; 2:22
v. 31: "Rather, this is happening so that the world may know that I love the Father, and that I do as the (A) Father has commanded Me. 'Get up! Let's get going!'"	A).Isaiah 50:5; John 10:18; Philippians 2:8
Chapter 15 **The True Vine**	
v. 1: "I am the real vine, and My Father is the gardener."	
v. 2: (a) "Every branch which is part of Me but fails to bear fruit, He cuts off; and every branch that does bear fruit, He prunes, so that it may (b) bear more fruit."	a).Matthew 15:13 b).Matthew 13:12
v. 3: (a) "Right now, because of the word which I have spoken to you, you are pruned."	a).John 13:10; 17:17; Ephesians 5:26
v. 4: (a) "Stay united with Me, as I will with you—for just as the branch can't put forth fruit by itself apart from the vine, so you can't bear fruit apart from Me."	a).John 17:23; Ephesians 3:17; Colossians 1:23
vs 5: "I am the vine and you are the branches. Those who stay united with Me, and I with them, are the ones who bear much (A) fruit; because apart from Me you (b) can't do a thing."	A).Hosea 14:8; Galatians 5:22–23 b).2 Corinthians 3:5
v. 6: "Unless a person remains united with Me, he is (a) thrown away like a branch and dries up. Such branches are gathered and thrown into the fire, where they are burned up."	a).Matthew 3:10
v. 7: "If you remain united with Me, and My words (a) with you, then (b) ask whatever you want, and it will happen for you."	a).1 John 2:14 b).John 14:13; 16:23
v. 8: (A) "This is how My Father is glorified—in your bearing much fruit; (b) this is how you will prove to be My *talmidim.*	A).Psalm 22:23; Matthew 5:16; John 13:31; 17:4; Philippians 1:11; 1 Peter 4:11 b).John 8:31

Gospel of Yochanan (John)	OT/NT References
Chapter 15 **Love and Joy Perfected**	
v. 9: "Just as My Father has (a) loved Me, I too have loved you; so stay in My love."	a).John 5:20; 17:26
v. 10: (a) "If you keep My commands, you will stay in My love—just as I have kept My Father's commands and stay in His love."	a).John 14:15
v. 11: "I have said this to you so that My joy may be in you, and (a) your joy be complete."	a).John 16:24; 1 John 1:4
v. 12: (a) "This is My (b) command: that you keep on loving each other just as I have loved you."	a).John 13:34; 1 John 3:11 b).Romans 12:9
v. 13: (a) "No one has greater love than a person who lays down his life for his friends."	a).Ephesians 5:2; 1 John 3:16
v. 14: (a) "You are My friends, if you do what I command you."	a).Matthew 12:50; 28:20; John 14:15, 21; Acts 10:42; 1 John 3:23–24
v. 15: "I no longer call you slaves, because a slave doesn't know what his master is about; but I have called you friends, because (A) everything I have heard from My Father I have made known to you."	A).Genesis 18:17
v. 16: (a) "You did not choose Me, I chose you; and I have (b) commissioned you to go and bear fruit, fruit that will last; so that whatever you ask from the Father (c) in My name He may give you."	a).John 6:70; 13:18; 15:19; 1 John 4:10 b).Matthew 28:19; Mark 16:15; Colossians 1:6 c).John 14:13; 16:23–24
v. 17: "This is what I command you: keep loving each other!"	
Chapter 15 **The World's Hatred**	
v. 18: (a) "If the world hates you, understand that it hated Me first."	a).John 7:7; 1 John 3:13
v. 19: (a) "If you belonged to the world, the world would have loved its own. But (b) because you do not belong to the world—on the contrary, I have picked you out of the world—therefore the world hates you."	a).1 John 4:5 b).John 17:14

Gospel of Yochanan (John)	OT/NT References
Chapter 15 **The World's Hatred Continued**	
v. 20: "Remember what I told you, (a) 'A slave is not greater than his master.' If they persecuted Me, they will persecute you too; (B) if they kept My word, they will keep yours too."	a).Matthew 10:24; John 13:16 B).Ezekiel 3:7
v. 21: "But they will do (a) all this to you on My account, because they don't know the One who sent Me."	a).Matthew 10:22; 24:9; 1 Peter 4:14; Revelation 2:3
v. 22: (a) "If I had not come and spoken to them, they wouldn't be guilty of sin; (b) but now, they have no excuse for their sin."	a).John 9:41; 15:24 b).Romans 1:20; James 4:17
v. 23: (a) "Whoever hates Me hates My Father also."	a).1 John 3:2
v. 24: "If I had not done in their presence (a) works which no one else ever did, they would not be guilty of sin; but now, they have (b) seen them and have hated both Me and My Father."	a).John 3:2 b).John 14:9
v. 25: "But this has happened in order to fulfill the words in their *Torah* which read, (A) 'They hated Me for no reason at all.'"	A).Psalm 35:19; 69:4; 109:3–5
Chapter 15 **The Coming Rejection**	
v. 26: (a) "When the Counselor comes, whom I will send you from the Father—The Spirit of Truth, who keeps going out from the Father—(b) He will testify on My behalf."	a).Luke 24:49; John 14:17; Acts 2:4, 33 b).1 John 5:6
v. 27: "And (a) you testify too, because (b) you have been with Me from the outset."	a).Luke 24:49; John 14:17; Acts 2:4, 33 b).1 John 5:6
Chapter 16 **The Coming Rejection Continued**	
v. 1: "I have told you these things so that you (a) won't be caught by surprise."	a).Matthew 11:6
v. 2: (a) "They will ban you from the synagogue; in fact, the time will come when (b) anyone who kills you will think he is serving God!"	a).John 9:22 b).Acts 8:1

Gospel of Yochanan (John)	OT/NT References
Chapter 16 **The Coming Rejection Continued**	
v. 3: "They will do (a) these things because they have understood neither the Father nor Me."	a).John 8:19; 15:21; Acts 13:27; Romans 10:2
v. 4: "But I have told you this, so that when the time comes for it to happen, you will remember that I told you. I didn't tell you this at first, because I was with you."	
Chapter 16 **The Work of the Holy Spirit**	
v. 5: "But now I am (a) going to the One who sent Me. Not one of you is asking Me, 'Where are you going?'"	a).John 7:33; 13:33; 14:28; 17:11
v. 6: "Instead, because I have said these things to you, (a) you are overcome with grief."	a).Matthew 17:23; John 16:20, 22
v. 7: "But I tell you the truth, it is to your advantage that I go away; for if I don't go away, the comforting Counselor will not come to you. However, (a) if I do go, I will send Him to you."	a).Acts 2:33
v. 8: "When He (a) comes, He will show that the world is wrong about sin, about righteousness and about judgment."	a).Acts 1:8; 2:1–4, 37
v. 9: (a) "About sin, in that people don't put their trust in Me."	a).Acts 2:22
v. 10: (a) "About righteousness, (b) in that I am going to the Father and you will no longer see Me."	a).Acts 2:32 b).John 5:32
v. 11: (a) "About judgment, in that (b) the ruler of this world has been judged."	a).Acts 26:18 b).Luke 10:18
v. 12: "I still have many things to tell you, (a) but you can't bear them now."	a).Mark 4:33
v. 13: "However, when the (a) Spirit of Truth comes, (b) He will guide you into all the truth; for He will not speak on His own initiative but will say only what He hears. He will also announce to you the events of the future."	a).John 14:17 b).John 14:26 Acts 11:28 Revelation 1:19
v. 14: (a) "He will glorify Me, because He will receive from what is Mine and announce it to you."	a).John 15:26

Gospel of Yochanan (John)	OT/NT References
Chapter 16 **The Work of the Holy Spirit Continued**	
v. 15: (a) "Everything the Father has is Mine; this is why I said that He receives from what is Mine and announce it you."	a). Matthew 11:27; John 3:35
Chapter 16 **Sorrow Will Turn to Joy**	
v. 16: "In (a) a little while, you will see Me no more; then, (b) a little while later, you will see Me."	a). John 7:33; 12:35; 13:33; 14:19; 19:40–42; 20:19 b). John 13:3
v. 19: "*Yeshua* knew that they wanted to ask Him, so He said to them, 'Are you asking each other what I meant by saying, "In a little while, you won't see Me; and then, a little while later, you will see Me"?'"	
v. 20: "Yes, it's true. I tell you that you will sob and (a) mourn, and the world will rejoice; you will grieve, but your grief will turn to (b) joy."	a). Mark 16:10; Luke 23:48; 24:17 b). Luke 24:32, 41
v. 21: (A) "When a woman is giving birth, she is in pain; because her time has come. But when the baby is born, she forgets her suffering out of joy that a child has come into the world."	A). Genesis 3:16; Isaiah 13:8; 26:17; 42:14; 1 Thessalonians 5:3
v. 22: "So you do indeed feel grief now, but I am going to see you again. Then (a) your hearts will be full of joy, and no one will take your joy away from you."	a). Luke 24:41; John 14:1, 27; 20:20; Acts 2:46; 13:52; 1 Peter 1:8
v. 23: "When that day comes, you won't ask anything of Me! (a) Yes, indeed! I tell you that whatever you ask from the Father, He will give you in My name."	a). Matthew 7:7; John 14:13; 15:16
v. 24: "Till now you haven't asked for anything in My name. Keep asking, and you will receive, (a) so that your joy may be (b) complete."	a). John 17:13 b). John 15:11
Chapter 16 **Christ Yeshua Overcomes the World**	
v. 25: "I have said these things to you with the help of illustrations; however, a time is coming when I will no longer speak indirectly but will talk about the Father in (a) plain language."	a). John 7:13
v. 26: "When that day comes, you will ask in My name. I am not telling you that I will pray to the Father on your behalf."	

Gospel of Yochanan (John)	OT/NT References
Chapter 16 **Christ Yeshua Overcomes the World Continued**	
v. 27: (a) "For the Father Himself loves you, because you have loved Me and (b) have believed that I came from God."	a).John 14:21, 23 b).John 3:13
v. 28: (a) "I came from the Father and have come into the world; again, I am leaving the world and returning to the Father."	a).John 13:1, 3; 16:5, 10, 17
v. 31: "*Yeshua* answered, 'Now you do believe.'"	
v. 32: (A) "But a time is coming—indeed it has come already—when you will be scattered, (b) each one looking out for himself; and you will leave Me all alone. (c) Yet I am not alone; because the Father is with Me."	A).Zechariah 13:7; Matthew 26:31, 56; Mark 14:27, 50; Acts 8:1 b).John 20:10 C).John 8:29
v. 33: "I have said these things to you so that, (A) united with Me, you may have *shalom*. (b) In the world, you have *tsuris*. But be brave! (c) I have conquered the world!"	A).Isaiah 9:6; Romans 5:1; Ephesians 2:14 b).2 Timothy 3:12 c).Romans 8:37; 1 John 4:4
Chapter 17 **Yeshua Prays for Himself**	
v. 1: "After *Yeshua* had said these things, He looked up toward heaven and said, 'Father, the (a) time has come. Glorify Your Son, so that the Son may glorify You.'"	a).John 12:23
v. 2: (A) "Just as You gave Him authority over all mankind, so that He might give eternal life to all those whom (b) You have given Him."	A).Daniel 7:14; Matthew 11:27; John 3:35; Philippians 2:10; Hebrews 2:8 b).John 6:37, 39; 17:6, 9, 24
v. 3: "And (A) eternal life is this: to know You, (b) the One true God, and (c) Him whom You sent, *Yeshua* the *Messiah*."	A).Isaiah 53:11; Jeremiah 9:23–24 b).1 Corinthians 8:4; 1 Thessalonians 1:9 c).John 3:34
v. 4: (a) "I gloried You on earth by (B) finishing the work (C) You gave Me to do."	a).John 13:31 B).Daniel 9:24; John 4:34; 19:30 C).Isaiah 49:3; 50:5; John 14:31

Gospel of Yochanan (John)	OT/NT References
Chapter 17 **Yeshua Prays for Himself Continued**	
v. 5: "Now, Father, glorify Me alongside Yourself. Give Me the same glory (A) I had with You before the world existed."	A).Proverbs 8:22–30; John 1:1–2; Philippians 2:6; Colossians 1:15; Hebrews 1:3
Chapter 17 **Yeshua Prays for His Disciples**	
v. 6: (A) "I made Your name known to the people (b) You gave Me out of the world. (C) They were Yours, You gave them to Me, and they have kept Your word."	A).Psalm 22:22 b).John 6:37 C).Ezekiel 18:4; Romans 18:4
v. 7: "Now they know that everything You have given Me is from You."	
v. 8: (a) "Because the words You gave Me I have given to them. (b) They have really come to know that I came from You, and they have come to trust that (C) You sent Me."	a).John 8:28 b).John 8:42; 16:27, 30 C).Deuteronomy 18:15, 18
v. 9: "I am praying for them, (a) I am not praying for the world, but for those You have given to Me, because they are Yours."	a).1 John:5:19
v. 10: "Indeed, all I have is Yours, and all (a) You have is Mine, and in them I have been glorified."	a).John;2:19
v. 11: (a) "Now I am no longer in the world. They are in the world, but I am coming to You. Holy Father, (b) guard them by the power of Your name, which You have given to Me, so that they may be one, (c) just as We are."	a).Mark 16:19; Luke 24:51; John 13:1; Acts 1:9; Hebrews 4:14; 9:24; 1 Peter 3:22 b).1 Peter 1:5; Jude 1:1–25 c).John 10:30
v. 12: "When I was with them, (a) I guarded them by the power of Your name, which You have given to Me; yes, I kept watch over them; and (b) not one of them was destroyed ((c) except the one meant for destruction, (D) so that the *Tanakh* might be fulfilled)."	a).Hebrews 2:13 b).John 6:39; 18:9; 1 John 2:19 c).Matthew 27:4–5; John 6:70; Acts 1:16–20 D).Psalm 41:9; 109:8; John 13:18; Acts 1:20
v. 13: "But now, I am coming to You; and I say these things while I am still in the world so that they may have My joy made complete in themselves."	

Gospel of Yochanan (John)	OT/NT References
Chapter 17 **Yeshua Prays for His Disciples Continued**	
v. 14: "I have given them Your word, (a) and the world hated them, because they do not belong to the world—(b) just as I Myself do not belong to the world."	a).Matthew 24:9; Luke 6:22; 21:17; John 15:19; 1 John 3:13 b).John 8:23
v. 15: "I don't ask You to take them out of the world, (a) but to protect them from the Evil One."	a).Matthew 6:12; Galatians 1:4; 2 Thessalonians 3:3; 2 Timothy 4:18; 2 Peter 2:9; 1 John 5:18
v. 16: "They do not belong to the world, just as I do not belong to the world."	
v. 17: (a) "Set them apart for holiness by means of the truth—(B) Your word is truth."	a).Acts 15:9; Ephesians 5:26; 1 Peter 1:22 B).Psalm 119:9, 142, 151
v. 18: (a) "Just as You sent Me into the world, I have sent them into the world."	a).John 4:38; 20:21
v. 19: "On (a) their behalf I am setting Myself apart for holiness, so that they too may be set apart for holiness by means of the truth."	a).1 Corinthians 1:2; 1 Thessalonians 4:7; Hebrews 10:10
Chapter 17 **Yeshua Prays for All Believers**	
v. 20: "I pray not only for these, but also for those who will trust in Me because of their word."	
v. 21: (a) "That they may all be one. (b) Just as You, Father, are united with Me and I with You, I pray that they may be united with Us, so that the world may believe that You sent Me."	a).John 10:16; Romans 12:5; Galatians 3:28; Ephesians 4:4, 6 b).John 10:38; 17:11, 23
v. 22: (a) "The glory which You have given to Me, I have given to them; (b) so that they many be one, just as We are One."	a).John 14:20; 1 John 1:3 b).2 Corinthians 3:18
v. 23: "I united with them and You with Me, (a) so that they may be completely one, and the world thus realize that You sent Me, and that You have loved them just as You have loved Me."	a).Colossians 3:14
v. 24: (a) "Father, I want those You have given Me to be with Me where I am; so that they many see My glory, which You have given Me (b) because You loved Me before the creation of the world."	a).John 12:26; 14:3; 1 Thessalonians 4:17 b).Matthew 25:34; John 17:5

Gospel of Yochanan (John)	OT/NT References
Chapter 17 **Yeshua Prays for All Believers Continued**	
v. 25: "Righteous Father, (a) the world has not known You, (b) but I have known You, and (c) these people have known that You sent Me."	a).John 15:21 b).John 7:29; 8:55; 10:1 c).John 3:17; 17:3, 8, 18, 21, 23
v. 26: (A) "I made Your name known to them, and I will continue to make it known; so that the love (b) with which You have loved Me may be in them, and I Myself may be united with them."	A).Exodus 34:5–7; John 17:6 b).John 15:9; Ephesians 3:17–19
Chapter 18 **Betrayal and Arrest in Gethsemane**	
v. 4: "*Yeshua*, who (a) knew everything that was going to happen to Him, went out and asked them, 'Whom do you want?'"	a).John 6:64; 13:1, 3; 19:28
v. 5: (a) "'*Yeshua* from *Natzeret*,' they answered. He said to them, 'I AM.' Also standing with them was (B) *Y'hudah*, the one who was betraying Him."	a).Matthew 21:11; Mark 1:24; 14:67; 16:6; Luke 18:37; 24:19 B).Psalm 41:9; Matthew 20:18; 26:21; John 13:21
Chapter 18 **Betrayal and Arrest in Gethsemane Continued**	
v. 6: "When He said, 'I AM,' they went backward from Him and fell to the ground."	
v. 7: "So He inquired of them once more, 'Whom do you want?' and they said, '*Yeshua* from *Natzeret*.'"	
v. 8: "'I told you, "I AM,"' answered *Yeshua*, 'so if I'm the one you want, let these others go.'"	
v. 11: "*Yeshua* said to *Kefa*, 'Put your sword back in its scabbard! (a) This is the cup the Father has given Me; am I not to drink it?'"	a).Matthew 20:22; 26:39; Mark 4:36; Luke 22:42
Chapter 18 **Yeshua Questioned by the High Priest**	
v. 20: "*Yeshua* answered, (a) 'I have spoken quite openly to everyone; I have always taught in a (b) synagogue or in the (c) Temple where all Jews meet together, and I have said nothing in secret.'"	a).Matthew 26:55; Luke 4:15; John 8:26 b).John 6:59 c).Mark 14:49; John 7:14, 28

Gospel of Yochanan (John)	OT/NT References
Chapter 18 **Yeshua Questioned by the High Priest Continued**	
v. 21: "So why are you questioning Me? (a) Question the ones who heard what I said to them; look, they know what I said."	a).Mark 12:37
v. 23: "*Yeshua* answered him, 'If I said something wrong, state publicly what was wrong; but if I was right, why are you hitting Me?'"	
Chapter 18 **In Pilate's Court**	
v. 34: "*Yeshua* answered, 'Are you asking this on your own, or have other people told you about Me?'"	
v. 36: (a) "*Yeshua* answered, (B) 'My Kingship does not derive its authority from this world's order of things. If it did, My men would have fought to keep Me from being arrested by the *Judeans*. But My Kingship does not come from here.'"	a).1 Timothy 6:13 B).Daniel 2:44; 7:14; Luke 19:4, 6; 1 Peter 2:22–24
v. 37: "'So then,' Pilate said to Him, 'You are a king, after all.' *Yeshua* answered, 'You say I am a king. The reason I have been born, the reason I have come into the world, (a) is to bear (B) witness to the truth. Every one who (c) belongs to the truth (d) listens to Me.'"	a).Matthew 5:17; 20:28; Luke 4:43; 12:49; 19:10; John 3:17; 9:39; 10:10; 12:47 B).Isaiah 55:4; Revelation 1:5 c).John 14:6 d).John 8:47; 10:27; 1 John 3:19; 4:6
Chapter 19 **Pilate's Decision**	
v. 11: "*Yeshua* answered, (a) 'You would have no power over Me if it hadn't been given to you from above; this is why the (b) one who handed Me over to you is guilty of a greater sin.'"	a).Luke 22:53; John 7:30 b).John 3:27 Romans 13:1
Chapter 19 **Behold Your Mother**	
v. 26: "When *Yeshua* saw His mother and the (a) *talmid* whom He loved standing there, He said to His mother, (b) 'Mother, this is your son.'"	a).John 13:23; 20:2; 21:7, 20, 24 b).John 2:4
v. 27: "Then He said to the *talmid*, 'This is your mother.' And from that time on, the *talmid* took her (a) into his own home."	a).Luke 18:28; John 1:11; 16:32; Acts 21:6

Gospel of Yochanan (John)	OT/NT References
Chapter 19 **Behold Your Mother Continued**	
v. 28: "After this, knowing that all things had accomplished their purpose, *Yeshua,* in order to fulfill the (A) words of the *Tanakh,* said, 'I'm thirsty.'"	A).Psalm 22:15
v. 30: "After *Yeshua* had taken the wine, He said, (A) 'It is accomplished!' And, letting His head droop, He delivered up His spirit."	A).Daniel 9:26; Zechariah 11:10–11; John 17:4
Chapter 20 **Mary Magdalene Sees the Risen Lord**	
v. 15: "*Yeshua* said to her, 'Lady, why are you crying? Whom are you looking for?' Thinking He was the gardener, she said to Him, 'Sir, if you're the one who carried Him away, just tell me where you put Him; and I'll go and get Him Myself.'"	
v.16: "*Yeshua* said to her, (a) '*Miryam!* Turning, she cried out to Him in Hebrew, "*Rabbani!*" (that is, "Teacher!")'"	a).John 10:3
v. 17: "'Stop holding onto Me' *Yeshua* said to her, 'because I haven't yet (a) gone back to the Father. But go to (B) My brothers, and tell them that (c) I am going back to My Father and your Father to (d) My God and your God.'"	a).Mark 16:19; Luke 24:5; Acts 1:9; 2:34–36; Ephesians 4:8–10 Hebrews 4:14 B).Psalm 22:22; Matthew 18:10; Romans :29; Hebrews 2:11 c).John 16:28; 17:11 d).Ephesians 1:17
Chapter 20 **The Apostles Commissioned**	
v. 19: (a) "In the evening that same day, the first day of the week, when the *talmidim* were gathered together behind locked doors out of (b) fear of the *Judeans,* *Yeshua* came, stood in the middle and said, (c) '*Shalom* aleikhem!'"	a).Mark 16: 14; Luke 24:36; John 14:27; 1 Corinthians 15:5 b).John 9:22; 19:38 c).John 14:27; 16:33; Ephesians 2:17
v. 21: "'*Shalom aleikhem!*' *Yeshua* repeated. (a) 'Just as the Father sent Me, I Myself am also sending you.'"	a).Matthew 28:18–20; John 17:18–19; 2 Timothy 2:2; Hebrews 3:1
v. 22: "Having said this, He breathed on them and said, to them, 'Receive the *Rauch HaKodesh!*'"	

Gospel of Yochanan (John)	OT/NT References
Chapter 20 **The Apostles Commissioned Continued**	
v. 23: (a) "If you forgive someone's sins, their sins are forgiven; if you hold them, they are held."	a).Matthew 16:19; 18:18
Chapter 20 **Seeing and Believing**	
v. 26: "A week later His *talmidim were once more in the room, and this time *T'oma was with them. Although the doors were locked, *Yeshua came, stood among them, and said, '*Shalom aleikhem!'"	
v. 27: "Then He said to *T'oma, 'Put your finger here, look at My hands, take (A) your hand and put it into My side. (b) Don't be lacking in trust, but have trust!'"	A).Psalm 22:16; Zechariah 12:10; 13:6; 1 John 1:1 b).Mark 16:14
v. 29: "*Yeshua said to him, 'Have you trusted because you have seen Me? (a) How blessed are those who do not see, but trust anyway!'"	a).2 Corinthians 5:7; 1 Peter 1:8
Chapter 21 **Breakfast by the Sea**	
v. 5: (a) "He said to them, 'You don't have any fish, do you?' 'No,' they answered Him."	a).Luke 24:41
v. 6: "He said to them, (a) 'Throw in your net to starboard and you will catch some.' So they threw in their net, and there were so many fish in it that they couldn't haul it aboard."	a).Luke 5:4, 6–7
v. 10: "*Yeshua said to them, 'Bring some of the fish you have just caught.'"	
v. 12: "*Yeshua said to them, (a) 'Come and have breakfast.' None of the *talmidim dared to ask Him, 'Who are you?' They knew it was the Lord."	a).Acts 10:41
Chapter 21 **Yeshua Restores Peter (Kefa)**	
v. 15: "After breakfast, *Yeshua said to *Shim'on Kefa, (a) '*Shim'on Bar-Yochanan, do you love Me more than these?' He replied, 'Yes, Lord, you know I'm your friend.' He said to him, 'Feed My lambs.'"	a).Acts 20:28; 1 Timothy 4:6; 1 Peter 5:2

Gospel of Yochanan (John)	OT/NT References
Chapter 21 **Yeshua Restores Peter (Kefa)**	
v. 16: "A second time He said to him, '*Shim'on Bar-Yochanan*, do you love Me?' He replied, 'Yes, Lord, You know I'm Your friend,' (a) He said to him, (B) 'Shepherd My sheep.'"	a).Matthew 2:6; Acts 20:28; Hebrews 13:20; 1 Peter 2:25; 5:2, 4 B).Psalm 79:13; Matthew 10:16; 15:24; 25:33; 26:31
v. 17: "The third time He said to him, '*Shim'on Bar-Yochanan*, are you My friend?' *Shim'on* was hurt that He questioned him a third time. So he replied, 'Lord, you know everything! (a) You know that I am Your friend!' *Yeshua* said to him, 'Feed My sheep!'"	a).John 2:24–25; 16:30
v. 18: (a) "Yes, indeed! I tell you, when you were younger, you put on your clothes and went where you wanted. But when you grow old, you will stretch out your hands, and someone else will dress you and carry you where you do not want to go."	a).John 13:36; Acts 12:3–4
v. 19: "He said this to indicate the (a) kind of death by which *Kefa* would bring glory to God. Then *Yeshua* said to him, (b) 'Follow Me!'"	a).2 Peter 1:13–14 b).Matthew 4:19; 16:24
Chapter 21 **The Beloved Disciple and His Book**	
v. 22: "*Yeshua* said to him, 'If I want him to stay on (a) until I come, what is it to you? You, follow Me!'"	a).Matthew 16:27–28; 25:31; 1 Corinthians 4:5; 11:26; Revelation 2:25; 3:11; 22:7, 20

PART 7:

GLOSSARY OF WORDS AND MEANINGS

The following words are taken from parts 4 and 6, the Scripture portions in the book. They were identified with an * and italicized for the reader within the scripture they were noted within. With the definitions of these words in mind, go back and reread the scriptures to possibly gain greater revelations of Yeshua's words and teachings.

Abba—some meanings for this word Yeshua referred Father God to in the garden of Gethsemane are "daddy" or "father" in a human essence. But since Father God is Spirit and divine, Yeshua's response, in context with the scripture Mark 14:36, where the word abba is used, is much deeper than a random "hey, Dad" per se. More fitting is "Father, I will obey You."

Adonai—the plural form of the Hebrew word Adon, which means "Lord" in English. Adonai gives us more of a hint about what the Lord's role is in our lives. Adonai means "master" or "Lord," showing God's divinity and sovereignty over us, yet lovingly draws us into.

Adversary—in context means Satan, as he is the father of all adversaries that influence sin and death toward humanity within the spiritual and physical realms.

Apostatize—a verb meaning "to renounce totally a religious belief once professed, to forsake one's church, the faith or principles once held or the party to which one has previously held."

Assarion—one-tenth of a drachma, which was valued at $.193 cents assarion value, or one-sixteenth of a denarius, which was valued at about $.14 cents or approximately a day's wage for a Roman soldier.

Avraham—Abram, as recorded in the Bible, was changed to Avraham in Hebrew or Abraham in English. Which means "Father of many nations." See Genesis 17:1–7. God appointed Abraham to be the progenitor of the Jewish and multiple nations. God tested Abraham, commanding him to offer up his son Isaac as an offering to God. Abraham's willingness to do so expressed his inner heart toward God, and he made ready the altar and his son Isaac. God, seeing Avraham's heart, intervened and provided a ram for the sacrificial offering. See Genesis 22:1–19. Abraham was father to Isaac, who fathered Jacob, whom God named Israel.

Ba'al-Zibbul—Beelzebub, written also "Baal Zebubb," the god of Ekron, whose oracle King Ahaziah consulted during his illness, provoking thereby the wrath of God (2 Kings 1: 2–16). The name of a Philistine deity, very offensive. Whose meaning is chief of demons.

Bat-kol—literally "daughter of a voice," refers to a heavenly voice that proclaims God's will or a divine judgment in a matter of legal dispute.

Beit-Anyah—Bethany, a city near Jerusalem.

Beit-Pagei—means "house of unripe figs." Aramaic. It is the place in ancient Israel from which Yeshua sent His disciples to find a colt upon which He would ride into Jerusalem a week before His crucifixion.

Beit-Tzaidah—Bethsaida means "house of the hunt." It was condemned by Yeshua for not repenting of their sins in spite of the mighty works the Lord did in them.

B'rakhah—means "blessing" and "an expression of praise and thankfulness to God."

B'rit-milah—means "covenant of circumcision" and is a commandment by God starting with Abraham. See Genesis 17:9–14. A religious ritual through which male babies are formally welcomed and dedicated into the Jewish people on the eighth day of life by means of circumcision. Jewish parents are obligated to have this ritual done while also offering a threefold blessing for the child:

1. a life enriched by Torah study and obedience unto God,
2. the wedding canopy (chuppah) for the continuance of multiplying and subduing the world as God commands,
3. good deeds come forth from faith and a sound conscience.

Though commanded by God in the physical, Yeshua and especially Rav Sha'ul in the epistles expressed the greater need for a spiritual circumcision of the heart by an individual.

Caesarea Philippi—a city on the northeast of the marshy plain of el-Huleh, 120 miles north of Jerusalem, and 20 miles north of the Sea of Galilee, at the "upper source" of the Jordan, and near the base of Mount Hermon. It was the northern limit of Yeshua's public ministry.

Cohanim—plural for "priests." They are given the first Aliyah (being called up to the Torah) when the Torah is read in synagogue, and during some services they reenact the giving of the priestly blessing. See the book of Exodus and Leviticus for deeper understanding of their standing and duties.

Cohen—its meaning is fairly straightforward; it means "priest," indicating the bearers of this name are (usually) members of the priestly clan, descendants of Aaron, the high priest.

Cohen Gadol—high priest who held the holiest position in Judaism. His role extended through history, from Aaron in ancient times until the destruction of the second temple. His job was to oversee the temple service and act as spiritual leader to the Jewish people. His prominent responsibility was entering the Holy of Holies on Yom Kippur. The annual national day of repentance and atonement. When the most sacred time, person, place, and God converged.

Davening—means "to recite meaningful Jewish liturgical prayers." However, in the context of its use in Luke 11:47, Yeshua expresses the Torah teachers are doing this at great length as a means to impress others who can see them. Our prayers, though encouraged corporately, are more pleasing to Father God when done in one's own prayer closet in His presence. Scriptures teach us we are to come boldly, confidently, and with great humility into the throne room of God with our continual prayers and petitions.

Denarius—a small silver coin issued during the Roman Empire, equal to ten asses/donkeys. The standard daily labor wage—worth approximately $20.00 in bread during times of antiquity.

Drachmas—Greek currency now replaced with Euro.

El'azar—Lazarus, whose name means "God has helped." A very fitting name for Lazarus, a friend of Yeshua whom He raised from the dead after four days in a grave site. See John 11:38–44. There are many accounts of men in the OT with prominent position or tasks with this name. It is also a rightful name for the beggar in Luke 16:20.

Elisha—a Hebrew prophet found in the Tanakh (OT) whose name means "God is salvation" and who was the successor of prophet Elijah.

Elohim—its meaning is "the God, the living God or gods." A more basic but not less encompassing meaning is "one of strength or power of effect." Elohim is the infinite, all-powerful God who shows by His works that He is the Creator, sustainer, and supreme judge of the world. Psalm 7:9, "Adonai, who dispenses judgment to the peoples, judge me, Adonai, according to my righteousness and as my integrity deserves." Singular is Eloah, and Elohim is the plural of the One, noted as the God of Israel and all who are born of or grafted into Israel. See the Sh'ma in Deuteronomy 6:4. The name is used over 2,500 times in the Tanakh (OT).

Ebyatar—an Israelite high priest whose name means "the great one is father." Another meaning is said to be "the sprout that lived on."

El or Eli—means "are high," "elevated," or "my God." It could also mean "my God" when it's a derivation of other biblical names, such as Elijah, Elias, Eliezer, Elimelech, etc.

- El is the name that is used in the Bible as a name for the God of the Israelites and is the suffix for the genitive form ("mine").
- "Eli! Eli! L'mah sh'vaktani and Elohi! Elohi! L'mah sh'vaktani" is believed to mean "My God! My God! Why have you forsaken me?"

- In the context of Matthew 27:46 and Mark 15:34 are specific references used by Yeshua for His Father God. But did God really forsake Yeshua, or was Yeshua possibly asking, "My God, why have You spared Me?"? Or "My God, how much longer must I be here?"?
- See "Commentaries" for further investigation of the 2000-year-old linguistic and theological debated meaning of both these statements used in both Gospels regarding Yeshua's cry out to Father God in His last minutes while on the cross.

Eliyahu—Elijah, the prophet found in the Tanakh (OT), whose name means "my God is Lord."

Elohim or Elohi—the plural form of El or Eloah, one of the oldest designations for divinity in the world. The Hebrews borrowed the term El from the Canaanites; it can refer either to the true God or to pagan gods. The word El is used more than 200 hundred times in the Tanakh. Elohim is used more than 2,500 times.

- Elohi, used in Mark 15, is a specific reference used by Yeshua for His Father God.

Emmaus—Hebrew meaning is "hot spring" and alternatively in Greek "spring of salvation." Heading toward the city of Emmaus, two disciples were walking on the road after Yeshua's death and resurrection. Yeshua came upon them, walked with them, and shared everywhere in the Tanakh He was prophesied.

Evil eye—ayin ha-ra—found in Matthew 6:23 and Luke 11:34. In some realms it can mean a supernatural belief in a curse brought about by a malevolent glare, usually given to a person who is unaware of causing misfortune or injury. The evil eye dates back 5,000 years and adorned some drinking vessels and other things. However, in the scripture found in Luke 11:34, it means "one who is stingy" not just in their giving but also in their hearts toward God and other people. The greatest in the kingdom of God are the ones who serve as Yeshua, our example in all things, who was a suffering servant to all mankind. It's a heart issue, as one will not serve if the eyes of one's heart are filled with selfishness versus selflessness.

Execution stake—literally the "cross" on which Yeshua was crucified. Those born again in spirit are on the very stake in Yeshua. We died with Him, were buried with Him, resurrected with Him, and will join Him in heaven at the appointed time.

- See "Part 9: Inclusion—הללכה—in the Resurrected Life of Jesus the Messiah" for further understanding.

Father God—very difficult to define God, as there aren't enough words known to man that could possibly express the breadth and fullness of His essence and being. But for the sake of trying to understand, He is Yeshua's Father, and in Yeshua's context regarding Father, He means "YHWH—God—I am will be what I am will be" (many will dispute YHWH as God's name, and I am not here to dispute them). All things come from within Father God, including Yeshua. Whether seen or unseen, understood or not understood, and known or unknown. I encourage every reader to seek counsel from the Holy Spirit, as He is Father God's Spirit, for understanding and wisdom regarding who and what Father God is to you personally. As Yeshua came to return the chosen in this world back to Father and His Kingdom. Father God would so that all would come into the saving belief and knowledge of His Son, Yeshua, and be saved in Yeshua's resurrected life.

Galil—Galilee, which means "rolling hills." It is a region of Yeshua's birth and ministry, a mountainous region in the north of Israel.

Gan-'Eden—Hebrew term for garden of Eden/paradise. The place of creation of man and all living things on earth, including man's intimate relationship with God and fall to sin as well.

Gat-Sh'manim—Gethsemane—the literal meaning is "winepress." In the New Testament, it refers to the Garden of Gethsemane.

- The place where Yeshua led His disciples after their Passover Seder meal so He could pray to Father God regarding His willful sacrifice and death on a cross for all humanity's sins.

- It is here that Yeshua was deceived by Judas into the hands of the Sanhedrin's temple guards.

- It is also the first place Yeshua spilled His blood for the sake of mankind. By sweating out blood through the pours of His skin onto the ground. Due to His great stress and sadness and sacrifice on the cross, He would have to make. He said to His disciples He could die contemplating what was being required of Him.

- But as He stated in Matthew 26:39, "Going on a little farther, He fell on His face, praying, 'My Father, if possible, let this cup pass from Me! Yet—not what I want, but what you want!'" What an unimaginable decision and willingness to go forward with His selfless sacrifice to forgive every person and possibly save them, born of this earth.

Gei-Hinnom—literally the valley of Hinnom, located just to the southeast of the Old City Jerusalem. It joins the Kidron Valley also just to the southeast. In the lower part of the Hinnom Valley and Kidron Valley, it was an ugly place where ugly things happened. It became the city dump. Dead animals from the temple sacrifices were thrown there to rot and be eaten by worms and maggots. City sewage was dumped there as well. The place was literally crawling with worms, full of rot and disease. Many Israelites sacrificed their children to the false gods of Molech and Baal in this valley in the times of antiquity. See Leviticus 20:2—the New Testament translates it as hell!

Get—or gett—a divorce document. Moses in Deuteronomy 24:1–4 allowed for divorce, though God abhors it. Divorce is a legal term. In biblical times men were divorcing their wives and leaving them destitute. So Moses, showing mercy toward the wife to be divorced, had the husband write a bill of divorce. Which are terms that take care of the woman who is being divorced, as in those days a woman had no way to support herself without a husband.

Good eye—tov ayin—found in Matthew 6:22 and Luke 11:34. Yeshua said this, which appears to be a Hebraic idiom that was used to describe a person's outlook toward others. A person with a "good eye" was a person who looked at others with compassion and had a generous spirit and gave to others as needed. In Proverbs 22:9, "he who is generous is blessed, because he shares his food with the poor." Understanding this idiom helps us understand the context of Matthew 6:19–24, which begins with "do not store up for yourselves wealth here on earth," then talks about the good/evil eye, and ends with "you can't be a slave to both God and money." All three of these sayings are part of a greater teaching on having the right attitude toward money and Father God's will.

Goyim—this is the word in Hebrew that refers to non-Jewish peoples. Goyim is not and should not be taken as an insult—it simply is the plural of the word goy, which means nation. Example:

- God uses the word goy as it relates to Isra'el as found in Exodus 19:6, "'And you will be a kingdom of Cohanim for Me, a nation set apart.' These are the words you are to speak to the people of Isra'el."
- It is better understood as any pagan nation outside of the nation of Isra'el.

Ha'Elyon—"Most High." Elyon appears thirty-one times in the Old Testament. All in the book of Daniel. It is translated as "Most High." When preceded by El, it is translated as "God Most High."

HaG'vurah—in context of the scripture Yeshua quoted in Matthew 26:64, it can mean "the power of God, His right hand of justice and righteous judgment."

Hametz—within the context, the spiritual inference is "rising up of sin." Fermented or fermenting dough, leavened bread was probably a common article of food among the ancient Israelites. It refers to food prepared from five species of grain—wheat, barley, oats, spelt, and rye—that has been allowed to leaven. God forbids, however, leavened bread to be used during the annual appointed festival of Passover or Pesach. Leavened bread was prepared when required at short notice. Such bread was designated "the bread of affliction" because of its association with Egyptian slavery. With few exceptions, leaven was forbidden in sacrificial offerings. In later times, "leaven" and "corruption" were regarded as synonymous terms.

Hevel—Abel, which means "vapor or breath," second son of Adam and Eve, brother to Cain, who took Abel's life.

Hippatach—literally means "be opened." It can refer to the physical but, more importantly, the spiritual opening of ears and eyes to the gospel of Yeshua. See Isaiah 61:1.

Hoshana Rabbah—meanings can be "saved," "day of salvation," "divine judgment." It is the seventh and final day of God's appointed feast of Sukkot (festival of booths). It is a day of saving and remembrance of when God led the Israelites out of Egypt and tabernacled with them in the wilderness on the way to the promised land. It was given to the Israelites as a festival but is also a festival for all peoples taken out of their individual wilderness journeys onto the path of life in Yeshua that are also invited to participate in.

Hutzpah—Chutzpah, a Hebrew word that has been adopted into Yiddish and then English. Chutzpah has been defined as audacity, insolence, impudence, gall, brazen nerve, effrontery, incredible guts, presumption, and arrogance. Something is missing from all these words. It can be destructive and ugly or vital and fantastic, but never in-between.

Isra'el—the nation of Israel, God's chosen people, as well as the Gentiles. In the book of Ephesians, it is explained that both peoples were being hostile toward God. Through Yeshua, they became one new man, messianic (followers of the way) in God's kingdom.

- The Torah teaches salvation to the Israelites first, then the Gentiles. Messianic and Christian faiths were born out of the Torah of Spirit, not the Torah of legalism.

Judeans—are citizens of Judah. A city named after Judah, the fourth son born to Jacob and his first wife, Leah. Whose name means, "Praised, let him be praised." He became one of the twelve tribes of Isra'el.

Kefa—Peter or Simon Peter (same as Shim'on Kefa), meaning "rock" or "small stone." A fisherman by trade, called by Yeshua to follow Him and become His disciple. Father God revealed to Kefa that Yeshua is the Son of God. It was at this time Yeshua said Shim'on (Peter) would be called Kefa, "rock," from that time forward.

K'far-Nachum—city called Capernaum, established during the time of the Hasmoneans, located on the northern shore of the Sea of Galilee. A fishing village named after prophet Nahum.

Korazin—Chorazin is located northwest of the Sea of Galilee near Capernaum. Condemned by Yeshua for not repenting of their sins in spite of the mighty works the Lord did in them.

Korban—a variety of sacrificial offerings described and commanded in the Torah. The object sacrificed was usually an animal that was ritually slaughtered and then transferred from the human to the divine realm by being burned on an altar as a means of doing homage, winning favor, or securing pardon.

K'riot—Kirioth or Kerioth, which means "cities" and is the plural in the Hebrew Bible. A town in the south of Judea found in Joshua 15:25 and Moab in Jeremiah 48:24, 41.

Levi—a male who claims patrilineal descent from the tribe of Levi. The tribe is named after Jacob's and Leah's third son, Levi. They were selected to serve God in the holy temple. Most served in peripheral roles, playing music, opening and closing the gates, and standing guard. This tribe did not receive a parcel of land to settle, and therefore it actually accompanies (lives among) the other tribes. A perfect example of a name foreshadowing future destiny. The personal name Levi means "to join."

Levi Ben-Halfai—the name referenced in the gospels of Mark and Luke is for Matthew, the tax collector Yeshua called to follow Him. As noted, the Hebrew name of Levi means "to join." However, this Levi, a tax collector, is not to be confused with a Levi who was the priest in the parable of the Good Samaritan.

Lot—son of Haran, Abraham's nephew, whose name means "covering, veil."

"Man"—or manna—which means "portion, dose, or ration." An edible substance that God provided for Israelites and peoples who joined them in leaving Egypt during their forty-year exodus travels to the promised land. In the context of John 6:49, "man" refers to manna.

Maneh—or mina—a monetary form of metal currency along with the talent that was units of account and remained so during the second temple period when the shekel became a coin denomination.

- Weight variously estimated, probably about two point five or three pounds.
- A simple table: 1 talent = 60 maneh = 3,000 shekels.

Manim—plural for maneh, which was about three months' wages in biblical times.

Marta—Mary, sister to El'azar (Lazarus) and Martha. The name means "lady."

Martha—sister to Mary and Lazarus, found in Luke 10:42. CJB uses the word Miryam for Martha, which means "mistress or myrrh."

Mashiach—meaning "our Anointed One or Messiah." Messiah is a word quite familiar to followers of the Jewish, Messianic, Christian, and Islamic faiths. It is intended for the reservation as an official title for Yeshua (Jesus), though some faiths would disagree. It has the designation for some of a Messiah that will come, has come, and will come again. However, Yeshua wasn't the only one in the Bible described as messiah. For Jewish people of biblical antiquity, the word "messiah" was primarily used during the Hebrew tradition of anointing a new king, as well as a Messiah that is yet to come and certainly will.

Mattiyahu—Matthew, whose name means "gift of the Lord," was a tax collector who left his work to follow Yeshua. In Mark and Luke, he is called by his other name, Levi.

Matzah—God-instructed, unleavened brittle flat bread prepared and eaten at Passover meal.

Messianic—Jewish people who come to the knowledge that Yeshua is the Son of God and are born again into His resurrected life while continuing to celebrate and adhere to the written Torah of Moshe and of God's Holy Spirit and appointed feast times in freedom. As well as Christians who come to realize that, though saved by the grace of God. He has appointed weekly and annual feasts to be participated in and celebrated in His presence as well as understand the Torah of the Spirit are not laws of legalism and judgment to be abolished but rather observances to be taught and adhered to that bring life, joy, and salvation to a person and community in God's care.

Messiah—same meaning as Mashiach, with references of Father God and Yeshua, Son of God, as both are one according to God within the commandment of the Sh'ma found in Deuteronomy 6:4. As well as biblical prophecy found in the books of the prophets, psalms of King David, and eyewitness accounts within the apostolic gospel scriptures from the disciples that actually walked with Yeshua.

Miryam—means "bitter" as a reflection of the bitter oppression under which the people lived at the time in Egypt.

- In the OT she was the sister to Aaron and Moshe, under Egyptian rule.
- In the NT she was the sister to Mary and Lazarus, under Roman rule.
- Both times were years of great oppression, but God heard the cries of His beloved people/person and intervened. Lifting the oppression of slave labor and even death unto resurrection.

Mitzvoth—the commandments of law given by God to Moses for the Israelites and all peoples born again into the kingdom of God.

Moshe—Moses in English, which means "drawn out of the water"; some interpretations say "savior." He was the miracle-working leader of the nation of Israel and the greatest prophet who ever lived. Chosen by God to take the Israelites out of Egypt more than 3,300 years ago. Moses transcribed the first five books of the Torah, the foundational text of Judaism and the womb, if I may use that term, through which, eventually, the Messianic community and Christians were birthed.

Na'aman the Syrian—Naaman, a descendant of Benjamin, also an Aramean (Syrian) general, whose name means "pleasantness."

Natan'el—Nathanael, which means "God has given," who became a disciple of Yeshua and was the brother of Philip, who also was a disciple of Yeshua.

Natzeret—Nazareth meaning "a shoot or sprout." It is a city situated among the southern ridges of Lebanon on the steep slope of a hill about fourteen miles from the Sea of Galilee and six miles west of Mount Tabor.

- This city is not mentioned in the Old Testament. It was the home of Joseph and Mary, and it was here an angel of the Lord announced the virgin birth of the Messiah Yeshua.

- The birthplace of Yeshua, where He grew up and was called to His ministry by Father God. Beginning within the synagogue as a child, where the priest was amazed at his knowledge of Torah, and as an adult, where some of the same priests and people were so offended that they sought to cast Him down from the precipice whereon their city was built.

- Twice they expelled Him from their borders, and He finally left the city, where He stopped doing miracles because of their unbelief.

Ninveh—the capital of the ancient kingdom and empire of Assyria. A city located in modern-day Iraq.

Noach—Noah means "to lead to a rest." In the broader sense, it means to lead to a rest as we see in the Holy Scriptures God's promise that He would lead Israel into repentance and into the promised land.

- Noah found grace in the sight of God. See Genesis 6:8.

- The role that Noach played prior to the flood was as a leader, one who was to guide others to repentance and rest. A rest from the toils and troubles of the days prior to the flood.
- He was the builder of the ark of God.
- He and his family only were the redeemed and second beginning of humanity post-flood.

N'tilat-yadayim—literally means "on the washing of hands" or "washing hands." This is a ritual using a two-handled cup, which the Jewish people partake in many times of the day, not just before eating. After the hands are washed, a blessing in Hebrew is recited. Jewish tradition calls for the washing of hands every morning, which serves as a reminder to use them for holy purposes.

- Individuals are understood to be in a state of impurity at many points during their day. To rid themselves of such contamination, one must wash their hands using a "washing cup" or running water. Following the ritual helps Jewish individuals be as sanctified as they possibly can be, which allows them to be prepared for the time that the Messiah arrives.
- Messianic followers of the way and Christians partake in physical hand washing many times during the day. But they believe spiritually the shed blood of Yeshua as Messiah and His sacrifice for forgiveness and resurrection to a new life daily sanctifies them and makes them clean eternally.

Nu—is a Yiddish word that is in common use in Modern Hebrew. It means, "Well, go on!"

Nudnik—means "someone who is constantly asking you for something or otherwise taking up your time or a boring person."

'Olam haba—meaning "the world to come, the spiritual afterlife." This term is also used to refer to the Messianic age to come or a higher state of being in Judaism. The Messianic and Christian communities believe the afterlife means residing in the resurrection of Yeshua, Son of God, as Messiah in God's kingdom, which Father God has given over to Yeshua as well as all authority.

'Olam hazeh—meaning literally "this world" or, in Jewish theology, "present life on earth." Another Jewish Rabbinical definition is, though olam hazeh is full of misery and injustice, one's view of life is transformed by realizing, according to the Mishna (code of Talmudic laws), that "this life" is but an antechamber where one prepares oneself to be admitted to the banquet hall that is "the world to come."

Parush—an individual Pharisee from a class of priests within the Sanhedrin.

Pesach—Passover, a festival appointed by God, commemorating the Israelites' exodus and liberation from slavery in Egypt and the "passing over" of the angel of death. It is foundational in the story of the Jewish people, as well as to people of Messianic and Christian faiths. God hears the cries of His people and answers with the Messiah. Moshe was a type and shadow of the Messiah to come, and Yeshua, the Son of God, is the Messiah. It is an annual feast that will be celebrated in perpetuity now as well as in God's kingdom to come. See Exodus 12, Leviticus 23, and Deuteronomy 16 for history and commanded instruction from God to Moses for all peoples in God's kingdom to keep. See Luke 22 for Yeshua's last Pesach Seder meal with His twelve disciples prior to being deceived by Judas and taken into custody prior to His crucifixion. Jews and followers of the way alike continue to eat of the Seder meal at Pesach, but Yeshua will not eat of it again until His second coming and He establishes His kingdom here on earth as it is in heaven.

Pool of Shiloach—the name means "sent." It has biblical roots and is the name applied to the waters of the Gihon spring in Isaiah 8:6. Talmudic sources refer several times to Shiloa. From the Middle Ages onward, the name Shiloach referred to the village on the eastern slope of the Kidron Valley. The village was a suburb of Jerusalem, and the citizens worked the fields on the hill of Ophel. In 1884, Jews from Yemen established themselves in part of the village but were forced to abandon their homes due to Arab riots in 1936. In 1967, after the Six-Day War, Shiloach was incorporated into the Jerusalem municipal area.

Psalm—means "a sacred song or poem." It is an ancient book of anthological poetic prayers originally written in Hebrew by various writers. The most well-known is King David as well as Solomon, his son. The book expresses the heart, circumstances, emotions, and prayers of its writers. The poems and songs were and are used as liturgical materials in various ritual contexts in ancient and modern Israel. As well as Messianic and Christian congregations.

P'rushim—Pharisees, a class of priests within the Sanhedrin.

Rabbi—in Hebrew, the word means "my master." A rabbi is a religious leader and teacher of the Torah to both Jewish and messianic peoples. Some rabbis lead synagogues and some congregations, others are teachers, and yet others lead informally. Rabbinic ordination is known as semichah. In common parlance, a rabbi with advanced training in practical Jewish law (Halachah) is known as a rav.

Rabbani—means "teacher or master." A Hebraic word of deep respect applied especially to spiritual instructors and learned persons of Torah.

Ruach HaKodesh—the Holy Spirit in both the OT and NT. It is the very Spirit of God and is God. There are exhaustive resources on the internet regarding definitions. Some say the breath of life, creative force within creation, counselor, and comforter. As God He is boundless, all-knowing, omnipresent, the power and helper Father God sends in Yeshua's name to those born again.

The Holy Spirit sanctifies and transforms people into Yeshua's image within Yeshua's resurrected life. Please do a personal study and prayerfully ask Father God to send the Holy Spirit to you in Yeshua's name.

Sanhedrin—the Jewish Supreme Court consists of seventy-one rabbis today. God had Moses appoint only seventy. They were the only ones who, in biblical times, could try the king and extend the boundaries of the temple and Jerusalem and were the ones to whom all questions of law were finally put and judgments rendered.

Satan—or ha Satan—meaning "adversary, one who resists, prince of evil spirits, evil inclination." Adversary of God in Judaism, Messianic, Christian, and Islamic faiths. Satan is traditionally understood as an angel, Lucifer, who rebelled against God and was cast out of heaven with other "fallen" angels before the creation of humankind. Most religions see Satan as the cause of humankind's expulsion from the garden of Eden. He was evil from the beginning, says Yeshua. As well as a liar, thief, and destroyer of humanity who especially targets God's peoples.

Schmooze—talk with someone in a lively and friendly way, typically in order to impress or manipulate them.

S'dom (Sodom) and Amora (Gomorrah)—Canaanitish cities, known as Sodom, meaning "to scorch or burn," and Gomorrah, meaning "the speaker or the interpreter," where God rained down fire and brimstone completely destroying all of the city's inhabitants due to their relentless sinning.

- Both towns were completely destroyed by the raining down of burning sulfur sent by God from heaven above.
- With the exception of Lot, who was Abraham's nephew, along with his wife and two daughters. Unfortunately, Lot's wife did not heed the warning from the angels not to look back upon the city, and for doing so she was turned into a pillar of salt.

Sectarianism—is a noun meaning "adherence to a separate religious sect or party, especially excessive partisan or denominational zeal." We must keep in our hearts and mind there are no separate sects, parties, or denominations in heaven. Only the kingdom of God of which Yeshua is King and has full authority.

Seder—an appointed annual ceremonial dinner held on the first evening of Passover in commemoration of the exodus of the Israelites from Egypt.

Sekhel—in modern Hebrew and seykhel in Yiddish, it can mean intelligence, smarts, brains, reason, common sense, cleverness, or even wisdom.

Shabbat—is a verb meaning "to cease, rest." It is the appointed seventh day of creation, Saturday, not Sunday. It is the day of rest and abstention from work as commanded by God. Shabbat involves two interrelated commandments: to remember (zachor) and to observe (shamor). See the book of Leviticus 23:1–3.

Shalom—both in a greeting and a departure, the word is used as a blessing of "peace" from one to another. A more accurate translation of the word is "more than harmony." It means completeness, soundness, welfare, and to live in peace with another. Being a spouse, children, neighbor, community, or nation to nation.

Shalom aleikhem—a spoken greeting meaning "peace be upon you."

Shekel—means "to weigh" and was used as a unit of measure for measuring the weight of gold, silver, or copper in biblical and present times. The common standard both of weight and value in Israel for 1 Israeli New Shekel = $0.29381 American Dollar in exchange rate at the time of this writing, January 2023. The value of a "Shekel" in either time span depended on the metal being weighed.

Sh'eilah—means "to ask a question," "request," or "things asked for."

Shiloach—has biblical roots and is the name applied to the waters of Gihon spring in Isaiah 8:6. Talmudic sources refer to several times in Shiloach, and according to John 9:7, Yeshua sent a blind man to the "pool of Shiloach," and he was healed. From the Middle Ages onward, the name Shiloach referred to the village on the eastern slope of the Kidron Valley, a suburb of Jerusalem. The inhabitants worked the fields on the hill of Ophel.

Shim'on—Peter (Kefa)—Simon Peter (Shim'on Kefa), all the same person, a disciple of Yeshua. Whose name means "one who is trustworthy."

Shim'on Bar-Yochanan—Simon (Peter or Kefa), son of John, a fisherman who Yeshua referred to as the "rock" and called him to be a disciple.

Shlomo—Solomon, son of King David, whose name means "peaceable or man of peace." He built the first temple circa 990–931 BCE.

Shofar—a ram's horn for blowing or signaling like a trumpet. Jewish religious services use it during the high holy days of Rosh Hashanah services, every day except Shabbat during the preceding month of Elul, and the end of Yom Kippur.

- The four sounds of the shofar are tekiah, shevarim, teruah, and tekiah gedolah—reminding the people of a crying voice. See YouTube videos to hear the blowing of the shofar if you do not attend a synagogue.

- Hearing the shofar's call is a reminder for us to look inward and repent for the sins of the past year on Yom Kippur. It can be blown daily as well for the same reason.

- It is also a reminder to us of the Torah portion that is read on Rosh Hashanah. The story of the binding of Isaac, Abraham's son, as a sacrifice at God's command. God relented and saw the love in Abraham's heart and willingness to ultimately obey God, no matter the cost. God instead provided a ram stuck in the bush that Abraham ultimately sacrificed to God instead of Isaac.
- The great shofar will be blown by angels at the second coming of Yeshua and heard by all worldwide.

Shomron—capital of the Northern Kingdom of Israel. Known as Samaria or, in media, the "West Bank." Which means "place of watchkeeping." Here Yeshua met the Samaritan woman at the well.

Synagogue—Beit Knesset, meaning "house of gathering," is also the main and only place of worship and sacrifices of praises being verbally lifted up to God since the second temple's destruction in 70 CE. It is also referred to as a shul, a Yiddish word related to the English word "school," thus named since the Torah is studied there as well. Synagogues can be found virtually wherever there are Jewish peoples and have been in use since the Babylonian exile.

S'mikhah—can mean "transference," "authority," "anointing," or "ordination." The original was the formal "transmission of authority" from Moses through the generations. This form ceased between 360 and 425 CE. Since then, it has continued in a less formal way.

Talent—a measured form of metal currency in biblical times. Not to be compared with a coin. A talent is formed in the shape of a huge ingot, that is, a heavyweight with a handle on top for ease of transport (think of the shape of a kettlebell at a gym for a visual reference). A single talent weighs seventy-five pounds—over thirty-four kilograms. It weighs 6,000 denarii and represents the salary of 6,000 days' work. Sixteen and a half years.

Talita, kumi—which means, "Little girl, I say to you, get up!"

Tallit—means "prayer shawl/undergarment" and is a large rectangular shawl made of wool, cotton, or synthetic fibers. The corner fringes called tzitzit on this ritual garment remind the wearer of all the commandments in the Torah. The origin and its meaning are biblical and can be found in the book of Numbers 15:38–40.

Talmid—disciple, stresses the relationship between rabbi (teacher or master) and talmid/disciple (student).

Example:

- Rav Sha'ul (apostle Paul), in some of his epistles, referred to himself as a "slave" to Yeshua as found in Romans 1:1, Philippians 1:1, Titus 1:1. In his other epistles, he refers to himself as an emissary and prisoner and united with Yeshua. These words express the depth of Sha'ul's relationship he believed he had with Yeshua as his rabbi and, most importantly, his Savior, God, and Messiah that has come and will come again.

- Talmidim—Hebrew noun, plural meaning for "disciples."
- Tanakh—first five books of the Bible, writings of the prophets, and King David. Hebrew/Jewish Bible (Torah), the books Christians call the Old Testament.
- There are 365 prophecies within the OT scriptures that are fulfilled in the NT referring to Yeshua as the Son of God, Messiah, and God.
- Please keep in mind that there is no New Testament without the Old Testament. Both testify and are witnesses one to the other.

T'fillin—leather straps and boxes containing scrolls of parchment inscribed with verses from the Torah, which are worn by observant Jews and some Messianic Jews during weekday prayers.

T'oma—Thomas, the one who doubted that Yeshua had risen and was alive. Unless he could see the nail marks in His hands and put his finger into Yeshua's side, he refused to believe. Of course, Yeshua, showing up in the room behind locked doors, accommodated Thomas and told him to put his finger on his hand and look, then take his hand and put it into Yeshua's side.

Yeshua said, "Don't be lacking in trust (faith) but have trust (faith)!" Thomas looked and believed! See John 20:24–29.

Torah—this word has a wide spectrum of meaning. It can refer to one verse, a selection of verses, a book, and the first five books of the Bible. The entire OT/Tanakh or the whole Bible. Unfortunately, many Christians have been taught to believe its meaning is "law" with a negative pejorative as some form of "bondage" and "legalism." However, in Hebrew the word does not mean "law"; it actually means "instruction, teaching, guidance, or directives." In its broadest sense, it is believed to be the substance of divine revelation to Israel, Jewish teaching, culture, and practice; the arrow from an archer toward a target; or the teachings and instructions from a parent to a child. Training them up in the way God wants them to go or a teacher to a student in civic, moral, and judicial codes.

Torah experts—typically means "lawyer."

Torah teacher—a person who is an expert teacher in the commandments, a lawyer, and a continual student of the Torah themselves.

T'shuvah—for all Jewish peoples, this term has a critically important meaning. In Hebrew, the word translates literally as "return" and describes the return to God and with our fellow human beings that is made possible through repentance of our sins. In Christianity, the word "repent" is defined as "to turn away from sin." But this misses the mark in essence, as one cannot turn away from their sins without the power of Yeshua's resurrected life living in them by the Holy Spirit. So the deeper meaning for both groups of peoples is to return to the "Redeemer" of themselves and humanity, Yeshua, Son of God, and Messiah.

Tursis—meaning "trouble."

Tzaddik—in Judaism the title is given to a person considered to be the most human among humans. It carries the weight of doing what is correct and just. The personality of the tzaddik is calibrated to God's original specifications so that everything about this person is just as the Creator meant it should be, and all a tzaddik desires is what his Creator desires.

Tzara'at—commonly mistranslated as leprosy or Hansen's disease, this ailment described in the Bible cannot be healed by doctors. In the Bible, tzara'at is a skin disease that can take many different forms and, in particularly bad cases, can manifest itself on one's clothing, belongings, and house in addition to the skin. According to the rabbis, tzara'at is caused by sin. This makes it a disease like no others, part medical condition, part spiritual pathology. Chapters 13 and 14 within the book of Leviticus teach us about most variations and the required treatments.

Tzarfat—a biblical placement that may refer to Sarepta in Lebanon. In later times, it came to be identified with France. It is still the name of France in Modern Hebrew.

Tz-dukim—Sadducees, one of the two main groups in the religious establishment of Yeshua's time (the other being the Pharisees [P'rushim]). They tended to be more Hellenistic and more willing to cooperate with the Roman conquerors than the Pharisees. In Yeshua's references to them, it seems His point was that they considered themselves more righteous than others in their own minds.

Tzedakah—righteousness, fairness, or justice and is commonly used to signify charity.

Tzidon—an ancient fishing city of Phoenicia on the Mediterranean Sea in present-day southwest Lebanon.

Tzitziyot—specially knotted ritual fringes, or tassels, attached to the four corners of the tallit (prayer shawl/undergarment) worn by observant Jews. Some Messianic Jews and Christians wear it as well to remind them of God's commandments toward life.

Tziyon—meaning "Zion," a Hebrew place name used in the Hebrew Bible as a synonym for Jerusalem as well as for the land of Israel as a whole.

Tzor—a great sea trading city, meaning "rock." However, God gives Isaiah a prophecy about Tzor found in Isaiah 23:1–18.

Ya'akov—Jacob, Isaac's son and grandson to Abraham, whose name means "held by the heal, supplanter." He wrestled with a man he testified was God, whom he saw face to face, and yet his life was spared. God changed his name to Israel. Genesis 32:22–32.

- The same Hebrew name is also used for the name James. Who was one of the sons of Zebedee, a fisherman, and called by Yeshua to be His disciple. James means "my gift."

Yericho—city of Jericho, which means "place of fragrance." A fenced city in the midst of a vast grove of palm trees in the plain of Jordan over against the place where the Israelites crossed that river. See Joshua 3:16. Its site was near the 'Ain es-Sultan, Elisha's Fountain. See 2 Kings 2:19–22. About five miles west of Jordan and twenty-five kilometers northeast of Jerusalem.

Yerushalayim—Jerusalem, a holy city in Israel according to the Holy Scriptures, where God resides. See Psalm 9:11, Psalm 76:2, Psalm 132:14, Psalm 135:21, Joel 3:17, Joel 3:2, Zechariah 8:3.

Yesha'yahu—the biblical prophet Isaiah, whose name means "God is salvation."

Yeshua—Jesus, Son of God, Son of Man, God, whose name means "salvation and Deliverer." Born of the Holy Spirit and Mary.

Y'hudah—Judah. There are multiple biblical uses for the word.

- The fourth son of Jacob and Leah and the forebear of one of the tribes of Israel and whose descendants were to be Yeshua the Messiah.
- The tribal territory of his descendants became the nucleus of King David's kingdom, and after the kingdom had been divided into Israel and Judah, the southern kingdom of Judah had Jerusalem as its center.
- An ancient kingdom of southern Palestine between the Mediterranean and the Dead Sea. It lasted from the division of Palestine around 930 BC until the destruction of Jerusalem in 586 BC.
- Its meaning is "to throw your hands out or up in praise and awe or in a reaction of wow: 'Will you just look at that!'" This is the Hebraic understanding of "praise."
- Or Jude, one of four half-brothers to Yeshua and brother of Ya'akov. Writer of the book of Jude.
- There is more that would be fun research.

Y'hudah Ben-Shim'on—Judas, the one who betrayed Yeshua to the Sanhedrin for thirty pieces of silver. This is the one Yeshua was referring to in John 6:71; 13:21, 26–27.

Yochanan—known as John the Baptist or Immerser. Whose name means "God is gracious." He is Yeshua's cousin, son of Zechariah—a priest—and Elizabeth. He baptized Yeshua in the Jordan.

Yonah—for the most part, Jonah is a male name; however, the Yiddish translation of "dove," Toibah, is a female name. It is the name of a biblical prophet whose story is read on Yom Kippur, the annual Day of Atonement. The book of Jonah tells about the prophet's refusal to fulfill God's mission to call on the people of Ninveh to repent. After a long and frightening ordeal, Jonah regretted not obeying God's command when called upon. However, he did change his mind and went to tell the city to repent.

Yud—a dot. The expression is used to mean something very tiny, but it doesn't mean it is insignificant.

Z'kharyah Ben-Berekyah—Zechariah, which means, "Yah remembers, Yah's male." From the verb zakar (to remember or review) and Yah, the shortened name of the Lord. Father of Yochanan the Immerser (John the Baptist). Husband to Elizabeth, a priest who Yeshua testified was murdered by hypocritical Torah teachers and P'rushim between the temple and the altar. See Matthew 23:35.

Zakkai—Zacharia, whose name means "pure, intelligent." He was a tax collector hated by the Jewish people. Because paying a tax to the Roman government was considered giving homage to a pagan god. Some believe Zacharia climbed into the tree when Yeshua was walking by because Jewish zealots were known to carry knives in their clothing and attack tax collectors or anyone who supported the Roman empire and then sneak away. Is this a fact? Not sure, but it is logical and could make for some good research.

Zavdai or Zawdee—Zebedee, a fisherman, whose name means "God has bestowed." Father of two sons, James and John, who left their father's enterprise to follow Yeshua when called to do so and became disciples.

PART 8:

COMMENTARIES

*I*t is important the reader understands that there was no written NT/B'rit Hadashah when Yeshua walked and taught amongst humanity in His days on earth. As you read and come to know, many of His teachings are referenced directly from the OT/Tanakh. Yet additionally Father God spoke directly to Yeshua from the beginning to the end of His earthly life and ministry, revealing His will and teachings in and through Yeshua to those around Him as told in John 12:46–50, and thus became the writings of the NT/B'rit Hadashah through the apostolic writers, who were witnesses and inspired by the Holy Spirit. Unless otherwise specifically noted, all commentaries are those of the author.

Part 4: p. 28—Matthew 3:15, Luke 3:21-22. Yochanan (John) Baptizes Yeshua. Since God—the Father—the Son, and the Holy Spirit are One. I put these scriptures in, as all three are One in the same place at the same time. Yet they are but One voice. (See CJB—Deuteronomy 6:4, the "Sh'ma," John 12:46–50, John 14:15–31.)

Part 4: p. 49—Luke 17:6. And p. 76—Luke 7:9. Trust—the English word "trust" is abstract (cannot be sensed by five senses). Yet it is defined as "firm belief in the integrity, ability, safety, or character of a person or thing: confidence or reliance. A charge or duty imposed in faith or confidence or as a condition of some relationship."

But Hebrew is a concrete-oriented language where each word is associated with something that can be sensed by one or more of the five senses. Examples:

- *chasah*—Strong's #2620—means "to lean on"; see Psalm 18:2
- *betach*—Strong's #982—means "to cling"; see Psalm 565:4
- *yachal*—Strong's #3176—means "to hope, not as into wonder but as into know"; see Isaiah 51:5
- *aman*—Strong's #539—means "to be sure of" (see Isaiah 22:23) or "to be very firm" (see Micah 7:5)

Its meaning is deep. Yet the implied meaning in the English Scriptures is accredited to as "faith." In the Bible, the definition of the word "faith" is given in the book of Hebrews 11:1—now faith is confidence in what we hope for and assurance about what we do not see.

- Faith to believe in God is not something a person is born with. It is given as a measure in the essence of a spiritual awakening and is a free gift. We must take in this measure of faith God gives as all of our life's needs and blessing are included in it, I believe. As we live, worship, and serve God in faith, our lives manifest the good works God already has in store for us to produce. The productions create a very deep "trust" with God in us.

Also, see examples in the books of Ephesians 2:8–9 and 1 Corinthians 12:4–11 for wisdom concerning "faith" given to a person who is born again in Yeshua Messiah according to God's Word.
Part 4: p. 71-72—Matthew 7:21–23, Luke 13:25–30, 32–33.

Not everyone who says to Me, "Lord, Lord!" will enter the Kingdom of Heaven, only those who do what My Father in heaven wants. On that Day, many will say to Me, "Lord, Lord! Didn't we prophesy in Your name? Didn't we expel demons in Your name? Didn't we perform many miracles in Your name?" Then I will tell them to their faces, "I never knew you! Get away from me, you workers of Lawlessness."

These are some of the most sobering scriptures in God's Holy Word. The emphasis Yeshua is putting on the people here is what Father God wants. Which is more about a person's character transforming into the image of Yeshua's character than just prophesying, expelling demons, and performing miracles. Which may or may not be a means that leads another person to salvation or possibly as a means of credit, attention, or influence on themselves versus God's Son and His teachings. Yeshua is the embodiment of Father God's law. He fulfilled it and never once or ever will abolish it. How can we know some of the character traits of Christ according to Scriptures? Please ask the Holy Spirit's help for discerning wisdom as revealed in the following scriptures found in the Gospel of Matthew.

Read backward in Matthew from the following scriptures in this numbered order:

1. 7:15–20
2. 7:13–14
3. 7:12
4. 7:7–11
5. 7:6
6. 7:1–5

7. 6:25–34	9. 6:16–18	11. 6:5–13
8. 6:19–24	10. 6:14–15	12. 6:1–4

Interestingly what Yeshua calls lawlessness in Matthew He calls it wickedness in Luke. Willful and consistent unbelief that Yeshua is the Son of God and the only means by which a person returns to Father God, along with disobedience of Torah's law (observances and directives for living) and Yeshua's teachings, will lead to wickedness, lawlessness, and separation from God. This is not what Father God wants! The narrow path of life is a hard one, and few find it, Yeshua tells us. So we need to take it seriously as difficult as it may be at times. We need the Holy Spirit's power, counsel, comfort, and leading to stay on it and out of the weeds where the enemy of our soul roams daily seeking to destroy us like a roaring lion.

Part 4: p. 102—Matthew 10:34, Luke 12:49. Yeshua did not come to bring peace to the land. He came to bring a sword! Not a forged-in-fire, man-made sword but rather the living sword of the Spirit in God's own being. His Son, Yeshua, is also the living Word (Holy Scriptures). As found in the book of Hebrews 4:12. See, the Word of God is alive! It is at work and is sharper than any double-edged sword—it cuts right through to where soul meets spirit and joints meet marrow, and it is quick to judge the inner reflections and attitudes of the heart.

- All followers of the way of Yeshua need to train themselves by listening to the Holy Spirit within, exercising faith, continued study, discipleship, and obedience. So they will properly know how to handle the sword of the Spirit, which is the living Word of God.

Part 4: p. 155—Mark 9:7 and Luke 9:35. I included these verses where Father God on the Mount of Transfiguration speaks to Yeshua and a few of His disciples in the presence of Moshe and Elijah. Father God's voice and Yeshua's are always One in context. CJB and all other language transliterations of the Bible.

Part 4: p. 181—Matthew 19:24, Mark 10:25, Luke 18:25.

The word used for camel here is Gamala which actually refers to a "heavy rope" rather than a "camel" which also spelled gimel-meem-lamed-alop. Greek scholars puzzled over a camel passing through the eye of a needle, which is a physical impossibility. Yeshua is clearly not saying a rich man can't enter, or He would not "love" this one! The "heavy rope" lesson teaches about a rich man entering into heaven after he "unravels" his fortune strand by strand as Yeshua instructs. If his wealth was bound tightly and strong like a rope, it is to be unwound like threads which will pass through the eye of a needle. Careful attention is required to thread a needle; so are the rich obligated unto YHWH for how their wealth is acquired and dispersed. Theological attempts to "prove" the eye of the needle to be a geographical location have utterly failed, see Matthew 19:4 & Mark 10:25.

Andrew Gabriel Roth, author of the Aramaic English New Testament (AENT), p. 59, CR#199.

Part 4: pp. 203-205—Luke 14:7–14. Take the Lowly Place—I put this here for further context; the Holy Spirit tells us not only to accept the invitation when called to the banquet table by Father God but also how we are to handle ourselves in Their presence at Their table.

Part 4: p. 205—Luke 14:14. "How blessed you will be that they have nothing with which to repay you! For you will be repaid at the resurrection of the righteous."

Part 4: p. 212—Matthew 12:37, Mark 12:29. Sh'ma Yisra'el, Adonai Eloheinu, Adonai Echad: Hear, O Isra'el, the Lord, our God, the Lord is One. God gives this commandment to Moses, found in the book of Deuteronomy 6:4—it was given to the Israelites and a mix of foreigners with them who were led out of Egypt by God on the way to the promised land.

For them to explicitly "hear" and "know" that God is One. The same commandment applied to the Jewish people Yeshua was talking and teaching to, and it is the same commandment today for all peoples of the world.

Part 4: p. 255—Matthew 26:13, Mark 14:9. Mary anointing Yeshua with perfume. Remember this is the Mary of Bethany, sister to Martha and her brother, Lazarus, who died and Yeshua raised from the dead. She followed Yeshua and helped in preparation for His burial.

Yeshua declares her memory and story will be shared when the gospel is shared throughout the world.

- The expensive perfume was a symbol of preparation for Yeshua's soon-coming burial after His death on the cross. A smell of life for the living versus death for the dead. Dead people don't wear perfume. Knowing her heart, Yeshua accepted her anointing and love for Him.

- Have you given everything of your past life to Yeshua so He may turn the memories of sin and death into a new, inclusive, resurrected life? Or are you possibly still holding onto the lie of exclusion or something in secret? Give everything to Yeshua so you may be included in His resurrected life that He will give to you.

- Have you remembered to share the story of Mary when sharing the gospel of Yeshua Messiah to another?

Part 4: p. 266—Luke 22:62. He went outside and cried bitterly—"he" referring to Kefa, a.k.a. Peter, the disciple of Yeshua.

- I had to include v. 62 for context, reminding us who are born again not to think too much of ourselves. We, too, could be capable of such denial.
- However, like Peter, let us repent and return to Yeshua daily. As Yeshua forgave and restored Peter, so, too, will Yeshua forgive and restore us daily.
- Let us not be quick to judge one another. But rather, in the power of Yeshua Messiah, seek to lift up and restore one another in love and the Spirit of Torah.

Part 4: p. 269—Matthew 27:46 (Eli! Eli! L'mah sh'vaktani) and Mark 15:34 (Elohi! Elohi! L'mah sh'vaktani). Note: Perhaps no two scriptures evoke more emotion than the cry of Yeshua from the cross in this verse. How is it possible that these powerful words have been misunderstood for nearly two millennia? For many, Yeshua's last utterance was either understood as a cry of desperation or a declaration of His messiahship from Psalm 22:1 (AENT): "My El, My El, why have you forsaken Me." Greek versions attempt to transliterate the Psalm as Eli, Eli, lama sabacthani. However, the Aramaic Peshitta NT reads, "Eli, Eli lemana shabakthani," while the Hebrew Psalm reads, "Eli, Eli lama azbatani." Greek transliteration reflects the Aramaic word as does the Peshitta. However, there is a key difference between azbatani, which only means "to forsake," and its Aramaic counterpart shabakthani, which has multiple meanings but also includes the same concept.

Even so, does this mean Yeshua is quoting Psalm 22?

> Yeshua is clearly aware of the reasons for His death, and therefore to use other options would allow for inadequate options like, "why have you kept me around" or "Why have you reserved Me for this purpose." Since He fully knows the reasons for His sufferings, the preferred choice is "Why have you spared Me" or "I've been here for six hours and will die for this cause, but how much more time will this take?" In

response to this question Scripture tells me that Yeshua dies shortly thereafter, thus validating the original Aramaic context.

Andrew Gabriel Roth, author of the AENT—Aramaic English New Testament

See Andrew Gabriel Roth's commentary "My El! My El! Why have you spared Me?" in AENT, p. 912.

- Personally, I agree with Andrew Gabriel Roth's understanding of the word context within these scriptures and the implied meaning of "spared me" versus "forsaken me." Prior to ever reading Andrew's commentary found in His AENT transliteration, I never believed Father God would forsake His Son at any time. The very One He sent to free the world from sin and restore humanity back to Father God and His kingdom. Was Father at the last minute to have a change of mind and forsake Yeshua, even though it pleased Him to crush Yeshua? That just never made sense to me. Irregardless of Yeshua's humanity in a suffering state on the cross as some argue. He was filled with the fullness of Father God's Holy Spirit. The Spirit that led, empowered, and enabled Yeshua to see and hear Father God, thus doing His will. If anyone in the relationship would have forsaken the other, it could have been Yeshua, but He did not! Instead, He was willingly beaten beyond human recognition, the prophet Isaiah tells us—see Isiah 52:14. He could have bled out but didn't, tapped out but didn't, called for angels to come get Him and take Him up to heaven but didn't. Why? Because He was the required legal sacrifice, filled with Father God's Holy Spirit and power! The same Spirit Yeshua promises to send to every born-again believer to give us power to do God's will in our lives! He had to make it to the cross; there was no other option for Him, and He knew it. No one or nothing in heaven would or could forsake Yeshua. Only those here on earth and below. Remember He was already crucified in heaven prior to the founding of the world see Revelation 13:8. So it's not like He didn't know what was expected of Him or what was coming or the outcome before coming to earth as a Son and Ambassador of Father God in heaven and as the legal atonement and Savior for the world.

Part 4: p. 272—Luke 24:30. "As He was reclining with them at the table, He took the matzah, made the b'rakhah, broke it and handed it to them."

Question from the author: Do you frequently sit at the table with Yeshua to talk, get to know Him, say thank You, and give praises or to receive instruction, correction, and assurance for your life?

Part 4: p. 272—Luke 24:31. "Then their eyes were opened, and they recognized Him. But He became invisible to them."

Question from the author: Are your eyes being opened up yet to whom and what Yeshua really is to you? Is He revealing Himself and His kingdom to you with just His words, teachings, and inclusion in His resurrected life? Or is He still invisible to you? I pray not.

Part 4: p. 272—Luke 24:32. "They said to each other, 'didn't our hearts burn inside us as He spoke to us on the road, opening up the Tanakh to us?'"

Question from the author: Does your heart burn inside when you read His living words and teachings, prayerfully talking with Him? Has the Holy Spirit opened up your heart to receive Yeshua's way, truth, and resurrected life for you? I pray this is so!

Part 4: p. 273—Luke 24:45. "Then He opened their minds so that they could understand the Tanakh [OT]." This is an especially important scripture in my opinion. Because timing is everything in the order of God's will for a person. The word "then" in v. 45 is the bridge to the end of Yeshua's physical ministry on earth, which, shortly, was passed onto the disciples on the day of Pentecost. Which is the exact same day called Shavuot. The day on Mount Sinai, 1,200 years to the day prior, when God gave Moshe the law (Ten Commandments) to the peoples as a marriage covenant.

We need to personalize and put ourselves in the upper room in Luke 24:45, when Yeshua comes in and shows Himself to His disciples in His resurrected body. Grasp the fact that the disciples walked and witnessed Yeshua in all manners of teachings and miracles for three-plus years, approximately from the time He called them to be His disciples until they were in that upper room. But…

- As it says in Luke 24:45, it was "*then*" in the upper room after His resurrection that He opened their minds to the fulfillment of prophecies in the Tanakh/OT regarding Himself. Before filling them with the Holy Spirit and again with power of the Holy Spirit on the day of Pentecost ten days later.
- It was "*then*" they came into an understanding of Him they couldn't fully grasp before prior to that day and moment. Within their spirit and hearts, I believe they,

like I do, often during their time following Yeshua, pondered, *Just who and what is this man really?*

- For this reason and many others, we must not be quick to judge another but rather test the spirit.

So this begs some questions to the reader:

- Have you had your *"then moment"* yet? If not, are you ready for it now?
- Do you still see and feel excluded within yourself by possible people, places, and tyrannical things that have enslaved you?
- Do you feel as though you are walking in a wilderness alone or perhaps with others, but you really don't want to be there?
- Whom or what do you worship?
- Has your mind been opened up to who Yeshua really is and what He wants from you, a personal, loving relationship in His resurrected life? Not religion, man-made traditions, or your own imagination that can bind or restrict you from God. Rather a real and intimate relationship that includes you with God, His people in His Kingdom already prepared for you.

Then cry out to Him right now! Ask Him to lose you from the sins of yourself and others! Ask Him to come into your life and be your Savior, Lord, and Master. He wants to be the King of your heart.

- He is waiting—it's up to you—and He loves you so much! By His willful sacrifice, death on the cross, and resurrection to eternal life, you are already "forgiven," hallelujah, but are we really "saved" at the moment of forgiveness, or is something else required?
- Yes, technically we are definitely saved by the shed blood of Yeshua upon the cross of His legal sacrifice and death prescribed and required by Father God for the atonement of humanity's sins. But salvation unto eternal life is much more than just being forgiven, though it cost Yeshua everything this side of heaven. Father God's willful and desired salvation for a person rests in the ascension of a person's spirit into the reality of the resurrected life of Yeshua. God forbade forgiveness to come

and then lay dormant, being held captive in the grave only. He gave Yeshua the command and power to raise Himself to life. Within a relationship with Father God and Yeshua, we are given the same power to be raised to eternal life within Yeshua's resurrected life. As He alone is the first fruit of all fruit from the tree of life living in heaven. If not, then there's a greater probability the gift of forgiveness unto salvation might become a memory only that could fade away within a person versus a promised life-changing reality. Forgiveness has to ascend into life for it to become a viable promised reality of salvation, and it is!

- There has to be a promise and call to life and action to be saved from the grave into the accession of the resurrection. Let's clear something up first; you don't need to clean yourself up to try and be worthy. Just accept the call on your life from Father God, the inner voice your spirit hears. Then take into yourself the free gift of faith given by Father God. So you can believe and trust Yeshua is indeed Father God's Son sent to forgive, save you, and give you a new eternal life. Yeshua also adds that you must believe in and trust that Father God is indeed God! That He is the One who sent Yeshua to forgive and save you. Believe and trust these truths earnestly in your heart and confess them with your mouth, and you will be saved, as they are One. Upon that, Yeshua will then send Father God's Holy Spirit to live inside of you, to counsel and comfort you as you start walking out your new resurrected life into the transformation of Yeshua's image yet to be fully known and understood. But is a certainty of promises we can hold to found in 2 Corinthians 3:18, 1 John 3:2, 1 Corinthians 15:46–49, Romans 8:29–30, Philippians 3:21, 2 Corinthians 5:17, Philippians 2:13, Colossians 3:10, Ephesians 4:13, Romans 8:17, Colossians 1:22, Genesis 1:27, 1 Peter 1:17–19, Genesis 1:26, 1 John 3:31, 1 Peter 1:15–16, John 14:15, Romans 8:3–4, Romans 8:10–11, Romans 8:13, 2 Peter 1:4, 2 Peter 3:18, and 2 Peter 3:18.

- A new life that is an inclusive daily progression of sanctification unto transformation into the image of Yeshua. The baptism of the Holy Spirit is the fire that comes and lives within a person, eliminating everything old within a person's spirit, soul, and fleshly nature. The power of the Holy Spirit is the given new resurrected life to keep the old life from trying to raise itself up from the grave over and over again. The gifts of the Holy Spirit are the new desire and abilities as appropriated to each individual by God's will to share the life-changing gospel of the resurrection of Yeshua with others in need, as the harvest is ripe.

- A time of learning the Torah (instruction and directive teachings, not laws of punishment to be abolished) and Yeshua's love within the Bible, not man-made teachings and traditions that can and will enslave if given power.
- You will inherit a new family of believers who, prior to the cross, were just like you. Desperate for the need of forgiveness, eternal salvation, and a new resurrected life that creates life according to God's will and purpose for you that will help you and others.

So please ask Yeshua for these things and watch your life change and give power to an abundant way, truth, and life in Yeshua and all God's kingdom has in store for you. See, everything you will ever need in this life is installed in the free gift of faith God has given you to believe and trust. Not just money and man-given power, position, and prestige that can never be taken to heaven with you! The riches in a relationship with Yeshua are immeasurable by human standards. If you ask, seek, and knock, you will find. I'm praying with Yeshua and coming into agreement with Him that you will be born again!

Side note: Some readers might not realize that the day of Pentecost in the NT/B'rit Hadashah is on the same exact day as the day of Shavuot in the OT/Tanakh. Which is the giving of the law, really a marriage covenant between God and His people. After being brought out of Egypt by God, when in the wilderness, on Mount Sinai, God gave Moshe the law (Ten Commandments or words). However, since Moshe was gone from the people for forty days, the people thought something happened to him and He wasn't coming back. See the book of Exodus 32. So what did they do? They got busy demanding Moses's brother Aaron make a golden calf to worship as a god. Well, of course, God, from atop of Mount Sinai with Moshe, saw this, became infuriated with the people, and told Moshe to go down and straighten them out quickly as His anger was going to burn against them.

Moshe goes down and sees the "golden calf" abomination that was created and throws the law written by God on stone tablets at the peoples who were worshipping this false god at the foot of Mount Sinai. Moshe stood at the entrance of the camp and shouted, "Whoever is for Adonai, come to me!" All the descendants of Levi rallied around him, and they put the sword to 3,000 people who were in rebellion that very day.

Fast forward 1,200 years later to the very same day in Jerusalem within the upper room where the disciples were gathered. On the day of Pentecost, ten days after Yeshua was in the upper room, they were given their "then moment." That opened up their minds to who and what Yeshua really was as He also breathed the Holy Spirit into them. As promised, Yeshua sent the power of the Holy Spirit to the disciples ten days later. Filled, they then proclaimed the gospel of the kingdom of God, who is Yeshua, and the inclusion in His resurrected life. The fact that He is the Messiah that has come. To the Jewish people in Jerusalem, who were there for the celebration of Shavuot (the giving of the law), 3,000 souls were gained for the Kingdom that day. Thus the church was born. Only God can create that script and timing and make it happen.

He also has a created script specifically written for you; are you reading and understanding it yet? I pray you are, as it is already written within you based on His forgiveness due to the cross. Are you ready to come alive by His inclusion and power in His resurrected life? If, by the free gift of faith, you choose to believe and trust in God, this will be done.

PART 9:

INCLUSION—הללכה—IN THE RESURRECTED LIFE OF JESUS THE MESSIAH

*R*egarding the two men hanging on their cross alongside Yeshua at His crucifixion, which one do you see yourself as?

Luke 23:39–43:

One of the criminals hanging there hurled insults at Him. "Aren't You the Messiah? Save Yourself and us!" But the other one spoke up and rebuked the first, saying, "Have you no fear of God? You're getting the same punishment as He is. Ours is only fair; we're getting what we deserve for what we did. But this man did nothing wrong." Then he said, "Yeshua, remember me when you come as King." Yeshua said to him, "Yes! I promise that you will be with me today in Gan-'Eden."

Regarding the two men hanging on their crosses alongside Yeshua at His crucifixion and reading their conversations with Him, which one do you see yourself as?

This is a conjunctive writ. I must first accredit an anonymous writer unknown to me, who wrote "Living in the Resurrected Life of Jesus" at some time unknown. In keeping with their original four-page outline, along with prayer and additional scriptures given to me by the Holy Spirit, I was inspired to produce this new work, "Inclusion—הלללכה—In the Resurrected Life of Jesus the Messiah." Now a single yet collaborative written text, which I pray blesses you.

We are all the same in the process of being or having been led to the sacrificial death side of the cross of Christ. But are we all the same on the other side—the resurrection side? I must ask you this question regarding the two men hanging on their cross alongside Yeshua on the day of His crucifixion—which one do you see yourself as?

We are all given free will by God. However, we must realize that God's mercy and grace have two dominions: heaven and earth. His justice has three: heaven, earth, and hell. Eternal separation and hell were never meant to become an option for humanity, but unfortunately, it is for some who choose that destination.

There's a much better path and option for you. Know that you, too, may also receive the same promise Yeshua gave to the second man. It's a free gift within the resurrected life of someone who loves you so much—Yeshua. Most heard or know of Him as Jesus, the Son of God. But do they or you really know Him? Please read on to know more about this divine person and to what end His resurrected life is understood thus far for all who come to Him and accept Him as Lord of their lives. With much more to be revealed by Father God's sovereign will and timing. Father's free gift of faith in grace to forgive and save by means of His Son, along with inclusion and love, is especially for you versus exclusion. So you, too, may make the better, wiser choice today.

I pray you embrace this forthcoming teaching and gain the needed understanding and wisdom to live your life within the truthful and transforming loving realm of inclusion—הלללכה—in the resurrected life of Yeshua HaMashiach. To be first in God's kingdom is to become a servant. We must shed ourselves from the dead skin of our old nature and put on the new skin of His divinity in the resurrected life in Yeshua. Becoming a servant to God, people, and creation in both kingdoms of heaven and earth.

It is in the preaching of the cross and resurrection of Yeshua that we find power to live!
First Corinthians 1:17–18:

> For the Messiah did not send me to immerse but to proclaim the Good News-and to do it without relying on "wisdom" that consists of mere rhetoric, so as not to rob the Messiah's execution stake of its power. For the message about the execution-stake

is nonsense to those in the process of being destroyed, but to us in the process of being saved it is the power of God.

The cross implores those who are born again to preach, teach, and disciple others about what happened to Yeshua in His willful sacrifice, death, burial, and resurrection for all of humanity's sake.

- It's important we understand why. With prayer and counsel from the Holy Spirit, may we learn to what end we are to be born again.

The Holy Scriptures in the Torah teach that all believers in Yeshua were and are "included" in Yeshua's crucifixion:

- Galatians 2:20, "When the Messiah was executed on the Cross as a criminal, I was too; so that my proud ego no longer lives. But the Messiah lives in me, and the life I now live in my body I live by the same trusting faithfulness that the Son of God had, who loved me and gave Himself up for me."

Yeshua's death:

- Romans 6:8, "Now since we died with the Messiah, we trust that we will also live with Him."

Yeshua's burial:

- Romans 6:4, "Through immersion into His death we were buried with Him; so that just as, through the Glory of the Father, the Messiah was raised from the dead, likewise we too might live a new life."

Being made alive again with Yeshua:

- Ephesians 2:4–5, "But God is so rich in mercy and loves us with such intense love that, even when we were dead because of our acts of disobedience, He brought us to life along with the Messiah—it is by grace that you have been delivered."

Yeshua's resurrection:

- Ephesians 2:6–10:

  That is, God raised us up with the Messiah Yeshua and seated us with Him in heaven, in order to exhibit it in the ages to come how infinitely rich is His grace, how great is His kindness toward us who are united with the Messiah Yeshua. For you have been delivered by grace through trusting, and even this is not your accomplishment but God's gift. You were not delivered by your own actions; therefore no one should boast. For we are of God's making created in union with the Messiah Yeshua for a life of good actions already prepared by God for us to do.

First, we need to understand Father God's will for humanity. Do the Holy Scriptures teach that it has always been God's will for all of humanity to be saved, not just one but all? If so, then by what means and for what purpose?

- First Timothy 2:1–6:

  First of all, then, I counsel that petitions, prayers, intercessions, and thanksgivings be made for all human beings, including kings and all in positions of prominence; so that we may lead quiet and peaceful lives, being godly and upright in everything. This is what God, our Deliverer, regards as good; this is what meets His approval. He wants all humanity to be delivered and come to full knowledge of the truth. For God is One; and there is but One Mediator between God and humanity, Yeshua the Messiah, Himself human, who gave Himself as a ransom on behalf of all, thus providing testimony to God's purpose at just the right time.

- Yochanan (John) 5:19–34:

  Therefore, Yeshua said this to them: "Yes, indeed! I tell you that the Son cannot do anything on His own, but only what He sees the Father doing; whatever the Father does, the Son does too. For the Father loves the Son and shows Him everything He does; and He will show Him even greater things than these, so that you will be amazed. Just as the Father raises the dead and makes them alive, so too the Son makes alive anyone He wants. The Father does not judge anyone but has entrusted all judgment to the Son, so that all may honor the Son as they honor the Father. Whoever fails to honor the Son is not honoring the Father who sent Him. Yes indeed! I tell you that whoever hears what I am saying and trusts the One who sent Me has eternal life—that is, he will not come up for judgment but has already crossed over from death to life! Yes, indeed! I tell you that there is coming a time—in fact, it's already here—when the dead will hear the voice of the Son of God, and those who listen will come to life. For just as the Father has life in Himself, so He has given the Son life to have in Himself. Also, He has given Him authority to execute judgment because He is the Son of Man. Don't be surprised at this; because the time is coming when all who are in the grave will hear His voice and come out—those who have done good to a resurrection of life, and those who have done evil to a resurrection of judgment. I can't do anything on My own. As I hear, I judge; and My judgment is right' because I don't seek My own desire, but the desire of the One who sent Me. If I testify on My own behalf, My testimony is not valid. But there is someone else testifying on My behalf, and I know that the testimony he is making is valid—you have sent to Yochanan, and he has testified to the truth. Not that I collect human testimony; rather I say these things so that you might be saved."

- Yochanan (John) 6:37–40:

Everyone the Father gives Me will come to Me, and whoever comes to Me I will certainly not turn away. For I have come down from heaven to do not My own will but the will of the One who sent Me. And this is the will of the One who sent Me: that I should not lose any of them on the Last Day. Yes, this is the will of My Father: that all who see the Son and trust in Him should have eternal life, and that I should raise them up on the Last Day."

- Yochanan (John) 6:44, "No one can come to Me unless the Father—the One who sent Me—draws him. And I will raise him up on the Last Day."
- Yochanan (John) 6:63–65:

"It is the Spirit who gives life, the flesh is no help. The words I have spoken to you are Spirit and life, yet some among you do not trust." (For Yeshua knew from the outset which ones would not trust Him, also which one would betray Him.) "This," He said, "is why I told you that no one can come to Me unless the Father has made it possible for him."

- Yochanan (John) 8:47, "Whoever belongs to God listens to what God says; the reason you don't listen is that you don't belong to God."

Truth, promise, and a rebuke? Holy Spirit, please open our eyes, ears, and mind to the way, truth, and life according to the Holy Scriptures. Doesn't a person who is sick and knows they need medical attention seek out and find the help they need to get well? Or does the fear of sickness and death hold them back from doing so?

- Luke 5:31–32, "It was Yeshua who answered them: 'The ones who need a doctor aren't the healthy, but the sick. I have not come to call the "righteous," but rather to call sinners to turn to God from their sins.'"
- Yochanan (John) 10:1–18:

"Yes, indeed! I tell you, the person who doesn't enter the sheep-pen through the door, but climbs in some other way, is a thief and robber. But the one who goes in through the gate is the sheep's own shepherd. This is the one the gatekeeper admits, and the sheep hear his voice. He calls his own sheep, each one by name, and leads them out. After taking out all that are his own, he goes on ahead of them; and the sheep follow him because they recognize his voice. They never follow a stranger but will run away from him, because strangers' voices are unfamiliar to them."

Yeshua used this indirect manner of speaking with them, but they didn't understand what He was talking to them about. So, Yeshua said to them again, "Yes, indeed! I tell you that I am the gate for the sheep. All those who have come before Me have been thieves and robbers, but the sheep didn't listen to them. I am the gate; if someone enters through Me, he will be safe and will go in and out and find pasture. The thief comes in order to steal, kill, and destroy; I have come so that they may have life, life in its fullest measure. I am the good shepherd. The good shepherd lays down His life for the sheep. The hired hand, since he isn't a shepherd and the sheep aren't his own, sees the wolf coming, abandons the sheep and runs away. Then the wolf drags them off and scatters them. The hired worker behaves like this because that's all he is, a hired worker;

so, it doesn't matter to him what happens to the sheep. I am the good shepherd; I know My own, and My own know Me—just as the Father knows Me, and I know the Father—and I lay down My life on behalf of the sheep. Also, I have other sheep which are not from this pen; I need to bring them, and they will hear My voice; and there will be one flock, one shepherd. This is why the Father loves Me: because I lay down My life—in order to take it up again! No one takes it away from Me; on the contrary, I lay it down of My own free will. I have the power to lay it down, and I have the power to take it up again. This is what My Father has commanded Me to do."

- Second Kefa (Peter) 3:9, "The Lord is not slow in keeping His promise, as some people think of slowness; on the contrary, He is patient with you; for it is not His purpose that anyone should be destroyed, but that everyone should turn from his sins."

There's still a lot more to break down. Is the willful sacrifice of Yeshua an NT/B'rit Hadashah concept only, or is it also found in the OT/Tanakh? Let's continue and take a look:

- B'resheet (Genesis) 49:18, "I wait for your deliverance, Adonai."
- Sh'mot (Exodus) 15:2, "Yah is my strength and my song, and He has become my salvation."
- Sh'mu'el Alef (1 Samuel) 2:1, "Then Hannah prayed; she said: 'My heart exults in Adonai! My dignity has been restored by Adonai! I can gloat over my enemies, because of my joy at Your saving me.'"
- Sh'mu'el Bet (2 Samuel) 23:5, "For my house stands firm with God—He made an everlasting covenant with me. It is in order, fully assured, that he will bring to full growth all my salvation and every desire."
- Divrei-HamYamim (1 Chronicles) 16:35–6, "Say: 'Save us, God who can save us! Gather and rescue us from the nations; so that we can thank Your holy name and glory in praising You. Blessed be Adonai, the God of Isra'el, from eternity past to eternity future!'"
- Z'kharya (Zechariah) 8:7–8, "Adonai-Tzva'ot says, 'I will save My people from lands east and west; I will bring them back, and they will live in Yerushalayim. They will be My people; and I will be their God, with faithfulness and justice.'"

- Yeshua 'yahu (Isaiah) 45:11–25, Thus says Adonai, the Holy One of Isra'el, His Maker:

"You ask for signs concerning My children? You give orders concerning the work of My hands? I am the one who made the earth! I created human beings on it! I—My hands—stretched out the heavens and directed all their number. I am stirring up Koresh to righteousness, I am smoothing out all his paths. He will rebuild My city; and he will free My exiles, taking neither ransom nor bribe," says Adonai-Tzva'ot. Here is what Adonai says: "the earnings of Egypt, the commerce of Ethiopia, and men of stature from S'va will come over to you and become yours; they will come in chains and follow you. They will prostrate themselves before you; they will pray to you: 'surely God is with you; there is no other, other gods are nothing.'" Truly, you are a God who hides Himself, God of Isra'el, Savior! The idol-makers will be ashamed, disgraced, all of them; they will go dishonored together. But Isra'el, saved by Adonai with an everlasting salvation, you will never, ever, be ashamed or disgraced. For thus says Adonai, who created the heavens, God, who shaped and made the earth, who established and created it not to be chaos, but formed it to be lived in: "I am Adonai; there is no other. I did not speak in secret, in a land of darkness. I did not say to the descendants of Ya'akov, 'It is in vain that you will seek me.' I, Adonai, speak rightly; I say what is true. Assemble, come, and gather together, you refugees from the nations! Those carrying their wooden idols are ignorant, they pray to a god that cannot save. Let them stand and present their case! Indeed, let them take counsel together. Who foretold this long ago, announced it in times gone by? Wasn't it I, Adonai? There is no other God besides Me, a just God, and a Savior; there is none besides Me. Look at Me, and be saved, all the ends of the earth! For I am God; there is no other. In the Name of Myself I have sworn, from My mouth has rightly gone out, a word that will not return—that to Me every knee will bow, and every tongue will swear about Me that only in Adonai are justice and strength." All who rage against Him will come to Him ashamed, but all the descendants of Isra'el will find justice and glory in Adonai.

- Tehillim (Psalm) 98:1–4:

A Psalm: Sing a new song to Adonai because He has done wonders. His right hand, His holy arm have won Him victory. Adonai has made known His victory; revealed His vindication in full view of the nations, remembered His grace and faithfulness to the house of Isra'el. All the ends of the earth have seen the victory of our God. Shout for joy to Adonai, all the earth! Break forth, sing for joy, sings praises!

- Tehillim (Psalm) 67:2–4, "God, be gracious to us, and bless us. May He make His face shine toward us, so that Your way may be known on earth, Your salvation among all nations. Let the peoples give thanks to You, God; let the peoples give thanks to You, all of them."
- Etc., etc., etc., by God's mercy unto grace through His unique Son, Yeshua, at a determined time revealed and to come again!

So what can we determine then by these truths? That God definitely has a plan of inclusion for all humanity within forgiveness and salvation unto a resurrected life!

- Romans 8:28–39:

Furthermore, we know that God causes everything to work together for the good of those who love God and are called in accordance with His purpose; because those whom He knew in advance, He also determined in advance would be conformed to the pattern of His Son, so that He might be the firstborn among many brothers; and those whom He thus determined in advance, He also called; and those whom He called, He also caused to be considered righteous; and those whom He caused to be considered righteous He also glorified! What, then, are we to say to these things? If God is for us, who can be against us? He who did not spare even His own Son, but gave Him up on behalf of us all—is it possible that, He would not give us everything else too? So, who will bring a charge against God's chosen people? Certainly not God—He is the One who causes them to be considered righteous! Who punishes them? Certainly not the Messiah Yeshua, who died and—more than that—has been raised, is at the right hand of God and is actually pleading on our behalf! Who will separate us from the love of the Messiah? Trouble? Hardship? Persecution? Hunger? Poverty? Danger? War? As the Tanakh puts it, "For your sake we are being put to death all day long, we are considered sheep to be slaughtered." No, in all these things we are super conquerors, through the One who has loved us. For I am convinced that neither death nor life, neither angels nor other heavenly rulers, neither what exists nor what is coming, neither powers above nor powers below, nor any other created thing will be able to separate us from the love of God which comes to us through the Messiah Yeshua, our Lord.

Are you then a wild branch grafted into Isra'el? Or perhaps even a native branch of the vine, yet might be lacking understanding? If either-or, please prayerfully read the book of Ephesians in the NT/B'rit Hadashah and come to realize who and what you are. Then understand what we are together as one in Yeshua Messiah. As one with each other in Christ, we have become God's new man, according to Father God's many-sided wisdom.

We read and can see a glimpse that the will of the Father God for the salvation of mankind was established since the beginning of His creation and all things. His plan is certainly intentional, but it needs to be legal according to His own Torah. This will require a willful bloody sacrifice unto death on an execution stake, burial, and resurrection to a new life from Yeshua. This is so Father God can legally remove our sins, allowing humanity to be forgiven and hopefully ultimately saved within the inclusion of Yeshua's resurrected life if one believes this to be true. A new life that only God can give!

Yeshua, who is without sin, willfully decided to take our sins and death within Himself on the cross; He became our substitute. He took our place, identifying with us on the cross. He became what we are: people filled with sin and sickness, leading to misery, death, and eternal separation from Father God and His kingdom. Yet, Yeshua's death became our personal death in all manners of our lives. In His resurrection the Holy Scriptures clearly teach that all of humanity was forgiven so we could then potentially become saved and included with Yeshua within His new resurrected life.

It's imperative that we realize that when life was given back to Yeshua through His resurrection, it was given back to us as well. Because Yeshua was there for us as us. Our greatest enemy, "death," has been conquered. For the wages of sin lead to death, and we can boldly profess, "Oh death, where is your sting now?" This should be a very personal and liberating significance for all peoples who hear the powerful message of the gospel (good news). Holy Spirit, please minister this way, truth, and life into our spirits!

Yeshua's new life was given to us legally by His willful sacrifice unto resurrection. But this new resurrection life requires something from us that decides whether or not an individual can receive it: faith to believe it and trust in Yeshua as the Son of God and belief in the One who sent Him, Father God.

Nakdimon, a rabbi, questions Yeshua about this very thing in John 3:1–21. Let's take a read of their conversation:

> There was a man among the P'rushim named Nakdimon, who was a ruler of the Judeans. This man came to Yeshua by night and said to him, "Rabbi, we know it is from God that you have come as a teacher; for no one can do these miracles you perform

unless God is with him." "Yes, indeed." Yeshua answered him, "I tell you that unless a person is born again from above, he cannot see the Kingdom of God." Nakdimon said to him, "How can a grown man be 'born'? Can he go back into his mother's womb and be born a second time?" Yeshua answered, "Yes, indeed, I tell you that unless a person born from water and the Spirit, he cannot enter the Kingdom of God. What is born from the flesh is flesh, and what is born from the Spirit is spirit. Stop being amazed at My telling you that you must be born again from above! The wind blows where it wants to, and you hear its sound, but you don't know where it's going. That's how it is with everyone who has been born from the Spirit." Nakdimon replied, "How can this happen?" Yeshua answered him, "You hold the office of teacher in Isra'el, and you don't know this? Yes, indeed! I tell you that what we speak about, we know; and what we give evidence of, we have seen; but you people don't accept our evidence! If you people don't believe Me when I tell you about the things of the world, how will you believe Me when I tell you about the things of heaven? No one has gone up into heaven; there is only the One who has come down from heaven, the Son of Man. Just as Moshe lifted up the serpent in the desert, so must the Son of Man be lifted up; so that everyone who trusts in Him may have eternal life. "For God so loved the world that He gave his only and unique Son, so that everyone who trusts in Him may have eternal life, instead of being utterly destroyed.

"For God did not send the Son into the world to judge the world, but rather so that through Him, the world might be saved. Those who trust in Him are not judged: those who do not trust have been judged already, in that they have not trusted in the One who is God's only and unique Son. Now this is the judgment: the light has come into the world, but people loved the darkness rather than the light. Why? Because their actions were wicked. For everyone who does evil things hates the light and avoids it, so that his actions won't be exposed. But everyone who does what is true comes to the light, so that all may see that his actions are accomplished through God."

Now trust can't be activated until a person accepts and takes into themselves the free gift of faith. One must believe Yeshua is indeed Father God's Son and that Father is God who sent Him into the world to forgive humanity of its sins and raise those up who believe into an eternal life, a resurrected life.

- First Peter 1:3, "Praised be God, Father of our Lord Yeshua the Messiah, who, in keeping with His great Mercy, has caused us, through the resurrection of Yeshua the Messiah from the dead, to be born again to a living hope."

Is now a reasonable time to ask if Yeshua's death on the cross and resurrection into eternal life means more for the unsaved or saved person? I pray it is becoming obvious it is for the unsaved, sinful, and spiritually dead. However, equally as important is the constant reminder to the saved of their new identity and position in Yeshua's resurrection life, which He freely gives only to all who believe.

As followers of the way (Jewish people who believed in Yeshua as Messiah called Messianic as well as Gentiles labeled Christians historically), upon being born again, we are called to walk and live by the presence and power of the Holy Spirit and the Torah.

- Romans 6:4–11:

    Through immersion into His death we were buried with Him; so that just as, through the Glory of the Father, the Messiah was raised from the dead, likewise we too might live a new life. For if we have been united with Him in a death like His, we will also be united with Him in a resurrection like His. We know that our old self was put to death on the execution-stake with Him, so that the entire body of our sinful propensities might be destroyed, and we might no longer be enslaved to sin. For someone who has died has been cleared from sin. Now since we died with the Messiah, we trust that we will also live with Him. We know that the Messiah has been raised from the dead, never to die again; death has no authority over Him. For His death was a unique event that need not be repeated; but His life, He keeps on living for God. In the same way, consider yourselves to be dead to sin but alive for God, by your union with the Messiah Yeshua.

A note about the word "immersion" versus "baptism"! The above is not talking about something that happens to us when we are water baptized only. The word "baptism" in the Greek is baptizo. The word was not translated from Greek to English in the KJV. The word actually means "to immerse." Scriptures refer to several immersions or baptisms besides water baptism. We can be immersed in the Holy Spirit subsequent to the new birth.

At the new birth, we are immersed in or put into Christ Yeshua spiritually as one in union with Yeshua. At the moment of the new birth (being born again), we are united to and immersed into Christ Yeshua. The results of His death and resurrection go into effect for us vitally in all manner.

Baptism with water, however, has a prefigured meaning that Kefa (Peter) makes understood in the NT/B'rit Hadashah:

- First Peter 3:20–22:

To those who were disobedient long ago, in the days of Noah, when God waited patiently during the building of the ark, in which a few people—to be specific, eight—were delivered by water. This also prefigures what delivers us now, the water of immersion, which is not the removal of dirt from the body, but one's pledge to keep a good conscience toward God, through the resurrection of Yeshua the Messiah. He has gone into heaven and is at the right hand of God, with angels, authorities, powers subject to Him.

- As we ought to be also.

What, then, is the glory of the Father that raised Christ Yeshua and us in Him from the dead? It is the very life of God. Not as a being, as Father God is an unseen and incomprehensible Spirit yet revealed in Yeshua. So, on earth, the God-man Yeshua lived His life by Father God's fullness dwelling in Him.

- Colossians 1:18–23:

Also He is head of the Body, the Messianic Community—He is the beginning, the firstborn from the dead, so that He might hold first place in everything.

For it pleased God to have His full being live in His Son and through His Son to reconcile to Himself all things whether on earth or in heaven, making peace through Him, through having His Son shed His blood by being executed on a stake. In other words, you, who at one time were separated from God and had a hostile attitude toward Him because of your wicked deeds, He has now reconciled in the Son's physical body through His death; in order to present you holy and without defect or reproach before Himself—provided, of course, that you continue in your trusting, grounded and steady, and don't let yourselves be moved away from the hope offered in the Good

News you heard. This the Good News that has been proclaimed in all creation under heaven; and I, Sha'ul, have become a servant of it.

In Yeshua's resurrection, He was justified and made alive in spirit again. That life was given to us at the moment of our new birth—being born again.

- First Timothy 3:16, "Great beyond all question is the formerly hidden truth underlying our faith: He was manifested physically and proved righteous spiritually, seen by angels, and proclaimed among the nations, trusted throughout the world, and raised up in glory to heaven."
- First Peter 3:18, "For the Messiah Himself died for sins, once and for all, a righteous person on behalf of unrighteous people, so that He might bring you to God. He was put to death in the flesh but brought to life by the Spirit."

Our sins had made dead men and women of us all, and Father God, in giving life to Christ Yeshua, gave life to us too. He gave us the very life of Christ Yeshua, the same new life with which He quickened Him.

- Ephesians 2:5, "That, even when we were dead because of our acts of disobedience, He brought us to life along with the Messiah—it is by Grace that you have been delivered."

Grace is not as simple as a statement of unmerited favor from God toward man as some are taught to think. It is intentional, Father God's will! Which cost Yeshua His very life for humanity's sake! This is why a person needs the free gift of faith to believe, as this understanding does not exist in a man's own conscience without God's spiritual revelation. Again, it is the power of God!

- Ephesians 1:19–20, "And how surpassingly great is His power in us who trust in Him. It works with the same mighty strength He used when He worked in the Messiah to raise Him from the dead and seat Him at His right hand in heaven."

This power in us is the same as the mighty strength that He used when He raised Christ Yeshua from the dead. This is the good news of the Gospels! Fantastic life-changing news! How tremendous is the power available to all who believe in God sending His Son, Yeshua, to us because He loves and includes us.

- John 3:16, "For God so loved the world that He gave his only and unique Son, so that everyone who believes in Him may have eternal life, instead of being utterly destroyed."

- Most people leave out the part of being utterly destroyed when quoting this scripture. Because some think they will offend another or turn them off to God. The truth is some people refuse to take into themselves the free gift of faith, so they may be able to believe this. Because many people suffer in their life from exclusion versus inclusion in many aspects of their lives. Whether in private or public, secretly or openly, which draws them away from God's calling on their life. They exclude themselves from the option for God's love, mercy, and grace. Choosing to compare a potential relationship with a sinless God to relationships with sinful people, which is one of the greatest deceptions of Satan, the world, and even a person's own sinful nature called the flesh. Unless a person repents—that is, to return to the only redeemer option, Christ Yeshua. They are already under judgment. However, as we continue to read, there is good news of redemption!

So now we have in our resurrected spirit the life of God. Life that has already conquered death. The life of God is powerful to destroy and will destroy our greatest enemy: death! Yeshua's life is a light that shines through the darkness, and the darkness can never extinguish it.

- John 1:4–5, "In Him as life, and the life was the light of mankind. The light shines in the darkness and darkness has not suppressed it."

Ultimately, the power of the resurrected life will transform our current physical body and make it just like Yeshua's eternally new, resurrected, glorified body.

- Philippians 3:20–21, "But we are citizens of heaven, and it is from there that we expect a Deliver, the Lord Yeshua the Messiah. He will change the bodies we have in this humble state and make them like His glorious body, using the power which enables Him to bring everything under His control."

Through the resurrection Yeshua was freed from the dominions of the devil, world, and death. When life came back into Yeshua's resurrected spirit, soul, and body, death could no longer hold Him. Hallelujah!

- Romans 6:9–10, "We know that the Messiah has been raised from the dead, never to die again; death has no authority over Him. For His death was a unique event that need not be repeated; but His life, He keeps on living for God."

If truly we say we believe in Yeshua, are in union, and love Him, the Holy Spirit indwelling us will produce love and willful obedience to Yeshua and the Torah in us—if we submit ourselves daily to both. Legally, when Yeshua was freed from the dominion of death and the devil, we were too. Hallelujah! That freedom became our vital inclusion and possession in all manner at the new birth. Receiving spiritual life releases us from spiritual death and the dominion of the devil.

- Colossians 2:15, "Stripping the rulers and authorities of their power, He made a public spectacle of them, triumphing over them by means of the cross."

The law of the spirit of life in Christ Yeshua has made us free from the law of sin and death.

- Romans 8:1–2, "Therefore, there is no longer any condemnation awaiting those who are in union with the Messiah Yeshua. Why? Because the Torah of the Spirit [new resurrected life], which produces this life in union with Messiah Yeshua, has set me free from the 'Torah' of sin and death [old unresurrected life]" (italics added, mine).

What is the law of sin and death? People who are guilty of sin are under the dominion of death; that is the law.

- Romans 6:23, "For what one earns from sin is death; but eternal life is what one receives as a free gift from God, in union with the Messiah Yeshua, our Lord."

Before we were saved, we were a fallen race. In sin and away, we were guilty of sin, and death rightfully reigned over us and in us. Because of the law of sin and death (not the teachings and observances of the Torah, which Yeshua fulfilled and did not abolish), we didn't have to pray or fast or use faith to get sickness, depression, fear, guilt, lack, etc. They became ours in the fall of Adam and Eve.

Because our sins have been paid for, death has no more dominion over Yeshua or over us!

- Romans 6:9, "We know that the Messiah has been raised from the dead, never to die again; death has no authority over Him."

If you are not guilty of sin, death cannot hold you, and we have been given witnesses to this fact.

- Acts 2:24–25, "But God has raised Him up and freed Him from the suffering of death; it was impossible that death could keep its hold on Him. For David says this about him: 'I saw Adonai always before me, for He is at my right hand, so that I will not be shaken.'"
- Acts 2:26–28, "For this reason, my heart was glad; and my tongue rejoiced; and now my body too will live on in the certain hope that You will not abandon me to Sh'ol or let Your Holy One see decay. You have made known to me the ways of life; You will fill me with joy by Your presence."
- Acts 2:32, "God raised up this Yeshua! And we are all witnesses of it!"

We are not guilty of sin anymore because Yeshua willfully paid the price for our sins and satisfied the wages of sin against us. Just as receiving life broke the dominion of death over Yeshua, inclusion in His resurrection life broke its dominion over us. Hallelujah!

We were legally united with Yeshua at the cross. We have life and are in union with Yeshua. The life of Christ Yeshua has broken the dominion of sin and death over us, and that's the law of the Spirit. A new resurrected life in our spirit. The wages of sin, lust, ego, sickness, fear, pain, depression, guilt, shame, lack, etc., are all trespassers now to us. We have the legal right and power in Christ Yeshua to resist them in Yeshua's name. And because we were raised up with Yeshua and seated with Him in heavenly places, we now have the authority to command them to go.

To live the resurrected life, we must understand what the cross has provided and how it is provided:

- When Yeshua, sinless and incarnated, took on a full human form (spirit, soul, and body), every part of Him was put to death on the cross. This means every part of us was crucified with Him.
- At the cross, from the standpoint of God, we were legally executed for our sins.
- At the resurrection we were legally included and given new life. Raised up from the dead free from sin and all its consequences—free from the law of sin and death.

- Both death and life come to us through the cross, death to the old man/nature, and resurrection life for the new man/nature.
- When you make Yeshua Lord of your life, what happened at the cross goes into effect immediately. But the vital results affect each part of our makeup—spirit, soul, and body differently. This needs to be understood because this is where many new and still older (not yet wiser in some cases) believers get confused and their joy of salvation is snatched up from them by Satan given the opportunity.
- At the new birth, the Holy Spirit comes into us, and instantly we are made anew. He counsels, leads, and comforts us.
- Together we begin contending against our old spiritual and fleshly nature, which leads to death. However, the benefit of the cross affects our body differently from our spirit and soul.
- Our body is still alive with the natural human life, which is corrupt. In our flesh there are still selfish, sinful desires that the body wars against our spirits directly and also through our soul. Because the body (referred to as our flesh) is still subject to sickness, sin, misery, separation from God, and death. The fact that, along with our spirit, our soul and body were crucified with Yeshua means that the dominating power of our flesh was broken.
- The fact that our body was crucified with Yeshua means that sin, sickness, disease, etc., have lost the "legal right" to dominate us. But that doesn't mean they are going to easily give up continually trying.
- The spirit and flesh are constantly battling one another on this side of heaven. The soul stands in between the spirit and the flesh; our daily choice to live in the flesh or live in the Spirit becomes the deciding factor for our victory and freedom. We share in this regard Yeshua's sufferings. For He was tempted in all aspects as are we but did not sin.

We must now appropriate and enforce by faith through Yeshua's death, burial, and resurrection. This choice is our free will to take action. To appropriate means to come into physical possession of the benefits of the cross and resurrection. This means we must believe we are included in them before we see, feel, or understand them.
Diseases, sickness, and sins were put on Yeshua, and He took them to the grave and left them there.

- Isaiah 53:4–5, "In fact, it was our diseases He bore, our pains from which He suffered; yet we regarded His a punished, stricken and afflicted by God. But He was wounded because of our crimes, crushed because of our sins; the disciplining that makes us whole fell on Him, and by His stripes we are healed."

When Yeshua was raised to a new resurrected life, He was freed from our sins, sicknesses, diseases, etc., and so were we legally. Through the new resurrected birth, we now have power in our spirit. From God's point of view, we are healed, legally and vitally, in all manner.

- First Peter 2:24–25, "He himself bore our sins in His body on the cross, so that we might die to sins and live for righteousness—by His wounds you were healed. For you used to be like sheep gone astray, but now you have turned to the Shepherd, who watches over you."

Therefore, though your spirit and soul are now being made eternal, your body is still mortal and, therefore, subject to sin, sickness, and disease. Now, the invisible spiritual reality you have in your spirit (healing and eternal life) can become a visible physical reality in your body and soul as God's will.

This is available, as we know what happened to us at the cross and new resurrected birth and agree with God about what He has done for us through His Son Yeshua's willful sacrifice.

- Yet, at times, in our sanctification journey to transformation into Christ's image, this can be a difficult belief to hold onto that might contend against our faith. If this is ever the case, let us pray this prayer fully trusting in God's timing and provision for us.

Prayer: Thank You, Father God, that Yeshua bore my sin, sicknesses, diseases, and death on the cross. I realize and choose to believe that I am now forgiven and free from them. Eternal death no longer has its sting. Thank You that I am included in His healing and set free because of Yeshua's resurrected life. I am now empowered to live above all my circumstances. Despite what I once believed were immovable anchors to my body and soul. May I praise You forever. Amen!

- Psalm 43:5, "My Soul, why are you so downcast? Why are you groaning inside me? Hope in God since I will praise him again for being my Savior and God."

Then the Holy Spirit brings the reality of it into your physical body. The life of Christ Yeshua is manifested (made active), and it produces physical results. Again, in God's timing and will.

- Romans 8:11, "And if the Spirit of the One who raised Yeshua from the dead is living in you, then the One who raised the Messiah Yeshua from the dead will also give life to your mortal bodies through his Spirit living in you."

Are His mercy and grace still not recognizable even now that He gives the breath of life to our mortal bodies while we still sin while living in this fallen world in a state of grace? How much more will He give us in our sinless transformation in His great mercy and love? He still promises us so much more that will become manifest in all manners for our lives!

Even though we are born again, there are still selfish, sinful desires in our flesh because they are still animated by natural human life.

- When we feel sinful desires coming out of our old natural life—either our body or soul—we must count on the fact and agree with the fact that our old man is crucified with Christ Yeshua.
- Thank You, God. Once we choose to deny our flesh, these desires are crucified with Christ and no longer have the right or power to dominate us despite the temptations around or within us.

The Holy Spirit living in us will provide a way to come out of the temptation and put to death the evil desire and give us the experience of the freedom that the cross provided.

- Romans 8:13–17:

> For if you live according to your old nature, you will certainly die; but if, by the Spirit, you keep putting to death the practices of the body, you will live. All who are led by God's Spirit are God's sons. For you did not receive a spirit of slavery to bring you back again into fear; on the contrary, you received the Spirit, who makes us sons and by whose power we cry out. "Abba!" [That is, "Dear Father I will obey You."] The Spirit Himself bears witness with our own spirits that we are children of God; and if we are children, then we are also heirs, heirs of God and joint-heirs with the Messiah—provided we are suffering with Him in order also to be glorified with Him.

According to the Bible, we must reckon ourselves dead to sin and alive to God. To reckon literally means to take an inventory—to consider or to count the cost. We must assess who we are, what happened to us, what will happen to us according to God's Living Word, the Holy Scriptures.

- Romans 6:11, "In the same way, consider yourselves to be dead to sin but alive for God, by your union with the Messiah Yeshua."

To live a resurrected life, we must understand the two-sided benefit of the cross for us. We were crucified with Christ, yet we are made alive and included within the new resurrected life in Christ Yeshua.

- Galatians 2:20, "When the Messiah was executed on the cross as a criminal, I was too; so that my proud ego no longer lives. But the Messiah lives in me, and the life I now live in my body I live by the same trusting faithfulness that the Son of God had, who loved me and gave himself up for me."

We must reckon or count it so, despite what we see, feel, or understand. The number one way we count it so is with the words of our mouth—words that agree with what God's Word says and has done to us (by crucifying and raising us up with Christ Yeshua). Then the Holy Spirit gives each of us who do this the victory in the physical and spiritual realms.

- Your confession is not to make it happen. Your confession is because it already has happened in the spirit but not always immediately in the physical!

Conclusion—as we close, let us together consider these points:

- The crucifixion was a means to an end—so God could legally execute us for our sin, releasing us from eternal death and then start over by inclusion, giving us a new resurrected life by a new birth, His eternal life.

- To live a resurrected life means to live with an awareness of sin's power of unbelief, a sinful nature, sickness, and death that was broken or cut off at the resurrection. This new life now means to live with God's awareness of the power and inclusion that was given to us in Yeshua's resurrection—the power of God to recreate us, empower us, live and work in us, and bring to pass everything the cross provided. He wants us in His family!

To live the resurrected life, we must do these things; in Christ we worship and serve God and others as we become teachable, studious, obedient, and prayerful. We live in the world but no longer desire to be a part of its priorities and enticements in our flesh and come out of it being led by the Holy Spirit.

- First Corinthians 1:18, "For the message about the cross is nonsense to those in the process of being destroyed, but to us in the process of being saved it is the power of God."

Ask God to give understanding of what has happened to you because of the cross.

- Ephesians 1:16–20:

  I have not stopped giving thanks for you. In my prayers I keep asking the God of our Lord Yeshua the Messiah, the glorious Father, to give you a spirit of wisdom and revelation, so that you will have full knowledge of Him. I pray that He will give light to the eyes of your hearts, so that you will understand the hope to which He has called you, what a rich glory there are in the inheritance He has promised His people, and how surpassingly great is His power working in us who trust Him. It works the same mighty strength He used when He worked in the Messiah to raise Him from the dead and seat Him at His right hand in heaven.

- Philippians 3:10, "Yes, I gave it all up in order to know him, that is, to know the power of His resurrection and the fellowship of His sufferings as I am being conformed to His death [*and ultimately raised into Yeshua's image, hallelujah!*]" (italics mine).

Focus your attention on unseen realities through looking at God's Word.

- Colossians 3:1–3, "So if you were raised along with the Messiah, then seek the things above, where the Messiah is sitting at the right hand of God. Focus your minds on the things above, not on things here on earth. For you have died, and your life is hidden with the Messiah in God."
- What are the things above we are to think of if we've never been there? God's promises!

Affection is the word "mind" in the Greek. We are to keep our mind focused on God's Word so we won't be moved when what we see and feel contradicts God's Word. Whoever looked at the type of Christ on the cross was healed. Looking has the idea of gazing continually, constantly seeking the face of God.

- Numbers 21:8, "And Adonai answered Moshe: 'Make a poisonous snake and put it on a pole. When anyone who has been bitten sees it, he will live.'"
- John 3:14–15, "Just as Moshe lifted up the serpent in the desert, so must the Son of Man be lifted up; so that everyone who trusts in him may have eternal life."

Hold fast to speaking what God says about your new resurrected identity and position of inclusion (because of the crucifixion and resurrection of Christ Yeshua), despite what you see, feel, think you understand, or don't yet.

- Revelation 12:11, "They defeated Him (Satan) because of the Lamb's blood and because of the message of their witness. Even when facing death, they did not cling to life."
- Hebrews 10:23–27:

    Let us continue holding fast to the hope we acknowledge, without wavering; for the One who made the promise is trustworthy. And let us keep paying attention to one another, in order to spur each other on to love and good deeds, not neglecting our own congregational meetings, as some have made a practice of doing, but rather encouraging each other. And let us do this all the more as you see the Day approaching. For if we deliberately continue to sin after receiving the knowledge of the truth, there is no longer remains a sacrifice for sins, but only the terrifying prospect of Judgment, of raging fire that will consume the enemies.

Four things can hold us back from living a resurrected life:

1. Deciding not to receive the free gift of faith to believe Yeshua is the Son of God or Father who is God that sent Him. This is a free-will decision, and "your choice" will invoke consequences. Again, read Yeshua's words and teachings for

what those could or will be. Eternal death or eternal life, each person has a say in their own fate in this life and into life hereafter.

2. Lacking knowledge of the Torah (God's teachings and observances, not man's laws of judgment and traditions unto enslavement) understanding in the spirit.

3. Lies, thievery, and destruction from the devil.

4. If truly born again, still choosing not to stay the course until we are fully convinced and persuaded of what we cannot see in the physical but is an absolute reality in the spiritual.

It's not about getting God to do something. It's believing and knowing what has already been provided for every person born again and included in a new resurrected life in Yeshua Messiah!

Now, as I end, I thank you for your patience at my seeming redundancy. It's just that I want to see you saved and set free eternally within an intimate personal relationship with Yeshua.

May we all be born again and included in Yeshua's crucifixion and resurrection of spirit, soul, and body. With power from Father God, counsel and comfort from the Holy Spirit, and teachings regarding life from the Torah. Let us love and encourage one another in this miraculous new life now and in the life to come. Let us who are Messianic, Christians, or followers of the way always remember that there are no separate religious denominations, factions, fellowships, or racism in heaven! What man makes or believes without the inclusion of Christ will be left behind in this world. What God and people born again create always goes forward with Christ into God's kingdom here on earth as it is in heaven yet to be revealed. There is only one bride who loves, worships, and serves Father, Son, and Holy Spirit and our neighbors as ourselves.

Because they are One and so immeasurably in love with us!

D'varim (Deuteronomy) 6:4–5, "Sh'ma, Yisra'el! Adonai Eloheinu, Adonai Echad [Hear, Isra'el! Adonai our God, Adonai is ONE] and you are to love Adonai your God with all your heart, all your being and all your resources."

Blessings on your inclusion—הלֵלכה—in the resurrected life of Yeshua HaMashiach if you choose to be!

Shalom,
Michael, in conjunction with an
unknown author

PART 10:

MICHAEL'S TESTIMONY

This portion of the book is certainly the most difficult for me to write. Why? Because it requires honesty and transparency, and I would prefer to write about Yeshua than myself. Yet, Matthew tells us in his gospel account 7:13–14, "Go in through the narrow gate; for the gate that leads to destruction is wide and the road broad, and many travel it; but it is a narrow gate and a hard road that leads to life, and only a few find it."

I was born on the opposite road, the broad road, through the wide gate on November 13th, 1957. As a young boy, I sensed the presence and peace of God once a week only while in church. My childhood was filled with verbal, physical, and spiritual violence inside my home. No faults of my parents, as their childhood was even more so to the best of my understanding. As I grew up, a deep, intense sense of betrayal had me feeling and believing I was excluded, lonely, and unlovable. Yet at times I clearly heard the call of God and would cry out to Him. I remember watching Billy Graham's messages on TV, being deeply moved to tears, listening, and watching thousands of people responding to the gospel message of Yeshua as Savior and Lord. I felt the desperate need to be saved, and I desired to be an evangelist like Billy Graham.

My desire to become a formal evangelist did not come to be. Instead, I became a barroom evangelist. After high school I became a teamster in San Francisco, California, working alongside my dad. As a young man, a lot of money was put in my hands; I grew up fast and hard with the guys around me. The world started calling me, and I answered the call. I will not share details about the chaotic side of my life living in this world. It's enough to know it's been filled with childhood sexual abuse, drugs, alcohol, witchcraft, fornications of many different kinds, adultery and abominations, pride, rebellion, lying, strongholds of my imaginations, fear, anger, hatred, death of one of my daughters, marriages and divorces, many masks, resentment, bitterness, loneliness, depression, anxiety, self-loathing, therapy, etc. The constant burden of believing I needed to be like others versus my authentic self, which died within myself as a child, etc., etc. And, of course, church once in a while. Which I came to resent as an adult because I never believed or felt I could live up to the standards I was told were a "Christian."

As an adult, unlike my childhood, the weekly refuge of church had become a place of confusion, judgment, and comparatives, all of which I could not live up to. So I judged myself endlessly and found solace in the offerings of the world to many bitter and unstable ends at the expense of my relationships with God, others, and myself. I have had many regrets. I know what the inside of a mental health unit, while bound in a strait jacket for days, or a cell inside a jail looks like. All while hiding behind self-made masks that carried disingenuous smiles of "grace." I was praised at times for the things others thought I got away with. But I never got away with anything, as many times my decisions and actions continually created loathsome internal judgments.

As I grew as an adult, leaving the blue-collar world and entering into the white-collar world, I tried hard to be "successful" as the world deems success, with many things available to me.

Including different denominations and faiths as I sought to be approved of, liked, or loved. Rejection, fear, anger, and judgment were the constant cornerstones I carried with me everywhere I went in my personal, business, and religious lives. Yes. Indeed, they were all separate, and I lived and, at times, loved them as such. Thus, the need to create masks and change them if and when needed to suit whatever situation. I would make sincere attempts to go to church and become a part of God's people. I just couldn't do it sustainably. The warfare in my spirit, soul, and body was relentless and much in secret, as I couldn't let anyone see many of my doings or sufferings. Church people are overcomers in Christ, right? "Do more, be more" was the message I received. Thoughts of taking my own life at different times were real, but with my many self-constructed masks, I couldn't let others see that. Yet a few did at times to my deep regret for the sorrow and torment I put on them.

I cried out to God one day after an angelic visitation; yes, that's right, they do happen—at least it happened to me. I was told the life I was "choosing" to live was not what God wanted for me. I responded, "I am just a man, and that is all I am, and I am failing at that—please help me." God intervened immediately and set me on a pathway of sobriety and years of deep therapy. But everyone around me in the world hates a quitter, and the church wasn't prepared for people like me. So back on the cycle I would go with a leg standing on each gate on each road, being split in half, ugh.

After multiple marriages and divorces, my wife at the time, and I got married on November 12, 2006, and were born again into Christ Yeshua on July 12, 2009, at 9:00 a.m. That day we both went through the narrow gate to the hard road, the path of life. This I know for a fact: that God appoints guardian angels while Satan has assigned demons to my life. I have too many accounts of both for this not to be true. I never prayed for the things that were going to happen to happen because I didn't know how to pray. Other than beg God to save me or take me. This narrow road did not relieve me of demonic pursuit or oppression at times. But it did bring me into a deep desire to get into the reading of the Bible and times of prayer to the Holy Spirit for wisdom, counsel, and comfort and, most importantly, a very personal, intimate, one-on-one relationship with Yeshua. My spirit has literally been taken into rooms to have conversations with Yeshua as well as into the depth of the deep black darkness at the entrance of hell. I've been given the revelation of the prison system each person creates within themselves from the first time they cast a judgment, criticism, or curse on another and don't repent for doing so. My wife and I were quickly moved out of the Baptist denomination into a fellowship of Apostolic Pentecostal folks. Where God showed us great signs, miracles, prophecies, and move of the Holy Spirit for a minute. He told me, "Michael, don't ever put Me into a box, as I live outside the box of everyone's understanding!" We were called to the ministry of the homeless, addicts, and hopelessly battered both physically and spiritually.

Then we heard a couple at church give their testimony. He was an orthodox Jew who came to accept Christ as his Savior, and His wife was a born-again Christian. The timing of this was perfect, as are all things in God's timing and will. Both our hearts were stirred—my wife regarding the seventh day Sabbath, which is Saturday, and myself regarding my unspoken and denied reality by both my parents that I have more Jewish blood versus being mostly Italian as I was taught and lived by growing up. My wife and I both did the ancestry test and came to find out I/we both indeed have Jewish blood. However, being of Jewish or Italian descent wasn't what was important. What was important was that I was lied to about this growing up. Processing this, I could easily say now I am more American, being the third generation born here. Yet even that may or may not appease the sense of understanding of others born here. What I know for certain now is I am a son of the most high God, and this world is not my home but is a temporal dwelling place. My true home and destiny is the kingdom of God in heaven and, for now, earth.

The Holy Spirit put it on our hearts to seek out a Messianic fellowship. At the beginning we had no idea what that even meant. We were led to one, and we both felt as though we were home. We were embraced and started to learn what words like Torah meant, God's appointed feasts, and Old Testament prophecies regarding Yeshua being fulfilled. Well, needless to say, our Christian family had great difficulty accepting this regarding us moving into the Messianic faith. As we learned, we offered ourselves up to the ministry of being a bridge between Jewish, Christian, and now Messianic faiths.

In our hearts we only wanted to know more about the Jewishness of Yeshua, our Messiah, and what Israel is to the world according to the Holy Scriptures. What it means to be grafted into Israel and, most importantly, being included into Yeshua's resurrected life. Has the walk in this lane been easier? Not always. Why? Because the sufferings I/we suffer for in Christ now are of a much different purpose and internal perspective. While walking in the weeds of this world or some man-made denominations and traditions of the "church." Where, sadly, many have become enslaved while some churches have become a business of a spiritual trade for worldly works and rewards. Versus vessels of truth and growth on the pathway to the life for those who seek to be a follower of the way.

As Solomon assures us in Ecclesiastes 12:13–14, "Here is the final conclusion, now that you have heard everything; fear God, and keep His mitzvot [commandment]; this is what being human is all about. For God will bring to judgment everything we do, including every secret, whether good or bad."

Because like any other road a person journeys on in life, there are other people. Some who come along, some who get along, and some who disregard the reflection in their own mirror and keep casting stones. I don't blame anyone else for my shortcomings and free-will choices. For at the end of each day, I realize I am the sum total of my own individual choices irregardless of choices that others may intentionally or unintentionally impose on me. Looking back, I realize it seemed easier at times for me to bear and yield a greater harvest by my walk in the wide path of the world than the narrow, hard road of the path of life. In my experience both roads are sometimes filled with comparatives, scrutiny, professed love, grace, individual agendas, and I can assure you, many masks other than my own. Reality is we all come to the cross of Christ broken and in desperate need of life, forgiveness, and salvation as we are the walking dead in the wages of our sins until we accept the path of salvation in Yeshua if indeed we do. I am to encourage and bring up brothers and sisters in the kingdom and to test the spirits in the world.

So why do I walk and cry out to God and encourage others to do so? Because there are only two alternatives: eternal life in the resurrection of Yeshua and God's kingdom or eternal death and separation from God because of the wages sin produces that lead to eternal spiritual and physical death in hell. Due to unrepented belief, which begets wages of sinful, faithless works. I've known death, and I know life. I choose life in Christ, and the sufferings I may suffer are adjoined to the sufferings of my risen Savior and accredited to His victories and glory. I am nothing without Him! I try to keep my walk real and transparent as a daily goal I have with the Holy Spirit. It's a battle, and I don't win everyone or any in the spirit by myself. But I am one with the Holy Spirit living within me, and He is my comfort and counsel. I run my race of this life to attain the goal of overcoming and winning. How? Only by submission to God's power, not reliance on anything of myself that excludes Yeshua. Like going to the gym daily for temporary health benefits, as my body will die one day despite this. I do my best one day at a time to discipline myself and not to get ahead of God. The good work Yeshua started in me He promises to finish.

Which is an eternal promise, as are all of His promises. For Scripture tells us in Proverbs 16:9, "A person may plan his path, but Adonai [God] directs his steps."

What the end image will look like and be is yet to be revealed. He is my "yes and amen," regardless of what my warring flesh, other people, or this world system may see, hear, or think of me. God's love is very different from humanity's love, and it's still something I press into God for an understanding of every day.

I was given the assignment to author this book that listed only the words and teachings of Yeshua over ten years ago. He had me add the collaborative writ with an unknown author regarding inclusion in Yeshua's resurrected life. My assignment is complete, and it's to God's glory, not mine, I pray. As time and time again, I would pick up the task only to be sidetracked by something or another. I now realize Satan, this world, and my old fleshy nature did not want me to complete this assignment, as it would become a means to their ends in my life. Reality is living in Yeshua's resurrected life now; they are all actually dead to me already. They only live when I choose to give them power to do so. I've learned the hard way at times; however, this I know for certain. *You don't place a shovel in your dead man's grave so he can try and dig his way out!*

Reading and writing out just the words and teachings of Yeshua. This book has given me a much better, growing understanding of Him and His love and will for me. As well as a promised peace I can access any time if I choose. Which I struggled to embrace and have before. It's become all about submission for me. My being out of control for so many years led me to try and be in control. Which only led me to be trapped in variant levels of fear most days.

Which led to being tormented by strongholds of my imagination and a false perspective of my authentic self. Which I now only seek in Christ. I try hard to embrace 1 John 4:18: "There is no fear in love. On the contrary, love that has achieved its goal gets rid of fear, because fear has to do with punishment; the person who keeps fearing has not been brought to maturity in regard to love." I am charged to share and to guard this holiness of God's love and promised peace.

This isn't an easy task for me or any born-again follower of the ways of Yeshua. It's a day-by-day work of sanctification that Yeshua promises to finish within each of His followers. My salvation has to be about submission and eternal rest. Because of works and wages of sin within my fleshly nature, this world's system and Satan can only lead to ungodly burdens that could result in eternal death. I am clear that Yeshua is the only free gift sent by Father God, who loves the world and me beyond my understanding that changes death to life!

I encourage you as the writer of the book of Hebrews encourages me in Hebrews 10:21–39…

We also have a great Cohen over God's household. Therefore, let us approach the Holiest Place with a sincere heart, in the full assurance that comes from trusting—with our hearts sprinkled clean from a bad conscience and our bodies washed with pure water. Let us continue holding fast to the hope we acknowledge, without wavering; for the One who made the promise is trustworthy. And let us keep paying attention to one another, in order to spur each other on to love and good deeds, not neglecting our own congregational meetings, as some have made a practice of doing, but, rather, encouraging each other. And let us do this all the more as you see the Day approaching. For if we deliberately continue to sin after receiving the knowledge of the truth, there no longer remains a sacrifice for sins, but only the terrifying prospect of judgement, of raging fire that will consume the enemies. Someone who disregards the Torah of Moshe is put to death without mercy on the word of two or three witnesses. Think how much worse will be the punishment deserved by someone who has trampled underfoot the Son of God; who has treated as something common the blood of the covenant which made Him holy; and who has insulted the Spirit, giver of God's grace! For the One we know is the One who said, "Vengeance is My responsibility, I will repay," and then said, "Adonai will judge His people." It is a terrifying thing to fall into the hands of the living God! But remember the earlier days, when, after you had received the light, you endured a hard struggle with sufferings. Sometimes you were publicly disgraced and persecuted, while at other times you stood loyally by those who were treated this way. For you shared the sufferings of those who has been put in prison. Also, when your possessions were seized, you accepted it gladly; since you knew that what you possessed was better and would last forever. So don't throw away that courage of yours, which carries with it such a great reward. For you need to hold out; so that, by having done what God wills, you may receive what He has promised. For "There is so, so little time! The One coming will indeed come, He will not delay. But the person who is righteous will live his life by trusting, and if he shrinks back, I will not be pleased with him." However, we are not the kind who shrink back and are destroyed; on the contrary, we keep trusting and thus preserve our lives!

Who really wants to suffer? No one I believe. I know I didn't. But at times I surely did by listening to the programming of my own flesh and the narratives of this world's system. I lied to myself as did the world telling me, "Hey, come here or go over there. I have the answer or fix for you," and next thing you know, it's just another tentacle of enslavement, despair, and shame. I'm not just talking about drugs, alcohol, sex, etc. It was also about relationships with people and things that I idolized and lifted up in higher esteem giving more time to them than I did God. Different geographic changes, only to have internal secrets always follow. For no matter where we go, there we are. The worldwide internet came along and is filled with many people, places, things, beliefs, social media, chat forums, likes and dislikes, egos, godly and evil doorways to knowledge. Some are good and informative portals, while some are not, etc. Looking back, I realize I spent much of my time building my own imagination like a construction site. Where strongholds were being firmly established. Remember Satan is a liar, thief, and destroyer. He teaches everyone very well and calls daily to the evil inclination of our flesh nature whether we respond or not. We choose to be in agreement intentionally or unintentionally.

Yeshua's resurrection gives life in abundance, not condemnation and shame. His gospel is not the world's prosperity gospel, created by selfish, self-seeking men and women using Yeshua's name to guide and misdirect vulnerable folks into giving their hard-earned money to them.

Many of our world governments perpetuate lies, manufacturing and handing out mind-altering enslaving drugs, false narratives, exclusions masked as inclusion, and many types of free passes that are not meant for the betterment of a person's life or soul experience here on earth. But as much as they all can and will do to others, the reality is a person's own free will is ground zero or the delta. Every one of us is more alike in our sins and our sufferings before we are born again.

However, many are being spiritually awakened by Father God and choosing to become vastly different in Yeshua's resurrected life versus their eminent graves leading to hell and eternal torments. So cry out to Father God and give Yeshua a real chance to reveal Himself, His life plan, a new identity, and life position for you that's undeniable. On the days you suffer, know He suffered more because He loves you more.

I am sixty-six at the writing of this testimony. On July 12, 2009, at 9:00 a.m., a true rebirth occurred. I seek Father God's face and will, which causes me to press into a relationship with Yeshua. His teachings and inclusion in His resurrected life are bringing out His authentic self for me to see and experience. The process of realized sanctification unto transformation. My heart aches for the lost and praises God for the saved! I pray the sincerity of my testimony will and has somehow, someway, related to you. Whether you are still in the world, a follower of Yeshua, or deciding to become a follower of Yeshua. My intentions were to give you hope and inspiration to give Yeshua a real chance in your life. I can say with assurance, though, I fight battles daily as we all do. My life is absolutely worth living because Yeshua has forgiven and saved me by already winning the war over my eternal life!

May the Lord bless you and keep you; may the Lord make His face shine upon you and be gracious to you; may the Lord lift up His countenance upon you and give you peace! Numbers 6:24–26.

Shalom,
Michael

"It's one thing to know the word of the Lord; it's another to know the Lord of the Word!"

>Rabbi Greg Hershberg
>Beth Yeshua International
>Macon, Georgia, USA
>(Cited with permission)

PART 11:

CONCLUSION

John 3:16–18:

> For God so loved the world that He gave His only and unique Son, so that everyone who trusts [believes] in Him may have eternal life, instead of being utterly destroyed. For God did not send the Son into the world to judge the world, but rather so that through Him, the world might be saved. Those who trust in Him are not judged; those who do not trust have been judged already, in that they have not trusted in God's only and unique Son.

First Peter 1:3–9:

> Praised be God, Father of our Lord Yeshua the Messiah, who, in keeping with His great mercy, has caused us, through the resurrection of Yeshua the Messiah from the dead, to be born again to a living hope, to an inheritance that cannot decay, spoil, or fade, kept safe for you in heaven. Meanwhile through trusting, you are being protected by God's power for a deliverance ready to be revealed at the Last Time. Rejoice in this, even though for a little while you may experience grief in various trials. Even gold is tested for genuineness by fire. The purpose of these trials is so that your trust's genuineness, which is far more valuable than perishable gold, will be judged worthy of praise, glory, and honor at the revealing of Yeshua the Messiah. Without having seen Him, you love Him. Without seeing Him now, but trusting in Him, you continue to be full of joy that is glorious beyond words. And you are receiving what your trust is aiming at, namely, your deliverance.

Romans 8:1–2:

> "Therefore, there is no longer any condemnation awaiting those who are in union with the Messiah Yeshua. Why? Because the Torah of the Spirit [resurrected life], which

produces this life in union with Messiah Yeshua, has set me free from the 'Torah' of sin and death [un-resurrected life]."

First Peter 1:22–25:

> Now that you have purified yourselves by obeying the truth, so that you have a sincere love for your brothers, love each other deeply, with all your heart. You have been born again not from some seed that will decay, but from one that cannot decay, through the living Word of God that lasts forever. For all humanity is like grass, all its glory is like a wildflower—the grass withers, and the flower falls off; but the Word of Adonai lasts forever. Moreover, this Word is the Good News which has been proclaimed to you.

PART 12:

SPACE FOR PERSONAL NOTES

Part 12: Space for Personal Notes   401